Labour Law in Greece

Labour Law in Greece

Second Edition

Viktoria Sp. Douka
Vasileios Th. Koniaris

This book was originally published as a monograph in the International Encyclopaedia of Laws/Labour Law and Industrial Relations.

Founding Editor: Roger Blanpain
General Editor: Frank Hendrickx
Volume Editor: Frank Hendrickx

Wolters Kluwer

Published by:
Kluwer Law International B.V.
PO Box 316
2400 AH Alphen aan den Rijn
The Netherlands
E-mail: international-sales@wolterskluwer.com
Website: lrus.wolterskluwer.com

Sold and distributed in North, Central and South America by:
Wolters Kluwer Legal & Regulatory U.S.
7201 McKinney Circle
Frederick, MD 21704
United States of America
Email: customer.service@wolterskluwer.com

Sold and distributed in all other countries by:
Air Business Subscriptions
Rockwood House
Haywards Heath
West Sussex
RH16 3DH
United Kingdom
Email: international-customerservice@wolterskluwer.com

Printed on acid-free paper

ISBN 978-94-035-1741-4

e-Book: ISBN 978-94-035-1784-1
web-PDF: ISBN 978-94-035-1832-9

Printed in the United Kingdom.

The Authors

Dr Viktoria Sp. Douka is Professor Emeritus of the Faculty of Law of the Aristotle University of Thessaloniki, Hellas. She has held academic positions at the National School of Judges, the Police Academy and the University of Macedonia in Hellas. Her academic interest, and field of specialty, lies in new forms of employment and collective labour relations. She has served in several academic and administrative roles in a plethora of institutions, such as President of the Organization for Mediation and Arbitration (Organismos Mesolavisis & Dietisias – (OMED)), Member of the Board of Directors of the 'Teloglion Foundation of Art' of the Aristotle University of Thessaloniki, Scientific Director by the Executive Committee for European Union (EU) Presidency Conference in Athens, Hellas (2003), Member of Legislative Preparatory Committees of the Ministry of Labour and Social Security and Ministry of Education, Research and Religious Affairs. She has been Member of Thessaloniki Bar Association since 1974, appointed by the Supreme Courts of Hellas, practising mainly in the field of labour law. Speaker in numerous congresses and conferences, in Hellas and abroad, on topics of labour law and labour relations. Titles of some of the publications she has written: *Employment Contracts in Public Services: Contribution to the Study of the Individual Labour Relations of the Employees in Public Services*; *The Transfer of Enterprises and Its Impact on Individual Labour Relations*; *Part-Time Employment: The Legal Status in the Private Sector*; *The Protection of Personal Data and the Employment Contract* (books), Personal data, working relations and General Data Protection Regulation (GDPR), the labour relations and the proposal for gross domestic product (GDP), 'From "flexicurity" to "flexiprecarity"? The case of the "more atypical" employment and of the hybrid contract of the "employee-shareholder", 'Subcontracting, outsourcing and their impact on labour relations', 'Prohibition of discrimination, Law and law case', 'Decent work – Convention No. 189/2011 and Recommendation No. 201/2011 for domestic workers' (studies).

The Authors

Dr Vasileios Th. Koniaris is a researcher working for the Centre of International and European Economic Law, in Thessaloniki, Greece. He holds a PhD from the Department of International and European Studies, University of Macedonia, Thessaloniki, Greece. He holds a bachelor's degree in International and European Studies (2007), a master's degree in Accounting and Finance, with emphasis on Corporate Social Responsibility (2008) and a Master in General Management at the Vlerick School of Management in Leuven, Belgium (2010). His academic interest, and field of specialty, lies in European Industrial relations with an emphasis on European trade unions. He is the co-author of *European Works Council – Hellas* in the International Encyclopaedia of Laws.

Table of Contents

Table of Contents

List of Abbreviations

ADEDY	Civil Servants' Confederation
AP	Supreme Civil Court (*Areios Pagos*) – Third Degree Civil Court
APDPX	Hellenic Data Protection Authority
APol	Supreme Civil Court Plenary Session – Third Degree Civil Court
ASE	Supreme Labour Council
ASKE	Representative Conference of Social Control of 'Socialized' Enterprises
ATA	Automatic Price Index Re-adaptation of Employees' Income
CC	Civil Code
CHSE	Committee for the Health and Safety of the Employees
CVT	Continuing Vocational Training
DA	Arbitration Award
ECB	European Central Bank
EEC	European Economic Community
EED	Labour Law Survey (Periodical, Fortnightly)
Ef.	Second Degree Civil Court
EIE	National Institute of Labour
Eir.	Magistrate's Court
EKE	Internal Labour Code – Works Regulations
EL	Emergency Law
EPA	National Employment Monitoring Service
ESC	Economic and Social Committee
ESEE	Hellenic Confederation of Commerce and Entrepreneurship
ESF/EKT in Hellenic	European Social Fund
ESM	European Stability Mechanism
ETAM	Unified Fund of Salaried Employees Insurance
ETCHS	European Financial Stability Facility
ETUC	European Trade Union Confederation

List of Abbreviations

Preface

Labour relations constitute life for a large part of population in Hellas, who are employees, and labour law is the law that regulates them. In fact, labour law directly covers and regulates the professional life of employees and, therefore, indirectly determines their personal life.

In addition, labour law influences and determines the life of the unemployed and applicants for work, while it also tends to conceive of labour relations in a wider spectrum that concerns an even bigger part of population, all those who do not work independently.

It is generally accepted that the regulations of labour law, perhaps more than the regulations of other laws, consist of political choices and are determined by the expediencies that these choices serve.

In 1975, the new Constitution, adopted after the fall of the military junta in 1974, introduced, for the first time, provisions relating to work, such as the recognition of the right to work, the trade union freedom (SD), the right to strike and to collective negotiations (Articles 22, 23).

The national legislation is supplemented by the International Labour Organization (ILO) Conventions (Hellas has ratified the majority of ILO Conventions)[1], the European Court of Human Rights and the EU legislation. The influence of the legislation of the EU is considerable and gave new impetus to improving the national system of protection of workers. Hellenic labour law provides answers to almost all current questions relevant to work. Provisions regulating labour relations have, however, not yet been codified into a Labour Code.

The impact of the wider socio-economic environment and historical process on the configuration of the content of the regulations of labour law is obvious. In Hellas, this has been more than obvious in recent years during which the new laws on labour issues have reflected the policy choices imposed by (a) the Troika, meaning the EuroZone Member States (Eurogroup), the European Central Bank (ECB) and the International Monetary Fund (IMF), following the accession of the country to the Financial Stability Mechanism (FSM) established by the Troika and (b) later by the so-called the Institutions, meaning the lenders.

It is common knowledge that since 2010 Hellas has gone through the most significant social, political and economic crisis since the *Metapolitefsi* in 1974 (transition to democracy after a seven-year period of military junta). In 2010 the economic crisis began, quickly evolved into a debt crisis and led to the accession of

1. *See* Annex 2.

for the first time will be paid 84% of the minimum basic wage set by the NGCA, and social security contributions will be subsidized by Organization of Employment of the Labour Force (OAED).

Underage persons from 15 to 18 years old, under apprenticeship contracts will be paid 70% of the minimum basic wage for a period of one year in order to enable them to acquire skills and provided that maximum weekly working time is up to forty hours for persons aged 16 to 18 and up to thirty hours for those aged 15 to 16.

Flexibility of employment is further enhanced against security; e.g., the employer's right to unilaterally impose work by rotation was reinforced in cases where his business activities decline; the maximum period that an employee of a Temporary Employment Agency (TEA) can be employed with an indirect employer increases to thirty-six months.

The remuneration for overtime is reduced by 5% to 20%.

Time limits on obligatory rest are reduced from twelve to eleven continuous hours every calendar day.

The distribution of annual leave can be divided into more than two periods, one of which must be a period of ten or twelve continuous days for those employed on a five-day or six-day working week.

Individual dismissals became cheaper as a result of a reduction in the notice period and an increase in the probation period from the first two to the first twelve months of the labour contract. Given that the amount of severance pay is related to the length of the notice period, the significant reduction in the latter resulted in an indirect reduction of severance pay, determined by law, by (*circa*) 50%.

The new law lowers the thresholds for collective dismissals. Until 2010 enterprises employing between 20 to 200 employees were allowed to dismiss up to four employees per month and those employing more than 200 employees up to 2% per month. Under the new law (Law 3863/2010) enterprises employing from 20 to 150 employees are allowed to dismiss up to six employees per month and those with more than 150 employees up to 5% and no more than 30 employees per month.

The system of collective negotiations and collective agreements and the system of mediation and arbitration, as a means of resolving collective conflicts and as a mechanism for regulating labour standards in favour of the employee, were significantly revised and have been decentralized from the national general and sectoral level to the enterprise level.

The principle of the 'implementation of more favourable provision' or 'favourability principle' according to which an employee's remuneration, terms and conditions of employment were determined by the most favourable clauses of the collective agreements, has been lifted, as a general rule, in favour of the enterprise-level collective agreement.

The new regulations have shifted the centre of gravity of the procedure for defining the remuneration, terms and conditions of labour from the collective back to the individual level leaving room for the regulatory power of the freedom of contracts on the basis of the individual labour contract.

The new legislation includes a package of reforms that essentially demolish the current system of retirement benefits, e.g., the age for a full pension was, as a general rule, 65, and effectively not more than 62, and now the minimum age is of 67; pensionable earnings used to be calculated on the basis of the wages earned in the last five or ten last years of a person's career, most often those with the highest wages, thus increasing the amount of pension and now the new law requires that pensionable earnings are calculated on the whole career average.

People aged 55 to 64 who have been dismissed have the right to insure themselves for social security purposes. That right must be exercised within two months of the termination of their employment contract (irrespective of whether it is a mass redundancy or an individual dismissal), provided they remain unemployed, and the employer is obliged for a period of three years after the dismissal to participate in the cost of such a self-insurance scheme by up to 50% for persons aged 55 to 60 and 80% for persons aged 60 to 64. However, it is not permitted for this category of dismissed persons to exceed 10% of the total number of people dismissed; otherwise all dismissals will be invalid. Law 4093/2012 increased the retirement age by at least two years for most categories of insured people unless they were due to retire under the old provisions by the end of 2012.

Laws 4472/2017 and 4475/2017 adopt measures for drastic pension cuts for those already retired, and, at the same time, the amount of the social insurance contributions of self-employed persons is increased. More specifically Law 4472/2017 stipulates from 2019: (a) reduction by 18% of the personal excess amount of wage paid in connection to all primary and supplementary pensions; (b) abolition of family allowances (spouse and children); and (c) freezing of all pension increases until December 2021.

The new legislation has brought about a major shake-up in public sector employment relations both for public employees and civil servants, in the form of the following changes: the increase in weekly working time from 37.5 to 40 hours without a proportional pay rise; the introduction of optional part-time employment by up to 50% on a daily or weekly basis and for up to five years, with a proportional wage cut; the introduction of intersectoral mobility of civil servants; the introduction of the opportunity to take unpaid leave of absence for a maximum of five years; the introduction of interdepartmental mobility of public sector employees and the introduction of the 'labour reserve' scheme for staff close to retirement, offering them a proportion of their salary for a period of between three and five years without having to work; reductions in earnings, severance pay, benefits and all kinds of remuneration by up to *circa* 50%.

While numerous laws have brought about continuous reductions in employees' wages, the country's poor economic situation has also caused a big drop in purchasing power. In addition, there has also been a great increase in part-time employment, casual work, fixed-term labour contracts and unemployment, especially among women and young people. Reducing the protection level that labour law provides for employees cannot guarantee jobs and, therefore, cannot contribute to the economic recovery of the country and to confronting the economic crisis.

On 11 July 2018, the European Commission adopted a decision to activate the enhanced surveillance framework for Greece. This decision entered into force after the conclusion of the European Stability Mechanism (ESM) stability support programme on 20 August 2018.

The effects of this programme on labour law and industrial labour relations in Greece remain to be seen.

General Introduction

Chapter 1. General Background

Vasileios Th. Koniaris

§1. The Significance of Hellas for Industrial Relations

1. Relationships between and within workers, working groups and their organizations and managers, and employers and their organizations are defined as industrial relations. They cover all aspects of the employment relationship and its associated institutions and socio-economic environment. These work relations, based on new institutions, have become a subject of importance to legislators and other interested parties. Labour had been distinguished from other objects of transaction and is now considered as a human product. After the industrial revolution in Britain in the eighteenth century, the use, primarily, of machines in production and the social unrest that this provoked, the state has tried to limit the abuse of rights by the employers in labour relations, by enacting labour law and industrial relations provisions. The self-organization of the workers and employers created the first trade (labour) unions and employers' organizations as well as works councils. They are considered to be institutions created under industrial capitalism and according to the law of the land. In Hellas, the institution of collective negotiations and collective agreements (but not of a European-scale collective agreement) is one recognized way of formation of labour relations between workers and employers.[6] Although not evident now, it is expected in the future that cultural capitalism (in a world of networks and interconnections) will set aside the competitive interests of the employees and the employers and lead to the adoption of means that are more cooperative and more oriented to the building of consensus.[7]

2. Labour law[8] in Hellas follows the labour laws of European countries, which were the interpretation of certain clauses and were the result of states power. Labour law, adjusted to the necessities of the state each time, expresses the current views and tendencies of state policies. It treats of persons in their capacity as workers or as employers, as including the employment relationship between a worker and an

---

6. R. Blanpain (ed.), *Comparative Labour Law and Industrial Relations* (Kluwer, 1982); T. Koniaris, *Labour Law in Hellas*, originally published as a monograph in the International Encyclopaedia of Laws/*Labour Law and Industrial Relations* (Kluwer Law International, 2002), pp. 170 et seq.
7. J. Rifkin, *The Age Access: The New Culture of Hypercapitalism, Where All of Life is a Paid for Experience* (Putnam Publishing Group, 2000).
8. *See* A. Marsh & E. Evans, *The Dictionary of Industrial Relations* (Hutchinson, 1973), p. 182.

employer arising from the contract of employment and the problems of job security connected with its termination, collective negotiations and collective agreements, statutory provisions in relation with particular conditions of employment, trade unions, industrial conflict, strikes, lockouts and membership of trade unions and works councils. Labour law follows the operations of private economy, both individual and collective, but the intervention of the state leads it towards public law and international or European law. From a different point of view, Hellenic labour law together with laws on social policies are considered as social law by many lawyers, because they enact exact social evaluations which concern the individual relation, not in abstract, but in a concrete social environment, national or international (or more strictly European) under social justice. Labour law has its own institutions, its own principles and its own methodologies. Legal documents of the European Union (EU) concerning labour law of all its member countries, and Hellas is a member of EU, and international conventions proposed by International Labour Organization (ILO) and ratified by Hellas as a Member State of the United Nations (UN), make up an integral part of the law of the land.[9]

3. Trade unions and employers' organizations, from an international perspective, lead the development of labour law at high speed, in order to keep up with the most important changes in the European labour economic environment. Since 1 January 1981, Hellas, as a member of the EU, has incorporated into national law the new European legal setting.[10]

4. The official spoken language in the country is Hellenic. The Hellenic language, which has journeyed for more than four thousand years, reached the peak of its development in a dialect form, mainly Ionian, with the poetry of Homer (900 BC). In a second phase, there was the emergence of the Attic *koine* which was the spoken and written Hellenic language in the extended area of the Hellenic rule following the conquests of Alexander the Great. This language evolved into the Hellenic *koine* which is preserved in the New Testament. The meeting of Hellenic thought with Christian faith, which prevailed under the name of Orthodoxy, made the Hellenic language the vehicle for the ecumenical ideal, formerly in Homeric epics, later in the New Testament.[11]

5. Since ancient times Hellas has undergone many changes. Philosophy was born in Hellas, and Hellenic society through the centuries has preserved and elaborated philosophical thinking by creating and implementing general clauses in legal interaction between the Hellenic city-states and throughout its evolution up until the communes under the Turkish occupation. Some general terms most representative of the Hellenic continuous legal experience are freedom, justice, equity, autonomy,

9. D.A. Morse, *The Origin and Evolution of the ILO and Its Role in the World Community* (Ithaca New York: New York State School of Industrial and Labour Relations, Cornell University, 1969).
10. T. Koniaris, *European Works Council – Hellas* (The Hague: Kluwer Law International, 1999).
11. P.L. Jr. Drew (The George Washington University) 'Logos' in: *The Philosophy of Logos*, 7th International Conference on Greek Philosophy (Samos-Patmos, August 1995) p. 56; M. Z. Kopidakis (ed.), *Istoria tis ellinikis glossas (History of the Hellenic language)* (Athens: Elia, 1999); G. Thomson, *To aithales dhendro (The evergreen tree)* (Athens: Kedros, 1999) pp. 280-294.

equality, good faith, concord, solidarity. During the second half of the eighteenth century and under the Turkish occupation, Hellenic society had, at communal level and under a mercantile collectivism, institutions of labour relations which caused astonishment among foreign travellers-writers of those days.[12] There were works regulations, worker shareholders, workers' participation in the profits of international enterprises, social policy schemes for all in the Community. The study of those institutions might help to solve problems of labour law and industrial relations today.[13]

§2. Geography and Population

6. Hellas lies at the southern end of the Balkan Peninsula. It is bordered to the north by Albania, Fyrom and Bulgaria, to the east by Turkey and the Aegean Sea, to the south by the Mediterranean and to the west by the Ionian Sea. Hellenic territory now covers an area of 131,957 km^2, of which the 43 big inhabited islands and the smaller inhabited ones cover 24,808 km^2.[14] The population, according to the last census of March 2011, is 9,903,268, though the short-term population projection of Hellas (1944–2004) for the year 2004 was 10,690,000.[15] This difference is mainly attributed to a change in the statistical method used to calculate the population and to immigration caused by the economic crisis in 2009. Athens is the capital, and there are 228 urban agglomerations and cities with more than 10,000 inhabitants.[16]

7. Hellenes, in spite of the scepticism or the opposition of the rest of Europe, in the beginning liberated some Hellenic territory. In accordance with the London Protocol of 1830 and the Constantinople Convention, the first territory of the independent Hellenic State comprised of 47,516 km^2. The territory grew after the Protocol of London of 1864 to 50,211 km^2, while after the Balkan Wars, in accordance with the Protocols of London and Bucharest of 1913 and the arbitration of the Big Powers in 1914, the territory grew to 121,794 km^2. After the Lausanne Convention of 30 January 1923, the Hellenic territory grew to 129,794 km^2, while Hellenes totalling 1,222,000 (according to the census of 1928, five years later) had moved into

12. H. Holland, *Travels in the Ionian Isles ... During the Years 1812 and 1813* (London, Longman, Hurst, Rees, Orme, and Brown, 1815); W.M. Leake, *Travels in Northern Greece* (London, J. Rodwell, 1835), p. 387; F. (de) Beaujour, *Tableau du Commerce de la Grece* (Paris, Renouard, 1800) volume I, p. 287; E. Dodwell, *A Classical and Topographical Tour Through Greece* (London, Rodwell and Martin, 1819), volume II, p. 108; H. Tozer, *Researches in the Highlands of Turkey* (London, J. Murray, 1869), p. 62; D. Urquhart, *Turkey, Its Resources, Its Municipal Organisation, Its Commerce* (London, Saunders and Otley, 1835), volume B, pp. 75, 100 et seq.; F. Boulanger, *Ambelakia ou les Associations et les municipalites Hellenique* (Paris, Librairie de Guillaum, 1875).
13. T. Koniaris, Mercantile Collectivism of Ampelakia: A Liberal Proposition, in: Society for Macedonian Studies and Thessaloniki Bar Association (eds.), *Tribute to Kostantinos Vavouskos,* Vol. D (Sakkoulas, 1991), pp. 461–484.
14. Hellenic Military Geographical Service, in *Concise Statistical Yearbook of Greece 1994,* National Statistical Service of Greece (Athens 1995), Table I: 4.
15. News release, Hellenic Statistical Authority, 31 Jul. 2012; The Hellenic population in accordance with Eurostat is higher, because the Hellenic Statistical Authority uses different statistical methods.
16. *Concise Statistical Yearbook 2012,* Hellenic Statistical Authority, pp. 44–50.

Hellenic territory from the agricultural lands of Asia Minor, Eastern Thrace, the Black Sea territories, Constantinople and other places. Lastly, after the decision of the Allied Powers in Paris of 27 June 1946, which was ratified by the Hellenic-Italian Convention of 10 February 1947, the territory grew to what it is today (131,957 km^2).[17]

8. While during 1828 the population was 753,400 persons, according to the census of that year, in 1920 it was 5,017,000 persons, and in 1971 the population was 8,769,000 persons, which means an annual rate of increase of 1.10%. Besides the natural increase, additional factors contributed to this rate. During the period of 1920–1928 the population of Hellas had an annual increase of 2.7%, while during the war years until 1947 the rate fell to 0.25%. The national rate of increase in population averaged 1.20% between 1955 and 1960. An increase of 4.5% during the period 1961–1971, unusually low in comparison with international averages, was mainly caused by emigration. During the period 1971–1981, there was an increase in the population of 11.1%. Later, in the period 1981–2001, there was an increase in the population of 6%, which reached 10,964,020 in 2001.[18]

9. Emigration was rising rapidly to more than 71,500 persons per annum (average 1961–1962) reaching a peak during 1965 (117,167 persons in accordance with the National Statistical Service (NSSG)), while during 1970 emigration reached a figure of 92,681 persons. From 1901 to 1921, 398,767 Hellenic people emigrated overseas (95% to the USA). This number compared with the total Hellenic population of 1901 (about 2,500,000) was destined to inflict permanent damage on the size of the Hellenic population.

10. Concerning immigration, in accordance with the *2012 Statistical Yearbook of Hellas*, for the year 2001, there was an inflow of 347,919 immigrants, mainly from countries of Southern Europe and Balkans.[19] Today (2014), there is an estimation of more than a million immigrants in Hellas, because of the increase of immigration from Balkan, Asian and African countries[20] while this number shows signs of decreasing because of the current economic crisis.

11. Until 1974 the real increase in population was lower than the natural increase. It was higher only in the district of Greater Athens (where Athens, the capital of the country, is located) and in the districts of Central and Western Macedonia. All other areas of the country did not retain the increase in population due to the natural rate of increase, because emigration was leaving a negative balance. It

---

17. J. Koliopoulos & T. Veremis, *Greece: The Modern Sequel: From 1831 to the Present* (Washington Square, N.Y.: New York University Press, 2002); *see also* National Statistical Service of Greece, 1994, I: 4; Hellenic Statistical Authority, 2012, I: 4, p. 28.
18. *See* Hellenic Statistical Authority, 2012, p. 35.
19. It is disputed whether that figure is close to reality. Certain unofficial calculations consider the number of immigrants much higher.
20. 'OECD International Migration Outlook 2012: Greece', *OECD Publishing*. doi: 10.1787/migr_outlook_2012_21-en.

was only in 1977 that the real increase became 0.88% due to the increase in immigration compared with emigration. In recent years, an increased number of foreign immigrants have settled in rural areas, working mostly in agriculture. Urban areas also attract another high number of foreign immigrants.

12. By calculating the recent rates of natality and mortality, the population in Hellas, under the precondition of balanced migration, will increase at a very slow rate, the annual birth rate will diminish progressively and the death rate will increase relatively. This will mainly be the consequence of an increase in the population over the age of 65 years. While in 1971 the population of people over 65 years of age was 10.9% of the de facto population of Hellas, in 1991 it increased to 13.7% (which in real figures means about 1,377,000 persons), in 2001 it was 16.2%. Recent official data of 2009 show that the population of 65 years and over has reached 18.8% of the de facto population.

13. The percentage of de facto population by major age groups in Hellas was as shown in Table 1.[21]

Table 1 Hellenic Population

	1971	*1981*	*1991*	*2001*	*2009*	*2016*
0–19 years	33.0	31.4	26.8	24.2	19.4	18.5
20–64 years	56.1	56.8	59.5	59.6	61.7	60.59
65 years and over	10.9	11.8	13.7	16.2	18.8	20.91

14. In 2019, the density of population was 84.28 inhabitants per km^2. But Hellas manifests what is perhaps an exceptional phenomenon, namely the accumulation of about 60% of the whole increase in the country's population, since 1961, in the area of Greater Athens. This area contains more than half of the inhabitants of the Hellenic cities and more than a quarter of the total Hellenic population.[22]

§3. Political System

15. Modern Hellas has been a democracy, a democracy with a king, with a short interval of dictatorship, and a presidential democracy since 1975. In the past decades, there have been military movements, *coup d'états* and dictatorships. The first governor of Hellas was Ioannis Kapodistrias (1823–1831). After 1832, Hellas

21. *See* Hellenic Statistical Authority, 2012, p. 37.
22. *See* National Statistical Service of Greece, 1994, II: 14, p. 47.

became a kingdom and passed through the stages of absolute monarchy to democracy with a monarch. The kingdom of Hellas lasted until the Declaration of Democracy by Alexandros Papanastassiou in 1924, after a period of unrest and military movements, the most important of which were on 15 August 1909, introduced by Eleftherios Venizelos and on 15 September 1922 by Nicolaos Plastiras. New military movements followed but finally a *coup d'état* by Ioannis Metaxas restored the king and promulgated a dictatorial state in 1936 until the German occupation. Hellas was a kingdom again after World War II and survived as such during the communist guerilla war that lasted until the summer of 1949.[23]

16. In 1967 an 'updated' *coup d'état* took place 'to avert the danger of a communist threat against the nation'. A referendum took place under the military regime in 1973 and Hellas was changed into a republic. A new *coup d'état* took over in 1973 until the final collapse of the military dictatorship on 23 July 1974. On 8 December 1974, a new referendum on a republic was proclaimed and 69.2% of the valid votes attested the preference of the electorate for a republican regime and not for a king.[24] On 28 May 1979, Hellas acceded to the European Community[25] (EU after the Maastricht Treaty of 7 February 1992) and became a member of the Eurozone on 1 January 2001.

17. Since 1844, the principle of separation between legislative power, executive power and judicial power has been in all the constitutions of modern Hellas. In accordance with the Constitution of 1975, revised for the third time in 2008 and currently in force, Article 26 promulgates:

(a) legislative power shall be vested in Parliament and the President of the Republic;
(b) executive power shall be vested in the President of the Republic and the government;
(c) judicial power shall be vested in the courts of law, the decisions of which shall be executed in the name of the Hellene people.

18. General elections are normally held every four years for all seats of the Parliament (300 seats in total). Parallel to the election of 300 seats of the National Parliament, the voters express their preference, in a further election, by votes which are cast for the 21 seats Hellas holds in the European Parliament after the Lisbon Treaty. The most recent elections for the European Parliament were of 25 May 2014 and for the National Parliament were of 17 June 2012. Every citizen over the age of 18 is entitled to vote. The government must have the confidence of the Parliament. Also, the President of the Republic is elected by the Parliament for a period of five years by a special majority and a special procedure.

23. *See* Koliopoulos and Veremis, pp. 101–102.
24. G.I. Rallis, *Politikes Ekmystirefseis 1950–1989 (Political Confidences 1950–1989)* (Athens: Proskinio, 1990).
25. Official Journal of the European Communities, L 291, Vol. 22, 19 Nov. 1979. *Documents concerning the accession of the Hellenic Republic to the European Communities.*

19. Two consecutive elections (January and September) made in 2015 brought into power *Syriza* (coalition of radical left) bringing an end to a traditional two-party system in Greece since the *Metapolitefsi* (period after the political junta of 1967–1974). The parties of the Hellenic Parliament after the last elections (September 2015) compared to the percentages of the elections of the 25 January 2015, are as shown in Table 2.[26]

Table 2 Seats in the Hellenic Parliament

	25 January 2015		*20 September 2015*	
	%	*Seats*	*%*	*Seats*
Coalition of Radical Left (SYRIZA-EKM)	36.34	149	35.46	145
New Democracy (ND)	27.81	76	28.10	75
Panhellenic Socialist Movement (PASOK)	4.68	13	6.28	17
Independent Hellenes (ANEL)	4.75	13	3.69	10
Golden Dawn (XA)	6.28	17	6.99	18
Communist Party (KKE)	5.47	15	5.55	15
The River	6.05	17	4.09	11
Centre's Union	–	–	3.43	9

20. The results of the last elections of May 2014 for the European Parliament after the entry into effect of the Lisbon Treaty, compared to the results of 7 June 2009, were as shown in Table 3.

Table 3 European Parliament

	7 June 2009		*30 May 2014*	
	%	*Seats*	*%*	*Seats*
Panhellenic Socialist Movement (PASOK)	36.64	8	8.02	2
New Democracy (ND)	32.29	8	22.72	5
Communist Party (KKE)	8.35	2	6.11	2
Popular Orthodox Rally (LAOS)	7.14	2	2.7	–
Coalition of Radical Left (SYRIZA-EKM)	4.7	1	26.57	6
Golden Dawn			9.39	3
The River (Social Democrats)			6.60	2
Independent Hellenes			3.46	1

26. *See* the website of the Hellenic Ministry of Interior, 2015, available at www.ypes.gr/en/Elections.

21. It should be mentioned that until the economic crisis there were three major national groups or parties, which under different names have dominated the Hellenic political scene: rightists and liberal-democrats, now under the party of New Democracy, socialists and/or social democrats, now under the Panhellenic Socialist Movement, leftists and/or communists under the Communist Party, the 'Coalition of the Radical Left' and the Democratic Left. In the present Parliament, there are also the political parties of the Independent Hellenes (democrats), Golden Dawn (extreme rightists), The River (Social Democrats) and the Centre's Union (Social Liberals).

22. The Supreme Court in Hellas is the *Areios Pagos*. Judicial power in Hellas is vested in courts having regular judges. Article 87 of the National Constitution states that:

(a) Justice shall be administered by courts composed of regular judges who shall enjoy functional and personal independence.
(b) Judges shall in the discharge of their duties be subject only to the Constitution and the laws; in no case whatsoever shall they be obliged to comply with provisions enacted in abolition of the Constitution.
(c) Regular judges shall be supervised by judges of a superior rank and by the Public Prosecutor and the Deputy Prosecutor of the Supreme Court; Public Prosecutors shall be supervised by Supreme Court judges and Public Prosecutors of a superior rank, as specified by law.

23. The courts comprise administrative, civil and criminal courts and they are organized by special laws. The courts are bound not to apply laws, the contents of which are contrary to the Constitution. Thus, the courts in Hellas have the power not to apply acts passed by the legislature, if they rule them to be non-constitutional.

24. The Council of State is the Supreme Administrative Court. In accordance with Article 95 of the Constitution, the jurisdiction of the Council of State pertains mainly to:

(a) the annulment upon petition of executive acts of administrative authorities for abuse of power or violation of the law and;
(b) the reversal upon petition of final rulings of administrative courts, for abuse of power or violation of the law.

25. The Council of State is the supreme competent court of the state (there are also the other administrative courts) to rule on the legality of the actions of the government and the administration.

§4. THE ECONOMY

26. Hellas produces a variety of minerals in a crude state or concentrates and, since 1980, oil from the North Aegean Sea. However, the key sector of the economy is not manufacturing industry, though many efforts have taken place to promote the creation of competitive industry. The number of regions having more than the average percentage of industrial activity (mining, construction, factories and electric power) is very low, less than 35%. The main industries are confined to some of the major cities like Athens, Piraeus, Thessaloniki, Volos, Kavala, Patrai and consist of food, beverages, tobacco industries, textiles, clothing, chemicals, cement and oil refineries. But primary commodities such as tobacco, cotton and currants still constitute a large percentage of Hellenic exports. In general, while agricultural developments have not been satisfactory, industrialization remains a crucial and pressing problem. On the other hand, the public services sector has been oversized and disorganized.

27. Hellenic industry passed through the following stages:

(a) 1840–1874: a series of mining and metal companies developed at Lavrion; the last founded in 1874 was considered to be one of the most modern metal factories in Europe. They were competing with the best in Europe. During the years 1870–1874 unexpectedly heavy industry in its most advanced form was founded in Hellas. It was engaged in the production of all kinds of machinery. John MacDonald, founded in 1874, Vassiliadis, Argyriou and Coupa were among the first industries in Hellas.
(b) 1875–1922: for the first time in Hellas with the H. Trikoupis government (1875) and later with the E. Venizelos government (1910), industry found favourable conditions for development, regardless of the Balkan Wars of 1912–1922. This period has been called the 'infancy' of the Hellenic economy.
(c) 1923–1951: this is the 'juvenile' period of the Hellenic economy when giant industries and trusts, like those of cement and beer, were built up before World War II and after. The Marshall Plan (1948–51)[27] (the USA programme to help the recovery of western Europe following World War II) and the United Nations Relief and Rehabilitation Administration[28] put funds to many uses, including the building of highways, bridges, railroads, power installations, housing, factories and farm improvements.[29]
(d) 1952–2000: the industrial sector of the economy was assisted by foreign investment and aid in many ways, but organizational and commercial factors, as well

27. *See*, in particular, for Hellas: C.A. Munkman, *American Aid to Greece* (New York: Frederick A. Praeger, 1958).
28. The United Nations Relief and Rehabilitation Administration was the organization founded during the World War II to provide aid to areas previously occupied by Axis powers.
29. C. Ammer & D. Ammer, *Dictionary of Business and Economics* (London: The Free Press, 1977), p. 141.

as a high cost of production, did not make it competitive until 1965. It is mentioned that, in 1967, about 22.5% of the gross domestic product (GDP) (at factor cost) originated from agriculture, while secondary production (manufacturing) accounted for 29.3% and the tertiary sector of the economy for 48.4%. In 1975 the relative percentages (current prices) were 18, 30 and 52, in 1988, 14, 32 and 56%.

In the NSSG of the *Hellas Concise Yearbook* of 1994, the last data on manufacturing establishments are from the 1988 census. In accordance with these data, in 1988, there were registered 144,714 manufacturing establishments. These establishments presented a total average annual employment of 705,819 personnel. About 1.5% of these covered more than 60% of the total gross value of production. A total of 100 of these industries, in the form of limited companies, covered about 40% of the personnel, while the 10 larger companies covered 8%. At least four of these industries have been financed by foreign capital, American, German and French, while most of them were capital intensive and not labour intensive. As regards new enterprises, data released by the Industrial and Commercial Chamber of Hellas show that there were 3,337 new enterprises in 1987, compared to 3,263 in 1986 and 3,166 in 1985. New enterprises in the form of limited companies were: 155 in 1984, 205 in 1985, 235 in 1986 and 237 in 1987.

One of three profitable enterprises with its own capital managed a capital return 25.1% to 50%, and 26 enterprises showed a return on their own capital higher than 50%. In Hellas, the level of return on capital, in that period, was impressive. Hellas had been in the second place for profitability among the Organization for Economic Cooperation and Development (OECD) countries. Profits in 1999 reached 50% and increased further in 2000.

(e) 2001–2009: after the entry of Hellas in the Eurozone (1 January 2001), inflation was very low as well as interest rates. This provided industries with the capital to make investments.

(f) After 2009, the economic crisis changed the whole picture of the Hellenic economy.[30] Since the period between 2010 and 2017, Greece has lost approximately 22% of the GDP.

28. Since 2009, real wages have fallen and employees have lost more than 35% of their purchasing power. The average income from employment of a Hellene employed person is 80% of the European average. In accordance with Eurostat, in 2013, 34.6% of the population is at risk of poverty or social exclusion, even though Hellas is the 29th most developed of a total of 141 countries.[31] It should be mentioned that, in 1984, Hellas ratified the European Social Charter (which was revised in 1996) on a minimum income for the economically disadvantaged.

---

30. Hellenic Republic Ministry of Finance, *Hellenic National Reform Programme 2012-2015: Report on the progress towards Europe 2020 and the implementation of the Euro Plus Pact commitments*, Athens, April 2012.
31. UN, *Human Development Report 2011, Sustainability and Equity: A Better Future for All*, p. 126.

29. In a report published by ICAP in 2012,[32] the 300 biggest Hellenic industrial companies in 2009 showed a decrease in their gross profits by 9.24% (a decrease of EUR 1.6 billion). For the year 2011, the 250 biggest Hellenic industrial companies, with an annual turnover of more than EUR 3 million, showed total losses of EUR 1.75 billion. Recently, in a report published by ICAP, the 500 most profitable companies in the country demonstrated a significant increase in their turnover (9.5%), a trend that seems to continue for the next years.

30. Although Hellenic enterprises had succeeded in increasing their profits since 1991, historically, industrial companies showed losses in their balance sheet. In accordance with IOBE (the Hellenic Foundation for Economic and Industrial Research) the decrease in profits was the result of:

(a) decrease in consumption;
(b) decrease in turnover;
(c) decrease in the amount of banking loans for new investments.[33]

31. Sectors, like drinks and food, leather products and shoes, ready to wear clothing, tobacco industries, textiles (though textiles and basic metal industries as a whole have lost ground) and dairy products, cover more than 50% of the first 350 Hellenic industries in sales. In Hellas, as in other European countries, it is the service sector that develops and rising economic strength is found among entrepreneurs of the tertiary sector of the national economy. The role of services and especially of the financial sector of the economy is central (banks, financial services and insurances). Also, supermarkets have led to the disappearance of small-to-medium business.

32. The important thing is that the mainland of Hellas has not been equally affected by industrial and trade activities. In a hundred years Hellas has suffered unusual and abrupt changes; the establishment of new populations, war damage, an exodus of peasants to the cities, emigration to the rest of the world and recently immigration of Hellenic populations from countries of soviet republics.

33. The big fall in the number of jobs in recent pre-crisis years (before 2009), is attributable not only to companies' technological modernization but also to the interruption of the re-absorption of industrial capital. The incapacity of the Hellenic industrial sector to stand on its own feet internationally, as well as the evident trend towards under consumption, has negative consequences for industrial development.

34. Hellenic per capita income (or GDP per head) reaches now USD 2,003 billions,[34] but pronounced inequalities in the regional and personal distribution of

32. ICAP, *Greece in Figures, Greek Financial Directory 2012*, European Association of Directory and Database Publishers, 2012, p. 8.
33. IOBE, *The Hellenic Economy (3/2012)* 69 (October 2012): 17–18.
34. World Bank available at http://data.worldbank.org/indicator/NY.GDP.PCAP.CD.

national income are limiting the significance of the average. Wide disparities in living standards and expenditure, between urban and rural areas, as well as in the cities, are apparent. There are also changes in the GDP (at factor costs). In 2015, there is a high percentage resulting from the tertiary sector of 84.6%, only 12% from industry and 3.3% from agriculture.[35]

35. Since 1974 the Hellenic currency (drachma) had lost two-thirds of its buying power. In 1989, the yearly average inflation was more than 17%, the highest among the European Economic Community (EEC) countries, but for entering the monetary union, inflation has been pressed and remains below 4%. Since 2001, inflation remains on average 4%, but since 2009, it has shown high volatility, from a low of 0.3% to 5.1%, partially because of the increased Value Added Tax (VAT), indirect taxes, the high oil prices and the drop in domestic demand.[36] Recent figures indicate an inflation rate of 1% for 2019.

36. Productive investments had declined during the period 1975–1980. In agriculture, investments had declined from 8 billion drachmas in 1975 to 6 billion in 1980. This decrease led the national economy into a zero rate of growth. Also, the national economy lost its capacity to modernize its machinery and to re-orientate its production in a period of critical re-adaptation all over the world. During 1981–1987, the GDP had a yearly rise of only 1.2%, and since then it may be observed that the country is de-industrializing in the absence of new investments in production.

37. Since 2003 foreign direct investments in Hellas has remained at satisfactory levels, attracting capital mainly from Germany, France and the United Kingdom. Still, the majority of capital formation in Hellas (almost 80%) was driven by domestic private investment.[37] Despite the economic crisis, total gross capital inflows to the country totalled EUR 2.7 billion in 2010, EUR 3.2 billion in 2011,[38] while for 2013 Foreign Direct Investment (FDI) was EUR 2.9 billion mainly in the tertiary sector, caused by the liberalization of telecommunications. Recent figures indicate a stability in FDI flows, at EUR 3.60 billion following a significant increase after 2015.

38. After a strong period of growth from 2001 until the end of 2007, the Athens Stock Exchange Index dropped from 5,400 to 750 units in the end of September

---

35. *See* CIA, 'The World Fact book: Greece'; certain data, which comprise part of the National Accounts results for the period 2004–2012, are provisional. *See also*, Hellenic Statistical Authority, 2012, XXII, pp. 559 et seq.
36. Directorate-General for Economic and Financial Affairs, *The Economic Adjustment Programme for Greece*, European Economy, Occasional Papers 87/2011, Fifth Review-October 2011, pp. 11–12; Eurostat, News Release Euro Indicators, 145/2012, 14 Sep. 2012.
37. McKinsey & Company (Athens Office), *Greece 10 Years Ahead, Defining Greece's New Growth Model and Strategy* (Executive Summary), June 2012, p. 13.
38. UNCTAD, *Towards a New Generation of Investment Policies: World Investment Report 2012* (Geneva: United Nations Publication, 2012), p. 63.

2012, having reached its lowest in May, at 475 units. This drop can be further examined in two periods. The drop in the first period, from the end of 2007 until the beginning of 2009, can be attributed to the global financial crisis after the collapse of Lehman Brothers in 2008, while the drop in the second period is fully attributed to the Hellenic government debt crisis. Since September 2009, after the upwards change of the Hellenic deficit, the Supreme Labour Council (ASE) Index lost approximately 72% of its market capitalization. For the same period, the average amount of daily transactions dropped from EUR 250 million to EUR 63 million. The total market capitalization of the ASE Index in 2009 was EUR 295 billion[39] while for 2012, it was approximately EUR 27 billion. In 2019, the total market capitalization of the ASE Index is EUR 15.62 billion. In September 2018, foreign investors accounted for the 66.4% of the transactions in the ASE, while three years later in 2012 this percentage was 32%.[40] The banking sector has shown the biggest losses, although recently there are signs of recovery due to planned mergers and acquisitions and the amelioration of the economic climate of the country.

39. The corporate tax regime in Hellas has undergone significant changes during the past years as a consequence of an unstable tax policy, which continues until today. As a consequence of the economic crisis, the government has introduced an increased corporate taxation to increase the state's revenues. Concerning Public Limited Companies (SA), the applicable tax rate for undistributed profits is 26%. Distributed profits are subject to an additional income tax at 10%. Dividends paid to parent companies based in European countries are exempted from such tax.[41]

40. VAT is charged on every supply of goods and services by a commercial enterprise. The VAT rate is 24% except for specific categories of goods and services for which the tax rate is 13% and 6% respectively. The above rates are reduced by 30% in certain circumstances. Public services (health, education, insurance, etc.) are not subject to VAT.[42] In 2013, VAT was reduced for restaurants at 13% as a means to decrease the prices of the services offered because of the decrease of domestic demand and to support the tourism sector of the country.

41. The deficit of the state budget (ordinary and investments) was increased from GRD 22.5 billion in 1974 to GRD 190 billion in 1981. The relative deficit of the public sector, including the state budget, administering agricultural products and public enterprises, from GRD 128 billion in 1974, was GRD 350 billion in 1981. It reached GRD 2,500 billion in 1989 (which means that it had increased more than seven times since 1981). Recent figures for the deficit of the state budget indicate a gradual decrease, or a surplus, mainly caused by the cut in government spending because of the crisis.

---

39. Athens Stock Exchange, *Monthly Statistical Bulletin Exchange Developments*, September 2009, Table 2.
40. Axia Numbers, *Monthly Statistical Bulletin*, Issue 109, September 2012, p. 5.
41. L. 3943/2011; *see also*, Deloitte International, Greece Highlights Tax, 2012.
42. The Hellenic General Tax Code as it was revised by L. 3899/2010. *See especially*, Art. 4 of this Law concerning VAT.

42. The deficit of the current exchange increased from USD 932 million in 1976 to USD 2.3 billion in 1981. This happened under conditions of economic recession. The deficit reached a peak in 2009, 15.6% of GDP, and since then, it is decreased to 6% for 2012[43] mainly due to the decrease in the value of imports. During the same period, the general government gross debt and its interests were doubled. In 1989, the government debt was 105% of the GDP, which means that it was more than GRD 9,300 billion. In 2000 the debt reached 103.4% of the GDP, reaching 112.9% in 2008, 148.3%, or EUR 328,588 billion, in 2010 and 170.6% in 2011.[44] For 2012, the debt was decreased to 156.9% of the GDP.

43. The above-mentioned accumulated economic problems and their social consequences are accompanied by the super-centralization of the state, and by the ineffectiveness of public administration, which paralyses the state machine. The sad picture is accompanied by a non-democratic cultural system, socially, economically and culturally abandoned rural areas, inhuman conditions of life in the city and a poor quality system of social services, which has deteriorated.

§5. Research on Employment

44. Since 1975 the NSSG (now the Hellenic Statistical Authority) has launched an annual survey of unemployment. The research takes place in urban and semi-urban districts of Hellas, in order to organize a continuous sample survey of the employment of the population of the country.[45] The basic aim of this research on employment was the accumulation of the necessary data for the study of the structure of employment of persons, of age 14 and over, of households of urban and semi-urban areas of the country. Certain characteristics of the population (economically active and non-active population) are also included. The study of the labour force by branches of economic activity, occupational groups, position in the occupation and hours of work is also another target of the research, as well as the study of the length of unemployment in combination with age, sex, district and certain characteristics of the branches of economic activities. Members of collective cohabitations (e.g., nurseries, orphanages, military camps and prisons) or permanent hotel residents or alliance servicing at consulates, commissions or reserve officers living alone or with their families have been excluded.

45. Registered and hidden unemployment in the non-agricultural population remains a pressing problem, to which emigration offered some solution, but now immigration of Hellenes from Eastern Europe and foreign labour and emigrants from third countries have exacerbated the problem. The unemployment of educated

43. Hellenic Government, *Draft Budget 2013*, October 2012, p. 13; *see also* Annual Report of the Governor of the Bank of Greece 2009–2011.
44. Public debt and deficit statistics are in accordance with Eurostat http://epp.eurostat.ec.europa.eu.
45. Decision of the Ministers of Co-ordination and Programming and Economics No. 1616/B11/9 January 1975.

young people (high school and university leavers) is a very serious problem, while social scientists are talking about a 'new proletariat'.

46. Development laws have been implemented[46] without, however, reducing unemployment. Law 2784/2000 introducing greater deregulation of the labour market had the same results. Also, the Fund for Employment and Professional Formation, as well as European programmes,[47] had served in (but had also wasted resources for) the training of the workforce, the reduction of unemployment and the promotion of employment succeeding with very poor results.

47. The main reasons for unemployment are new technology, globalization that defies competitiveness, and the tough monetary, and monetarist, policy of recent years. These days, the expected development is based to a large degree on a form of capitalism that does not produce incomes, that does not conduct productive operations, that does not increase real earnings, that merely takes profits, while propping itself up on a market in delusory values and illusions.

48. Unemployment insurance covers persons in a dependent labour relation, for reward and as a main occupation, with a labour relation for unlimited or for defined time (permanent or temporary), and who are covered by health insurance with Institute of Social Insurance (IKA),[48] or another insurance organization.[49]

I. General Employment Status

49. Certain official indicators show that unemployment in Hellas was below 3% in 1980, and from 3.6% in 1983, reached 7% in 1987. These figures might not be compatible and unemployment may be much higher, because, as already mentioned, the method of measuring unemployment in Hellas is different from the methods of the other European countries. In accordance with the NSSG, in 1989 there were 296,000 unemployed persons.[50]

50. The census of 1991 and surveys conducted by the NSSG (*Concise Statistical Yearbook 1994*) show that a total of about 4,118,400 persons comprised the labour force of Hellas for 1993. From these, the employed persons were about 3,720,200 and the registered unemployed 398,200. Males in the labour force were about 2,584,000 and females about 1,534,400. There were about 2,419,500

---

46. For a detailed presentation of this issue of development laws *see*, in particular, Law 1892/1990.
47. T. Koniaris & A. Voyatzis, FORCE, Formation Continue en Europe, in R. Blanpain, C. Engels and C. Pelegrini (eds.), *Contractual Policies Concerning Continued Vocation Training in the European Community Member States* (Leuven: Peeters Press, 1994), pp. 189–203.
48. Now incorporated into a new First-level National Health Network (PEDY).
49. Until today, in order to receive the unemployment benefit of the Unemployment Insurance Organization (OAED), a person must have spent 125 days in employment that comes under OAED insurance, in the 14 months preceding the dissolution of the labour relation, without counting days of work in the two months previous to this.
50. *See* National Statistical Service of Greece, 1994, III: 6, p. 62.

employed males and 144,500 unemployed. Also, there were 1,300,700 employed females and 233,700 unemployed females. For the year 1997, there were 440,400 unemployed (10.2%) in a 4,294,400 labour force.

51. In 1999 recorded unemployment rate was 11.7% (523,374 persons), compared with 9.2% in the rest EU. Of the Hellenes recorded unemployed, 58.5% were long-term unemployed, 61.5% were females and 50% were young persons under 30 years of age. It is a fact that young persons under 30 years of age, as well as females, are the most vulnerable to unemployment.

52. Recent figures on unemployment suggest a major increase because of the financial crisis since 2007 and are as shown in Table 4.[51]

Table 4 Unemployment Figures (Thousand)

	2009	*2010*	*2011*	*2012*	*2013*	*2019*
Employed	4,506.5	4,401.3	4,092.2	3,763.1	3,635.9	3,843.9
Unemployed	472.8	629.6	883.6	1,261.6	1,345.3	875.9
Economically inactive	3,328.7	3,290.3	3,358.5	3,356.2	3,360.2	3,243.4
Unemployment rate %	9.5	12.5	17.8	25.1	27	18.6

II. Employment per Sector

53. As has been mentioned, during the 1980s, a population increase was evident in decentralized areas of the country where industry, services and especially tourist enterprises have developed. Official data from the two censuses of 1991 and 2001 provide a good picture of the transformation of employment per branch of economic activity.

Table 5 Employment by Economic Activity (Thousand)

Branch of economic activity	*1991*[52]		*2001*[53]		*Change*
	Number	%	Number	%	
Total	4,118.4	100	4,614.4	100	
Agriculture, livestock, forestry, fishing	793.9	19.2	599	12.9	–24.5

51. In accordance with the Hellenic Statistical Authority http://www.statistics.gr.
52. *See* National Statistical Service of Greece, III: 7.
53. *See* Hellenic Statistical Authority, 2012, p. 113.

Branch of economic activity	*1991*[52]		*2001*[53]		*Change*
	Number	%	Number	%	
Mining	19.3	0.4	12.2	0.2	–36.7
Manufacturing	977.3	23.7	530.5	11.4	–45.7
Electricity	39.6	0.9			
Construction and public works	261.4	6.3	375.6	8.1	43.6
Trade, restaurants and hotels	791.5	19.2	916	19.8	15.7
Transport and communications	249.3	6	286.0	6.1	14.7
Banks and insurances employed	220.8	5.3	109.5	2.3	–50.4
Education			257.9	5.5	
Other services					

54. Employment in the primary sector was also diminished in 1990 by 2.5%. This decrease of the labour force diminishes the total supply of work, because the contribution of the age group 15–64 years to the labour force is higher in the primary sector, than in total population. It is mentioned that the female contribution in this sector is higher than in the other sectors. Since 2009, there are signs of interested young persons returning to work in the primary sector because of high unemployment in urban areas.

55. The fall in production influenced employment. After a small increase in 1989, the stagnation of economy in 1990 followed. Nevertheless, despite the changes in economy the public sector continued to grow. In accordance with recent data from the Ministry of Economics, the increase of persons employed in the public sector developed as shown in Table 6.[54]

Table 6 Persons Employed in the Public Sector

	2001	*2002*	*2003*	*2004*	*2005*	*2006*	*2007*	*2008*
General government sector	301.2	308.8	318	355.9	347.4	380.1	400.8	392.3
Publicly owned companies	560	582.1	601.9	640.9	618	624.8	617.2	629.8
Public sector (total)	861.2	890.9	919.9	996.8	965.5	1004.9	1018.0	1022.1

54. ILO, Labour Statistics Greece laborsta.ilo.org 13 Nov. 2012.

56. It should, however, be mentioned that the most recent attempt to record the exact number of the employees in the public sector should be completed by the end of 2012, since the first census had poor results because only employees in the general government sector had been registered. Those employed in the publicly owned companies were not included.[55]

57. The contribution of the primary sector to the growth of GDP is negative, as is that of the secondary sector, while the tertiary sector has a positive influence. A decrease is recorded in the secondary sector, though for the years 1988 and 1989 its increase was evident, contributing to the GDP. The product of the primary sector followed a downward curve because of the lessening of returns and the negative economic cycle. The tertiary sector (also because of its link with underground or black economy) showed an increase.

III. Participation Rate

58. Participation rate or activity rate is the percentage of the total population in a given age group or sometimes the proportion of the civilian employees included register unemployed, which is in the working population (labour force). For Hellas, the employee participation rate remains one of the lowest in the EU.[56]

Table 7 Employee Participation Rate (%)

	2005	*2006*	*2007*	*2008*	*2009*	*2010*	*2011*	*2012*	*2018*
Male	65.0	65.3	65.2	65.3	65.2	64.9	64.3	63.9	65.0
Female	42.3	42.8	42.8	42.8	43.9	44.5	45	45.1	42.2
Average	53.4	53.8	53.8	53.9	54.3	54.5	53	53	51.7

59. The working ages of the persons who belong to the labour force of Hellas are between 15 and 65[57] years old. They are actively employed or seeking employment. Among them there are not included students, retired people, stay-at-home parents or people in prisons. The low participation rate in Hellas further affects the pension system of the country and has created extensive deficits since 1980.

55. Until 2 Nov. 2012, the number of employees in the public sector was 768,009 as is indicated at the registry of public sector employees of the Ministries of Administrative Reform and E-Government and Finance. However, this is not the final number since not all personnel information has been verified by their respective personnel divisions yet.
56. International Labour Organization, Key Indicators for the Labour Market Database and other data laborsta.ilo.org 13 Nov. 2012.
57. In accordance with L. 3863/2010, the retirement age becomes the 67th year, creating a new state of retirement for other categories (women, disabled, etc.) as well.

IV. Seniority of Employees

60. The principle of equal treatment of the employees by the employer is applied to equal situations.[58] Parallel to this, the institution of permanence has become a provision of work regulations, especially in big companies. Seniority rights are particular rights based on length of service or continuous employment which have been recognized and protected by Hellenic laws and court decisions. The will of the legislator is to promote tenure with recognized seniority rights in the labour relation. All data (e.g., court decisions) show the determination of employees to exercise their rights to tenure and seniority, but reliable data are missing as to the level of labour mobility. Of course, in highly specialized positions of work of large companies of the tertiary sector some mobility is evident, as in all large companies.

61. University research has shown that average seniority in ceramics industry (construction), before the year of the economic crisis of 2009, was two years for unskilled workers, four years for skilled and eight to ten years for white-collar employees and managerial personnel. In one clothing firm, average seniority was reported as being four to eighteen months for unskilled, forty-five to sixty months for skilled, twenty-four to forty-eight months for white-collar and permanent personnel, to the pension age for managers. In mass transportation services average seniority was thirty-five years for all personnel. In another textiles clothing firm, average seniority was: unskilled five-ten years and of white-collar and managerial personnel twenty years. Under the current economic reality of stagnation and the suggestions of the Troika, seniority rights will be in conflict with the new propositions for the recovery of the economy which consist in lowering higher salaries and employing new employees.

V. Degree of Education of the Labour Force

62. Unemployment occurs basically among the uneducated labour force. The number of educated and trained persons grows continuously, but the non-existence of occupational orientation creates large numbers of high school leavers and higher education graduates unsuitable for positions actually available. Also, there are shortages of trained/educated candidates for posts in other very crucial sectors of economy. A general conclusion is that industry employs proportionately more of that part of the labour force with lower educational attainments, in contrast to banks and other services which employ personnel of a higher educational level.

63. This is another indication of the unorthodox way in which the Hellenic economy is structured and functions, unable to adapt to occupational changes. By Law 2009/1992, the National System of Occupational Education and Training was founded for organizing and providing occupational training and awarding certificates and diplomas to its graduates. A list of recognized occupations and a report identifying the levels of training (in accordance with certification) was prepared by

58. *See* below para. 795.

the EU for all Member States to incorporate into their national legislation. During this period, we should also mention the FORCE programme for the development of continuing vocational training (CVT) in the European Community, which was adopted by the Council of Ministers on 29 May 1990 and launched on 1 January 1991. The main research goals were for factors enhancing and promoting CVT, but the research in Hellas showed very poor results.[59]

59. *See* in R. Blanpain, C. Engels & C. Pelegrini (eds), *FORCE: Contractual Policies Concerning Continued Vocational Training in the European Community Member States* (Peeters Press, Leuven, 1994), pp. 189–203.

Chapter 2. The Historical Background

§1. Individual Laissez-Faire and Mixed Trade Unions (1821–1909)

64. The proclamation of human rights in the Hellenic National Constitution of 1844 was a result of the new democratic ideas about individual freedoms protected and promoted by the state. On the other hand, Articles 212–215 of the Hellenic Penal Law, which correspond to Articles 291–294 of the French Penal Code, had proscribed the founding of unions and companies in general, without the prior permission of the administration. But many activities of workers testify to the fact that associations of workers had been founded as spontaneous reactions to new situations since 1821.

65. For the first time in modern Hellas, the Hellenic Constitution of 1864 recognized the freedom of association. The internal and external content of the 'new right', which was gradually absorbing unknown theories, principles, unknown systems of ideas and, in general, nineteenth-century trends, was to be regulated constitutionally, by basic guarantees and limitations, as a way of securing its growth and maintenance. But the new democratic form of government did not function properly until 1875.

66. In the elections of 1875, the clear victory of the bourgeoisie and the application of the principle of ratification and confidence in the government by the majority in Parliament heralded the beginning of a new era in Hellenic history. During this new period, freedom of association was recognized, subject only to the objective of the associations being legal. Thus, the completely free organization of trade unions in the economic sphere was granted. The founding of a trade union was not subject to a regulation by law. The common civil law of that period, considering at least three persons as enough for the founding of a union, facilitated in that way the creation of many labour unions. But the lack of any general movement, even in the same trade, characterizes this period, which is also marked by strikes for better working conditions and higher wages.

67. After 1900, labour movements in Athens, Piraeus and Patrai resulted in the founding of some 'workers' centres',[60] where different unions of the district came together, for the first time, compressing many elements of the bourgeoisie and some vague trade union programmes. The new liberal progressive force needed friends among workers. Thus, the basis of the unions had been laid through the help of known 'sociologists' and with the assistance of middle-class thinkers and writers. The revolution of 1909 formulated the goals for future union activity. These were broad reformist goals, representing the interests of the up-and-coming middle class, who opposed the old Hellenic land-owning class.

60. 'Workers' Centres' or 'Trade Unions' Centres' are second-level local trade unions.

§2. The Period of Individual Protection (1910–1917)

68. The period begins with the declaration of Alex Papanastassiou during the Pan-Hellenic Association of the Productive Unions: it distinguished the interests of workers and employers and stressed the autonomy of workers. One year later, the complete freedom of the legislature to pass special laws concerning the operation of the right of association often discussed in the Hellenic Parliament had materialized in the National Constitution of 1911. Law 281/1914, on unions, was passed and the application of special legislation then became necessary, in order to define to what extent trade unions could be freely created. Since then, special control on trade unionism has been channelled. The government, without contradicting the Constitution, can easily bypass such protection by placing restrictions on the right. This method of controlling trade union freedom (SD) was brought about in Hellas by registration of the trade unions, which gives effect to the wishes of the government and endows the trade union with legal status and other attributes.

69. Socialist propaganda was inexperienced and misinformed. Nevertheless, the struggles of workers for international solidarity for political rights and complete labour freedom began. The rule books of the trade unions were orientated towards the class struggle and the Socialist Labour Party. But the labour class, as a whole, did not respond 'properly'. The enemy was not only the bourgeoisie; it was also the unawareness and ill-considered actions of the people. Though Law 281/1914 heralded the separation of the workers from the employers and their unionization in their own trade unions, many workers continued to join mixed unions, under representatives comprised largely of employers.

70. During this period, the government passed labour laws establishing the protection of the individual worker, thus initiating the so-called phase of 'individual protection'. The end of the period was marked by the materialization of the First Pan-Hellenic Congress in Athens, which established the Greek General Confederation of Labour (GSEE). Until 1918, trade unions were organized on an occupational, craft or local basis. Certain workers' centres and two federations were active during the last years of this formative period. During those early years, the new Liberal Party, led by E. Venizelos, 'sought to change the course of modern Hellenic history by making material progress and social and cultural development advance side by side'. New trade union possibilities on a national level opened after the establishment of the GSEE, while activities on an international level had already been materialized by certain trade unions.

§3. Trade Unions and Interventionism (1918–1949)

71. The labour movement of Hellas won its national recognition at a time when the already existing differences between the leading groups of GSEE were provoking conflicts within the movement. But under the pressure of trade unions and the progressive government of Venizelos in 1920, the Constitution of the ILO was ratified. Under this Constitution, the first real application of SD had taken place. But ideological differences evoked more conflicts, especially between the two predominant beliefs, Marxists and reformists (socialists). In 1929, for the first time, two laws of the government of Venizelos were passed, permitting the abolition of those trade unions which had gone beyond their objectives and were considered as being communist in ideology. Many trade unions were abolished and trade union leaders were jailed and exiled. From this point on, the GSEE leadership was dependent upon the Hellenic government to attain the right of representation of Hellenic labour. This dependence enslaved the official labour movement to the state.

72. Until 1936, the dispersed labour forces developed into five distinct branches in Hellenic trade unions. However, in 1936, the different branches united and decided upon a common policy which augured well for workers. Unfortunately, the Metaxas dictatorship had secured power the day before the scheduled general strike of 5 August 1936.

73. The intervening dictatorship of Metaxas, which lasted until 1941, created the national GSEE. The government at the beginning appointed the leadership of GSEE, reduced SDs and exiled opposing union representatives. On the other hand, new protective labour legislation was passed. Law 694/1937 on the protection of workers' representatives in the institutes of social insurance was also passed.

74. During the German occupation of Hellas, the same situation continued, though newly appointed officials had taken over the GSEE. The Labour National Liberation Front (Labour EAM), which later came completely under communist control, included those who had opposed the Metaxas dictatorship and German control. It also worked for the failure of the 'draft' of Hellene workers to work in Germany. During this period, the Hellenic government in exile in England had voted Law 3127/1942, which provided for the restoration of SDs, abolished the dictatorial decrees and restored the previous legislation.

75. Labour EAM was recognized after the liberation as the official organization of trade unions in Hellas and won the elections of 1946, keeping control of the GSEE for a few months, until the guerrilla war divided the nation. This was the last time that leftist representatives had the GSEE under their control. Since then, the rightist or, recently, socialist governments and the GSEE leadership have kept communism in a minority position in the official trade union represented by GSEE.

§4. Features of Post-war Industrial Relations from the Perspective of History

I. Wages

76. Wages were never fair in Hellas. They did not correspond to higher productivity of work and the lowest wage never covered the basic needs of the family. But nominal salaries and wages were low, while inflation contributed to the further reduction of real wages. Thus, especially after 1942, employers were obliged to provide for their employees common canteens and other material benefits. In 1947 collective negotiations did not succeed. Thus, until 1952, ministerial decisions were only trying to restore some of the lost purchasing power of real wages. Wages were determined by a tripartite board, and when later another system was introduced for setting wages and salaries, which was completely unacceptable to union officials, they in consequence left the board.

77. Trade unionists continued to demand the re-establishment of collective negotiations as well as the government's fixing of minimum wages according to the basic needs of workers. Thus, in 1954, after pressure by trade unions, the introduction of new legislation on collective negotiations was announced. This legislation, however, was a failure. The Minister of Labour had absolute and total power over wages and conditions of work. During that period, unskilled work was divided into two categories by the Minister of Labour. Those unskilled workers who had not completed two years' work received smaller increases in wages than the other category of unskilled workers. This did not even correspond to the falling buying power of that period. Finally, Law 3239/1955 gave the means of regulating the procedures of collective agreements, including arbitration.

78. After the Second World War, real wages had fallen by about 25% in comparison with the pre-war period. Since then (in the post-war era) real wages have been kept below the real productivity of work (Hellenic labour using old machinery) and were also kept lower by the preference of the employers for unskilled labour (for reasons of low payment). It has also been declared many times, even by ministers of employment, that the steadiness of the Hellenic price index has been successful, thanks to the below-average level of employees' wages: it is declared that after the Allied liberation of the country, the attempt to improve the economy and the initiation of the programme for rehabilitation became a burden for the labour class.

79. In 1956 the General Secretary of GSEE wrote that the buying power of 832 drachmas, which was the regular monthly wage of an unskilled worker (namely 60% of Hellene workers), was not enough to cover the daily needs of the worker (let alone of the family). Since wages have not been raised by trade union action, one can assume that their level would be about the same without trade unions. In times when the economy was in trouble, the standard wages were clearly below the productive capability of work and higher wages were needed in order to strengthen the market.

80. Until 1959, the increase in nominal wages was about 55% while the increase in the cost of living for a worker's family was 72.3% according to GSEE. This meant a real decrease of about 17%, or according to other price indices 10–12%. This decrease in real wages occurred notwithstanding that the living standards of workers were already very low.

81. The increase in national income during that period of about 31.4% meant that employees, instead of benefiting by the increase in the national income, on the contrary had the purchasing power of their wages diminished through the increased cost of living.

82. Following the Allied liberation, the government forced GSEE to exercise restraint in its demands in order to increase national production. After the devaluation of the drachma in 1953 (by 50%) and the increase in the cost of living, the representatives of GSEE had to choose between two alternatives: to express the opposition of the labour class and in doing so to shake the general faith which was necessary for economic measures to achieve the expected happy results, or not to oppose devaluation and the rise in the cost of living, but to contribute to the creation of necessary conditions for development. They preferred the second. The indignation of the labour leaders was visible after GSEE's failure to achieve positive results by substituting a more long-term political rationality for short-term political reality. In Hellas, the demand by unions for higher wages has never corresponded to an increase in production or an increase in company profits. These demands have always meant that the workers and their families could not live on their wages and that a wage increase was needed in order to cover some (but not all) of the increased living expenses. The Hellenic working family tried to make ends meet by sending more family members out to work.

83. As from 1974, employers' organizations had unsuccessfully suggested the replacement of guaranteed weekly wages by an hourly payment, in order that more people could find work. Since 25 February 1975, national collective agreements have been signed relating to the lowest wages and salaries, the equal payment of men and women, the increase in the workers' vacations, the implementation of the forty-hour working week (1984) and the five-day working week (1985), but hourly payment has been excluded.

84. According to Article 8 of Decision 1/1982 of the Second Degree Arbitration Court[61] of Athens and the Law of Legal Content of 19 May 1982, Law 1346/1983 in Article 6 introduced the Automatic Price Index re-adaptation of employees' income (ATA) which had been decided in a collective agreement, an arbitration award (DA) or a Ministerial Decision. Since 1991, ATA has been abolished and free collective agreements have been reinstituted.

II. Relationship to the Communist Party

85. There have been many unsuccessful attempts to establish large labour organizations which could be more effective than the GSEE. The only labour organization capable of achieving success would be one supported by the Hellenic

61. Using the term 'Arbitration Court', one must have in mind that an 'Arbitration Court' is not a 'court' *stricto sensu* and does not solve legal disputes; it solves collective disputes (disputes of interests) between trade unions and employers' organizations.

Communist Party. The Communist Party had several elements conducive to a well-functioning organization. Not only did it have dedicated followers and an adequate amount of funds for certain needs, but it also had well-indoctrinated officials who would faithfully follow a direct party line.

86. After many unsuccessful attempts to get into GSEE's leading group, which had been maintained by reformists since 1947, the communists tried to collaborate with reformist officials who had been thrown out of GSEE and were opposing its leadership. In its twenty-five years of organized action, the Hellenic communist labour movement had applied the Leninist policy of alliances with the peasants and the middle classes of the city, 'where labour gains the leading role … having its own organized political party'. But the communists in Hellas were never thought of as a harmless group of activists. After the civil war, they had always been treated by Hellenic governments as being enemies of the state. The Hellenic conservative community treated them as the scapegoat for socio-economic failure.

87. The Communist Party did not influence the Hellenic trade unionist scene as much as it influenced the political scene. Since few union members, outside of the established 'labour fathers', showed an interest in running their union the militant communist officials did not find strong opposition in making headway into the GSEE leadership, by easily influencing all the dissatisfied non-communist union members. The Communist Party was the only political party to organize itself for elections within the unions. Well studied militant activists would have succeeded in the unions under two preconditions:

(a) that the voters in the trade union elections would not know or would not be interested in the candidates' politics;
(b) that the state would not police trade unions and their activities.

88. Due to state intervention, the Communist Party was never able to attain control of GSEE. The communist union movement, 'having been the leading force of the revolution against the democratic institutions and in the name of Democracy has been rightly excluded since the (allied) liberation of Hellas'. On the other hand, one cannot assume that the Hellene non-communist workers would have had the power to stop the communist domination. Perhaps Hellas did not need revolutionary trade unionism but the old reformism, which was the political expression of the labour movement. This led to the labour class opposition to the employers who had not adjusted to the new realities and principles of social law and democracy.

89. Post-war realities had a detrimental impact on communist ideology in Hellenic trade unionism. The communist unions, during periods of prosperity, e.g., the years 1964–1967, were only competing with the GSEE on its own terms. On the other hand, one does not know how many workers, following the so-called communist unions, accepted communist ideology. Considering the political elections in Hellas (the last one of June 2012), the majority of the workers voted against the Communist Party, even if one believes that the communist votes came from the workers and employees.

90. After the civil war, most Hellene workers acted in a conservative manner. Though they were not satisfied with the 'bourgeois' state, they preferred to express their rights through trade union struggles. They did not wish to become citizens of a socialist state similar to those of Eastern Europe. Now the legalized Communist Party, after the fall of the Soviet Union, has changed its strategy and attempts to establish communism in Hellas through the use of democratic procedures.

III. Trade Unions

91. The most important trade union in Hellas is the GSEE. In July 1918, 44 labour organizations totalling 60,000 members attended the First Pan-Hellenic Congress, which founded the GSEE in Athens. Very soon eight federations were founded. In 1919, 385 trade unions totalling 84,926 members were organized. They were represented regionally at workers' centres.

92. Official statistics on trade union membership are disputed, especially when unemployed and pensioners remain unionized. Certain data show that trade union membership amounts to 30% of the active employees, but in the private sector, membership is not more than 15% The degree of organization is much higher in service industries, like banks, and in the greater public sector. Civil servants are also free to organize their trade unions.[62] Their representative confederation is Civil Servants' Confederation (ADEDY).

93. There are three main syndicalistic fronts: PASKE leads the socialist trade unions, PAME organizes the communist trade unions and DAKE represents the liberal trade unions. Since last years, PAME officials have left their chairs at the executive boards of GSEE and ADEDY.

94. Managerial or supervisory personnel are kindly requested by their employers of the private sector not to become organized at all, although they are legally entitled to join trade unions and to bargain collectively. The Hellenic trade unions are organized on a craft or occupational basis.

95. The system of labour relations in Hellas cannot be understood unless one has grasped what is meant by 'trade union officials'. In Hellas, trade union officials are employees who carry out legal union activity: that is, at the same time that they remain in work they carry out their union duties in parallel.[63] Employers are obliged to grant paid leave to trade union officials for union purposes.

---

62. Article 46 of L. 2683/1999.
63. Articles 14 and 15 of L. 1264/1982.

IV. Representative Trade Unions

96. Under Hellenic law, a legal entity is an individual or a corporation. Unincorporated unions are not considered to be trade unions. One type of these unincorporated associations is the trade union from the time of the signing of its founding law and constitution by its members until its acquisition of a legal personality. Under certain conditions these associations are characterized as trade unions. A trade union, as the collective force of its individual members, is different in kind and separate from the sum of those who founded it and contribute to it. It is a legal entity, and as such, there are laws concerning its representative organs, its property and its power in the social, economic and political spheres. It is a legal person.[64]

97. Legislation on collective agreements has been passed by Hellenic governments, in order that trade unions may bargain collectively for their interests in free discussions, which also creates a sense of loyalty for every member in the union. The belief that individuals had equal rights before the law and were able to sign free contracts was proved invalid when class dynamics changed the law, especially in the economic sphere. Some second thoughts placed the control of the interests of the classes in the hands of the state, which had absolute power to pursue its ends. But the state, having been influenced by the interests of one or more social groups, has proved incapable of wielding absolute power. The state has been judging and controlling the powers in the state, trying to promote cooperation between classes and the dissolution of their contradictions. And the independent representative bodies of class interests have been necessary to undertake this mission.

98. Article 4 of ILO Convention No. 98, dealing with the encouragement and promotion of collective negotiations, 'enjoins governments to take measures appropriate to national conditions for the creation of conditions for successful voluntary negotiations between the two sides, employers and workers'. It is explicit that negotiations should take place between 'employers or their organizations and the organizations representing the workers'. Disputes as to which representative trade union has the right to sign collective agreements have been solved by the institution of the 'most' representative trade union, which has also been accepted by ILO. In Hellas, this institution had been distorted in order that certain trade unions, also representing the workers, may be excluded from collective negotiations. For the first time the terms 'representative' or 'rather representative' were used in Part XIII of the Versailles Convention and later in Article 3 paragraph 5 of ILO's Constitution, without their meaning being determined.

99. Hellenic legislation used the term in Emergency Law (EL) 866/1937 under Metaxas' dictatorship when it named the national GSEE as representative of all employees. Later, Law 1367/1938 used the term 'of more general importance', without determining the meaning or offering criteria for its characterization, although it was meant for the national GSEE and its unions.

---

64. *See* below para. 1032.

100. Hellenic jurisprudence considered as a trade union any trade union capable of signing a collective agreement. Of course, the criterion of the number of union members has always been of great importance, especially from the ministerial side, which is necessary to expand to non-signatories the results of an agreement, though the criterion of number poses some difficulties in its realization.

101. Legislative Decree (LD) 186/1969 had defined criteria for signing collective agreements by those trade unions who obtained at least 100 votes at the last elections or 5,000 if they were unions of trade unions. According to Article 2, a stated number of criteria had to be considered in the case of a dispute on representativeness (while governmental influence had been truly considered, implicitly by the law, the most prevailing of all criteria).

102. LD 73/1974, which modified the above law, also accepted the system of representative organizations, but defined the number of members as an absolute criterion of representativeness, thus abolishing all subjective criteria, which were considered as opposed to the principle of SD. Article 3 defined that the most representative union for a certain trade (or occupation) was the one prevailing in numerical power of members exercising the trade or their trades in a definite district or the country as a whole. The most representative union of labour unions, for a certain trade or trades, was the one which included the labour unions having in total the largest number of members exercising the trade or these trades in a certain district or the country as a whole. In Hellas collective agreements had to be published in the state gazette (this is no longer the case).

103. Approval by the labour authorities could be refused if the agreements were thought to be harmful to the economy or out of line with official guidelines on wages and conditions of employment. Article 2, interpreting Article 4 of ILO Convention No. 98, according to certain lawyers had abolished the right of the Minister of Labour to refuse approval on the above grounds.

104. The definition of the representative organization given by the above law also concerned the trade unions of employees under private law of public services. So a mixed legal status, which prevailed in this area of public services, had changed after having been orientated towards the legislation of EU countries.

V. Collective Negotiations

105. The reasons for the passing of different laws on collective agreements are various. Formerly, the state wished to follow and introduced the recognized rights of the employees by international conventions. However, because of the construction of these laws, the rights of the workers were overlooked or given secondary consideration.

106. Law 281/1914 permitted the signing of ‘group’ contracts which only bound the trade union and the signatory employer. However, not a single contract was signed under that law. Thus, for the first time collective agreements were adjusted by the EL of the 16–21 November 1935, pertaining to the regulation of collective agreements on labour. This basic law was modified many times (the most important modification was by EL 1367/1938). Most of the modifications were initiated through strong government intervention during the negotiation period, the application of the agreement on third parties, etc. Hellenic labour law has not been able to free itself from these restrictions.

107. The above law dealing with the regulation of collective labour differences attempted to impose solutions to disputes arising between employers with more than ten employees, and their workers. This law permitted arbitration by state officials and compulsory arbitration in cases of unsuccessful negotiations. It had remained valid since August 1936 when the under-Ministry of Labour was established for the true application of this law.

108. Because of the above-mentioned laws issued in 1935, collective labour law was introduced and applied in Hellas and the institution of collective negotiations and agreements between employees and employers was established.

109. During the German occupation government officials were given permission to regulate the level of salaries, setting aside the system of collective agreements.

110. The Civil Code (CC), which was introduced in 1946, did not consider the interests of the social groups but brought forth a new era in the Hellenic legal system. In 1947 the Hellenic government continued to set wages below pre-war standards.

111. For the first time after liberation, Law 2053/1952 dealt with the regulation of collective relations and differences of labour, while LD 3086/1954 referred to the modification, etc. of the regulation of collective relations and collective disputes. These laws were very strongly criticized and short-lived. Finally, Law 3239/1955 introduced a more liberal regime for regulating the collective labour disputes and established a National Committee of Social Policy. Since it was known that free collective agreements were going to establish wages and salaries and that wage parity no longer existed as a result of Law 3239, the free determination of salaries and wages under negotiations was still restricted. This law had been considered by union officials as a deviation of the system of wage levels.

112. LD 3755/1957 modified and completed Law 3239. Law 3239 was also modified by LD 186/1969 on collective agreements, by EL 435/ 1968 concerning the fixing of the wage scale by ministerial decisions, and by LD 1198/1972 dealing with wages of private law employees in government services, etc.

113. LD 435/1968 was abolished, while Laws 186/1969 and 1189/1972 were modified by LD 73/1974, which concerned the restoration of the national general collective agreements (NGCAs) of labour, and the abolition of the intervening rights on collective agreements, etc. The modification of Article 20 of Law 3239/1955 abolished the right of the government to modify or quash, in total or in part, the collective agreement or the arbitrator's decision. By this same law, NGCAs were again restored. The right to sign NGCAs was withdrawn from GSEE by the military government.

114. Collective negotiations were introduced as a process of reaching decisions involving the terms or the conditions of employment or the price of labour. It brought with it a new way of establishing rules and compulsory arbitration of binding decisions. In 1935 the process of instituting collective agreements was a convenient means of imposing this new institution, but the then-existing dictatorial regime did not assist in its application. The division of collective agreements into national general, national and local sectoral, national and local occupational and special has partly changed by Law 1876/1990 which replaced special collective agreements by enterprise ones.

115. The law states that a trade union should be a representative union of trade. In the case of competing unions, the competent organ[65] must decide which of the union is the 'foremost representative'.[66] Another task of the competent organ is the attainment of a solution when collective negotiations fail to settle a contract.

116. It is said that the impact of negotiations is a major contribution to the idea of democracy and equality in labour relations, while in a 'free contract' the worker is obliged to accept the terms of the employer. Another asset of collective agreements is the advantageous combination of economic factors for higher productivity, especially when the legislation extends the right to negotiations and the application of collective agreements.

117. The institution of collective negotiations, without government intervention, functions in many countries. However, in Hellas, it had been applied inappropriately because of the specific types of agreements and hampered the development of comparability in different enterprises which produced identical goods and provided identical services.

118. The law had also been criticized for compulsory arbitration. The trade unions had continually asked for the abolition of the 'suffocating' law on collective labour disputes, contending that this law was 'full of traps'. Under the above circumstances, no real collective negotiations could proceed. Now, there is an established opinion that Law 1875/1990 on Free Collective Agreements has provided solutions to many of the above problems.

65. The Committee of Art. 15 of L. 1264/1992.
66. *See* below para. 1072.

VI. Strikes

119. The unions use immediate action to back up their demands. Some of these actions take the form of a strike.[67] Theoretically there are numerous means of direct action, but in reality, the choice is very much constrained by differing conditions.

120. The laws of the military regime[68] and the proposed Plan of Labour Code had considered a strike as a pre-planned reduction in labour force productivity. However, the procedures required to proclaim a lawful strike were merely obstacles used to prevent the strike from ever materializing. Before 1910, Article 167 of the Hellenic Penal Law forbade strikes. But in 1920, Law 2111/1920, dealing with offences against the freedom to work, had already adopted the view that the right to strike had been constitutionally fortified by paragraph 1, Article 2.

121. LD 42/1974, concerning the restoration of SDs and the regulation of related topics, abolished LD 890/1971 and also abolished the legal status of labour union strikes and employers' lockouts. Thus, decisions of jurisprudence interpreting strikes, made before the rule of the military, become of great importance since strikes have never been regulated by special rules. Now, the right to strike is explicitly recognized in the Hellenic Constitution and Law 1264/1982. Nevertheless, Article 4 of Law 1365/1983 demanded a majority of the registered members of a union to decide on a strike in the socialized public nature or utilities organizations, until Article 1 of Law 1766/1988 abolished it.

122. From a socio-political point of view, most of the strikes which have been organized in Hellas have been directed by the elected union officials who wished to gain recognition or followed orders of the political leaders or political structures. As a result, elected union officials became the victims of their own actions, because the character of the trade union, as a pressure group, was overextended owing to extremist action resulting in the loss of control of the situation. Hellas has, several times, been an innocent victim of opposing pressure groups made up of not only employers but also military leaders, political party organizations and pressure groups representing the politically orientated economic leading class.

123. We must not forget that the dictatorship of the Metaxas regime was established before a general strike.[69] We must also not forget that the dictatorship of 21 April 1967 was founded a few days before a political rally in the city of Thessaloniki and when strikes were a daily event. From this evidence one can clearly see that it was the 'efforts' of the working class that paved the way for the rule of the military. But these dictatorships should be considered 'exceptions' to the usual 'regulatory' methods of maintaining the status quo of the working class.

---

67. *See* below paras 1317 et seq.
68. LD 185/1969 and LD 890/1971.
69. Gr. Kassimatis, *Lectures on Social Law and Social Policy* (Athens: Faculty of Law of the University of Athens, 1963), p. 354.

124. In Hellas, social struggles do not usually consist of conflicts between classes, but of short-term cooperation between social groups which attack the state and have little interest in government economic policy or consumer demands. Professor Kassimatis, past Minister in Hellenic governments, described the phenomenon by giving three examples of action:

(a) In an independent company, the employer is willing to give in to the demands of the employees after having been assured of expected profit. This guarantee is approved by the government at the indirect expense of the consumer.
(b) The management of the enterprise cooperates with its employees since the government-affiliated enterprise will not directly pay for the monetary demands of employees.
(c) In public institutions where the management and employees are civil servants, strikes are not directed against the state or the public but are used against another class of civil servant. Strikes also are a result of intra-union disputes, where the preservation of the present union leadership takes precedence over the real issues, e.g., union leaders feel that they can maintain their position by championing the cause of a strike.

125. The realization of these problems had led to the constitutional prohibition on strikes of public servants. One solution could be the undertaking of the responsibilities provided by the autonomy which a public servants' federation claims it can bear. But in Hellas, trade unionism has also been defined as the freedom to create pressure groups, which call upon the interests of the social classes, in order to achieve benefits which at times are irrelevant to the interests of their classes. When the mechanics of collective negotiations are used to solve a wide variety of problems or when strike action is deemed the only means of securing labour demands, one must not only consider that the union leader is responsible for these events, but also perceive that the ulterior motives of the union leader can be directly traced to non-economic objectives.

126. The law gives two reasons for striking (industrial action). According to Article 19, paragraph 1, of Law 1264/1982, a strike is recognized:

(a) for the protection or promotion of interests (vindication);
(b) as a declaration of solidarity with third parties whose strike has direct consequences for their interests (of solidarity).

127. Civil servants are free to strike. Article 46 of Law 2683/1999 considers the striking and negotiations rights of civil servants. But, in the case of striking at enterprises which are legal persons under public law, a social dialogue precedes and notice of a strike must be given four full days in advance. For other companies, a shorter period of notice is required (twenty-four hours). During strikes, security staff of the strikers guards the private enterprise, while for public enterprises, personnel for serving the immediate needs of the public are put under the direction of the employer, as decided at the beginning of each year.[70]

§5. The Impact of EU Membership

128. Since 1981, Hellas, as a member of the EEC and now of the EU, has followed the aim of promoting a decent quality of life and standard of living for an active, inclusive and healthy society. Hellenes, like other people in the EU, have access to one of the strongest social safety nets in the world. Competition for improved productivity and growth, based on strong solidarity between citizens, leads to a stable society and widely shared prosperity.

129. Though employment strategies and social policy are the responsibility of each Member State, the EU deals with social matters only in accordance with the principle of subsidiarity, which is when solutions on a European level are more preferable. The social partners, trade unions and employers' organizations play an improved role in the EU. Hellenic representative organs of employers and employees participate in their European counterparts: BusinessEurope, the European Trade Union Confederation (ETUC) and the European Centre of Employers and Enterprises (c). Since 1992, the social partners have become special advisers to the European institutions and, since 1997; the Amsterdam Treaty has made them joint decision-makers. Social partners' agreements may now be transformed into European law, which is also implemented in Hellas.

130. The new 'European employment strategy', which emerged out of the discussion on 'growth, competitiveness, employment', from 1993 onwards, has the aim of employability of job seekers, entrepreneurship, adaptability to economic and technological change and equal opportunities for all. The European Social Fund (ESF) has channelled European money into helping Hellas to meet the goals they have agreed together to create more and better jobs.[71]

§6. Employment and Competitiveness

I. Social Solidarity and Social Programming

131. The participation of trade unions in public life and their collaboration with the employers' organizations are the results of a long evolution in which the events of the Second World War and the following guerrilla war played a particular and important role.

---

70. *See* below paras 1350–1352.
71. EC, *European Employment and Social Policy: A Policy for People*, Europe on the Move, 2000.

132. At the start, the grave social problems 'either were ignored or buried … the Hellenic government, at least on this line, was absolutely led by the unscrupulous economic oligarchy, which thinks only of its gold', F. Makris, General Secretary of the GCEE, declared in his speech at the 12th Congress in 1955.

133. The entire social-economic situation in Hellas was characterized by the escalation, in recent years before the economic crisis, of the profits of the capital, while unemployment had risen to more than 12% of the active population.

134. The very high profits of banks, commerce and industry are mostly monetary and are not the result of increased production. These extravagant profits were the result of a greater than ever absorption of the income of the working classes.

135. Profitability in the company sector, taking 1987 as base 100, was in 2000, 120 in the EU and 140 in Hellas. This placed Hellas second only to the USA among OECD countries. The result had been that real wages had slipped back to their 1982 level, without any corresponding increase in investment. In an eighteenth-month period, the last six months of 1999 and the twelve months of 2000, 5.4 trillion drachmas (EUR 15.847 billion) were put on the Athens Stock Exchange. Only 15% of company profits are invested.

136. As early as 1984, Hellas ratified the European Social Charter for a minimum income for the economically disadvantaged. Nevertheless, the average Hellene approaches 69% of the standard of living of the corresponding EU citizen. About 2,150,000 Hellenes live below the EU poverty threshold. Of these two-thirds are pensioners and 17% wage-earners.

137. In Hellas there was no 'plan of social solidarity' establishing the principles on which a system of labour relations was built, covering wages, hours of work, social security, etc. In 1980, the Socialist Party (PASOK) came into power and tried to establish socialist working relationships in public life. Some early measures included the transformation of public enterprises into socialized enterprises; their administration had as members, representatives of the employees of the enterprise, representatives of trade unions, of municipalities, of the government, etc.[72]

138. This joint programming of the socialized enterprises, under which the social advances envisaged could be worked out against the background of a realistic assessment of the economic possibilities, was for the benefit of the people. The idea was that by working in concert and taking account of objective criteria, the employees' share in the growth of national wealth for the benefit of the people was 'programmed' over a certain fixed period. But this idea was not implemented in collective negotiations. The government tried to implement social programming by

72. There were also the representative conference of social control (ASKE) and the central and regional labour councils for each of these enterprises.

'creating governmental trade unionists' and attaching less importance to the social partners and the collective agreements which could have resulted from social understanding.

139. ATA was in effect up to 1990. Social dialogue for social programming never had the expected results, and the government decided to transform the co-determination at the administration level of socialized enterprises. The representative conference of social control of 'socialized' enterprises (ASKE) was turned into an opinion-giving committee.

140. On the other hand, collective negotiations did not have an important effect on the overall climate of labour relations. Only after the beginning of 1991 were free collective agreements, including negotiations within the enterprise, regenerated to reflect real actors such as employers and employees, labour relations, remuneration ceilings.

141. Public dialogue is now implemented,[73] even before a strike, on the initiative of employees' organizations or employers' organizations, leading to a social dialogue. The mediator tries to solve the crisis.

II. Deregulation and Flexibility

142. Deregulation and flexibility are the new criteria introduced into Hellenic labour relations, as in other countries of the EU.

143. Flexibility is seen especially in changes concerning the contact of replacement, the monthly payment of compensation for lack of notice in the case of dismissal for enterprises which are in economic difficulties, extension of the duration of the trial period for certain employees, works councils and committees for health, protection of wages, work regulations, closure of enterprises.

144. The government, in conformity with the wage freeze, adapted the automatic cost of living clause in relation to wage indexation (ATA), leading to a so-called healthy cost of living clause in which the price increases of certain goods and services were taken into account. A wage freeze was imposed, and any increases given through any agreement or unilaterally by the employer were forbidden.

145. The government continued to intervene, with ATA, on income and purchasing power up to 1991, determining the ceilings and the conditions of labour relations. Law 1876/1990 put an end to this automatic governmental regulation of incomes.

73. Article 3 of L. 2224/1994.

146. The fight against casual labour (informal work), especially in the construction industry and in agriculture is becoming more and more difficult. The cost of engaging illegal labour on the informal markets is very low, compared with that of official markets.

147. The law imposes penal sanctions and fines in cases of social fraud. Work cards have also been introduced, and every worker has to carry one when at work, but informal markets continue to flourish.

148. Law 2837/2000 introduced economic support for low wage employees. Employees meeting certain conditions prescribed by law do not pay their insurance contribution to IKA, but none the less continue to be insured.

149. By decisions of the Minister of Labour and Social Insurance, Organization of Employment of the Labour Force (OAED) contributes to the promotion of employment by creating jobs for certain groups of people, and also by helping enterprises in poor or remote areas of the country to employ workers,[74] or by contributing to the remuneration of persons with special needs. On the other hand, flexibility is provided by Article 5 of Law 2874/2000.

§7. Evolution of Hellenic Labour Law or a History of Hellenic Labour Law

150. It has been argued that in Hellas, labour law has been introduced by the legislator not to regulate an existing social or economic reality but in order to create one. This is why many difficulties have appeared in the application of labour regulations because the legislation was ahead of social and economic development under capitalism. The legal profession in Hellas believes that this method of law enforcement has been the main reason for two kinds of behaviour by workers and employers. One is to wait and accept from the state the solution to their differences; the other is to oppose the state in periods when its paternalistic labour policy is considered 'wrong'.

151. Hellenic labour law may be divided into six periods, and in order to provide better information on its present status, the drawing up of a list of labour laws is necessary. This description does not comprise all re-enactments and amendments of the Laws.

I. The Period until 1910

152. During this period, social-economic actors had not developed a situation where labour law could exist and legislation intervened only to forbid strikes, by Article 167 of the Penal Code.

74. Common Ministerial Decision 334/12090/1997.

153. Free Hellas after the Revolution of 1821 and the destructions that the war brought to the country, did not possess any heavy industry enterprises. The most common enterprises of that period were grain mills, olive mills, wineries, shipyards, tanneries, spinning mills, forges, soap mills, dye works and print shops. The total number of the employees in industrial and handicraft enterprises was 28,400 persons, of whom 5,735 were females.[75]

154. The above number of employees was relatively small compared to the population of the country and comprised mainly of employees from parts of the mainland that was not yet freed from the Turkish occupation such as Epirus, Macedonia and the Aegean Islands. The wages of these employees were very low, and child labour was a common phenomenon. For that period a twelve-hour daily working time was usually the case.

155. Although the right of association was stipulated by Article 11 of the Constitution, under the Constitutional National Assembly of 1864, this referred only to political and religious organizations. Trade unions appear to be founded and function in 1875.[76]

156. Since 1875, there were efforts for the first unions to be founded, in specific occupations and enterprises, and a specific statute to be introduced as a document signed by their members.[77] Among the demands of these early trade unions were the implementation of a ten-hour daily working time and stable wages for separate categories of employees of their sectors, e.g., craftsmen, workers of the shipyard of Syros. The same applies to tanneries where the demands of the workers focus on the unpaid two-hour work of Sunday and that the payment of the wage is made in a stable currency in accordance with the then revaluation.[78]

157. Until 1910, the emerging industry was followed by a significant increase in the number of the employees and the number of the trade unions.

II. The Period from 1911 to 1920

158. The main demands of the workers in that period were the eight-hour daily working time, the mandatory rest for all workers from the evening of Saturday and the whole Sunday, the protection of children in the workplace, the care for hygiene and safety in the workplace and the care for those workers that had accidents in the workplace.[79] From 1911 until 1914, a series of worker-friendly laws were enacted

---

75. I. Kordatos, *History of the Hellenic Labour Movement* (Athens: Boukoumanis, 1972), p. 13 (In Greek).
76. *Ibid.*, p. 44.
77. For example, the statute of the trade union titled Fraternal Connection of the woodworkers of the shipyard of Syros, was made as an agreement under a notarial act; *see* Kordatos, p. 23.
78. Kordatos, p. 32.
79. *Ibid.*, p. 157.

in the Hellenic Parliament under E. Venizelos facing the strong opposition from industrialists. This opposition was so fierce that basically prohibited the implementation of these laws.[80]

159. The large number of laws enacted under the government of E. Venizelos had the purpose of preventing the disruption of the harmony of the social relations in the country and led to the creation of a new social environment. Under the guidance and the support of the group of the 'sociologists', a group of Hellenic social scientists that had studied outside of the country, Venizelos adopts the demands of the workers and assign to these 'sociologists' to draft these laws that were, in spite of the strong opposition, voted in the Parliament.[81]

160. It is noteworthy that the cost of labour for that period was estimated at 20–25% of the total cost of production, the lowest in all the countries of Europe. The basic reason for that was the oversupply of unskilled labour and the uncontrolled labour of children and women.[82]

161. During that period, eight-hour working time is regulated for the printers of Athens and the miners of Lavrion. Gradually until 1936, this would apply to all sectors of the economy except the public sector.

162. This period demonstrates the enactment of a big number of protective and regulatory as well as collective labour laws.

A. *Protective Labour Law*

- 1911: Law 3934 on Sunday rest; Law 3834 on hygiene and security of the workers and hours of work;
- 1912: Law 4029 on the labour of women and children; Law 41 on the payment of salaries and wages;
- 1914: Law 271 on opening hours of shops;
- 1915: Law 551 on labour accidents;
- 1920: Law 2112 on compulsory termination of private employees' contracts. The law was completed by Royal Decree (RD) of 16–18 July 1920, in order to cover workers, technicians and domestic servants.

---

80. A. Tixier, Director of the Social Security Department of the League of Nations' International Labour Office, Interview in the newspaper *Akropolis* on 21 Apr. 1929.
81. Kordatos, p. 231.
82. *See* X. Zolotas, *Hellas at the Stage of Industrialization* (Athens: Eleftheroudakis, 1926) (In Greek).

B. Collective Labour Law

- 1911: under Article 11 of the revised National Constitution of 1864, under which freedom of association was guaranteed, freedom of an association pursuing trade union goals was also covered;
- 1914: the first substantial laws for the protection of unions were passed after the revolution of 1909. Regardless of the low level of the economy and the non-existence of an organized labour force, state social policy was established. Law 281 concerning associations, the only trade union law of the period, regulates the application of the constitutionally provided right of the freedom of association;
- 1920: Articles 5 and 8 of Law 2151 foresee the preconditions of issuing strike action and lockout. Articles 21 and 22 indirectly permitted unionization of the civil servants.

In the summer of 1920, Hellas became a member of the ILO and accepted basic international conventions of labour, ratifying them by the following laws:

- Law 2269 which ratified the international convention of Washington on limiting the hours of work in industry to eight daily and forty-eight per week;
- Law 2270 on ratifying the international convention on unemployment;
- Law 2271 on ratifying the international convention on defining the minimum age when children may be engaged in industry;
- Law 2272 on ratifying the international convention concerning children and night work;
- Law 2273 on forbidding the use of white yellow phosphorus in the match industry;
- Law 2274 on ratifying the international convention of Washington concerning maternity leave.

III. The Period from 1921 to the Introduction of the CC (1946)

163. This period can be further divided into two sub-periods, the first since 1922, after the catastrophe of the Hellenic population of Asia Minor until the crisis of 1932 and the second period from 1932 to 1946.

164. Following the Asia Minor catastrophe (1921), the internal market of the country was extended while the labour market increased with specialized and cheap personnel from the increased number of immigrants. Among these immigrants there were many entrepreneurs with capitals that started their own enterprises in Hellas.

165. The dictatorship of Ioannis Metaxas had the purpose to ease the opposition from the labour movements. For that reason, eight-hour daily working time was regulated for the private sector, while special attention was given to the founding of IKA for the social insurance of the employees.

166. The most important legislative work concerning labour relations of that period is the following.

A. Protective Labour Law

- 1932: Presidential Decree (PD) of 27 June, on codification of the provisions for the eight-hour working day; PD of 8 April, on codification of the provisions of laws regulating the hours of work in shops; PD of 14 March, concerning the health and safety of workers and employees at factories;
- 1945: Law 118, by which Law 2112/1920 was re-enacted; EL 539, establishing paid leave.

B. Collective Labour Law

- 1931: Law 4879 of 6 June, concerning the right of association of civil servants was passed, later fortified by Law 5403/1932;
- 1935: EL of November 16/21 and 16/20 regulating for the first time the Constitution of collective agreements and foreseeing arbitration for collective disputes. These laws were modified many times up to 1938;
- 1941: LD 310 introduced the system of defining salaries by ministerial decisions; Law 2785 regulating the question of trade unions; LD 424 introducing a system of work by turn and restricting the right of termination of labour contracts;
- 1942: Law 3200 of 31 October, concerning the re-establishment of SD was passed by the free Hellenic government in exile. Work regulations in the workplace were also established;
- 1945: EL 148 concerning trade union election procedures was supplemented by Article 2 of Law 274; Law 393 of 9 June promulgated an application of the law for the re-establishment of SDs;
- 1946: EL 986 modified certain topics of previous legislation concerning trade unions.

IV. The Period from the Introduction of the CC (1946) until 2000

167. After the end of the Second World War, the system of labour relations moves under the total control of the government with the creation of an autonomous Ministry of Labour. This effort was finalized by the military dictatorship of Papadopoulos in 1967. It is worth mentioning that for the period of 1964–1965, Hellas was ranked in the first place concerning strikes worldwide.

168. After the end of the military junta in 1974, the restoration of the right to organize followed with the restoration of the previous regime before the military dictatorship, concerning collective negotiations, minimum wage and elections for first-level and second-level trade unions.

169. Gradually, the role of the government in the intervention of labour relations was decreased, although it still played a major role due to the highly politicized character of the trade unions.

170. Concerning the legislation of that period, the following laws may be mentioned.

The CC in Articles 648–680 regulates in detail the individual relations between the employer and employee for independent work:

- 1955: Law 1836 on the protection of those released from the army; Law 3198 on modifying and completing regulations on the termination of the labour contract; Law 3464 on controlling group dismissals;
- 1966: Law 4504, LD 4547, RD 748 on Sunday rest, paid leave, etc.

On collective labour law:

- 1951: EL 1803 concerning the protection of union elected representatives (this applies only to the president and General Secretary);
- 1955: Law 3239 regulating collective labour disputes as modified later by LDs 3755/1957, 186/1969 and 73/1974;
- 1957: LD 3789 on works regulations.

In 1967, the military regime came to power and proceeded to abolish the previous legislation on trade unions:

- 1968: RD 667 which consolidated the legislation on trade unions;
- 1969: LDs 185 and 186. The first dealt with the right to organize and the right to strike, the dissolution of trade unions, etc. LD 186 (amended by LD 73/1974) dealt with collective negotiations and collective agreements, the settlement of disputes and the financing of trade unions;
- 1971: many laws were abolished by LD 795 on associations. LD 890 on trade unions also abolished other laws;
- 1974: the last trade union law of the military regime was LD 353 on the modification and completion of LD 890.

171. After the re-establishment of the Parliament and the SDs, LD 42 of 14 September 1974 abolished the laws of the period of the military rule (1967–1974) and re-established the previous legislation as a first step towards new legislation on trade unions:

- 1975: Law 6 regulates the carrying out of trade union elections; Law 46 on equal payment for equal work between men and women (ratified International Convention (IC) 100 of ILO);
- 1976: Law 330 on trade unions;
- 1977: Law 643 on trade union Activities by civil servants was issued after the provision of paragraph 2 of Article 23 of the National Constitution of 1975;

- 1978: Law 780 recognized the free unionization of journalists and their unions as trade unions;
- 1980: Law 1082 on paid public holidays, etc.;
- 1982: Law 1264 on the democratization of the union organizations of workers-employees (not employers). It abolished Laws 330/1976 and 643/1977, Law 1302 (ratified Article 6 of IC 103 of ILO) on the working rights of a mother-to-be;
- 1983: Law 1342 (codified IC of 1979 of UN) on equal payment for equal work between men and women. Law 1361 on the Peasants' Union Organization, Law 1365 on the socialization of the Public Nature or Utilities Organizations, Public Banks, etc., Law 1385 on Supervisors' Boards at mining enterprises, etc., Law 1387 on controlling group (collective) dismissals;
- 1984: Law 1414 on employment equality (incorporated Directive 76/207 of EC);
- 1985: Law 1545 on the National System of Protection from Unemployment and other provisions; Law 1566 (ratified IC 159/1983 of ILO) on employment of disabled persons; Law 1568 on the Health and Safety of Employees; Law 1576 (ratified IC 156/1981 of ILO) on equality of remuneration between the sexes, etc.;
- 1987: Law 1712 on the modernization of the occupational organizations of merchants, vocational and handicraft employers, etc.;
- 1988: Law 1767 (ratified IC 135/1971 of ILO) on Works Councils;
- 1989: Law 2676 on the system of social insurance; Law 1836 on the National Observatory of Employment; Law 1849 on the Organization of Workers' Home;
- 1990: Law 1892 on working time;
- 1993: Law 2160 on the National Work Institute;
- 1994: Law 2224 on paid leave after pregnancy, etc.;
- 1996: Law 2434 on the National Observatory of Employment, employment and professional training, etc.; PD 17 on labour protection and prevention from work accidents, etc.;
- 1998: Law 2639 on the labour inspection body (SEPE), working time, private work placement offices, etc.;
- 1999: Law 2676 about certain insurance themes; Law 2736 on the labour inspection body, etc.; PD 15 on protection and prevention services of workers;
- 2000: Law 2874 on the promotion of employment and other provisions.

V. The Period from 2001 until 2009

172. During the period from 2001 until 2009, as in all the countries of the EU the shocks for labour law that started from 1980 were becoming more evident. The principles and the ideals of labour law are questioned. The principle of the protection of the employee, which is achieved through the limiting of the contractual freedom of the employer and the employee, starts to recede, and the contractual freedom is once again prevalent in public order. This reversal is illustrated by the flexibility of labour relations and the legal provisions that promote this.

173. At the same time, the application of new (electronic) technologies for the provision of work put in doubt the 'traditional' criteria of the legal and personal dependence for the characterization of subordinate work. Under the impact of these two factors, labour law begins to transform from protective law to a law that regulates employment towards the direction of the flexibility of labour relations.

174. During that period (2001–2009), the regulations of labour law in Hellas, mainly concern the enforcement of flexibility, the incorporation of directives and regulations of the EU and the reorganization of public services with the aim to control the application of labour law.

175. From the legislative work of that period, the following laws may be mentioned:

- 2001: Law 2956 with provisions for the employment through Temporary Employment Agencies and the reorganization of OAED;
- 2002: PD 178 with provisions on the protection of the rights of the employees in case of a transfer of the enterprise, facilities or departments of facilities or enterprises in compliance with Directive 98/50/EC;
- 2003: Law 3144 with provisions on working time and annual holiday leave;
- 2003 and 2005: Law 3174 and Law 3250, respectively, which include provisions for part-time employment;
- 2001: PD 81 with provisions for the employees under a definite time contract, as amended by PD 180/2004;
- 2004: PD 164 with provisions for the employees under a definite time contract in the public sector;
- 2005: Law 3304 for the application of the principle of equal treatment regardless of racial or ethnic origin, religious or other beliefs, disabilities, age or sexual orientation which incorporated Directives 2000/43/EC and 2000/78/EC;
- 2005: Law 3385 with regulations for the decrease of the payment of overtime work and management of working time;
- 2005: Law 3429 with provisions for the possibility of less favourable treatment of the newly hired in public utility organizations and abolishing the general staff regulation in case of negative economic results in public enterprises;
- 2007: PD 40 with provisions for the protection of the employees in the case of insolvency of the employer in compliance with the Directive 2002/74/EC;
- 2008: PD 44 for the completion of the statute of the European Cooperative Society concerning the role of the employees in accordance with the Directive 2003/72/EC/22 July 2003;
- 2009: Law 3762 with provisions for the reorganization of the Labour Inspectorate Body (SEPE), regulation of issues or organizations under the auspices of the Ministry of Labour and Social Security and other provisions.

VI. The Period from 2010 until 2013: Impact of Globalization and Economic Crisis on Labour Law

176. By the end of 2009, as a result of a combination of international and local factors, the Hellenic economy faced the most severe crisis since the restoration of democracy in 1974. Aiming to fight the crisis, since February 2010, began a series of harsh economic measures imposed legislatively by Law 3833/2010 (15 March 2010) 'Protection of national economy – emergency measures to address the fiscal crisis'.

177. Even more, in order to avert the total economic collapse of the country, in May 2010, the other Eurozone countries and the International Monetary Fund (IMF) agreed to a rescue package providing Hellas loans (on bailout terms). For the purpose of securing the funding, Hellas was required to adopt harsh austerity measures to bring its deficit under control and have access to the Financial Stability Mechanism (FSM), established by the Eurozone Member States, the European Central Bank (ECB) and the IMF. On 3 May 2010, Hellas requested EUR 80 billion from the rest of the Eurozone countries and EUR 30 billion from the IMF. To realize the request, the country signed three memoranda on the austerity measures that should be taken (to be implemented) in order for the bailout package to be activated. Those were the Memorandum of Economic and Financial Policies, the Technical Memorandum of Understanding and the Memorandum of Understanding on Specific Economic Policy Conditionality. On 8 May 2010, the Loan Facility Agreement with the Member States and the Stand-by Agreement with the IMF were approved. All those agreements together are called memoranda.

178. Since then, successive renegotiations followed concerning the credit claim agreement, and in relation to these, Memorandum II and Memorandum III were voted in the Hellenic Parliament under the names of Medium Term Financial Strategy 2012–2015 on 29 June 2011 and Medium Term Financial Strategy 2013–2016 on 7 November 2012. The aim of these two memoranda was to impose more and harsher austerity measures on the Hellenic economy.

179. Indeed, after the memoranda measures of an economic nature were adopted and for their application, the following laws were voted:

- Law 3845/2010 on 6 May 2010, for Measures for the implementation of the support mechanism for the Hellenic economy by the euro area Member States and IMF;
- Law 4046/2012 on 14 February 2012, for the Approval of the plan of the Financial Assistance Facility Agreement between the European Financial Stability Facility (ETCHS), the Hellenic Republic and the Bank of Hellas, the plan of the Memorandum of Understanding between the Hellenic Republic, the European Commission and the Bank of Hellas and other urgent measures to reduce the public debt and rescue the national economy;
- Law 4093/2012 on 12 November 2013, for the Adoption of the Medium Term Fiscal Strategy 2013–2016 Urgent Measures for the Implementation of Law 4046/2012 and the Medium Term Fiscal Strategy 2013–2016.

180. In accordance with the above mentioned, the accession of Hellas to the FSM led (among other things) to a series of significant reforms to the country's labour legislation (more than 90 laws, degrees, etc.), labour relations and labour market. Over the last four years (2010–2013) measures adopted in labour law, both on individual and collective level, are as follows:

(a) Measures in the private sector:
  - reduction of the national minimum wage under the NGCA by 32% for workers under 25 years of age, and by 22% for other employees;
  - regulation of minimum wage (daily and monthly) with legal regulations and after consultations with the social partners;
  - facilitation of dismissal of an employment contract of indefinite duration, by extending from 2 to 12 months the minimum period of employment, necessary to constitute the employer's obligation to pay redundancy compensations after the termination by reducing the notice period and the cost of lay-offs, by restricting the limit of partial repayment from 6 months' salaries to 2 months, by increasing the limit for collective redundancies from 4 to 6 employees for businesses that employ 20–150 people and from 2% to 5% for larger enterprises;
  - reinforcement of flexible and precarious forms of employment based on a large variety of regulations, e.g., the extension of the maximum period for temporary employees from eighteen to thirty-six months, the extension from two to three years of the maximum period for the renewal of temporary employment contracts, the extension from six to nine months per calendar year of the duration of shift work (four-day and three-day work), the abolition of supplements in part-time salaries in cases of overtime and jobs with less than twenty hours per week.

(b) Measures in the public sector:
  - reduction of the number of public servants through the establishment of a 1:5 and 1:10 hiring and departure ratio, dismissals, abolition of public services;
  - reduction of salaries (20–50), complete elimination of the two salaries for those receiving salaries up to EUR 3,000, cut of many of the benefits.

(c) Measures in collective labour relations:
  - major reforms on Collective Bargaining Agreements;
  - abolition of a series of terms of collective agreements and DAs. Fundamental changes have also come to the law of insurances with the major one being the change of pension age and the decrease of pensions.

181. Data from the Labour Inspectorate showed an increase of part-time employment and rotation employment, as well as a transformation of the full-time contracts to part-time and rotation contracts. These are shown in Annex 1 of this monograph.

182. There have been intentions that new austerity measures and more legislative reforms are to be taken in the following years, e.g., for collective redundancies, right to lockout. However, these will face strong opposition in the Parliament, and the current majority (2014) is fragile in order to vote for these laws (153 seats of 300).

183. The reforms of labour law are included in the austerity measures and have been implemented with a view to creating a more competitive productive sector in the effort for fiscal adjustment and restoration of competitiveness of the Hellenic economy in conjunction with the country's obligations deriving from the loan agreement affect the income policy, employment policy and social protection. Work is the best means for combating poverty and, to this end, a number of policies, measures and legal interventions have been developed aiming at the increase in employment rates for all population groups.

184. However, these targets were not met. In the field of labour law, the memoranda reformed the protection of the worker by reducing the rights that the previous regime recognized to them. The new legislation raises questions about its compatibility with the Constitution of Hellas, the legislation of the EU – primary and secondary – and the international conventions ratified by Hellas especially after the fact that these measures were proposed, in contrast with the previous regime, by extranational actors that had not consulted with the social partners in the country.

185. The financial crisis, particularly the austerity package put forth by the EU and the IMF that led to Law 3845/2010, has been met with anger by the Hellenic public, leading to riots and social unrest. Employees, with more than forty strikes and five general mobilizations, have expressed their opposition to the adoption of the austerity measures.

186. Despite the adoption of the measures imposed by the memoranda, during the last five years, inflation had risen and finally dropped in 2014, unemployment reached unprecedented heights, especially for young people where unemployment has reached 60%, wages have decreased to almost poverty levels and Small and Medium-Sized Enterprises either close or marginally survive still facing the possibility of closure in the near future. Combined with the increase on taxation (incomes, real estate, etc.) and the rest of the economic measures, the negative consequences for the country are so intense, that they led to the ascertainment on July 2013 that the measures imposed by the first Memorandum were both inappropriate and destructive for the country.

187. The most important legislation that implemented the above-mentioned measures concerning labour relations is the following:

- Law 3846/2010 (11 May 2010), Guarantees against work insecurity and other provisions;
- Law 3847/2010 (11 May 2010), Redefinition of the benefits and allowances paid to retired civil servants for the Christmas and Easter holidays and licensed leisure;
- Law 3863/2010 (15 July 2010) New Social Security System, relevant provisions, regulations concerning the employment relations;
- Law 3871/2010 (17 August 2010) Financial Management and Accountability;
- Law 3899/2010 (17 December 2010) Emergency measures for the implementation of the programme to support the Hellenic economy;

- Law 3979/2011 (16 June 2011) e-Government and other provisions;
- Law 3986/2011 (1 July 2011), Emergency measures for the implementation of a medium-term fiscal strategy 2012–2015;
- Law 3996/2011 (5 August 2011), Reform of the Labour Inspectorate, regulation of social security issues and other provisions;
- Law 4024/2011 (27 October 2011), Pension regulations, uniform pay scale – rank scale, labour reserve and other provisions for the implementation of the medium-term fiscal strategy 2012–2015;
- PIS No. 6/2012 (28 February 2012), Provisions for the implementation of paragraph 6 of Article 1 of the Law 4046/2012;
- Law 4052/2012 (1 March 2012), Approval of the draft Financial Assistance Facility Agreement between the ETCHS, the Hellenic Republic and the Bank of Hellas, Plan of the Memorandum of Understanding between the Hellenic Republic, the European Commission and the Bank of Hellas and other urgent measures to reduce the public debt and rescue the national economy and other provisions;
- Law 4111/2013 (25 January 2013), Pension regulations, amendments of Law 4093/2012, ratification of the Law of Legislative Content Approval of the draft of the Amendment agreements of the main Financial Assistance Facility Agreement between the European Financial Stability Fund, the Hellenic Republic, the Hellenic Financial Stability Fund and the Bank of Hellas, with the title Main Agreement of Financial Assistance Facility of the Financial Assistance Facility Agreement between the European Financial Facility Fund, the Hellenic Republic and the Bank of Hellas, with the title 'PSI LM Facility Agreement and the Financial Assistance Facility Agreement between the European Financial Stability Fund, the Hellenic Republic and the Bank of Hellas', with the title 'Bond Interest Facility', provision of authorizations for the signing of the contracts and other important provisions;
- Law 4139/2013 (20 March 2013), Law on addictive substances and other provisions;
- Law 4152/2013 (9 May 2013), Emergency measures for the implementation of Laws 4046/2012, 4093/2012 and 4127/2013;
- Law 4172/2013 (23 July 2013), Income taxes, urgent enforcement of Law 4046/2012, Law 4093/2012 and Law 4127/2013 and other provisions.

188. Besides the above legislation, a series of laws have regulated issues concerning labour relations, many of which incorporated directives of the EU, such as:

- Law 3850/2010 (2 June 2010), Ratification of the code of Laws for the health and safety of the employees;
- Law 3863/2010 (15 July 2010), New insurance scheme and relevant provisions, regulations concerning labour relations;
- Law 3896/2010 (8 December 2010), Application of the principle of equal opportunities and equal treatment between men and women on issues concerning work and employability – Harmonization of the current legislation with the Directive 2006/54/EC of the European Parliament and the Council of 5 July 2006 and other relevant provisions;

- Law 4071/2012 (11 April 2012), Provisions for local development, local authorities and decentralized authorities – Incorporation of Directive 2009/50/EC;
- Law 4096/2012 (23 November 2012), Ratification of the amendment of Article 20 paragraph 1 of the Convention for the extinction of all types of discrimination against women as adopted by the meeting of the Member States to the above Convention on 22 May 1995 and approved by the General Assembly of the UN on 22 December 1995 (A/RES/50/202/23 February 1996);
- Law 4097/2012 (3 December 2012), Application of the principle of equal treatment between men and women engaged in an activity in a self-employed capacity – Harmonization of the legislation with the Directive 2010/41/EU of the European Parliament;
- PD 80/2012 (14 June 2012), Granting of parental leave and leave of absence to employees with a contract of working at sea on cargo vessels flying the Hellenic flag, in accordance with the implementation of the revised Framework Agreement on parental leave concluded by BusinessEurope, the European Association of Craft, Small and Medium-Sized Enterprises (UEAPME), CEEP and ETUC and with the repeal of the Directive 96/34/EC.

§8. The Role of the Government: Intervention Versus Autonomy

I. Labour Relations under Intervention

189. The relations between employers' organizations and trade unions in Hellas never resembled what in Europe is considered the autonomy of the social partners. Accusations launched from both sides had created a very problematic situation. Labour relations were left to be organized by the government and were very much controlled by the strongest pressure groups, which, in Hellas, were never the trade unions. Fotis Makris, non-communist General Secretary of GSEE, dominated the Hellenic trade union scene for a very long period (1945–1969) except for a few short intervals. In 1955 he wrote that the government was led by the economic oligarchy. But Hellas was facing the same situation already since 1947:

> Not only were [they] left free and undisturbed to continue the job of the exploitation of the people and of the appropriation of very valuable resources of the country, but they (the industrialists) succeeded, also, in using, in a new way, political power in order to cover, with the envelopment of the typical legitimacy, their unjust and antisocial actions. And the State, having been the unfortunate organ of private interests, did not take one measure to limit the unlawful profits, which sprang from the exploitation of the misfortune of the Hellenes, but also accepted this impertinent demand and channeled this gold into the pockets of the insatiable speculators.[83]

83. K. Varvaressos, Report on the economic issue of Greece, (Athens: Savvalas, 2002) (In Greek).

190. Even later Hellenic economists made reference to the employers' pressure groups and their attitudes towards social democracy in an extremely derogatory way. Professor X. Zolotas, later Prime Minister of Hellas, wrote:

> The industrial enterprise factor (industry) often followed, in the past, the logic of short-term exploitation of the chances of easy profit and was less interested in the programming of its productive capability, in a manner which would safeguard the long-term growth and productivity of its enterprise. This mentality was one of the main characteristics and causes of industrial underdevelopment and it is incompatible, not only with the contemporary spirit and the demands of the industrial duty from a private economic view, but also with the more general pursuits of the socio-economic development.[84]

191. The government plays a primary role in the shaping of labour relations: its real function is to impose a solution on suggestions coming from strong pressure groups, though most of the time these suggestions are ironically commented on. The Chamber of Commerce and Industry suggested in February 1973 that:

> The problem of prices, and of their control, and also arguably their readjustment, is the first and main aim, which emerges not only from the present monetary reclassification, but also from all the monetary devaluations of world economic history. The second is the payments (salaries and wages). This aim as mirrored in the social side of the economic policy, is more elastic and is susceptible to many manipulations among which are margins of postponement; of course, after explaining to the interested parties their limited sacrifice, for a time, and the more general need which excuses it.

192. A later Minister of National Economy, Athanasios Kanelopoulos, commenting on the above wrote:

> In other words the prices and the profit of the industrialists and of the merchants cannot be lowered. Only salaries and wages can be lowered which are susceptible to many manipulations. This recommendation reminds one of the drunkard who was cutting all other expenses, but not that for wine. ... [85]

193. In Hellas, many delays were caused because of the idea that the state would be responsible for all the 'serious' or 'unpleasant' decisions on social policy matters. But now the scene has changed, and the involvement of the social partners in development is considered necessary. The legislative foundations for a new period of labour relations have been laid, but the results are not yet available. The right to conclude collective agreements used to belong to the employers' organizations, even in cases where the collective agreement concerned employees of one firm only. Now, new laws demonstrate the will of the legislature for a complete liberalization

---

84. X. Zolotas, *Monetary Equilibrium and Economic Development* (Athens: National Bank of Greece, 1964), p. 227.
85. The newspaper *To Vima*, 'O akroatis', 25 Mar. 1973.

of collective negotiations and arbitration (only compulsory arbitration was formerly recognized) from that state intervention which was the case under Law 3239/1955 on collective agreements. Recently, under Law 1876/1990, the social partners were free to decide their course of action when they bargain to conclude a collective agreement or voluntarily choose recourse to arbitration, according to Law 2403/1996.

194. Thus, after Law 1767/1988 on works councils, by which the IC 135/1971 of ILO was ratified, Law 1876/1990 on collective agreements, by which the right is also extended to a single employer who may sign for himself or herself collective agreements with the trade union of his or her firm, and after the Development Law 1892/1990 defining work time (full and part-time work), hurried steps taken by the Hellenic government have prepared Hellas for full compliance with EU standards and regulations. Labour legislation already allows the social partners flexibility in their activities and free choices. Of course, the social partners are free in accordance with the law, but they lack experience and training for these new responsibilities. In certain areas (e.g., contractual CVT), the social partners have not undertaken any distinguishable formal joint innovative activity.

II. Government Institutions

195. The growing role of the state in the labour field is reflected in the progressive increase of different services for preparatory works and the implementation of labour law and industrial relations. The Ministry of Labour and Social Insurance is the organ at governmental level.

196. The Ministry of Labour was founded in 1935. Its organization was re-enacted by Law 400/1976, PD 1156/1977 and PD 368/1989. The Ministry carries the main responsibility for studying the resolution of social problems, for shaping and administering labour law, industrial relations and, after 1995, social insurance. Its services have been divided into central services and peripheral services. By PD 372/1995, the General Secretariat of Social Insurance was incorporated into the Ministry of Labour from the Ministry of Health. The current name of the Ministry is Ministry of Labour, Social Security and Social Solidarity in accordance with P.D. 134/2017.

A. Central Services

197. The central service of the Ministry is divided into services and departments, and divisions. The Ministry is comprised of the Political Offices of the Minister, Deputy Ministers, Substitute Minister, General Director, General Secretary for Social Solidarity, General Secretary for Social Security, General Secretary for Management of European and other funds, Special Secretary for the Labour Inspectorate, Special Secretary for Social and Solidarity Economy and Special Secretary for Roma social inclusion.

1. The General Directorate of Administrative Services and Electronic Governance

198. This has services and departments: the Department of the Administration of the Staff, the Department of the Professional Development of the Human Resources, the Department of Electronic Governance, the Department of provision of quality services, the Department for the organization of the Ministry's services and the Department for the funding of the services.

2. The General Directorate of Work Conditions and Hygiene of Labour

199. This Directorate[86] is considered to play an important role in the scientific construction and implementation of regulations of work. It covers the area of industrial hygiene, the area of medical surveillance of work, the area of security of work, the area of training and treatment and the design and implementation of the National Strategy for Health and Safety at work. External private services, inspected by a committee of the Ministry, which advises the competent General Directorate of the Ministry, are now also covered by PDs 17/1996 and 95/1999.

3. The General Directorate of Labour Inclusion

200. This is the part of the Ministry with competencies ranging from the employment terms (individual labour contracts, working time and equality) to the design and implementation of the national action plan for the employment and vocational training.

201. There is also the National Council for Social Care, which was established in accordance with Article 8 of Law 2646/1998, certain committees of the Ministry of Labour and Social Insurance, e.g., the Committee of Article 15 of Law 1264/1982 on the protection of trade union leaders, the Regional Committee of Professional Training and Employment, of Article 2 Law 1836/1989, the Advisory Committee on matters concerning the issue of operating permits to External Services for Protection against and Prevention of Occupational Hazards.

B. Peripheral (Regional) Services

202. The peripheral or regional services include certain inspectorates or offices. There are departments of the Labour Inspectorate of Employment and units for the Technical Labour Inspectorate. The Labour Law Inspectorate, as a service of the Ministry of Employment, comes under the direction of a high official of the Ministry. Its main task is to superintend the reasonable application of labour laws and

86. Article 21 of P.D. 134/2017.

contracts (collective or individual) as well as to examine complaints and accusations made against employers or workers. It is very difficult to fulfil these tasks. The Inspectorate is badly understaffed and cannot operate efficiently. The defective functioning of the service will never succeed in establishing a spirit of responsibility, even if all the other sectors of labour law relations evolve towards models.[87] Perhaps this is the main reason for the continuous reorganization of the institution.

203. By Article 6 of Law 2639/1998 a service with the title Body of Labour Inspectors, SEPE is formed within the Ministry of Labour, Social Insurance and Welfare, directly answerable to the Minister of Labour and Social Insurance. There is also established the recallable post of Special Secretary,[88] who superintends this service. Recently, PD 134/2017 in Articles 41–49 provides for the organization of the services of the Labour Inspectorate.

204. According to paragraph 2 of Article 41 of PD 134/2017, the Labour Inspectorate has as its principal tasks:

(a) the supervision and inspection of the application of the provisions of labour legislation;
(b) the amelioration of employment relations and health and safety at the workplace;
(c) the establishment of a climate of reconciliation between employees and employers;
(d) the investigation, parallel to and independent of the insurance organizations, of workers' insurance coverage;
(e) the provision for employers and workers of information, advice and recommendations on fully effective compliance with the relevant provisions;
(f) the investigation, discovery and prosecution, parallel to and independent of the police authorities, of illegal employment.

205. By Article 2 of Law 3996/2011, the Labour Inspectorate inspects all companies and all workplaces in the private and public sectors or places where it is conjectured that workers are employed. It is to proceed with any necessary examination, inspection or investigation to ascertain compliance with and application of the provisions of labour legislation concerning terms and conditions of labour, in particular limits on working hours, earnings and other benefits provided and workers' health and safety. The inspectors have the right to enter a place of work at any hour of the day or night, without prior notification to the employer. They may temporarily suspend the operations of any company or part thereof if it is judged that there is immediate danger to the health and safety of workers and may recommend its final and definitive closure to the Minister of Labour and Social Insurance. They take direct administrative measures to impose the administrative penalties provided by law or to have recourse to judicial authority for the imposition of penal sanctions.

87. *See also* EED, Vol. 48 (1989), pp. 895 et seq.
88. Article 28 of L. 1558/1985.

206. The Labour Inspectorate may take direct action, in accordance with the relevant provisions, when illegal employment is detected. It has access to the records and documents of the company, as well as to the production process infrastructure. It may gather any information from the company books and registers and may take copies of these. It investigates fatal and serious accidents at work and draws up reports on these. It investigates the causes and conditions of the appearance of work-related illnesses and recommends measures for their prevention.

207. The Labour Inspectorate is immediately to inform the insurance organization of any breach of insurance legislation that it may detect. It may proceed with the taking of samples and their analysis, the taking of photographs and the measurement of naturally occurring, chemical and biological factors in the working environment.

208. The Labour Inspectorate examines any notification or application submitted to the service that has to do with the correct application of labour legislation. It intervenes in a conciliatory role for the resolution of individual or collective disputes arising at work. It draws up and submits an annual report to the ILO in accordance with the obligations of Hellas under the 1981 International Labour Agreement.[89]

209. The competencies of the Inspectorate cover the whole of the national territory and are exercised by its central and regional services. It cooperates and exchanges information on matters to do with its mission, with other services within the country or abroad.

210. Article 15 of Law 2874/2000 makes an important extension to the competence of the Labour Inspectorate: its competencies henceforth will include the ratification of companies' rules of work, under the provisions of LD 3789/1957, the acceptance or rejection of complaints lodged by workers' organizations against provisions of codes of labour regulations, in accordance with paragraph 3 of Article 2 of LD 3789/1957 and the extension of the obligation to ratify internal codes of labour regulations to companies employing fewer than seventy but not fewer than forty persons.

211. Under Article 42 of PD 134/2017, the Inspectorate comprises the Central Service, who administers this service, and Peripheral Services. In all, there are 970 posts of Labour Inspectors, classed as Social Labour Inspectors, Technical Labour Inspectors and Labour Health Inspectors.

212. The services of the Labour Inspectorate operate every day of the month and its employees, given the nature of the object of its work, exercise their competence to carry out inspections throughout the twenty-four hours and every day of the week

89. L. 3249/1955.

and are obliged to undertake overtime, Sunday, holiday and night work, being on duty at any place or time, in accordance with the operating regulations of the Labour Inspectorate.

213. Employees of the Labour Inspectorate must maintain confidentiality with respect to information and data which come to their knowledge in the course of the execution of their duties, even after leaving this work. They must also maintain confidentiality with respect to the sources of denunciations and complaints that are brought to their notice.

214. The personnel of the Inspectorate are trained on entry to this employment and at regular intervals thereafter. Training programmes are set up by the Central Service after taking the opinion of the Council of Common Inspection of Labour Inspection which is provided for by Article 13 of this law. The training and continuing instruction of the personnel of the Inspectorate may be carried out in cooperation with the Institute of Education of the National Centre for Public Administration. Inspectorate personnel may be sent for training to schools or training centres in the public or private sectors within the country or abroad, in accordance with the particular needs of their mission. There is also established, within the Labour Inspectorate, a service of Special Labour Inspectors with competencies covering the inspection of the operation of the Inspectorate's services, of places of work anywhere in the country, etc.

III. Autonomous Organizations

A. Organization of Employment of the Labour Force

1. Introduction

215. The OAED was founded by LD 212/1969. Because of the lack of coordination, both at the national and enterprise level between workers and employers to promote economic development, the government organization for development coordinates information and guides the movement towards better distribution of employment. This is the organization which replaced and reorganized the previously existing government employment offices.[90] Offices belonging to this national organization offer advices to people for the employment opportunities all over the country and about studies at rapid training centres, assist in the free movement of workers to areas of economic expansion, help employers in their search for labour, handle terminations of contracts of employment and collect statistical data about work.

90. L. 2961/1954.

2. Government

216. A board and a governor govern the Manpower Employment Institute. The board is made up, besides the governor, of two high officials from the government, three representatives of the employers' associations and three of the workers' trade unions. These representatives hold office for two years, while the office of the governor is for three years. The governor is appointed by a decision of the national government. There are certain committees which assist the work of the board.

217. There are branches which are subordinate to the services of the government of the Institute and these branches are further subdivided into sections, e.g., the Directorate of Inspection, having more sections of employment services and of education, the General Directorate of Labour Force, with branches on the technical education of young people and apprenticeship. There are also inter-district services, on the level of prefectures, such as the service of Labour Force with branches of employment and insurance, careers guidance, vocational training and maintenance. In every prefecture, there are also offices of employment, insurance, maintenance and other services.

3. Goals

218. OAED, as the main organ of government policy on employment for ensuring the precondition of balancing supply and demand of labour, is considered to be the basic mechanism for implementation of government development programmes. OAED, besides preparing and training the labour force or assisting in the free movement of employment and protecting the unemployed, is no longer the only legal organ, according to paragraph 3 of Article 1 of LD 212/1969, but the main organ for facilitating the placement of workers and employees.

4. Activities

219. The Manpower Employment Institute is active in the field of employment through its offices all over the country for technical, educational and vocational training. But only 15% of the placements were done by OAED. In Athens and some big cities special offices giving advice on career guidance already existed. Careers' advisers are occupied with the interviewing and guidance of the students and employees towards occupations, which will give security and the best salary, and advising them of their rights. OAED issues an employment card to all, in accordance with Article 2 of Law 2434/1996. Both employed and unemployed persons must be provided with such a card, by Article 3 of Law 1545/1985.

220. The target of the apprenticeship branch is the technical education of young people of 14 to 20 years old by providing them with courses in general education at apprenticeship schools, in combination with practical education in work establishments. After two to four years, according to their skill, the students are ready to work as specialists in their chosen field. In Hellas there are more than fifty-two apprenticeship schools and half of them are in Athens and Piraeus. Students for more than thirty-one trades are being educated at them now. For those students coming from the rural areas there are hostels where students live under the supervision of trained staff. Free board is provided there. During this education the students receive remuneration.[91]

221. Programmes of creating new positions of work for the unemployed, for assisting persons with special needs (disabled, youngsters, women), for new entrepreneurs, for the temporary mobility of seasonal workers and communal public works have the financial support of the ESF. By Law 1545/1985, OAED is the competent institution for the implementation and functioning of the National System of Protection from Unemployment (ESPA). OAED also supervises the unified system for the administration of training Activities (ESDEK) and certain programmes of continuous training for unemployed persons.

5. Economic Means

222. The funding for OAED basically consists of contributions from employers and the workers:[92]

(a) for the fund assisting those workers who are doing their military service, the contribution of the employer is 1 to 2% on any kind of payment to his or her employees;
(b) for the unemployment fund, the contribution of the employer is 2% and of the employee who will benefit from this insurance 1%;
(c) for the family assistance fund, employers and employees each contribute 1% of every payment to the employees.

223. Other responsibilities of OAED are related to dismissed persons[93] and the payment of allowances for military service as well as the completion up to the level of ordinary remuneration of allowances for pregnancy and maternity which are provided by the IKA, allowances to persons of 20 to 29 years old, special allowances to seasonal workers, to Hellenes returning from abroad, etc.

B. The Institute for Workers' Welfare, Ergatiki Estia (OEE)

224. The Institute for Workers' Welfare (*Ergatiki Estia*, OEE or Workers' Fund) was founded in 1936. Law 3467/1965 was one of the main laws concerning OEE and under Law 678/1977, according to which its primary target was to promote the

---

91. *See also* Laws 1346/1983 and 1404/1983.
92. These contributions apply until the printing of this book. There are indications that the contributions of employers and employees to OAED will be abolished after the summer of 2014.
93. Article 4 of L. 1172/1981.

welfare of employees (as well as pensioners) and members of their families. Under the implementation of the austerity packages this institution was abolished.

C. *Workers' Housing Organization*

225. The Institute for Housing for Workers or the Workers' Housing Organisation (OEK) had as its primary objective to provide homes for workers and employees. The Institute also allocated home purchase loans to workers and employees who meet the preconditions for buying a house or an apartment. The founding Law was LD 2963/1954, which had been completed and modified many times. Under the implementation of the austerity packages this institution was abolished.[94]

D. *Important Tripartite Institutions*

1. The Supreme Council of Labour

226. By Law 3239/1955 the Supreme Council of Labour was founded.[95] Based in the Ministry of Labour, with a board comprised of representatives of the government, the social partners and specialists, it is an advisory body which issues opinions on any labour matters, such as remuneration and hours of work of the private sector, settlement of disputes on paid leave and unhealthy work conditions, work regulations.

227. The Supreme Council of Labour operates also under the name of the Council of Hygiene or Health and Safety at Work. By Article 15 of Law 1568/1985, the Council of Hygiene and Safety at Work was founded as a new department of the Supreme Council of Labour and as an advisory body of the Ministry of Labour on workers' health and the protection of hygiene and safety at work. Among the fifteen members of the board, three are nominated by GSEE, three by employers' organizations, one is a representative of the Pan-Hellenic Medical Association and one of the Association of Chemists.

2. The National Council of Occupational Training and Development of Human Resources (ESEKAAD)

228. By Law 4485/2017, ESEKAAD was founded at the Ministry of Education as an advisory organ to the government on occupational training and employment at a national level, on promoting coordination among agencies implementing occupational training and employment programmes, etc. In its eleven-member board,

94. Article 1, para. 6 and Art. 2, para. 1 of L. 4046/2012. The successor of these two institutions is OAED in accordance with Art. 35 of L. 4144/2013.
95. *See also* LD 184/1969, Law 1568/1985, PD 368/1989, PD 296/1991, Law 1414/1984.

there are one representative of GSEE, one of cooperatives, one of occupational and handicraft organizations and one of Hellenic Federation of Enterprises (SEV).

229. To best achieve the above ends, the National Institute of Labour (EIE) and Occupational Training of Human Resources is founded to operate autonomously on a tripartite basis at the Ministry of Education. It is a legal person under private law with economic, administrative and operational autonomy. Its mission is the study and investigation of work as a means of procuring a livelihood and as a factor in production and social progress. Another function is the study and investigation of Hellenic labour markets in general, together with the consequences of international development and the unification of the EU as well as the connection between Universities and the labour market. The Institute was the product of an all-party agreement.

3. The National Employment Monitoring Service

230. The National Employment Monitoring Service (EPA) was founded under the authorization of Law 1836/1989 and Article 14 of Law 2434/1996 together with Decision 31699/1993, as modified by Decisions 33347/1996 and 33244/1997 of the Minister of Labour and Social Insurance. The purpose of the foundation of the Monitoring Service was similar to that of the EIE, especially as regards study and data collection, as in the study of the demand for and supply of labour, of professionals and of skilled workers and the cooperation with other monitoring services in EU states.

231. By Article 19 paragraph 2 of Law 2874/2000 the personnel of the Institute were transferred to the EPA with their labour relation and insurance rights and obligations unchanged. Work contracts concluded with the Institute remain valid and bind the Monitoring Service.

232. In addition, all movable and fixed property (real estate) of the Institute passes to the Monitoring Service which takes on all rights and obligations of the Institute. The manner and procedure for the transfer of property, the competencies, and all other matters are to be settled by PDs yet to be issued. Any law or provision allocating resources to the Institute is considered valid in respect of the EPA.

4. The Organization for Mediation and Arbitration

233. The Organization for Mediation and Arbitration (OMED) is an independent legal entity operating according to the provisions of the law,[96] the PDs and regulatory laws, which are issued under authorization of Article 18, paragraph 2 of Law 1876/1990, as well as by decisions of its board of directors in exemption to

96. Article 17 of Law 1876/1990 as amended by Art. 14 of Law 3899/2010 and Art. 20 para. 23 of Law 4019/2011.

legal regulation applying to public sector legal entities. OMED is administered by an eleven-member board of directors composed of five members representing five employers' organizations (the SEV; the Hellenic Confederation of Professionals, Craftsmen and Merchants (GSEVEE); the Hellenic Confederation of Commerce and Entrepreneurship (ESEE); the Greek Tourism Confederation (SETE); the Federation of Industries of Northern Greece (FING)), three workers' representatives from GSEE five members representing the third-level most representative trade union GSEE, one expert on labour field as President of the board, chosen by the unanimous decision of the other members. On the board sits one representative of the Ministry of Labour as an observer without entitlement to vote.[97] Their term of office lasts five years.

234. The mission of OMED is to support free (with no charge at all) collective negotiations by the provision of mediation and arbitration services to trade unions, employers' organizations and independent employers. In view of its mission, OMED may:

(a) organize administrative services to support mediation and arbitration proceedings;
(b) undertake information and training programmes on collective negotiations, labour relations and labour economics addressed mainly to the representatives of trade unions and employers' organizations;
(c) undertake scientific/academic research and studies on issues related to its mission;
(d) issue annual reports covering the activities of the year to be submitted to the board of directors of the trade union and employer's organizations appearing on the board as well as to the Minister of Finance and the Minister of Labour, Social Security and Welfare.

235. According to Article 18 of Law 1987/1990 the resources of OMED include funding from the OEE, from the budget of the Ministry of Labour, from donations, publications and fees charged to those having recourse to OMED's services. OMED used to be funded only by the OEE. Therefore, after the abolition of OEE, there was a great economic problem for the existence of OMED.

236. Article 22 paragraph 2 of the Constitution allows the legislator to set up a system of arbitration as is seen fit in order to ensure peaceful cooperation between the social partners.[98] Therefore the entrusting by law of arbitration to a legal person under private law is not unconstitutional if the arbitration bodies provide a reliable, correct and objective judgment.

97. Article 17 para. 3 L. 1876/1990 as amended by Art. 37 L. 4144/2013 and Art. 41 L. 4554/2018.
98. *See also* Art. 94, paras 3 and 4, and Art. 95 and para. 1a of the Constitution.

5. The Council of Expert Advisers on Employment and Social Security

237. By Article 2 of Law 2874/2000 the Council of Expert Advisers on Employment and Social Security is founded. For the last seven years another advisory body, the Council of Social Security, should have been operating, but the institution remained unused. The new advisory body has been established under another name but has the same responsibilities.

6. The Economic and Social Committee

238. The Economic and Social Committee (ESC) was formed by Law 2232/1994 as a legal person under private law. By Article 1 paragraph 2, its task is the formulation of reasoned opinions on matters of particular importance to do with labour relations, social insurance, fiscal measures and with socio-economic policy in general, particularly on matters of regional development, investment, exports, consumer protection and competition. The budget is not included within the scope of the matters referred to.

239. On the above matters, the expression of an opinion by the ESC is obligatory before the passage of corresponding legislation. A decision of the Council of Ministers, following an opinion from the ESC, may rule that further matters also require an opinion from the ESC. The ESC may on its own initiative express an opinion on other matters of socio-economic policy. It may also pronounce an opinion on any other matter on which, by reason of its gravity, the ESC's opinion is sought by the competent Minister.

240. The competent state body seeks the opinion of the ESC on each suitable occasion, and the opinion is issued to a set deadline. In order that its opinions may have validity, the ESC forms research groups of experts, cooperates with ministerial services and various bodies, and may enter into any agreements that it sees fit.

241. The ESC is composed of its chairperson and forty-eight other members, which form three groups each with an equal number of members. The first represents the employers, the second the workers, while the third represents other categories, such as agricultural cooperatives, bars of lawyers, chambers of trade and municipalities. Members serve for three years, renewable. The bodies within the ESC are the general meeting of all members and the executive committee composed of the chairperson and the three vice-chairs. The General Secretary, appointed by the Minister for the National Economy, administers all the services of the ESC.

7. The Municipal Consultation Committees

242. By Article 76 of Law 3852/2010, in every municipality of the country with more than 10,000 habitants, a consultation committee may be created comprised by representatives of the local community such as from the local trade and occupational associations, scientific associations, local associations of employers and employees, parents' associations, youth councils. The municipal consultation committee is chaired by the mayor of the municipality. In practice, very few of these types of committees have been created.

8. The Regional Consultation Committees

243. Similar to the municipal consultation committee, under Article 178 of Law 3852/2010, every prefecture of the country may create a regional consultation committee. This committee is comprised by the mayors of the municipalities of the prefecture and representatives from employers and employees associations, chambers of commerce, cooperatives, public services that have their headquarters in the prefecture, etc. The role of the Committee is opinion giving and examines possibilities for the economic and social development of the prefecture. Like the municipal consultation committee, this institution has not yet worked in the country.

Chapter 3. Sources of Labour Law

244. Sources for labour law fall into two categories: first, the usual sources of law in general, that is, law and custom, and second the autonomous occupational sources or rules, which are comprised of collective agreements, DAs and other sources, such as trade union statutes.

§1. Common Sources of Law

I. EU Legislation

245. Hellas, as a member of the EU, is bound by EU law, both primary and secondary. It follows that Hellas is bound by EU conventions, the Charter of Fundamental Rights of the EU, regulations, directives and so forth. In compliance, Hellas has incorporated all those directives concerning labour law into national law.

II. The Constitution of Hellas

246. The Constitution of Hellas, voted in by the Fifth Revisionary Parliament of the Hellenes on 9 June 1975, entered into force on 11 June 1975, and was revised on 6 March 1986, on 6 April 2001 and on 27 May 2008.[99] It follows the line of most liberal constitutions, being based on ideological plurality and human values. Provisions of the Constitution having enforceable validity and numerous of them refer to work, SD, collective agreements and strike.

247. Concerning labour relations, the most important articles are the following:

(a) Article 22 paragraph 1 section a recognizes the right to work for all citizens and the duty of the state to protect this right by creating conditions of employment and by pursuing the moral and material advancement of all the working population, stipulating that 'Work constitutes a right and shall enjoy the protection of the State, which shall care for the creation of conditions of employment for all citizens and shall pursue the moral and material advancement of the rural and urban working population.'
(b) Article 22 paragraph 4 prohibits compulsory work, stipulating that 'Any form of compulsory work is prohibited. Special laws shall determine the requisition of personal services in case of war or mobilisation, or to face the defence needs of the country or urgent social emergencies resulting from disasters or which are liable to endanger public health, as well as the supply of personal work to local government agencies to satisfy local needs.'

99. The process of a new revision of the Constitution has begun.

(c) Article 22 paragraph 1 section b recognizes and stipulates the right to equal pay for work of equal value,[100] stipulating that 'All working people, irrespective of sex or other distinction, shall be entitled to equal pay for work of equal value rendered.'
(d) Article 23 recognizes and stipulates the right to unionize and strike, stipulating that '1. The State shall adopt due measures safeguarding the freedom to unionise and the unhindered exercise of related rights against any infringement thereon within the limits of the law. 2. Strike constitutes a right to be exercised by lawfully established trade unions in order to protect and promote the financial and the general labour interests of working people.'[101]
(e) Article 22 paragraph 2 underwrites collective agreements and free collective negotiations, stipulating that 'General working conditions shall be determined by law, supplemented by collective agreements contracted through free negotiations and, in case of the failure of such, by rules stipulated by arbitration.' According to jurisprudence and legal theory, the true meaning of this provision is that working conditions, including remuneration, shall be determined by law only if these are of general and great importance; otherwise they shall be determined by collective agreements. The law is subsidiary to collective agreements.
(f) Article 12 paragraphs 1, 2 protects free association, stipulating that '1. Hellenes shall have the right to form non-profit associations and unions, in compliance with the law, which may never subject the exercise of this right to prior permission. 2. An association may not be dissolved for violation of the law or of a substantial provision of its statutes, except by court judgment.' Article 12 has complementary validity for trade unions since they are protected separately by Article 23.

248. Other articles of the Constitution that are important to labour relations are:

(a) Article 4 paragraphs 1 and 2 where equality before and under the law is enacted. Those paragraphs state '1. All Hellenes are equal before the law. 2. Hellene men and women citizens have equal rights and equal obligations.'
(b) Article 5 paragraph 1 which secures the freedom of the persons and economic and social rights,[102] Article 17 paragraph 1 which promulgates the protection of property but not its abusive use and Article 106 paragraph 2 on exercising economic freedom without damaging human dignity, etc.

---

100. AP 272/2017.
101. The same article stipulates that 'Strikes of any nature whatsoever are prohibited in the case of judicial functionaries and those serving in the security corps. The right to strike shall be subject to the specific limitations of the law regulating this right in the case of public servants and employees of local government agencies and of public law legal persons as well as in the case of the employees of all types of enterprises of a public nature or of public benefit, the operation of which is of vital importance in serving the basic needs of the society as a whole. These limitations may not be carried to the point of abolishing the right to strike or hindering the lawful exercise thereof.'
102. According to settled case law (e.g., APol 7/2015, APol 6/2015), this provision makes engaging in economic activity in general an individual right while also safeguarding economic freedom. A particular manifestation of economic freedom is the freedom to work, that is to say, an individual's right to work without hindrance and to choose for themselves, without restrictions, the type, place and length of their employment (Art. 22 para. 1 of the Greek Constitution).

(c) Article 25 paragraph 3 stipulates that 'the abusive exercise of rights is not permitted'.
(d) Article 25 paragraph 1(c) of the Constitution states that 'These rights also apply to the relations between the individuals that they personalize.' In accordance with this last provision, within the framework of legal relations under private law, as in the labour contract, the employer is obliged to respect the fundamental personal and social rights of the employee, given that these are objective values that are applied in the whole field of law. Furthermore, under Article 25 paragraph 1(c) of the Constitution, it is stipulated that 'Any type of limitations that may be imposed in accordance with the Constitution to these rights must be either directly provided for by the Constitution or by the law, since there is prejudice in favor of that, and must respect the principle of proportionality.'

III. ICs of the ILO

249. Hellas has ratified almost all the international Conventions of ILO, which, according to Article 28 paragraph 1 of the Constitution, prevail over any contrary provision of the law.[103]

IV. The Typical Law

250. The term 'law' indicates the Acts of the Legislature, namely of the Parliament (Law) and the President of the Republic PD, RDs (remaining from the period of the Kingdom of Hellas, the system of government in Hellas before the dictatorship of 1967–1974), LDs and obligatory acts (remaining from abnormal political periods when the function of the Parliament was suspended), regulatory ministerial decisions, etc.

251. Because of the great number of laws, efforts have been made to codify labour law in general or in particular, as yet without result, mostly because of the fear that such codification could change and diminish the rights of the workers.

V. Customs

252. Customs are of very limited validity as a source of labour law, compared with other, normal provisions of labour law.

103. *See* the table of ratified conventions in Annex 2.

§2. Jurisprudence

253. Jurisprudence, namely the previous decisions of courts, is not deemed to be a 'source' of law in Hellas. Though jurisprudence may be significant to the interpretation of legislation and in many cases, with its final broad interpretation of labour law, has effectively contributed to the protection of employees, the decisions of the courts are not binding on the judgment of subsequent similar court cases.

§3. Sources of Occupational Origins (Autonomous Sources): Collective Agreements and DAs

254. Law 3239/1955, LD 3755/1957, LD 186/1969 and LD 73/1974 were the laws on collective agreements. Since 1990 Law 1876/1990, as amended and supplemented, has been in force.[104]

255. Collective agreements acquire legal power, even though they are not products of the state legislature. In cases a collective agreement is not achieved there may be an DA. DAs, acquire legal power, are assimilated with collective agreements.

§4. Hierarchy and Conflict of the Sources of Labour Law

256. There is a hierarchical order for the sources of the labour law. This hierarchical order is determined by the extent to which each source is important in formulating the employment relationship. Considering the hierarchy of provisions and factors, regulation from a higher source is more powerful, binding and normative than provisions of a lower source. In general, provisions of a lower source should not conflict with those of a higher source. Exceptions are valid when specific provisions from a lower source regulating matters at a lower level are more favourable to employees.

257. In the case of a conflict of rules of labour law from different sources, the choice of the applicable provision is made on the basis of the principle of favourability. According to Article 7 paragraphs 2 and 3 of Law 1876/1990, provisions of law prevail over the provisions of a collective agreement, unless those of the latter are more favourable to employees. On the same grounds, the terms of a labour contract or the practice followed by the enterprise are valid and prevail over the provisions of law if they are more favourable to the employees.

104. *See* below Part II, Chs 1, 5, 7.

§5. Special Kinds of Sources

I. Local Employment Agreements

258. The year 1998 saw the legal establishment[105] of the possibility of concluding special collective agreements called 'Local Employment Agreements', with the aim of addressing the development needs of poor regions of the country in which special programmes with the use of national or European funds were being applied or were to be applied.

259. The purpose of these agreements is the promotion of employment in viable and competitive activities and so to reduce unemployment by creating new job positions.

260. The relevant provision of law is as follows:

1. Bodies in the public sector, of local administration, and social partners, within the meaning of Article 3 of Law 2232/1998, on the basis of the need to develop the disadvantaged areas of the country, in particular AREA C as defined in paragraph 1 of Article 4 of Law 2601/1998, for which are implemented or for which it is envisaged that there will be implemented special programmes, for which national and community funding is available and of which the aim is to meet the goals of the promotion of employment in viable and competitive activities, the combating of unemployment and the creation of new posts of employment, may conclude, for the realization of the above aims, special collective agreements having to do with the execution of a particular project or the exercise of a particular activity of an economic, social or cultural nature, in which there are specified the period of validity and all the terms of their application. In these agreements it is permitted to regulate the minimum levels of salary or daily wage and in general the terms of employment of the personnel who will be employed for the execution of the project or the activity (Local Employment Agreements).

   These terms may not be in breach of rules concerning the health and safety of workers or of the minimum levels of protection specified by the currently valid provisions of labour law or of NGCAs, but nonetheless take precedence over any other relevant regulation when these terms are included in the proper individual work contact of the employed person and on the condition that in the concluding of the local employment agreement the most representative Workers' Centre should have taken part, by Article 6 paragraph 2 of Law 1876/1990. Local Employment Agreements are valid only if ratified by the Ministers of the National Economy, of Labour and of Social Insurance.

105. Article 4 of L. 2639/1998.

2. From the date of publication of the present law and up to the 31st December 2001, in companies operating within the areas referred to in the previous paragraph, and with the aim of the achievement of the goals therein, it is permissible to establish, either by company collective work contracts or by individual work contracts, either for the first time or after twelve months have passed since the worker's last day in employment (long-term unemployed), levels of recompense for labour equal to those provided for by the currently valid NGCA and for a maximum period of one (1) year.

261. The agreement is concluded between agents of the public sector, the local authority, and the social partners that participate in the ESC and represent interests of the specific local level, such as employers' associations and trade unions, professional associations, consumer associations, educational and research institutions, any agent of the public and private sector. It may concern the completion of a specific project or the exercise of a specific activity of an economic, social or cultural nature.

262. By these agreements, issues concerning the scheduling of the project, or the activity where these will be applied, may be regulated, as well as the minimum salary or wages and work conditions in general for the personnel who will be employed for the completion of the project, its defined duration and all the terms of its implementation.

263. Regulations that concern the terms of work may not breach rules for employees' health and safety, or the minimum safety standards that are stipulated by Law and the NGCA.

264. If these terms are included in the individual labour contract concluded in writing with every employee, and if the conclusion of the local agreement took place with the participation of the most representative Workers' Centre of the region, then these terms shall prevail over any other related provision.

265. Local Employment Agreements apply only if they are approved by the Ministers of National Economy and Labour and Social Security.

266. In practice, Local Employment Agreements have found very limited application, while there is a strong critique of them for their scope and for being contrary to the Constitution, specifically to Article 22.

II. Work Regulations at Enterprise Level

A. General Remarks

267. Rules that regulate labour relations are also formed at enterprise level. With these rules, it is aimed, within the framework of the normative provisions (law, collective agreements, etc.) and complementary to these, to shape labour relations in ways that take into account the specific conditions that apply to the enterprise. As is self-evident, these rules apply only for the employees of the specific enterprise and are regulated by enterprise-level collective agreements, agreements between the works council and the employer. Work regulations (named also internal regulations of work or personnel regulations) as well as regulations for the health and the safety of the employees are established by collective agreements or agreements between the works council and the employer.

B. Work Regulations

268. Work regulations are established, as mentioned above, by enterprise-level collective agreements or agreements between the works council and the employer.[106] Their provisions have a normative effect. By LD 3789/1957, the employer is obliged to establish a work regulation in enterprises of more than seventy employees. This regulation is established by the employer individually and ratified by a Ministerial Decision. After Law 1876/1990, concerning collective agreements, and Law 1767/1988, concerning works councils,[107] this obligation of the employer applies only if the possibility of co-defining the regulation with the employees does not exist.

269. Work regulations usually define the relations that are formed in the course of the execution of work and are intended to ensure fair and uniform terms, coherent policy, just disciplinary authority, equal treatment for employees. Work regulations may also define issues concerning hiring, such as the manner in which hiring takes place and the skills required of the applicants, the organization of the personnel, such as their positions and duties, hierarchy in the enterprise and the prerequisites for development within the hierarchy, disciplinary actions and sanctions, preconditions for the termination of contracts.

C. Enterprise's Customary Practices

270. A customary practice in an enterprise is one that has been formed by a long-term, similar handling of certain issues that are related to the relationship between the employer and the employee. This happens when the employer either explicitly promises to the employees future benefits under certain conditions, or without an explicit promise, continuously offers such benefits. The acceptance of these benefits by the employee is the basis of a contractual commitment and negates individual reversible will. For the existence of a customary practice, it is necessary that the behaviour of the employer be general and impersonal, meaning that the same issue must have been dealt with in a similar, general way in the long-term. It is also possible that such a custom may refer to the acknowledgement of employees' previous

---

106. In public sector enterprises, legal stipulations may also be made.
107. *See* below paras 1105 et seq.

work experience.[108] Customary practice is not, of itself, a source of claims; however it may become so on the basis of a tacit agreement.[109]

271. Customary practice usually refers to benefits provided voluntarily by the employer, by his or her behaviour towards the employees, and by the manner in which work is managed.

108. AP 1263/2005, AP 2/1992.
109. AP 1146/2004.

Chapter 4. Private International Labour Law

§1. The International Jurisdiction of Hellenic Civil Courts

272. In accordance with Article 3, paragraph 1 of the KPolD (Code of Civil Procedure), if there is competency by a Hellenic court, all Hellenes and foreigners come under the jurisdiction of the civil courts. By this provision there is established, as a special rule, the international jurisdiction of Hellenic civil courts on private international disputes, since these are connected with the Hellenic state by the element of competency of the Hellenic court, in accordance with the provisions on general and specific jurisdiction,[110] if no other provision exists, such as Article 9 of the Regulation of the Council of the EC 44/2001, of 22 October 2000, on international jurisdiction for civil cases.[111]

§2. Applicable Procedural and Substantive Law

273. In these cases, the Hellenic courts always apply the Hellenic civil procedural law and the substantive law of the country that, in accordance with the prevailing provisions, is deemed to be applicable.[112]

274. From the aforementioned provision, in combination with the provisions of Articles 42, 43 and 44 of the KPolD, it is concluded that the international jurisdiction of the Hellenic courts can be excluded over existing disputes and, provided that this is defined in writing and in a clear manner, over future disputes that may arise from a specific relationship. By this agreement, in accordance with the general principle of autonomy of the will, the parties express their will and proceed to the designation of the applicable civil court. This agreement is legal unless other reasons of legal infringement exist.[113] Its validity and type is judged under *lex fori*, while the right to propose it is not subject to the limitation of the abusive use of right.[114]

275. It is common today that the individual labour contracts include elements which involve interests in more than one countries; for instance, when the country where the contract is signed differs from the country of work performance. In such cases the question arises of which legislation is competent.

§3. The Basis for the Determination of Applicable Substantive Law

276. The applicable substantive law can be determined on the basis of the following:

110. AP 803/2000, AP 108/1988.
111. AP 37/2012.
112. AP 803/2000.
113. APol 4/1992, AP 1288/1994, AP 880/1989.
114. AP 1288/1994.

(a) Labour contracts made before 1 January 1991: in accordance with Article 25 of the CC, the contracting parties, the employer and the employee, may agree, explicitly or implicitly, on the country whose substantive law will govern their contract.[115] Under the prevailing opinion in theory and on jurisdiction, it is necessary for a link to exist between the contract and the chosen law. When such agreement does not exist, the applicable law is that which is imputed to the contract by factors such as the place of the supply of work, the location of the occupational activity or the headquarters of the employer, the nationality of the contractual parties.[116] However, as set out by Article 33 of the CC, a provision of a foreign law is not applicable if it is contrary to accepted customs or public order in Hellas in general. By rules of 'public order', we mean those that reflect the fundamental views of the Hellene legislator. As for labour law, it is not considered that public order is affected by the application of provisions of foreign law that have to do with the protection of employees.[117]
(b) Labour contracts made after 1 January 1991: since 1 January 1991, in accordance with Law 1792/1988, the 19 June 1980 Convention of Rome on the law applicable to conventional obligations of EEC Member States has been in effect. Since 1 January 1991, Article 25 of the CC has applied only to labour contracts that are not covered by the above Convention. For labour contracts, the applicable law is that chosen by the contracting parties or the law of that state which is more strongly connected with the contractual relationship.

277. Following the implementation of the European Convention, freedom of choice of applicable law is the general rule for contracts of employment. The contracting parties are free to choose the applicable law.

278. The choice must be expressed or demonstrated with reasonable certainty and must not result in depriving the employee of the protection afforded to him or her by the mandatory regulations of the law of Hellas, which are binding upon the Hellene judge.[118]

279. Labour contracts made after 17 December 2009. Since 17 February 2009, Commission Regulation 593/2003 on applicable law in contractual obligations has been in effect (Regulation Rome I). In accordance with Articles 28 and 29 of the Regulation, this is applicable to contracts concluded after 17 December 2009. In accordance with Article 3, the law applicable to a labour contract is that chosen by the contracting parties.

280. However, in accordance with the same article:

(a) the choice of the contracting parties must not violate the provisions of community law, as these are applied in the country of the presiding judge; and

115. AP 7390/1991, AP 1206/1982.
116. AP 7390/1991, AP 1206/1982.
117. AP 1206/1982.
118. *See also* Protocols 89/128 EEC and 89/129 EEC; AP 906/2004.

(b) the court may not apply the law chosen by the contractual parties if the agreement has been made in such a way as to violate Hellenic law.[119]

§4. Posted Workers

281. In cases of the posting of workers to other EU Member States, Directives 96/71/EC and 2006/123/EU apply; these were incorporated into national law by PD 219/2000, PD 101/2016 and by Law 3844/2010, respectively.

§5. Hellenic Employees in Asia and Africa

282. Specific legislation[120] applies to Hellenic employees who perform their work in countries in Asia and Africa. The provisions of this Law are applied in employment relations between:

(a) Hellene nationals that are hired, irrespective of the place of hiring, in order to be employed in Asian and African countries, and
(b) enterprises that have their base or economic interests in Hellas.

283. The labour contract, as well as any other agreement between the employee and the enterprise referred to the previously mentioned articles, is concluded in writing in the Hellenic language and the language of the country of employment. In case of any difference (conflict) between the two contracts, the Hellenic one shall supersede. The contract shall include the terms, conditions and remuneration of the employment, which are not allowed to be unfavourable for the employee as compared to those provided for by Hellenic *jus cogens*, unless they would otherwise be contradictory to rules of public order of the country of employment. A contract subjected to foreign law is valid only if this law is more favourable to the employee than the applicable Hellenic law, as a matter of the employee's choice.

284. Any subsequent contract or change of the original contract is void unless it is more favourable to the employee. This limitation ceases to exist three years after the start of employment. Any agreement that excludes the jurisdiction of Hellenic courts concerning disputes that arise from the employment relationship, or from any other cause arising from this relationship, is void.

---

119. AP 1302/1998, which judged that an agreement for the application of a foreign law was concluded in order to violate Hellenic law and that the transfer of the employee to a different country was not genuine and had the aim that the foreign law should apply to his dismissal; the judgment dismissed a decision of a Court of First Instance that had not taken the employee's claims into account. Similar is the decision of Eir. Athens 858/1996.
120. Articles 1–10 of L. 1429/1984.

Part I. Labour Law: The Individual Labour Relation

Chapter 1. Labour Law: Definition and Legal Nature

Viktoria Sp. Douka

§1. Social Law

285. In Hellas, labour law is the one part of social law. The other part is social security law.[121] Social security law provides for a compulsory social security system, which covers:

(a) compulsory insurance in the case of illness and disability, the health care sector;
(b) compulsory insurance in the case of illness and disability, the benefits sector;
(c) family allowances;
(d) retirement and survivor's pensions;
(e) insurance against accidents at work;
(f) insurance against occupational diseases.

§2. Labour Law

I. General Remarks

286. In Hellas, the term 'labour law' refers to the part of law that regulates the relationship between the employer and the employee. Employee is the person who carries out his/her labour in a subordinate position. Therefore, labour law is the law of the subordinate work, and the 'subordination' is the element key to ensure that the employee is covered by the regulations and the protection of labour law.

287. In this field, 'work' refers to the voluntary engagement of the employee and the right of everyone to freely choose whether to work or not, whether to conclude an individual labour contract or not and with whom, is part of the freedom of work

121. The terms 'individual labour relation', 'individual labour contract', 'labour contract', 'employment relation', 'employment contract' are used as equivalents.

protected by the Article 22 paragraph 1 of the Constitution. Compulsory work is prohibited by paragraph 4 of the same article.

II. Subordination of the Employee

288. The concept 'subordination' refers to the obligation of the employee to follow the directions of the employer concerning the place, the manner and the time of work, to accept the supervision and the control of the employer for the compliance with these directions. In order for subordination to exist, the above obligation must exist.[122] In conjunction with his/her position and the duties, the employee develops initiatives and the above obligation may be either broad or of limited nature.[123] The type of the remuneration and the way of its definition is without legal consequences;[124] e.g., these are not criteria for the existence of 'subordination'.

289. With the labour contract, the employee provides his/her work to the disposal of the employer in order for the employer to utilize it to his interest (in accordance with the law, the collective agreements and the individual labour contract). For that reason, the employee is not held responsible for the result of his/her work,[125] nor does he/she bears responsibility for the course of the enterprise (investment risk).

290. This subordination is characterized as 'personal' when the fact that the employee is set to the disposal of the employer is underlined, and 'legal', when the fact that the employer manages, supervises and controls the provision of work is underlined. Respectively, there is the 'theory of personal subordination' and the 'theory of legal subordination'.[126]

291. The courts base their judgments for subordination on the real facts under which the work is performed, even if the parties (employer and employee) have explicitly agreed that there is or there will be no subordination. The characterization from the contracting parties, the employer and the employee, bears no legal consequences.[127]

292. Jurisprudence accepts and applies both these theories and in combination.[128] The facts that jurisprudence seeks, in order to find whether subordination exists (criteria of subordination) are many and abundant. Such facts may be, for instance, whether the employee, during his/her work, uses the facilities and the means of the employer, whether he/she provides his/her work in person or whether

122. AP 2084/1984, AP 528/1971.
123. AP 893/1986, AP 914/1987.
124. AP 125/1998, AP 914/1987, AP 1888/1993.
125. This must not be confused with the responsibility of the employee when because of inefficiency or wilful misconduct produces a defective product (thing or service).
126. AP 677/2017.
127. APol 19/2007, AP 720/2013, AP 672/2000, AP 1575/1999.
128. AP 451/2013, AΠ 1681/2012, AP 58/2010, AP 45/2010, AP 1469/2007, AP 602/1988.

the employee provides his/her work to one employer or multiple employers. Each one of them is an indication for the existence of subordination but it is not a proof. The final evaluation for the existence of subordination is based on their general and combined evaluation of all the facts.[129]

293. During the last decades, given the changes in the terms of the employment relationship, e.g., more flexible terms, more initiatives of the employee, the distinction between the employee and those working independently as self-employed, is becoming more and more blurred and there is a problem whether some of the regulations of labour law should cover not only employees but self-employed as well.

294. In some cases, under the pretext of a self-employed person, there may be a contract of subordinate labour. In that cases, in order to facilitate the distinction of a labour contract as a subordinate one, the legislator stipulates that the 'agreement between an employer and an employee for the provision of services or work, for a definite or indefinite duration, especially in the piece-rate system, teleworking, work-at-home, it is assumed that a subordinate contract exists, since work is provided in person, exclusively or primarily to the same employer for nine consecutive months'.[130] This provision creates a presumption of the existence of a subordinate labour contract, which is, however, refutable, meaning that the employer may prove that in a specific case the contract is not a subordinate labour contract.[131]

§3. Parts of Labour Law

295. Labour law is considered in two parts, individual labour law and collective labour law.

I. Individual Labour Law

296. Individual labour law is mainly concerned with the individual relationship between the employer and the employee, such as for:

(a) categories of employees (blue-collar, white-collar, temporary employees, etc.);
(b) the employment contract (individual labour contract between the employer and the employee), such as categories, form and content, legal capacity of the parties;
(c) the rights and duties of the parties (employer–employee) during the operation of the employment contract;
(d) working time, overwork, overtime, holidays, Sunday rest, etc.;
(e) suspension and termination of the work contract;
(f) inventions by employees;

129. APol 28/2005, AP 1686/2007, AP 977/2000.
130. Article 1, para. 1 of L. 2639/1998 as replaced by Art. 1 of L. 3846/2010.
131. AP 1681/2012, AP 297/2012, AP 1935/2008.

(g) settlement of labour disputes.

II. Collective Labour Law

297. Collective labour law is mainly concerned with collective labour relations (industrial relations), such as trade unions and their activities, employers' organizations, collective negotiations and collective agreements and strikes. The most important topics which come under collective labour law are:

(a) SD and its protection;
(b) trade unions and employers' associations;
(c) institutionalized relations between employees, employers and the government at the national level;
(d) collective negotiations and collective agreements;
(e) strikes and (no) lockouts.

§4. The Scope and the Legal Nature of Labour Law

I. The Legal Nature of Labour Law

298. At its early stage labour law was only for the protection of the employees. Since the decade of 1980, it has also been oriented to the organization of industrial relations in general.

299. Labour relations, individual and collective, are relations between private persons (the employer and the employee, the trade unions and the employers' organizations) and cover their private interests. Therefore, labour law falls under private law. Thought for some academics, the fact that many regulations in labour law have an 'imperative' legal nature or are rules of public interest leads to the conclusion that labour law has a special legal nature, i.e., it falls partly in private and partly in public law. In public law falls the part of labour law that regulates the state organs and services competent for labour relations.

300. Labour law is not part of civil law, because it has its own institutions, principles and methodology.

II. The Scope of Labour Law: The Protection of Employees

301. Labour law is compulsorily applied in all cases that subordinate work is provided, even if the parties of the labour contract have decided differently. It applies not only in valid individual labour contracts but in void individual labour contracts as well.[132]

302. In accordance with the employee protection principle, which governs the labour law,[133] new laws regulating work conditions for the protection of employees, e.g., on working time, rules of work, remuneration, are immediately applied, because they are considered to be for the social interest. They are applied even to labour contracts in progress in relation to their future consequences. Agreements between the employer and the employee, as well as terms of collective agreements that are opposite to legal provisions related to these issues, are void. The invalidity is in favour of the employee, meaning than only the employee can claim it. If the employee wishes for invalidity to be recognized by a court decision, he must bring an action before a court in fair time and invalidity applies *ex tunc*.

303. Terms that regulate employment relationships introduce rights in favour of the employees with the aim to provide to the employee a minimum and absolutely necessary protection. Such terms may be those that defined maximum work time per day or week, those regulating minimum wage, severance pay, etc. These terms are of unilateral *jus cogens*, which mean that it is allowed with terms of a collective agreement or with an agreement between the employer and the employee to form the relevant work terms in a more favourable manner for the employee, but it is prohibited to form in an unfavourable manner. In that way, higher remuneration may be agreed, but not lower, fewer work hours per day or week but not more, etc.[134]

304. In order to safeguard the protection of the employee, it is prohibited for the employee to resign of the rights that the law sets in favour for him/her, concerning terms of employment. It is also prohibited for the employee to resign of his/her rights that are regulated with terms of *jus cogens* concerning any other issue. This prohibition concerns any agreement or unilateral action of the employee which bring the resignation of the above rights when the contract is concluded or during the execution of the contract or when the contract is terminated.[135]

305. On the basis of the principle of the employee's protection, when similar work terms are regulated by law, a collective agreement and an agreement between the employer and the employee, the provision that is more favourable for the employee shall apply.

132. A void labour contract creates a 'labour/employment relation' like a valid labour contract. *See* paras 367–369.
133. APol 8/2015, AP 316/2017.
134. The issue of the 'management of working time' is a special institution that is accompanied by assurances in favour of the employees.
135. AP 1691/2012, AP 677/2012, AP 75/2003, AP 1159/1999.

§5. Prescription of Employees' Claims

306. Any claims made by the employee concerning remuneration and his economic claims in general towards the employer, are invalidated after five years that start from the end of the calendar year that they were created.[136] But, the claim for severance pay must be made in a period (mandatory time limit) of six months and the claim for default wages in a period (mandatory time limit) of three months.

§6. Employees of the State and the Public Sector

307. Labour law is concerned with the private sector. But since the state and the rest of the holders of the public sector are employers, because they hire employees to work in public services, public organizations and enterprises owned by them,[137] labour law is concerned with the public sector too. However, there are many special laws regulating labour relations in public sector in a different manner. Given that the staff in public services and public organizations are in principle civil servants (covered by administrative law), there are problems arising due to this duality of the personnel in this area. This monograph refers only to the employees in the private sector.

§7. Persons Who Are Not under the Scope of Application of Labour Law

308. Those who provide their work as independent professionals, businessmen, members of a company, civil servants (who are employed by the state or government institutions under public law and whose employment is regulated by administrative law) are not subject to labour law.

309. Hellene seamen employed on merchant ships, in view of their special type of work and their unionization, are considered by Hellenic law as a totally separate category of employed persons. Their work is not subject to labour law but to the Code of Private Maritime Law and laws on collective agreements in marine employment. Their unionization also comes under different legislation concerning seamen's trade unions (e.g., Law 330/1976).

§8. Distinction Between Labour Contracts and Related Contracts

310. Labour law regulated labour contracts, namely the dependent work contracts, because of the need to provide special protection to the persons that provide their work under a subordination regime. Contrary, it does not regulate contracts for

136. Articles 250 and 253 of the C.C.
137. The state or the holders of the public sector own at least the 51% of the shares.

the provision of work, when the work is not provided under the subordination regime as this has already been described above.

311. Such contracts are mainly the following:

(a) The contract for the provision of independent services: a contract for independent services exists when the service provider is not under the direct control and supervision of the employer, concerning the time and place of the provision of service, and without being obliged to comply with the instructions of the employer concerning the time and the manner of his/her service provision.[138]
(b) Contract of work: a contract of work exists when the contracting parties seek the completion of a final agreed result, whose completion entails the automatic termination of their contractual relationship.[139] In this type of contracts, the contractor is not under the personal subordination of the employer and his/her binding instructions but has the freedom to choose the place, time and the way of the completion of the work. The only obligation that arises from this type of contract is for the contractor to complete the agreed work and to deliver it in a defined time limit or the designated payment day.[140]
(c) Contract of company: a contract of company exists when each of the contracting parties (partners), assumes the obligation to submit a specific contribution, which may also be personal work, with the aim to work as partners for achieving a common goal, mainly economic. The partners assume all the risks from the function of the company.[141] It is possible, however, that one of the partners will conclude a labour contract with the company for both of the contracts to exist simultaneously.[142]

§9. Requirements for the Conclusion of an Individual Labour Contract

I. The Type of Employment/Labour Contract

312. As a rule, an individual labour contract is concluded informally. It may be concluded orally or, even, tacitly.[143]

313. The parties may agree on a certain type, e.g., a contract in writing.

314. The law requires the type of a private document in specific cases such as for part-time employment, the renewal of a labour contract of definite period.

138. AP 297/2012.
139. AP 1672/2010, AP 1618/2003.
140. Article 681 of the CC; AP 1734/2002.
141. AP 1705/1987; Article 741 of the CC.
142. AP 1364/1990.
143. The terms 'employment contract' and 'labour contract' are used as equivalents.

Rarely, the law requires the type of a public document. Contravention of such legal requirements is not permitted; any such contravention renders the contract void.

315. In all cases where a contract is entered into verbally, its written form is simply evidential of the hiring and the conditions of the agreement.

II. The Legal Capacity to Conclude an Individual Labour Contract

316. All persons above the age of 18 have the capacity to conclude an individual labour contract, as an employee or as an employer, whenever and with whomsoever they wish. Minors under the age of 18 have the capacity that special provisions give them.

III. The Employer's Freedom to Select the Employee

317. Employers and employees, in accordance with contractual freedom, may freely choose their counter-parties. In Hellas, a closed-shop clause in a collective agreement is considered null and void. Certain limitations on the freedom of specific employers to select the employee are established by Law 2643/1998.

IV. The Procedure for the Conclusion of an Individual Labour Contract

318. In accordance with the provisions of Law 2656/1953, as amended by LD 4504/1966 and Law 3144/2003, the employer is obliged to choose among applicants listed as unemployed by OAED. However, if the employer decides otherwise, there are no sanctions that might be applied. If the employer decides otherwise and does not use the services of OAED, but hires an employee in a different manner, such as a simple choice from among interested applicants or through private employment agencies, the employer is obliged to notify OEAD of the hiring immediately; otherwise, the employer is liable to administrative and legal sanctions.[144]

319. The possibility of concluding a labour contract through the intervention of an individual as a third party was first set out in Law 2639/1998. Today the law in force regulating this issue is Law 4052/2012 Articles 98–109 as amended by Law 4093/2012. These provisions give to individuals or private legal persons the capacity to found a Private Employment Agency (PEA) as well as branches of the same. The prerequisites and the procedure for the founding of such agencies are there defined, as are their organization, the terms of their function and the sanctions, administrative or penal, that are imposed in the case of their breaching the law.

144. Article 5 of L. 3144/2003.

320. An object of the activity of a PEA and its branches is to act as an intermediary for the conclusion of labour contracts between employers and those seeking work, i.e., Hellene nationals, EU nationals or legally residents in Hellas holding a work permit, under the condition that these specific activities are not otherwise regulated. Further to this, PEAs are allowed to act as advisors or vocational trainers, in accordance with the terms and provisions of any applicable legislation. The activity of a PEA and its branches may not be transferred to another individual or private legal person.

321. Hiring via a PEA must be made without any economic charge to the employee. The PEA must provide job applicants for whom mediation is undertaken with the following services:

(a) to provide them with any relevant information concerning the job sought, in relation to their skills and qualifications;
(b) to provide exact information as to the object of the work that they will execute, as well as the skills required for that specific work;
(c) to evaluate their skills and qualifications via personal interview;
(d) to inform them in detail about the exact content and terms of the contract that they are about to conclude on their behalf.

322. Illegal operation of a PEA incurs administrative and legal sanctions, such as the permanent cessation or temporary suspension of its operation.

V. Hiring Procedure

323. The employer has the right freely to choose the employee from among those whom he/she considers capable of the work that is offered.

324. Furthermore, the employer has the right to call on the applicants to present their formal and substantial skills, as part of the hiring process. In that case, the employer may freely choose an applicant or may decide that there are no suitable applicants for the position offered.[145]

325. A labour contract may be concluded subsequent to an examination or competition, meaning a test that is administered by the potential employer and that examines the skills and the capabilities of the applicant. This is common in large enterprises. The announcement of such an examination by the employer for the hiring of employees constitutes an invitation addressed to an indefinite number of applicants, by which the employer calls on the applicants to participate in the examination, promising that he/she will hire a specified number of them: that is, the successful applicants.

145. Ef. Athens 15/1998, Ef. Thessaloniki 2079/1998.

326. Any employer who has announced such a proposal is bound by it and may not recall it for the duration of the time that he/she has set for the submission of applications from interested parties to participate in the examination/competition, except if he/she, when organizing and announcing the competition/examination, has specifically mentioned his/her right to recall the proposal before the expiry of the stated deadline, or if it may be concluded that she/he has this right from the nature of the contract or from particular conditions under which the announcement of the competition was made.

327. The labour contract is presumed to be concluded, when the person interested to be hired has applied and participated in the competition under the terms and conditions that were included in the notice calling the competition. The final conclusion of the contract is under the precedent condition of the success of the applicant in the said competition. After the success, the applicant is considered as an employee of the employer.[146] If the employer who organized the competition has stalled in any way as to its completion, contrary to bona fides, the applicant is considered successful in the competition and is therefore an employee to the employer.[147]

328. Large enterprises and organizations hold competitive examinations, competitions, with terms that are publicly announced in the mass media.

VI. Employers' Duties During the Conclusion of the Labour Contract

329. During the pre-contractual stage, the employer is obliged to respect the principles of equal treatment and non-discrimination, and to respect applicants' personal data:

(a) Respect for the principles of equal treatment and non-discrimination: the employer is obliged to treat all applicants without discrimination. In that respect, discrimination on the basis of sex, race, religion or ideology is forbidden. Exceptions to the above apply only in those cases where the duties of the position offered are directly related to the above factors, such as in the cases of a model of male underwear or a wet nurse and so on.
(b) Protection of personal data:[148] the employer is permitted to pose questions only on issues directly related to the job offered, such as studies, experience, skills. The employer may send the applicant for tests in order to find out whether the applicant is suitable for and capable of duties involved in the position offered. Similarly, the employer may refer the prospective employee to specialized persons for medical examinations, tests measuring general and emotional intelligence and so forth.

146. AP 654/2000.
147. AP 674/2009.
148. *See* L. 2472/1997.

330. In all these cases, the employer must notify the employee, providing the reasons why the examinations are being carried out (the scope principle), while ensuring that no other less drastic measures exist that would reach the same conclusions (the principle of analogy).

331. If it is found that the applicant is an HIV carrier, this does not constitute a reason to refuse hiring; nor is it a reason for dismissal, as the virus is not transmitted through contact between employees in their workplace.

332. In certain cases, when the employee in carrying out his/her tasks could possibly present a threat to public health, as in the case of cooks, waiters, bar staff, nurses and others, it is a legal requirement that the employee undergo a medical examination. The possibility that the employer may refer the applicant for medical examination during the hiring procedure must not be confused with the fact that in some cases the employee is obliged to hold a health certificate provided by a doctor of the public sector, an insurance agency or a doctor of the private sector who is specialized as a general pathologist, an occupational doctor or a general practitioner. Such cases concern those employees who are in direct contact with packaged or unpackaged foodstuffs, with food preparation equipment and tools, or with surfaces that come into direct contact with foodstuffs.

VII. The Employer's Obligation to Inform the Employee: PD 156/1994

333. PD 156/1994 first established the employer's obligation to inform the employee of the terms which govern the contract or labour relation. The purpose of this decree was the harmonization of Hellenic labour legislation with the terms of Directive 91/533/EEC of the Council of the European Community of 14 October 1991 'on the obligation of the employer to inform the employee of the terms which govern the contract or the labour relation'. The provisions of this PD apply to every employee who is linked to an employer by contract or by a dependent labour relation but do not apply to employees whose total duration of employment does not exceed one month, or to employees in casual agricultural labour.

334. In accordance with Article 2 of PD 156/1994:

(a) The employer must make known to the employee the essential terms of the contract or labour relation.
(b) This information is to include at least the following:
  - information on the identities of the contracting parties;
  - the location where labour is to be provided, and the headquarters of the company or the residence of the employer;
  - the post or skill of the employee, his or her grade, the category of work and the object of his or her labour;
  - the start date of the contract or labour relation and its duration, in the case of a temporary (fixed/definite period) post;

– the duration of paid leave to which the employee has the right, as well as the means and timing of its provision;
– the amount of compensation to be paid, and the time limits to be observed by employer and employee, in the case of the ending of the contract or labour relation by revocation, always in accordance with current legislation;
– all remuneration of any type to which the employee has the right, and the timing of its payment;
– the duration of the employee's normal daily and weekly employment;
– reference to that applicable collective regulation which sets the minimum terms for the employee's recompense and labour.

(c) Information as to points (v), (vi), (vii) and (viii) may be given by reference to the current provisions of labour legislation.

335. In accordance with Article 3 of PD 156/1994, information on the terms of Article 2 is to be given to the employee within two months of the start of work, and in the case of those already employed, within two months of the coming into force of this decree. Information is given by means of the delivery to the employee of a written labour contract or other document, with the condition that this must include all the details referred to in the Article. If for any reason the contract or labour relation should have a duration of less than two months, the above document is delivered to the employee on its expiry.

336. Article 4 deals with work abroad. If the employee is employed abroad under a contract or labour relation established in Hellas, the documentation referred to in the previous article shall be delivered to him or her before his or her departure from Hellas (or within one month), in writing, and shall include at least the following further information:

(a) the duration of work abroad;
(b) the currency in which earnings are to be paid;
(c) any benefits of a financial or other nature which accompany his or her departure for abroad;
(d) any terms concerning repatriation.

337. In the case of any change in the above information, the employer shall draw up a relevant document and have it delivered to the employee within one month at the latest of the occurrence of the change. The failure of the employer to deliver this documentation does not entail the invalidity of the labour contract. A fine is imposed on any person who is in breach of the obligations they incur under the provisions of this PD, on a reasoned writ from the Labour Inspector, following a hearing instigated by the interested party.

§10. Legal Characterization of the Contract by the Court

338. In any case, the characterization of a contract is made after an evaluation of all the specific circumstances by the court, which judges on the legal relation of the contracting parties, regardless of the name that they have given to the contract.[149] The basic criterion for the characterization of the contract as 'labour contract' is the legal and personal subordination of the employee as derived from the whole context of the contract and the facts during the execution of the contract.[150]

§11. Imposition of Administrative and Legal Sanctions

339. The employer that breaches the provisions of labour law is liable to administrative sanctions from the Labour Inspectorate. The breach of many of the provisions of labour law stipulates penal offence and imposes sanctions in the criminal courts.

149. APol 16/2017, AP 677/2017.
150. APol 18/2003, APol 19/2009, APol 20/2009, AP 1290/2010, AP 556/2010, AP 1259/2009, AP 797/2008, AP 1618/2003, AP 177/1999.

Chapter 2. The Employment Relationship

§1. Definitions and Concepts

I. The Parties

340. The parties to the employment relationship are the employer and the employee.

A. *The Employer*

341. The employer may be an individual (natural) person, a corporation having a legal personality under civil law or public law. Particular laws give specific definitions of the employer, but these are for specific application only not for general use.

342. 'Employer' is considered to be the legal or individual (natural person) person in whose service an individual provides subordinate (dependent) labour in exchange for remuneration.[151] The employer is usually, but not inevitably, the owner of the enterprise whose interests are satisfied by the labour contract. If there is doubt concerning the identity of the employer, as employer is defined as the (legal or individual) person for whose profit the work is offered, that is usually the owner of the enterprise or, beyond this, the person who is responsible for the expenses and the risks of the enterprise.[152]

343. The employer is the holder of the authorities identified by law and of the responsibilities and obligations imposed on him/her by law.[153]

344. However, in some cases, there is a split in the person of the employer, meaning that the authorities, responsibilities and obligations are shared between two different persons.[154] Thus, an agreement between an employer (initial employer), the employee and a third party (subsequent employer) that the employee will provide his/her work to the third party for a shorter or longer time is legal. This arises from the combination of Article 651 of the CC, which stipulates that unless it is otherwise set out in the agreement or the circumstances, the employee ought to execute personally his/her obligations and that the claim of the employer is non-transferable, and the Articles 361 (referring to the right of persons to make contracts) and 648 of the same Code (referring to the elements of the labour contract).[155] In such cases, the labour contract is not terminated and the initial employer cannot reject the attribute of employer, while the third party that uses the

151. Ef. Crete 514/2007, Ef. Piraeus 714/1999.
152. AP 499/2016, AP 873/2009.
153. AP 259/2016.
154. AP 17/2012.
155. AP 286/1994, AP 1371/1990, AP 229/1990, Ef. Athens 3366/2001.

employee's services assumes the attribute of employer and exercises for the duration of the concession the managerial right with the limitations and content that would apply to the initial employer.[156] Unless there is a different specific agreement, the initial employer is the one solely responsible for the payment of the basic contractual salary or wages and is the only person who has the right to terminate the labour contract, while the subsequent employer is solely responsible for the satisfaction of the employee's claims in respect of overtime, overwork or work on Saturdays and Sundays, because these services are a matter of the specific relation between the employee and the subsequent employer.[157] In these cases, there is a genuine contract for the 'transfer' of the employee to a third person, which differs from a non-genuine contract for the 'transfer' of the employee to a third person, which is concluded with a Temporary Employment Agency (TEA), as stated below.

B. The Employee

345. Employees, e.g., persons who work under a labour contract, are subject to the provisions of labour law. However, in accordance with the kind of the work they offer, the sector of economy in which they work, their skills and qualifications (e.g., degree, master's degree, knowledge of foreign languages, experience, specialization), they are further distinguished into further categories that are subject to specific provisions. In the following paragraphs, the more important of these categories are described.

1. Blue-Collar and White-Collar Employees

346. Those employed with a labour contract are distinguished, using the criterion of the kind of the work that they provide, into white-collar or blue-collar employees. A white-collar employee is one who provides basically mental work, while a blue-collar employee is one who provides physical work. This distinction is important mainly when it is a question of the termination of a labour contract of indefinite period.

347. Since any labour is a combination of physical and mental actions, jurisprudence, in order to facilitate the evaluation of whether in a specific case the mental or the physical element takes precedence, has formulated additional criteria or indications, such as experience, theoretical training, expression of initiative, taking of responsibility for the execution of the work, and considers that the affirmative existence of these criteria favour the definition of a white-collar employee.[158] Thus it is judged that a cook, a foreman[159] or a hairstylist[160] are white-collar employees. This

156. AP 17/2012, AP 1009/2010.
157. AP 293/1994, AP 1133/1981, Ef. Thrace 290/1995.
158. AP 637/2005, AP 1481/1995, AP 1479/1995.
159. Ef. Thessaloniki 1958/1994.
160. AP 1181/1993.

distinction is made by applying these criteria. The parties of the labour contract cannot apply other criteria, and if they agreed differently, their agreement is without legal consequences.[161]

348. In recent labour legislation and in collective agreements, promises to deal with both categories in a uniform way have not yet been fully applied, but the idea of extending to manual labour the privileges of white-collar employees is clearly present.

2. Leading Personnel: Supervisors – 'Cadres'

349. Leading personnel, named 'directing employees', are considered white-collar employees under Hellenic law. As for 'leading personnel', these are considered those persons who have the right to hire or dismiss employees or who have, because of the employer's trust in them, the power to make decisions as to the functioning of the enterprise.[162]

350. The concept of 'directing employees' was formulated under jurisprudence in accordance with Article 2 of Law 2269/1920, which ratified the Convention of Washington of 29 October 1919 on the limiting of the hours of work in industrial undertakings to eight hours per day and forty-eight hours per week, and was included in Article 12 of the pre-draft of a Labour Code, issued by the Constituent Committee of Law 4345/1964, which, however, never became law.

351. 'Directing employees' are employees at managerial level. In practice, they manage the enterprise and are identified with the employer, so they are considered by the law as participating in the employers' legal responsibilities towards those working under their direction. Nevertheless, they are in a subordinate (dependent) labour relation and they are covered by labour law. However, because of their duties, they are exempt from certain provisions of labour legislation, such as those concerning working hours and the prohibition of Sunday work. Further, because of their duties, they have interests that are opposed to those of the employees and so do not participate in trade unions.

3. Apprentices

352. An apprenticeship agreement is one in the context of which one of the contracting parties assumes the responsibility of transferring to the other the necessary skills for the practice of the work.[163] Apprenticeship agreements, which can be

161. AP 257/1990.
162. AP 74/2011.
163. APol 19/1987.

signed for a definite or indefinite duration, appear in two forms, the genuine apprenticeship agreement and the agreement for subordinate (dependent) employment of the apprentice.

353. In a genuine apprenticeship agreement, the significant element is the training of the apprentice, and his/her work is carried out only for training reasons and not for the execution of substantial work. In this agreement, the special provisions for apprentices and the provisions of labour law will apply on the condition that they are not in conflict with the nature of the agreement.[164] There may be an agreement that the employer will pay to the apprentice a wage (lower than the wage of a skilled salaried person) for the benefits that the employer gains from the work of the apprentice or that the apprentice will receive no wage or that the apprentice will pay a specified fee for his/her apprenticeship.[165]

354. In the agreement for subordinate (dependent) employment of the apprentice, the apprentice provides dependent labour in parallel with his/her training, which does not constitute an object of specific obligation for the employer. This contract is subject to all the provisions of labour law.[166]

4. Homeworkers

355. Homeworkers are employees who supply their work for the needs of the employer's enterprise, but their workplace is their own home and not a place provided by the employer, such as the facilities of the enterprise or the employer's home.[167]

356. Homeworkers are subject to the provisions of labour law unless these are in conflict with the special circumstances under which they supply work.

357. When the homeworker has also signed a contract for teleworking, he is also subject to the special provisions for these types of contracts.

5. Domestic Workers

358. Domestic workers are those who under a contract of subordinate (dependent) labour provide to the employer services which concern employer's domestic needs, personal care, the care or personal needs of the employer's family members. All these are evidenced by the combination of the provisions of Articles 647, 663 of the CC, Article 3 paragraph 1 of RD 17 July 1920, Article 1 paragraph 2 of OA 539/

164. Ef. Patrai 390/2006, Ef. Athens 5386/1996.
165. APol 19/1987, AP 1268/1988, Ef. Athens 5386/1996.
166. AP 1592/2009.
167. AP 1955/2007.

1945, Single Article subparagraph (c) of RD 376/1971, Article 2 paragraph 1 of RD 748/1966, Article 43 of Law 1836/1685 and Article 1 paragraph 1 of Law 1876/1990.

359. Using the criterion of whether these domestic workers reside in employer's household or not, they are classified as 'live-in domestic workers' or as 'non-resident domestic workers'.

360. Due to the particular nature of the services provided by domestic workers and the special circumstances under which they provide these, e.g., they work inside the domestic environment of the employer, under circumstances of special trust between the employer, employer's family and employee and under special care for the employee, the work relation of domestic employees is not governed by the special provisions concerning working time for salaried persons, that is, for Sunday work, holidays, rest days, overtime and overwork. Furthermore, the minimum salaries and wages regulated by law or NGCA are not applicable, but the wage is regulated by agreement; where this is not the case, the customary wage is due.[168]

6. Commercial Travellers

361. Commercial travellers are white-collar employees engaged in finding and visiting clients with the aim of negotiating and concluding transactions on behalf of and in the name of their employer. Insurance agents are not regarded as commercial travellers.

362. A commercial traveller is an intermediary and not a party to the agreement, which is concluded between his or her employer and the client. According to Hellenic jurisprudence, if they exercise their profession personally, for an enterprise, permanently and continuously, dependently though maybe not exclusively or full-time, then this constitutes a relationship of employment.

363. A commercial traveller is regarded as an employee unless the employer can prove that there is no subordination. The law establishes rules on the payment of the commission, indemnity for dismissal, and the covenant of non-competition and arbitration, as well as rules on social insurance.[169] Commercial travellers who develop initiatives are independent professionals (self-employed, providers of independent services, etc.), as with traders, etc. and are excluded from IKA insurance.

---

168. AP 1955/2007.
169. Article 4, para. 2(c) and (d) of L. 180/1990.

7. Employees under Special Provisions

364. Special provisions, above the generally applicable provisions of labour law, are applicable for employees in hotels, professional athletes and certain other groups of employees.

§2. Employment Relationship and Individual Labour Contract

I. Labour Contract (Contract of Subordinate Labour)

365. According to Article 648 of the CC and Article 6 of Law 765/1943, in the labour contract the employee is obliged to provide, under subordination, the work required by the employer for a definite or indefinite period, while the latter is obliged to pay the wage.

366. The concept of the labour contract has at least five principal features:

(a) dependence of the employee on his or her employer;
(b) obligation of the employee to perform the work;
(c) obligation of the employer to pay wages (remuneration);
(d) additional secondary obligations of the parties;
(e) duration (definite or indefinite).

II. Employment Relationship: Void Labour Contract

367. The labour contract establishes a contractual relationship between the employer and the employee. This relationship introduces the employee to the business of the employer, and it is considered to be the legal link by which rights and duties for both parties are established.

368. However, work can be provided even when the contract is void.[170] A labour contract is void when it goes against the rules of *jus cogens*, and in such cases the court examines ex officio the invalidity of the contract.[171] The void contract, if no contrary finding applies, is as if it had never been made. In these cases, a de facto relation is created between the employer and the employee, called an 'employment relationship' or a 'simple work relation'.

369. The employee is in need of protection concerning such relations. For that reason, many provisions of labour law use the term 'employment relation' to imply that the rights that they enact are also applied to employees with a void labour contract, such as rights under legislation on group dismissals,[172] provisions for

170. AP 768/2018.
171. AP 622/91, AP 501/91, AP 358/1990, AP 1620/1988, AP 661/1984.
172. Article 2, para. 1 of L. 1387/1983.

minors,[173] provisions for additional remuneration for work on Sundays and holidays,[174] provisions for holidays benefits[175] and provisions for accidents in the workplace.[176] In general, the employment relationship is considered as a valid labour contract for as long as it lasts.

III. Different Approaches to the Employment Relation as Compared to the Valid Employment Relationship

370. A different approach to the employment relation, as compared to the valid employment relationship, can be manifested in the following two cases.

371. The first refers to the remuneration of the employee. In accordance to a well-established position of jurisprudence, if the employer does not offer the remuneration to the employee, the latter cannot demand the whole remuneration, but only that part of it connected to the benefit the employer gains from the employee's work. This claim is based on provisions concerning unjust enrichment.[177] This benefit has to do with the cost that the employer would necessarily bear, in the specific case of the execution of the service of the employee, meaning that remuneration, in accordance with the circumstances of the time and place of the execution of work, that would be offered to a different person hired with a valid labour contract (with the legally defined skills and qualifications) and who would be employed in the same circumstances as avoided because of the invalidity of the hiring. Remuneration because of personal skills and qualifications, such as seniority or marital status, is not included in this benefit. However, legal theory opposes the above and claims that the employee has a valid claim to full remuneration. Moreover, theory contends that, even if the case for the attribution of benefit is accepted, in this benefit there should be included the remuneration due to the personal qualifications of the employee and that the enrichment of the employer exists even if the conclusion of a valid labour contract was not possible. The amount that is offered as alleged benefit is not 'remuneration', in the legal concept of the word, and for that reason it is not protected by the law as such.[178]

372. The second refers to the termination of the employment relation. An employment relation of definite time can be terminated without the need for a significant reason.[179] An employment relation of indefinite time can be terminated in the same way as a valid labour contract of indefinite time. However, if the termination of the relation of indefinite time is made by the employer and if the termination is void, the employer is considered to be in default and the employee has the

173. Article 15 of L. 1837/1989.
174. Article 2, para. 1 of LD 3755/1957 as amended by Art. 2 of L. 435/1976.
175. Ministerial Decision 19040/1981.
176. L. 551/1915.
177. Article 904 of the CC.
178. AP 1596/1983.
179. AP 419/1995.

right to claim the compensation provisioned by law. In such cases, the employee may not claim default wages or the continuation of the employment relationship.

§3. Different Kinds of Labour Contract

I. Typical and Atypical (Non-typical) Labour Contract

373. There are more types of labour contracts. A distinction of fundamental significance is that between typical contracts and atypical contracts. Further distinctions are dependent on multiple criteria, and the most important type of labour contracts are reported below.

A. The Typical Labour Contract

374. The labour contract that is projected as a standard by legislation is drawn up informally, is drawn up directly between the employee and the employer who accepts the work, does not comprise a trial contract, the employee is not a trainee, is a contract of indefinite duration, the employee is occupied for the longest time limits allowed for by the law, the employee provides the same kind of work throughout the duration of the contract with his/her duties and tasks being unaltered, the work is provided in a place determined and controlled by the employer, which usually is the place of the enterprise, and the work is provided with the use of means provided by the employer. The contract that assembles these characteristics in aggregate comprises the standard contract as formulated by labour law and is called 'typical labour contract'. For the conclusion of such a contract, the agreement of both parties for the provision of subordinate work and the determination of the kind of work to be provided is sufficient. The typical labour contract gives to the employee all the rights stipulated by labour law and social security law, while at the same time it comprises that standard that directs legal thinking on the resolution of general problems that may arise in its context, as well as the standard that directs legislation on the formation of generally applicable stipulations of labour law as well as those of social security law.

B. The Atypical Labour Contract

375. Those labour contracts that do not include one or more of the above characteristics that comprise the typical labour contract are called 'non-typical' or 'atypical labour contracts'. The conclusion of atypical labour contracts does not hold as a prerequisite any specific legislation that allows the conclusion or that dictates the content of the contract. Both the conclusion and the content are covered by the contractual freedom. For this reason, all types of atypical labour contracts are 'reversible', meaning that the contracting parties, the employee and the employer, may agree on new contractual terms and modify it to a typical labour contract.

376. Atypical labour contracts appear with a variety of terms, as many as the inventiveness of the parties can come up within their efforts to adjust the terms of the labour contract to their multiple, multifaceted and altering needs, mainly to the needs of the employer. For instance, atypical labour contracts are the part-time labour contracts, the contracts for casual work, the triangular employment relationships for the 'transfer' of the employee to a third person,[180] the on-call labour contracts, the group employment or group labour contracts,[181] contracts with variable remuneration or with flexible or rotating or scaled working hours, shift work labour contracts, contracts for homeworkers and for teleworking, etc. It is not only excluded, but, on the contrary, it is all too common that an atypical labour contract deviates from the typical in a number of aspects, e.g., part-time employment in a definite term contract, full-time employment in combination with on-call,[182] part-time employment contracts in an on-call condition, a part-time employment contract in combination with group employment, definite term employment on shifts. The employees under atypical labour contracts are fully subject, as is self-evident, to the regulations of labour law. Employees under such contracts are subject to social insurance by the Institute of Social Insurance – Unified Fund of Salaried Employees Insurance (IKA – ETAM).

377. The provision of employment under the terms that are formulated in atypical employment contracts may appear also in contracts for the provision of independent work. In such cases it has been stipulated by a LD[183] that if the provision of work for a definite or indefinite period was agreed between the employer and the employee, in particular in cases of remuneration per work unit (piecework/outwork), teleworking or domestic work, it is legally inferred that a labour contract exists provided that the work is provided in person, exclusively or mainly to the same employer, for nine consecutive months.

II. Full-Time and Part-Time Employment

378. The labour contract may be either for full-time or part-time employment.

A. Labour Contract for Full-Time Employment

379. It is the provision of work during that legal working time which is stipulated by the legislation or under the terms of the collective agreement, with the payment of the corresponding remuneration, that comprises the concept of 'full-time employment'. This concept is determined by two elements, the working time and the remuneration, their magnitude and the relationship between them. In particular, it is determined by the duration of employment that is in effect as the maximum

180. AP 286/1994, AP 891/1989, AP 1794/1987.
181. Ef. Larisa 384/1992.
182. *See* Ef. Larisa 539/2000.
183. Article 1, para. 1 of L. 2639/1998 as replaced by Art. 1 of L. 3846/2010.

duration for the class of the employee and by the payment of the total salary that corresponds to this duration for this class.

380. Given that the stipulations, by which legal working time is stipulated, contain rules of unilateral *jus cogens*, it is possible to reduce the duration of maximum legal working time under terms agreed upon by the employer and the employee without a corresponding reduction of the salary.[184] In such a case, 'full-time employment with less working hours' may be mentioned, but not 'part-time employment', since the term 'part-time employment' implies the provision of work in a reduced working time with a corresponding reduction in remuneration, as mentioned below. In the context of contractual freedom it is also possible for salaries greater than the legal ones to be agreed upon. Thus, it is not excluded that full-time employment may take the form of employment for fewer hours than the maximum working hours with remuneration higher than the legally defined salary.

B. Labour Contract for Part-Time Employment

1. The Concept of Part-Time Work

381. The concept of part-time work is not legally defined in Hellas. It is accepted that the part-time work has to be of a shorter duration than ordinary working time. Ordinary working time is understood as being the maximum working time during which a full-time employee has to perform in a given enterprise or sector or profession. When concluding the labour contract or while it lasts, the employer and the employee may agree on a daily or weekly or fortnightly or monthly working hours less than the regular hours of 'full-time employment'.

382. A part-time contract is not a specific type of employment contract but a (normal) contract for an indefinite period or of a definite period and so on.

383. In accordance with those stipulations in effect (Article 38 of Law 1892/1990, as replaced by Article 2 of Law 2639/1998, Article 2 of Law 3846/2010 and Article 17 of Law 3899/2010, by which the Directive 97/81/EC was incorporated into national law), a part-time labour contract may be concluded only in writing, while generally for the conclusion of a labour contract a written form is not needed, it is concluded orally or even tacitly. The written contract must state the system and hours of part-time work agreed upon.

384. The part-time labour contract is inferred to cover a full-time employment relation if within eight days from its conclusion is not notified to the competent Labour Inspectorate.[185] However, the employer has the right to submit proof that the contract was in fact concluded as one of part-time employment.

---

184. AP 162/1993, AP 522/1957.
185. AP 1264/2012, AP 811/2012.

2. No Dismissal Due to Refusal of Part-Time Work

385. Dismissal on the grounds of non-acceptance by the employee of the employer's proposal for part-time employment is not valid.

3. Covering by Enterprise's Training Activities and Social Services

386. For those employees who are covered by a part-time employment contract the following are provided:

(a) the possibility of participating in professional training activities applied by the enterprise under conditions corresponding to those conditions concerning full-time employees and employees under contracts of indefinite duration;
(b) the same social services that are available to the other employees in the enterprise.

4. Work by Rotation

387. One form of part-time employment is 'work by rotation', that is employment for fewer (than five or six) days per week or for fewer weeks per month or for fewer months per year or a combination of the afore with full-time or part-time working hours daily. During the drawing up of this employment contract or during its duration, the employer and the employee may agree, in writing by means of a personal contract, upon whatsoever irregular form of employment.

388. The employer, instead of dismissal, may unilaterally impose work by rotation in the case that the activities of the enterprise are limited. In such a case, the duration of the work by rotation may not exceed nine months in the same calendar year, while prior notice to and consultation with the employees' representatives are required. 'Work by rotation' means an alternation of days of working and days of not working while the operation of the business is not interrupted.

5. Remuneration and Part-Time Work

389. The remuneration of employees under a part-time labour contract is calculated in the same manner as the remuneration of comparable employees and corresponds to the working hours of the part-time work. For part-time employees all the stipulations of labour law apply.

6. Part-Time Work and Additional Work

390. If a need arises for additional work beyond that agreed, the part-time employee is under the obligation to provide it, if he/she is in a position to do so and his/her denial would be contrary to bona fides. The part-time employee may decline to provide work beyond that agreed when that additional work is to take place in a usual manner.

7. Modification of the Labour Contract from Full-Time to Part-Time

391. Full-time employees who work in businesses that employ more than twenty persons, have the right, following the completion of one calendar year of work, to ask for the modification of the labour contract from a full-time to a part-time work, reserving the right to return to a full-time work, unless the employer is justified in refusing this due to the needs of the business. In submitting her/his application, the employee must set down the duration of the part-time employment and its type. If the employer fails to respond in writing within a month, the employee's request is considered as accepted.

8. Information of the Employees' Representatives

392. The employer is to inform the employees' representatives of the number of employees in part-time employment in relation to developments in the total of the number of employees, as well as of the prospects for hiring full-time employees.

9. Regulations by Enterprise-Level Collective Agreements

393. It is permissible to supplement or amend the regulations mentioned in the above paragraphs by enterprise-level collective agreements.

10. Job-Sharing Labour Contract

394. A job-sharing labour contract constitutes a particular case of part-time work under which the duties of a full-time post are shared between more than one workers and the associated rights and obligations are also proportionally shared.

C. Labour Contract for Group Work

395. Group work may be described as a certain form of work performed by a group of persons which is organized for this purpose, and where each member of the group is responsible for the combined work performed together by all the members of the group. Certain forms of group work exist in musical, acrobatic and other artistic occupations, as well as in the brick and tile manufacturing industries, in quarries and the fishing industry, in loading and unloading work, and in the work of funeral directors. We can distinguish between those groups organized on the initiative of an employer, who entrusts the creation of the group to a leader, and those groups that are autonomous.

III. Labour Contract for an Indefinite or a Definite Period

396. A labour contract may be of a definite or of an indefinite period or of mixed character.[186,187]

A. *Labour Contract of Indefinite Period*

397. A labour contract of indefinite period is one the duration of which has not been set or is not inferable from the kind and purpose of the work.[188] A key characteristic of the contract of indefinite period is that the parties do not know the time of the expiry of the contract.

B. *Labour Contract of Definite Period*

398. A labour contract of definite period is one the duration of which is defined either by an exact specification of a future time or by the type and the performance of the specific task or purpose that is to be accomplished.[189]

399. A key characteristic of the contract of definite period is that the parties know the time of the expiry of the contract with exactitude. The date of expiry or the duration of the contract must be precise and clear, for example, expiry on a set date, hiring for the duration of the Christmas holidays, hiring for the replacement of another employee who will be absent for a set time, hiring for the execution of seasonal work, hiring in a seasonally operating enterprise,[190] setting of an age for the employee after which the contract is *ipso jure* terminated, etc.

186. The terms 'contract of indefinite period', 'contracts of unlimited duration', 'contract of unlimited time', 'contract of indefinite period', 'contract of indefinite time', 'open-ended contract' are used as equivalents. The terms 'contract of definite period', 'contract of limited duration', 'contract of limited time', 'contract of definite period', 'contract of definite time', 'fixed-term contract' are used as equivalents.
187. APol 13/2017 analyses the concept of a labour contact of 'indefinite' and of 'definite' period.
188. Article 669, sub-para. B of the CC.
189. Article 669 of the CC.
190. AP 1576/2012.

C. Transformation of a Definite Period Labour Contract to an Indefinite Period

400. A contract for a definite period ends when the agreed upon period expires or when the work agreed upon has been completed. According to Article 671 of the CC, a contract of definite period is transformed into a contract of indefinite period, if the employee continues to work after the agreed period has expired or after the agreed work has been completed and the employer does not reject this continuation.

D. Labour Contracts of Mixed Character

401. The contracting parties, in accordance with contractual freedom, may agree on terms by which the contract has elements of both definite and indefinite time. For example, the parties may agree that the contract has a maximum duration, after the completion of which the contract is *ipso jure* terminated, while at the same time they agree that they have the right to terminate the contract for any reason. In such a case, if the contract is terminated before the agreed maximum duration, it is transformed into one of indefinite time.[191]

E. Labour Contract for More than Five Years

402. If the employer and the employee agree that the duration of the labour contract is for the lifetime of the employee or for more than five years, the employee has the right to offer his/her resignation after the completion of five years from the conclusion of the labour contract provided that he/she give a six months' notice to the employer.[192] The waiver of this right is void.[193]

F. The Differentiation of the Termination of an Indefinite and a Definite Labour Contract

403. The distinction between a labour contract of definite period and one of indefinite period is important especially in cases of dismissal, because of the provisions governing the termination of the labour contract. Fuller protection of job security is enjoyed by employees who have a labour contract of indefinite time. However, since the negotiations power of the employee is not the same as that of the employer, there is the risk that the employee may accept a definite period contract on the employer's demand and thus be deprived of the protection that he/she would have had if the contract had been one of indefinite period. To deal with this risk, Article 8 paragraph 3 of Law 2112/1920 stipulates that a contract of definite

191. APol 42/2002, AP 1479/2007, AP 778/1995.
192. Article 670 of the CC.
193. Article 671 of the CC.

period is to be considered as one of indefinite period, if the conclusion of the definite period is not justified by the nature or/and the purpose of the work or the needs of the enterprise or the benefit of the employee.

G. Successive Labour Contracts of Definite Period

1. General Remarks

404. In the case of successive labour contracts of definite period, the abovementioned danger is evident. Accordingly, in accordance with the previously mentioned Article 8 paragraph 3 of Law 2112/1920 the signing of successive contracts of definite period is an indication that the agreement for definite period is not objectively justifiable, but is undertaken in order to deprive the employee of the protection provided by the legislation on the termination of a labour contract of indefinite period; this may be described as an abusive exercise of employer's contractual freedom. Under settled case law[194] such successive contracts are considered as one single contract of indefinite period. The consideration of the totality of these contracts as one single contract of indefinite period constitutes a legally correct classification of the contract, which is a matter for a court decision, in the formulation of which the court is not bound by the qualifications set out by the contracting parties, but will rule after interpreting the content of the contracts as required by bona fides, the customary practices and the circumstances that applied during the signing of these contracts.[195]

2. The PD 81/2003 for Successive Labour Contracts of Definite Period

405. As regards the treatment of successive labour contracts of definite period and the principle of non-discrimination between employees with labour contracts of definite period and related employees with labour contracts of indefinite period, the relevant provisions are found in PD 81/2003, as amended by P.D. 180/2004 and Article 41 of Law 3896/2011, which incorporated Directive 199/70/EC of the Council of the 28 June 1999 into national law, concerning the framework of agreement on definite period work, signed between the inter-branch organizations ETUC, Union of Industrial and Employers' Confederation of Europe and CEEP.[196] This agreement pursues on the one hand the amelioration of the quality of work of definite period with the application of the principle of non-discrimination in relation to work of indefinite period and on the other hand the avoidance of any abuse caused by the use of successive contracts or work relations of definite period.[197]

---

194. AP 18/2013, AP 603/1994, AP 1431/1991, AP 1219/1988.
195. APol 18/2006, AP 18/2013.
196. EEL. 175/10 July 1999.
197. PD 164/2004 applies for employees in the public sector and municipal and community enterprises.

406. In accordance with this PD in the private sector as 'successive labour contracts', we refer to the contracts or work relations that are concluded between the same employer and the same employee, with the same or similar working terms, within a time interval shorter than forty-five days, including non-working days. As for groups of enterprises, for the application of the previous paragraph, the concept of the 'same employer' includes all the enterprises of the group.

407. The unlimited renewal of labour contracts of definite period is allowed, if it is justified by an objective reason. An objective reason especially exists if the definite period work:

(a) is justified by the kind of the provided work and/or the activity of the employer and the enterprise or by specific reasons or needs, when there is direct or indirect evidence from the said labour contract, such as the temporary replacement of a salaried person, the provision of work of temporary character or a temporary accumulation of work;
(b) is related to the training of the employee;
(c) is made in order to facilitate the transfer of the employee to a similar occupation;
(d) is made in order to execute a specific work project or programme;
(e) is connected to a specific event;
(f) has to do with air transport enterprises or enterprises that offer airport ground and flight services.

408. The reasons that justify the renewal of the contract or the employment relation of definite period must in every case be mentioned in the related agreement between the parties, which is to be concluded in writing, or may be directly evidenced by the agreement. A copy of this agreement must be promptly given to the employee after the start of the provision of her/his work. The written form of the above agreement is not required when the renewal of the contract or the employment relation has a casual character and is not for longer than ten working days.

409. If no objective reason, as described above, exists and if the duration of the successive renewals of the contracts or employment relations of definite period is more than three years, it is assumed that, by these renewals, fixed and permanent needs of the enterprise are being covered, so such contracts/relations are transformed into labour contracts or employment relations of indefinite period. It is up to the employer to prove otherwise.

410. Concerning the terms of employment, employees with a contract or employment relation of definite period are not to be treated, because of the sole reason that their contract is of definite period, less favourably than related employees on indefinite period contracts, with the only exception being the existence of objective reasons that justify this different treatment. When the rights of the employee depend on the duration of service to the same or to different employers, it is not accepted that there should be a treatment that differs according to the criterion of the contract's being of definite or indefinite period, unless objective reasons exist.

The required period of service or seniority related to specific conditions of employment is the same for employees of definite and those of indefinite period unless objective reasons justify a different period of seniority.

411. Employers are to inform the employees of definite period as to positions that are available in the enterprise or the undertaking, in order to ensure that these employees have the same opportunities to claim the positions of indefinite period as the other employees. This information is given via a general announcement posted in an appropriate place, inside the enterprise or the undertaking, or by any other appropriate means.

412. As far as possible, and taking into account the need for the normal operation of the enterprise, employers are to facilitate the access of their employees of definite period to proper opportunities for training, in order that the employees may strengthen their skills and progress in their careers and their professional mobility.

413. This PD is, however, not applicable in cases of:

(a) relations concerning basic vocational training or an agreement or contract of apprenticeship; and
(b) labour contracts or relations concluded in the context of a special training, entry or vocational retraining programme in the public sector, or supported by the public sector.

§4. On-call Labour Contracts

414. On-call contracts are those labour contracts by which it is agreed that the employee is bound to be at the disposal of the employer in order to provide his/her work whenever the need arises (on-call work). This contract appears in the following three forms:

(a) genuine on-call contract: this is a contract where the employee is present in the workplace, remaining vigilant in order to provide his/her work when needed; for example a firefighter in the enterprise, a nurse in the enterprise, etc. This contract is a normal labour contract;
(b) simple on-call contract: this is a contract where the employee is present in the workplace and may rest or do as he/she wants, but is obliged to provide his/her work upon the employer's request; for example, a night watchman in a factory who after checking the premises remains in a guardroom in order to rest, etc;
(c) on-call contract with the employee not present in the workplace: this is a contract where it is agreed that the employee will not be present in the workplace but will immediately come there upon a call from the employer in order to provide his/her work: for example, a hotel electrician who remains at home and comes to the hotel to work when necessary, a doctor employed by an enterprise who remains in his office and comes to the enterprise when called, etc.

415. As to the two latter forms, there is a prevailing opinion these contracts are normal labour contracts only for the duration that the employee actually provides his/her work. For the rest of the time the provisions of labour law do not apply; for example, the provisions for the minimum wage are not applied but the usual rate of pay is due for the working time, etc.[198]

§5. Teleworking

416. Teleworking is a form of organization of labour power and/or provision of labour by the employee. In teleworking the employee uses information technology and provides his/her work from any place out of the employer's premises, while the same work could be provided inside the facilities of the enterprise.

417. A teleworker is an employee who provides telework.

418. Teleworking has a voluntary character for the interested parties, the employer and the employee, and may be a part either of the employee's initial job description or of a subsequent agreement.

419. Concerning the circumstances and the terms of employment, teleworkers, since they provide their work under a labour contract, enjoy the same rights that are secured by current legislation and collective agreements for related employees working inside the facilities of the enterprise. Additionally, special provisions included in the NGCA of 2006–2007 and Article 5 of Law 3846/2010 apply for teleworkers.

420. All issues concerning work equipment, responsibilities and expenses are to be clearly defined before the onset of telework. The employer provides the teleworker with proper technical support, and when the telework is properly provided, covers all costs that are directly connected to it, especially communication costs.

421. In general, the employer is responsible for the provision, installation and maintenance of the necessary equipment properly to carry out telework, unless the teleworker is to use his/her own equipment.

422. The employer bears the responsibility for any expenses related to the loss or damage of the equipment and data that are used by the teleworker.

423. The teleworker looks after the equipment that is provided to him/her and does not collect or distribute illegal material through the Internet. It falls to the employer to adopt appropriate measures, especially concerning software, in order to ensure the protection of data that is used and processed by the teleworker for professional reasons.

---

198. AP 1262/2009, AP 962/2007.

424. The employer is to inform the teleworker of all the current provisions and rules of the enterprise that concern the protection of data. It is up to the teleworker to comply with these.

425. The employer informs the teleworker of any specific limitations on the use of the equipment or tools of informatics, such as the Internet, and of any penalties in case of non-compliance. The employer respects the private life of the teleworker.

426. In accordance with Article 5 of Law 3846/2010, the employer, when he/she concludes a labour contract for teleworking, must provide the employee in writing, within eight days, with all that information relevant to the execution of his/her work and specifically to the hierarchical connection to his/her superiors in the enterprise, his/her detailed duties, the manner of calculation of his/her remuneration, the manner of calculating his/her working time and the payment of expenses incurred during the provision of work (telecommunication costs, system and equipment faults, etc.).

427. If the contract includes an agreement for tele-on-call (on-call tele-availability), the time limits for this as well as the time limits for the employee's response must also be defined. If regular work is changed into teleworking, in the agreement there is defined a period of adaptation of three months, during which any of the parties, after they observe a deadline of fifteen days, may terminate the teleworking and the employee can return to his/her former work to a position corresponding to that he/she held. The employer assumes in any case the cost that is incurred by the employee from this type of work and particularly telecommunication costs.

§6. Labour Contracts for Gaining Professional Experience

428. In the particular case of young employees 18 to 25 years old, labour law provides for the signing of labour contracts of definite period for the gaining of professional experience.[199]

429. The duration of the contract may be up to twenty-four months. It is possible that more than one labour contract be signed with the same or a different employer during the twenty-four months that follow the signing of the first contract of professional experience. Such hiring must constitute an addition to the current staff employed by an employer.

430. Labour contracts for the acquisition of professional experience are to be notified to OAED and SEPE in the area of the employer's headquarters not later than the day following their signing.

199. Article 43 of L. 3986/2011 in combination with Art. 1 para. 1 of PIS 6/2012.

431. Professional-experience employees are to be insured in IKA-ETAM in the sectors of pension, illness (health provision) and occupational hazard.

432. In order for the employer to conclude such contracts, he/she must not have reduced the number of employees in the three months previous to the conclusion of the contract and may not reduce staff numbers during the duration of the contract. In the case of seasonal enterprises, the employer must not have reduced the seasonal staff in comparison with the respective month of the previous year, and must not implement staff cuts during the duration of such contracts.

433. Labour law provisions fully apply to these contracts.

§7. Contract for Temporary Work

434. Temporary work is considered to be non-permanent and is entered into voluntarily. As a legal concept, temporary work refers exclusively to subordinate work. The temporary worker is regarded as a full-fledged employee, enjoying the full protection of labour law and social security. The contract for temporary work is usually one of definite period.

§8. Temporary (Agency) Work and Temporary Employment Agencies

435. The concept 'temporary employment' is, also, used for the provision of work by an employee to an employer through a TEA. A TEA may be founded by a legal person or an individual on the declaration of its initiation/foundation to the Directorate of Employment of the Ministry of Labour and Social Insurance, to be accompanied by the proper legal documentation. Every TEA is obliged, in order to exercise the said activity, to deposit two letters of guarantee from a bank as financial guarantees, the first for securing the remuneration of the temporary workers, and the second for securing the workers' insurance contributions.

436. The first law that regulated this type of temporary work was Law 2596/2001 (Articles 20–25). This law has already been repealed by Law 4052/2012 (Articles 113 et seq.), which incorporated into national law Directive 2008/104/EC of the Council of 19 November 2008 concerning temporary agency work. Further amendments have been made under Law 4093/2012, Article First paragraph IA subparagraph IA.8. The law applies to employees with a labour contract or employment relation with a TEA who are assigned to a user enterprise in order to work there temporarily under their supervision and discretion.

437. In the application of this law 'temporary employment' refers to work that is provided for a person (indirect employer) different than the one who has concluded the labour contract as employer (direct employer). The work may be provided to the third person for a limited time.

438. The employment of the employee by an indirect employer under a temporary labour contract is not permissible when:

(a) It replaces employees who are exercising the right to strike.
(b) The indirect employer during the previous six months had dismissed employees of the same occupation for economic reasons or had carried out collective redundancies of employees of the same occupation during the previous year.
(c) The indirect employer is the public sector or a legal person of public law.
(d) The work, due to its nature, presents serious risks to the health and safety of the employees.
(e) The employee is subject to the special provisions concerning insurance of blue-collar construction workers.

439. The basic employment terms of employees with a contract of temporary employment, which include remuneration, during their assignment to the indirect employer, are those minima that would have been applied in the case that these employees had been hired directly by the said employer (the indirect employer) to be placed in the same position. Employees with a contract of temporary employment receive, concerning safety and health in the workplace, the same level of protection that is provided to the other employees of the indirect employer. The indirect employer, subject to the contractual provision for co-responsibility cumulatively with the TEA, is responsible for the conditions under which the work of the salaried person is executed and for any possible work accidents.

440. The duration of the placement of the employee with the indirect employer, including any renewals made in writing, cannot extend for more than thirty-six months. Should this time limit be exceeded, then the contract is transformed into a contract of indefinite period with the indirect employer.[200]

441. Temporary employees are to be informed of available positions in the indirect employer's enterprise, in order they should have the same opportunities as the other employees of the enterprise to be hired as permanent employees.

442. Any clause that directly or indirectly forbids or limits the permanent employment of the temporary worker upon the conclusion of a labour contract between the indirect employer and the temporary employee, after the expiry of the labour contract with the temporary agency, is void. Further, any clause which directly or indirectly limits the employee' union rights or encroaches upon their insurance rights is void.

443. The promotion of temporary workers in enterprises (by the indirect employer) is allowed only through the action of TEA that are also allowed to exercise the following activities:

200. AP 674/2012, AP 742/2009.

(a) mediation for the placing of a person in a work position that has been announced as available by the Directorate of Employment;
(b) evaluation or training of personnel in accordance with the current provisions;
(c) consultation and professional guidance in accordance with the current provisions.

444. For the provision of work as temporary work via TEA the existence of a previous written labour contract of definite or indefinite period is a prerequisite. The contract is concluded between the TEA (direct employer) and the employee and the contract must include the terms of employment, its duration, the terms of the supply of work to the indirect employer(s), the terms of remuneration and insurance of the employee, the reasons for the placement and any other elements that, as a matter of bona fides and in the circumstances, should be known to the employee in relation to her/his provision of work.

445. The remuneration of the employee that does not offer his/her work to the indirect employer must not be lower than that stipulated in the relevant NGCA.

446. If during the time when this contract is being drawn up, it is not possible to mention a specific indirect employer or to determine the time during which the employee will offer his/her work, then this omission must be mentioned in the contract, in the framework of the terms and conditions for the supply of work to an indirect employer.

447. Employment of the employee by the indirect employer is allowed only after the signing of the contract with the direct employer, in accordance with the previous paragraph.

448. Any breach by a TEA of the provisions of the law incurs administrative and legal sanctions.

§9. The Trial Clause

449. A labour contract may admissibly include a trial clause by which it is agreed that for specified fair time following the beginning of the contract, the contract will be qualified as having a trial character (trial time/probationary period) in order that the employer shall have the opportunity to decide whether the employee is capable of and suitable for the work that he/she is hired for.

450. This agreement may take either of the following two forms:

(a) It may be signed as a contract of indefinite period, while it is agreed that this will be in effect until the employer decides that the employee is capable and suitable. Depending on the manner in which this agreement is formed, the contract is subject to conditions for its dissolution or suspension.

(b) It may be signed as a contract of definite period, while it is agreed that on the expiry of its duration the employer will decide objectively, making a fair judgment as to whether the employee is suitable and capable. If the judgment is positive, the signing of the final labour contract will follow.

451. During the trial stage/period between the parties there exists a final labour contract, not an interim one; this means that during that stage the contract functions normally and is fully subject to labour law. The duration of the trial period is counted as part of the overall duration of the labour contract for the calculation of seniority and for the establishing of other employee's rights.

452. A contract with a trial clause is regulated by particular provisions of law; its duration is defined by the parties but must fall within those fair limits that are necessary for the employer to make an assessment of the suitability or otherwise of the employee. The fair period will be judged on the basis of the kind and nature of the work; thus, it could be as much as a year for a high-ranking cadre of the company.[201] Employers or their competent body are obliged to judge the suitability or otherwise of the employee at the end of the trial period, and this assessment must be based on the qualitative and quantitative efficiency of the employee on trial as well as his/her overall conduct in the workplace. If the judgment is negative, the contract is *ipso jure* terminated.[202]

201. Ef. Athens 4564/2009.
202. *See* AP 1719/2012.

Chapter 3. Rights and Duties of the Parties in the Course of Employment

§1. General Remarks

453. The contracting parties of a labour contract, that is, the employer and the employee, have obligations that arise from the provisions of the law, the terms of collective agreements, work regulations and the clauses of the labour contract, which may not by law be less favourable than the corresponding provisions of the NGCA or of any applicable DAs.

454. These obligations are classified as either primary or secondary. The primary obligation of the employee is the supply of work and that of the employer the supply of remuneration. Secondary obligations, as with other contracts, are enforced by bona fides and bind the employer and the employee, without overlooking their own interests, to heed the justified interests of the other party and to avoid actions and omissions that may harm these interests. The concept of bona fides means that the employee has a good faith obligation towards the employer, while the employer has a welfare duty, or duty of care,[203] towards the employee. These two types of obligations can be set out as more specific obligations which bind the two parties for the duration of the labour contract.

§2. Duties of the Employee

I. Duty Towards the Provision of Work

A. General Remarks

455. The main obligation of the employee is the supply of work.[204] This supply is determined as a specific type of work, its timing and its place. These characteristics are a result of an agreement between the employer and the employee. If the time and place of the work have not been agreed, they are regulated by law, by the terms of the NGCA and by the work regulations. If such provisions do not exist, they are a matter of the managerial prerogative.[205]

203. *See* below para. 492.
204. Article 648 of the CC.
205. *See* below para. 472.

B. The Personal Element for the Provision of Work

1. Substitution of the Employee

456. The employee is obliged to render his/her services personally unless agreed otherwise, or except when it is considered that a third person may be allowed to perform the work.[206] Any such substitution of the employee by a third party may be entered into through words or through conduct, either expressly or implicitly, in whole or in part, and as restricted to certain persons. The legal agreement, however, remains that between the employer and the employee.

457. The third person has only an indirect relation to the employer, regardless of whether or not the person is obliged to work under the command, authority and control of the employer, while the employer's duty to pay remuneration is to the third person.

2. Employees' Loan Contract (Contract under Which the Employee Provides His/Her Service to Another Person)

458. Employees have the duty to provide their services to the employer.[207] However, following an agreement between the employer, the employee and a third party (e.g., another entrepreneur, natural or legal person), it may be decided that the employee will provide his/her work to a third party for a definite or indefinite time (employee loan contract).[208] An employee loan contract may be explicit or silent (implicit), but its existence must be proven.[209] This contract does not affect the labour contract between the employee and the (first) employer, and for that reason, the employee provides his or her work in accordance with the terms of the labour contract.

459. The employer continues to bear the liability for the employee's remuneration and provision of leave and has the right to terminate the contract of subordinate work, etc.[210] The third party obtains the right to claim the supply of work and to exercise his/her managerial right concerning this supply. He/she is obliged to act in accordance with the law on work supply (such as legislation concerning the health and safety of employees) and with the welfare of the employees (such as the security of their personal belongings).

460. The third party also bears the costs of additional remuneration for possible additional work of the employee, such as overtime or Sunday work. Correspondingly, the employee is obliged to comply with the work terms applicable to the

---

206. Article 651 of the CC.
207. Article 651 of the CC.
208. AP 1426/2004, AP 272/1991.
209. AP 1157/2009, AP 923/2008.
210. AP 229/1990.

employees of the enterprise of the third party (such as rules of conduct, time for breaks). Possible agreements between the third party and the loan-contract employee concerning additional remuneration or change of the duties of the employee are legal but do not bind the employer. Employee loan contracts are common in the case of a group of undertakings. Directive 96/71/EC concerning the protection of the employees in the cases of employee loan contracts was incorporated into national law by PD 219/2000.

C. The Type of Work

461. The duty of the employee is fulfilled when the employee provides the certain kind of work which was agreed upon, generally or particularly, under the labour contract, which is interpreted in accordance with custom and bona fides.[211] The type of work is usually defined by the occupational identity of the employee.[212] The employer, on the basis of managerial right, further defines the kind of work and sets out the duties of the employee. The employer may require the supply of work closely related to the kind of work that has been agreed upon, but cannot demand a change in the kind of work unless such change is provided for in the subordinate employment contract.

462. The employee is obliged, unless a different agreement with the employer exists, also to supply work that, concerning its kind, is closely connected with the main duties, such as preliminary, complementary and 'attendant' services: for example, a waiter has to clear the tables and to keep the room clean, a chauffeur takes care of refuelling the car. For these additional services, the employee is not entitled to an additional remuneration since they are considered as part of his obligation to supply work.[213]

463. The employee is obliged to provide different work, though still similar to that undertaken in his/her usual work position, in case of an emergency.[214] For this kind of work, the employee is entitled to additional remuneration.[215]

464. If, according to a contract of dependent work, it is agreed that the employee will provide more than one kind of work, meaning tasks of different kinds (mixed work), remuneration is set on the basis of the primary work.

211. AP 406/1989.
212. Ef. Athens 1162/1986.
213. AP 118/1997, AP 1087/1984.
214. AP 927/1986.
215. AP 1129/1991, AP 858/1986, Art. 659 of the CC.

D. The Place of Work Performance

465. The place of work is defined by the contract of dependent work or the enterprise regulations, or else in accordance with managerial right.[216] The place of work does not necessarily coincide with the location of the head office of the enterprise.[217]

466. The employee's place of work may temporarily be changed by an instruction by the employer to work elsewhere than the usual base. Unless there is an agreement to the contrary or a contradictory terms in the work regulations, the employee is obliged to work temporarily away from the usual base. In such case, additional payment is provided to the employee for transportation (travel expenses). If the employee spends the night at the appointed place, he/she is entitled to an additional payment (payment for working away). The amount of this payment is 1/25 of the salary as defined by law or by the collective agreement or by DA for the specific type of employee; in the case of daily wages, the amount is defined in accordance with the law or the terms of the collective agreement or DA. This compensation is due regardless of whether the employee also received subsistence expenses.[218]

467. The place of work may be changed permanently (a transfer), either by an agreement between the employee and the employer, which can be made before or after the hiring, or unilaterally by the employer in the following cases:

(a) Under a contract of subordinate employment, it may be agreed that the employee may be transferred in the case that the enterprise has more than one facility (establishment) or is about so to have in the future. If there is no specific term in the subordinate employment contract or in the works regulations, and the enterprise has many facilities, the employer, in accordance with prevailing opinion in jurisprudence,[219] may, by exercising his/her managerial right, transfer the employee to a different facility. This capability exists even if the employee had no knowledge of the number of facilities of the enterprise.[220] There is, however, a differing theoretical opinion which insists that if at the time of hiring the enterprise had only one facility, the employee is obliged to provide his/her work only in that specific facility or in a different facility (establishment) in the same region.[221]
(b) In the case of a change of the place of where work is performed, because of the movement of the establishment to another area or location, employees have a duty to perform their work in the new place[222] if this is not considered as a serious change of the employees' duty and does not incur more expenses for them.

216. AP 1425/2002, AP 1157/1989.
217. AP 1165/1999, AP 540/1992.
218. APol 33/1975.
219. AP 127/2007, AP 1248/1993, AP 1480/1990.
220. AP 1145/1992, AP 1564/1987.
221. *See* Ef. Thessaloniki 49/1995. *See also* AP 1418/1980.
222. AP 141/1980.

If the district where the establishment is newly located is far from the employees' place of residence, they have the right to refuse to supply their work at the new location. In this case, because the employees may present themselves at the location of the old establishment in order to supply their work there, the employer has the right to terminate the contract, paying any applicable compensation to the employees.[223]

468. Under no circumstances is transfer abroad possible without the consent of the employee.

E. *The Method of Work Performance*

469. The employee is obliged to provide his/her work in accordance with the terms of the labour contract, the work regulations, the terms of the collective agreements or DAs and the instructions of the employer. These terms and instructions refer to the manner in which the work is provided and the employee's behaviour within the enterprise. The aim is better to utilize work for the better service of the enterprise, in relation to its productive aims and its general functionality.

470. The manner in which work is provided may be altered without any unilateral creation of a detrimental change of the terms under which work is supplied.

F. *Employees' Private Life*

471. Employees' work performance should be separated from the employees' private life. The employee is obliged to supply her/his work during working hours and is entitled to dispose of the rest of his/her time freely. The employee's political ideas or beliefs, freedom of speech and freedom to engage in political activities are part of the employee's personal rights, and no intervention by his or her employer is permitted.

G. *Managerial Prerogative*

472. Managerial prerogative is the right of the employer to define and specify the supply of work by the employee by defining the kind, the time and place of work, when these are not otherwise regulated by law, terms of the NGCA, work regulations, enterprise customs or the terms of the labour contract. Managerial right must be exercised fairly;[224] it is forbidden that it be exercised abusively.[225]

223. AP 1087/2008.
224. Articles 371, 372 of the CC.
225. Article 281 of the CC.

II. Duty of Loyalty

473. The most important secondary obligation of the employee is the 'duty of loyalty'. This duty used formerly to refer to the general obligation of the employee to act in a way that would secure, and not infringe, the just rights of the employer and the enterprise. Latterly, this duty specifies other subordinate duties that the employee bears, even if these duties are not explicitly mentioned in the contract. The limits of the duty of loyalty are defined in any specific case after balancing the conflicting interests, so as to secure the professional interests both of the employee and of the employer. The duty of loyalty finds its limits at that point where the employee has to secure his/her own interests. For example, the employee is entitled to press charges if the employer does not comply with those health and safety regulations applicable to the enterprise, but is, on the other hand, obliged to maintain peaceful working relations with his/her colleagues and not to disturb the internal order of the enterprise. The duty of loyalty usually expires at the end of the labour contract, though not during temporary pauses, as in the case of leave from work.

III. Duty of Confidentiality

474. One specific expression of the duty of loyalty is the duty of confidentiality, meaning the obligation of the employee not to reveal to third parties confidential material concerning the enterprise which has become known to him through his or her work. Such material might include planning for the future activities of the enterprise, its financial state, its suppliers and customers, the cost of production of its goods or services, production methods, employee training, the software used, etc. The duty of confidentiality does not cover any possible illegal activities on the part of the enterprise.[226] Special duties of confidentiality are imposed on the employees' representatives.[227] The duty of confidentiality extends beyond the expiry of the labour contract.

IV. Duty Not to Compete with the Employer

475. Another specific expression of the duty to good faith is the duty of the employee not to proceed with any actions competitive to the employer's enterprise.[228] This obligation, as with other secondary obligations, need not necessarily be explicitly agreed.[229] It may be breached even if the competitive actions of the employee are incidental and even if no damage has been caused to the employer. Further, the employee who discloses confidential enterprise information with the

226. *See also* AP 470/1944.
227. Article 4 of L. 1876/1990, Art. 13 of L. 1767/1988.
228. *See* AP 192/1992, AP 1285/1984.
229. AP 1192/1992.

aim of competing with or causing damage to the employer faces legal sanctions and incurs a liability to compensate the employer.[230]

476. A breach of the above obligation does not automatically occur when the employee seeks work in an enterprise in competition with the employer's or prepares to set up an enterprise in competition that he/she will manage after the end of his/her labour contract. The duty of non-competition remains in effect until the end of the labour contract. However, its effect may be extended beyond the end of the dependent labour contract by explicit clause(s) of agreement.[231] Since such clauses involve the curtailment of professional and economic freedoms, they are subject to judicial control, in accordance with Article 281 of the CC, which prohibits the abusive use of this right, as well as with Articles 178 and 179 of the CC, on potential conflicts with generally accepted ethical principles.

477. Within the framework of such judicial control, the following factors will be examined:

(a) whether by these agreements justified interests of the employer are served (such as whether the employee is in a position to intervene with the employer's customers);
(b) if the duration of the right that binds the employee is fair (e.g., agreements that bind the employee for an indefinite time are void);
(c) if compensation is provided for the employee;
(d) what the geographical scope for the duty of non-competition is;
(e) what the scope of the prohibited actions is.

478. The greater the commitment of the employee, the stricter the control of the agreement. Agreements that are deemed excessive are void. If, however, the employee breaches a legal, valid agreement, he/she is liable for compensation to the employer.

V. Liability

479. The employee is obliged to provide his/her work with diligence and is responsible for any damage caused to the employer as a result of negligence or wilful misconduct.[232] Even the slightest negligence on the part of the employee is included in the above. Damage may be a result of non-compliance with the orders of the employer, of illegal withdrawal the supply of work, of defective work or of a breach of the employees' obligations, as derived from the terms of the labour contract, of law and of bona fides.

230. Article 16 of L. 146/1914.
231. *See* AP 1591/2002.
232. Article 652 of the CC.

480. The degree of diligence that the employee must show is judged on the basis of her or his knowledge, skills or attributes, all of which are taken as being known to the employer. Their combined evaluation may lead to the lessening or to the intensification of an employee's liability.[233] In order to define the amount of compensation that the employee owes, co-liability of the employer is also taken into account, especially on the basis that a great part of the work supply is undertaken under the supervision of the employer, and that the employer provides the necessary equipment for the supply of work, manages the supply of work and, in general, is responsible for the whole framework of the supply of work.

481. A special case is constituted by work tasks that are considered 'prone to accidents', such as in the case of use of hazardous materials (e.g., explosives) or fragile materials (e.g., glass), or in the case of work involving monotonous repeated movements, or where the equipment in use is heavy and difficult to handle. In these cases, it is considered that the employer bears the liability for accidents and that the employee is not liable, or incurs reduced liability.

482. Agreements between the employer and the employee for reduced employee liability are legal and may be undertaken during the hiring of the employee or at a later stage.

VI. Prohibition of Smoking

483. In accordance with Article 3 of Law 3730/2008, smoking and the consumption of tobacco products have been prohibited as of 1 July 2009 in the workplace and in all enterprise locations, public or private, that are closed or roofed. Certain spaces specifically designated for smokers are exempt, in accordance with a decision of Minister of Health and Social Solidarity, as are spaces used for the production of tobacco products.

§3. Duties of the Employer

I. Duty to Pay Remuneration

484. The main duty of the employer is the payment of remuneration.[234,235] As already mentioned, the payment of remuneration is the compensation by the employer in respect of the provision of work by the employee. Non-payment of

233. Ef. Thessaloniki 1219/1995.
234. *See* Art. 9 of L. 4554/2018, which stipulates that when an entrepreneur (natural or legal person) entrusts, in the course of his business, the execution of a work or part of it (contracting party) to another natural or legal person (contractor), he is jointly and severally liable with the contractor to the employees of the latter for the salaries owed, the insurance contributions and any severance pay owed.
235. According to settled case law, salaries are primarily a means of earning a living, e.g., StEol 668/2012.

remuneration is justified when the employee arbitrarily does not provide his/her work, while the employer is obliged to pay the remuneration in cases where the non-provision of work is in accordance with the law.

II. Duty to Employ the Employee

485. An issue that has led to different opinions between jurisprudence and theory is whether the employer has a general duty of real employment of the employee. Theory unanimously supports the opinion that the employer has a general duty of real employment of the employee, because through the provision of employment, the personality of the employee develops and the constitutionally determined right to employment is implemented.[236] This opinion has also been supported by certain court decisions concerning this issue.

486. However, jurisprudence from *Areios Pagos* (the Supreme Civil Court), in accordance with Articles 648 paragraph (a)[237] and 656[238] of the CC, declares that the employer, by being the holder, in accordance with the managerial right, of the authority to regulate all issues concerning the organization and function of the enterprise in order to achieve its aims, is not, as a rule, obliged to employ the employee, unless an agreement to the contrary exists. In any case, however, the employer is obliged to pay the remuneration.

487. However, the denial, legal in principle, of the employer to accept the work of the employee, becomes illegal when this is an abusive exercise of employer's right or when it infringes the personality of the employee; in that case, the employer is obliged to pay compensation to the employee.[239] In accordance with these positions, the jurisprudence of *Areios Pagos* actually supports the view that the employer does not hold a general duty to employ the employee, though he/she is obliged to pay the wage even if he refuses to employ the employee.[240] Recently, Article 656 of the CC has been replaced by Article 61 of Law 4139/2013 and has acquired the following content: 'If the employer is overdue in the acceptance of the work, the employee has the right to demand real employment as well as the salary for the time period that he/she was employed.'

---

236. Article 22 of the Constitution.
237. 'With the employment contract, the employee is obliged to provide his work, for a definite or indefinite time, to the employer who is obliged to pay the agreed remuneration.'
238. 'If the employer is overdue concerning the acceptance of the provision of work, or if the acceptance of work for reasons related to him and not by force majeure, the employee has the right to demand remuneration without having the obligation to continue his work. However, the employer has the right to deduce from remuneration anything the employee took advantage of from his stoppage of work or from his supply elsewhere.'
239. APol 9/2011, AP 171/1009.
240. For the cases where the non-acceptance of work justifies the non-payment of remuneration *see* below paras 750 et seq.

III. Obligation to Respect Employees' Constitutional Rights

488. Fundamental individual and social rights are protected by a plethora of provisions of the Constitution, such as Articles 2 paragraph 1[241] (on human dignity), 4 paragraphs 1, 2 (equality) with the supplementary 116 paragraphs 1 and 2, 5 paragraph 1 (personality) with the similar 106 paragraph 2 on the means of action in business, 5A[242] (information), 9[243] (family asylum), 9A[244] (personal data), 10[245] (reference to the authorities), 11 paragraph 1[246] (right to convene), 12[247] paragraphs 1–3 (associations), 13[248] paragraph 1 (freedom of religious conviction), 14[249] paragraph 1 (freedom of opinion), 17[250] paragraph 1 (property), 19[251] paragraph 1 (privacy of correspondence), 21[252] paragraph 1 (family), 22[253] (work, collective agreements, DAs), 23[254] (union rights, strikes).

241. The respect and protection of the value of human life is the main obligation of the state.
242. Every person has the right to information, as stipulated by the law. It is possible for limitations to this right to be imposed by law only if they are absolutely necessary and justified on reasons of national security, fighting of crime or protection of rights and interests of third parties. 2. Every person has the right to participate in the Information Society. The facilitation of the access to information that are digitally handled, as well as of their promotion, exchange and dissemination is an obligation of the state, always abiding by the guarantees of Arts 9, 9A and 19.
243. 1. The residence of every person is an asylum. The private and family life of the person is inviolable. No research is conducted in a residence, unless and only as stipulated by the law and always in the presence of judicial authority representatives. 2. The violators of the above stipulation are punished for a breach of domestic asylum and for abuse of power and they are obliged to indemnify in full the suffering party, as stipulated by the law.
244. Every person has the right of protection from the gathering, processing and use, especially by digital means, of his personal data, as stipulated by the law. The protection of personal data is ensured by an independent authority, which is structured and operates as stipulated by the law.
245. Every person or many individuals together have the right, abiding by the laws of the state, to report in writing to the authorities, which are obliged to act soon according to the stipulations in effect and to respond justifiably to the person filing the report, according to the law.
246. Hellene citizens have the right to convene quietly and without guns.
247. Hellene citizens have the right to form associations and non-profit unions, abiding by the law, however not ever being able to hinge the exertion of this right to a previous permission. (2) The union cannot be dissolved due to the violation of a law or of an essential stipulation in its statutes, by any means other than a judicial decision. (3) The stipulations of the previous paragraph are applied accordingly also on unions of individuals that do not comprise a union.
248. The freedom of religious conscience is inviolable. The relish of individual and civil rights does not depend on religious beliefs of any individual.
249. Every person can express and disseminate orally, in writing and in press his contemplations abiding by the law of the state.
250. Property is under the protection of the state, yet the rights resulting by it may not be exerted at the expense of the general benefit.
251. The privacy of correspondence and free response or communication in whatsoever manner is completely inviolable. The Law stipulates the guarantees under which the judicial authority is not bound by privacy on reasons of national security or to investigate particularly serious crimes.
252. The family, as a foundation of the conservation and promotion of the Nation, as well as marriage, motherhood and childhood are under the protection of the state.
253. 1. Employment is a right and it is under the protection of the state, which seeks to the establishment of employment conditions for all the citizens and for the moral and material elevation of the working rural and civil population. All the employees, irrespective of their sex or other distinction, have the right for an equal remuneration for provided work of equal value. 2. The general terms of work are defined by the law, complemented by the employment collective agreements attached to free negotiations and should these fail, by the rules set by arbitration. 3. The Law stipulates the

489. Article 25 paragraph 1(c) of the Constitution states that 'These rights also apply to the relations between the individuals that they personalize.' In accordance with this last provision, within the framework of legal relations under private law, as in the labour contract, the employer is obliged to respect the fundamental personal and social rights of the employee, given that these are objective values that are applied in the whole field of law. Furthermore, under Article 25 paragraph 1(c) of the Constitution, it is stipulated that 'Any type of limitations that may be imposed in accordance with the Constitution to these rights must be either directly provided for by the Constitution or by the law, since there is prejudice in favour of that, and must respect the principle of proportionality.'

490. In accordance with the last provisions the employer, when he/she proceeds to the limitation of the personal and social rights of the employees with the aim of protecting his/her and the company's fair interests, is obliged to adopt all measures that are fruitful in order to achieve his/her aim, that are necessary for that and, given multiple available measures, to adopt those that are less intrusive for the employee. As it is evident, a plethora of employee rights consists of a particularization of her/his constitutional rights, many of which are also protected by provisions of labour law, such as the protection of labour in the form of the protection of the work position, with provisions regulating the termination of the labour contract by the employer.

491. In cases where the rights of the employees, which are included among the constitutional rights, are infringed by the employer, the protection that is pursued by the employee is reinforced with by claims not only under the special provisions of labour law but also by the related constitutional provisions. In accordance with Article 25 paragraph 3 of the Constitution, that stipulates that 'the abusive exercise

---

relevant to the conclusion of collective employment contracts by public servants and employees of organizations of local government or of other legal entities governed by the public law. 4. Whatsoever form of compulsory labour is prohibited. Specific laws rule the issues relevant to the requisition of personal services in case of war or recruitment or confrontation of needs of the defence of the Country or of a social emergency due to natural disaster or necessity that may jeopardize public health as well as in relevance to the provision of personal employment in the local government organizations to meet local necessities. 5. The state seeks the social insurance of employees, as stipulated by the law. Explanatory statement: The general terms of employment include the determination of the manner and the person liable to collect and pay to the labour unions the fees of their members provided for by their statutes.

254. 1. The state undertakes the dully measures for the ensuring of union freedom and unimpeded exercise of the relevant to it rights against every offence of them, within the boundaries of the law. 2. Strike is a right, exercised by the legally established labour unions for the preservation and promotion of financial and in general labour interests of the workers. Strike is prohibited in whatsoever form, for judicial servants and for those serving in the security corps. The right of public servants and of employees in the legal entities governed by public law as well as of the personnel of every type of businesses of public character or public utility, the operation of which is of vital importance for the service of basic needs of the society, to resort to a strike subjected to the particular restrictions of the law that regulates it. These restrictions may not reach up to the abolishment of the right to a strike or the obstruction of its legal exertion.

of a right is not allowed', the constitutional guarantee of a right does not mean that its exercise is without control, but that its abusive exercise is prohibited, as is in general every abusive exercise of any right.

IV. Duty of Care to the Employee

492. Employers have a duty of care to their employees, which means that they should take all steps which are reasonably possible to ensure their legally protected interests. That duty used to refer to a general duty of the employer to act in a way that does not infringe the fair rights of the employees. It was a counter-balance to the duty of good faith that the employee has towards the employer. The said duty takes different forms and content in relation to the specific circumstances and, in some cases, may coincide with the duty of the employer to respect the constitutional rights of the employee.

Nowadays this duty is analysed in various duties of the employer and may be further specified by law, by the terms of collective agreements or by DAs, customary commercial practices and work regulations. The breach of these duties creates claims in favour of the employee for the satisfaction of her/his rights that have been infringed in the said case, without excluding a further claim for compensation for violation of personality.

V. Duty to Protect the Personality of the Employee

493. The employer is obliged to respect the personality of the employee. This duty arises from the general application of provisions concerning the protection of personality[255] but is specified in relation to the specific dangers that threaten the personality of the employee because of the exercise of the managerial right and with the utilization of new technological means. Within this framework, employees may freely schedule their private life outside work, and any intervention by the employer is prohibited, as is any adverse discrimination against employees because of their private lives. In extreme situations, however, the employer may take into consideration elements of the employee's private life in order to define the work terms, such as any gambling problems for an employee who works as a cashier or a conviction for paedophilia for an employee working as a teacher.

VI. Non-exercise of Violence Against the Employee: Protection of the Employee's Personal Belongings

494. As an expression of the respect of employee's personality, the employer is obliged not to exercise, physical or psychological, violence against him/her and also to take the same care with regard to the actions of the employee's co-workers or third parties. If violence is exercised, the employer is obliged to take all appropriate

255. Article 5, para. 1 of the Constitution, Art. 57 of the CC.

measures to ensure that this will not happen again in the future. In a similar way, the employer has a duty of care to ensure that employees' personal belongings are safe in the workplace. The employee must feel safe while he/she provides work, and this can take place only if the employer fulfils these duties. Employers who judge that for the fulfilment of these duties the presence of security personnel is necessary must adopt such a measure.

VII. Obligation for Equal Treatment of Employees

495. This obligation is extensively analysed in a different part of this monograph.[256]

VIII. Protection from Sexual and Moral Harassment (Bullying) in the Workplace

496. The employee is subject to harassment when undesirable behaviour takes place against him/her that is related to her/his gender, race, ethnicity, religion, age or sexual orientation, and has as an aim or result in the infringement of his/her dignity and the creation of a threatening, hostile, demeaning or aggressive environment.

497. Sexual harassment exists when any type of unwanted verbal or non-verbal or physical conduct of sexual character is expressed towards the employee with the purpose or result in the infringement of his/her dignity, especially with the creation of a frightening, hostile, demeaning or aggressive environment towards the employee. These definitions are included in Article 2 of Law 3896/2010 on the 'application of the principle of equal opportunities and equal treatment of men and women on issues of work and employment and the harmonization of current legislation with Directive 2006/54/EC of the European Parliament and Council of 5 July 2006 and other related provisions' and Law 3304/2005 on the 'application of the principle of equal treatment regardless of racial or ethnic origin, religion or other beliefs, disability, age or sexual orientation', as replaced by Article 7 of Law 3625/2007.

498. Harassment and sexual harassment, as well as any less favourable treatment that is due to the acceptance or rejection of such conduct, constitute prohibited discrimination because of gender, race, ethnicity, age or sexual orientation. Harassment, in all of its forms, entails a breach of the principle of equal treatment of the employees, and for that reason all measures that concern equal treatment apply.

499. As appears in the above-mentioned definitions, the elements that constitute harassment are:

---

256. *See* below paras 781 et seq.

(a) behaviour that is unwanted by the employee, even if this is a single incident and not continuous behaviour;
(b) behaviour that is made verbally or in any other way, such as gestures, facial expressions, e.g., degrading expressions, biased evaluations, pretended dismissal or disciplinary action, contemptuous movement of the head or the hands;
(c) behaviour that has as a purpose or result in the infringement of the dignity of the employee or the creation of a negative environment that hinders or makes insufferable the provision of work.

500. The employer is obliged not to act in any way that is considered as harassment, to adopt all necessary measures to avoid harassment by the employee's co-workers, by clients and suppliers of the enterprise and by any third party who is in contact with the employee. In this framework, the employer is obliged to impose sanctions on those employees who harass their co-workers, to change their workplace or to alter their working terms in order to avoid similar behaviour in the future. Harassment primarily concerns actions that are individually addressed to the employee but it may also be caused by actions that are addressed to an indefinite number of employees that reduce their dignity individually.[257]

IX. Duty for the Protection of Personal Data

A. *General Remarks*

501. The employer collects personal data on job applicants and workers for a number of purposes: to comply with law; to assist in selection for employment, training and promotion; to ensure personal safety, personal security, quality control, customer service and the protection of property.

502. The employer processes a plethora of employees' personal data at all stages of the labour contract. The processing of personal data on the employees by the employer starts with their collection from the pre-contractual stage, during which, based on the practice used by the employer, there is either an application with the curriculum vitae of the applicant or an interview or simple conversation in which the employee orally presents to the employer his/her personal data as required by the employer, or a combination of all the above. During that stage, data are usually collected concerning the employee's knowledge, experience and skills, as well as any information necessary in order to define his capability and suitability to supply the work that he/she is being considered for.

503. Some of the data collected are those mentioned in the job application, for the employer to know the identity of the applicant and communicate with her/him, such as the first and last name, the home address, the phone number. In cases that the employee is submitted to psychological tests, to medical examinations or other

257. *See* AP 1765/1999.

similar examinations, his/her personal data are gathered concerning health, heredity and genetic information in general. At the stage of hiring, it is admissible that family data should be collected if the applicant is married or otherwise, the number and age of the children.

504. During the labour relationship, the collection of the employee's personal data continues and is extended, due to the updating of data already known, as in the cases of a divorce or marriage, the death or birth of members of the employee's family. The collection of such new data is deemed necessary for the execution of work, as for adding, removing or altering duties, for sending the employee for occupational training, for imposing disciplinary sanctions on the employee, for responding to a request by the employee for the provision of a special type of leave, such as that for supervising the school performance of children, for caring for disabled members of the family, because of health problems.

B. Processing of Personal Data: Lawfully, Fairly, for Reasons Relevant to the Employment

505. In each of the above cases, the adoption of the purposes entails the collection of personal data by the employer, without his/her having a specific intention of doing so. Finally, the employee's personal data is also processed during the stage of the expiry of the labour relationship, as in the case of retirement, or in the case of a criminal proceeding that affects the labour relationship, or other personal reasons concerning the employee. Even after the expiry of the labour relationship, the employer retains personal data on the employee that may be necessary either to the employer, such as in order to prove that he/she employed the employee, with the duration and the terms of the labour contract, or to the employee, such as in the case of his/her future need for a certificate of his employment with the particular employer, or so that the data may be used in court on a matter concerning his/her labour relationship.

506. The ways of collection of employees' personal data are numerous and are carried out by various means, such as conventional, mechanical and electronic means, medical and genetic analyses, measurement of biometric data. There may be the presentation of certificates of marital status or health, degrees, a permit to exercise a profession, any other documents with information on the personal data of the employee, data on entry to and exit from the workplace, data concerning the use of medicines or substances, monitoring of phone calls and/or use of electronic mail and use of the Internet, and surveillance of the workplace with the use of closed-circuit cameras, all these in real time or with the use of recordings.

C. Employees' Right to Informational Self-Determination and Employer's Right to Information

507. The processing of employees' personal data by the employer is connected, among other things, to the employees' right to informational self-determination and to the employer's right to information in relation to the employee's personal data. These rights are an expression of the constitutional rights regulated by Articles 5(a) and 9(a) of the Constitution. The balance of these conflicting rights, the terms and the preconditions under which, the employer may proceed to the processing of employees' personal data and the assurances for the protection of the employees are regulated by Regulation (EU) 2016/679 of the European Parliament and of the Council General Data Protection Regulation (GDPR), of general application. A national law for the supplementation and implementation of the GDPR is expected.

D. Preconditions

508. This processing is legal when the following preconditions are met cumulatively:

(a) Principle of expediency: the processing has a specific and legal aim that justifies it (principle of expediency). This aim is the target pursued by the processing of the personal data and is distinguished from the means that are used for its attainment, which are the manner in which this will be attained. It is also distinguished by the specific tool with which the means is applied, e.g., the purpose may be to ensure that in a specific place of the workplace, only specific employees will enter; the means for the achievement of this purpose will be the determination of the identity of the persons who are allowed to enter, and during their entry the technical tool that is used might well be to check the outline of the left hand or the iris pattern of their eyes. The purpose also functions as a point of reference around which the processing procedure is formulated and developed, and the maintenance of purpose until the completion of processing preserves the legitimacy of the processing. The definition (of purposes) is to precede the start of the data collection, which is the first step in processing.
(b) Principle of proportionality: the personal data that are required to be submitted for processing so as to achieve this purpose are defined in relation to the purpose of the processing,. The employer defines this data, which must be relevant to the purpose of the process, fruitful for its achievement and no more in quantity than required on each occasion. Similarly, the employer defines the collection method and the type of the processing to which this data will be submitted. When defining these data, the employer must proceed to the collection of those personal data which are absolutely necessary and must collect them and submit them to processing with the least possible intervention with the rights and interests of the employee (principle of proportionality).
(c) Principle of legitimacy: the methods of collection and processing, as well as the means that are used, must be legitimate and legal (principle of legitimacy). These elements are defined by the employer, as the person responsible for the

processing, who, in addition, is obliged to check the truth and accuracy of the data that he/she collects. When these data are provided by the employee, truth and accuracy must be considered as given and the employer bears no responsibility if these data are found to be false or inaccurate. However, the employee is not considered to be the provider of the data when the collection is made with or without his consent, but through third parties, e.g., when the collection is carried out through surveillance of the workplace, or by conducting medical examinations, or by the examination of employees' biometric data. In these cases, the employee, all too often without choice in the matter, sets himself at the disposal of the employer in order that the employer may acquire the data with the aid of specialized and technical means. For that reason, the employer is obliged to check, possibly with the aid of third parties whom he/she chooses on his/her own responsibility, the truth and the accuracy of the data that he/she collects. If it is necessary, personal data must be updated and are to be kept in a form that will allow the determining of the identity of the employee and only for the time period that is required in order to achieve the purpose of the processing.

(d) Principle of clarity: the employer is obliged to inform the employee (principle of clarity) of the following:
  - his identity and the identity of his/her representative, if there is one;
  - the scope of the processing;
  - the recipients or the categories of recipients of the information;
  - the existence of the right of access.

  The information must be communicated to the employee no later than during the time of the collection of the employee's personal data by the employer. The information must be expressed in a clear and easily comprehensible way, in such language and form of words as are appropriate to the employee's age, educational level and perceptive abilities and allowing sufficient time for the employee to understand it fully. The passing on of this information can comprise the employee's being informed individually, while if the information concerns further employees, this can take the form of the posting of a clear and legible notification on the notice board for the personnel, or by means of the distribution of printed material, or of the sending of the notification by e-mail, etc. When the employer collects personal data directly from the employee, the information must be expressed in writing.

(e) Securing of privacy: the employer is obliged to secure privacy during processing as well as the security of the employee's personal data.

(f) Consent of the employee: the consent of the employee for the collection of his/her personal data and their submission to processing is necessary in only a few cases. However, if none of the above preconditions is met, the employer is proceeding with illegal processing of the employee's personal data.

E. No Evaluation of the Employee by the Use of Automated Processing of Personal Data

509. The employer is prohibited from proceeding an evaluation of the employee or making decisions that affect the position of the employee and his/her service status, such as evaluation for promotion or demotion, for assignment or subtraction of duties, for dismissal, exclusively by the use of automated processing of the employee's personal data. This prohibition refers to decisions of the employer, or of the councils of the enterprise, or of employees that act within the scope of their competencies, if these decisions entail legal consequences at the expense of the employee and are solely based on an evaluation of the employee that was made automatically, whether this refers to the collection, use, interconnection or combination of the personal data or to their evaluation.

510. In contrast, decisions can be made that were formed after the inclusion of the data that were not collected automatically or with evaluations that were not made wholly automatically or do not bring legal consequences at the expense of the employee, such as decisions of a preparatory or advisory character.

F. The Rights of the Employee

511. The rights of the employee to protection during the processing of his/her personal data by the employer are as follows (any contradiction of these rights is void):

(a) The right of information: the right of information relates to the obligation of the employer to inform, as previously mentioned.
(b) The right of access: the purpose of the right of access is to provide the employee with the possibility of checking whether the preconditions for legal and legitimate processing have been met by the employer in accordance with those conditions previously mentioned. If the employee exercises this right, this does not mean that he/she provides his/her consent to the processing (in the few cases where this is necessary), neither does it mean that the employer has the right to ignore his/her obligation to inform the employee. The exercise of this right must be without expense for the employee and the employer is obliged to respond punctually within fifteen days, in writing, and in language comprehensible to the employee.
(c) The employer is obliged to inform the employee of all the data of personal character that concern him/her, as well as their origin, the purpose of the processing, the recipients or the categories of recipients of data, any developments in the processing in the time since the previous update, and the rationale for the automated processing. The right of access can be exercised by the subject of the data and with the aid of a specialized person, depending on the circumstances, for the correction, the deletion or the freezing of the data record on the grounds that its processing has not been in accordance with the provisions of current law,

especially because of the incomplete or inaccurate character of the data and their communication to third parties who have been notified of the data.

(d) The right to raise objections: the right of access is extended and supplemented by the right of raising objections. The purpose of this right is to provide the employee with the opportunity to intervene in processing, to insist on its legitimacy and to object to illegal or illegitimate processing. The employee is entitled to raise objections during the processing, at any stage, though not before the start or after its conclusion. These objections are addressed to the employer in writing and must include a request for a specific action, such as correction, temporary non-use, freezing, non-transfer or deletion. The employer is obliged to respond in writing to the objections within an exclusive deadline of fifteen days. In his/her response, he/she is obliged to inform the subject of the action(s) taken and of the reasons for which he/she may not have satisfied the employee's claim.

(e) The right to judicial protection:
   - provision of interim judicial protection: In any case, and in parallel to the interim protection provided by the Hellenic Data Protection Authority (APDPX), the employee has the right, if the preconditions of Article 682 KPolD for the adoption of interim measures are applied, to request their adoption (interim regulation of the case);
   - provision of regular judicial protection in accordance with Articles of GDPR: In the cases where the employer breaches the provisions of GDPR, it is possible that material or moral damage is created to the employee because of the breach of these provisions, e.g., because the employer has not complied with the above-mentioned preconditions for legitimate and legal processing, or has hindered the employee in the exercise of the above-mentioned rights.

512. The employer who has breached the provisions of GDPR faces penal and administrative sanctions.

G. The Hellenic Data Protection Authority

513. In ensuring compliance with Law 2472/1997 and in ensuring the legitimacy of the processing of personal data, an important role is played by the APDPX, which, in accordance with Article 9(a) of the Constitution, was founded by Article 16 of Law 2472/1997, which law incorporated Directive 95/46/EC into the national law, and has as its mission the supervision of the application of current law and other provisions that concern the protection of the individual from the processing of personal data, as well as the performance of such other competencies as may be entrusted to the agency.

514. The APDPX has broad competencies and by its decisions interprets the provisions of Law 2472/1997 and their specification, with the purpose, besides others, that these be applied correctly by employers during the processing of employees' personal data. For the same purpose, the APDPX issued the advisory function

Directive 115/2001 on the processing of employees' data and general application Directive 1/2011 concerning the use of video surveillance systems for the protection of persons and goods, Direction 1/2005 on the destruction of files of personal data after the expiry of the period that is required for processing and Directive 1122/2000 for the processing of personal data through closed circuits.

X. Specifically for the Surveillance of the Workplace with Cameras and Video Surveillance, for the Surveillance of Telephones (Tapping) and of Computer Systems and for the Use of Biometric Methods and Medical Examinations

A. General Remarks

515. The use of cameras and electronic surveillance systems by the employer to monitor the workplace has become a usual and widespread phenomenon, in real time with or without the recording of image and sound, and the storing of the recordings (video) for a long period. There is also the surveillance (tapping) of phones and personal computers and other communication channels used by employees, the use of biometric methods for the control of entry and exit to the premises of the company, and the submission of the employees to medical examinations.

516. With all these methods the employer collects employees' personal data and submits these to processing. In the light of this, this capability of the employer to use such measures is governed by the provisions of GDPR and the principles of expediency, legitimacy, proportionality and clarity, as mentioned above.[258]

517. Therefore, according, for instance, to the principle of clarity, the employer cannot proceed with the above-mentioned actions in secrecy but is obliged previously to inform the employee. According to the principle of expediency, the employer must be in a position to justify the adoption of these invasive measures, meaning the purpose that is pursued through their use, while in accordance with the principle of proportionality, the employer must explain why less onerous means could not be adopted.

518. In any case, the employer is not allowed to use the means that are mentioned above for reasons that are not connected to the employment relation, in a place that is not a workplace and in time that is not working time, such as breaks, or commuting time (even if this commuting is carried out with means that are made available by the employer), or the time before the start of and after the end of working hours.

519. In addition to those points that are of general application, and specifically for each of the methods of accumulation of personal data mentioned above, the following also apply.

---

258. *See* above para. 508.

B. Surveillance of Workplaces with Cameras and Video Surveillance

520. By such surveillance of the workplaces, the employer usually aims to prevent or avoid dangers, such as theft, robbery, acts of violence in general, harassment of the employees, the security of the enterprise's classified information.

521. The APDPX, in order to facilitate the application of Law 2472/1997 in such cases, issued Directive 1/2011, applicable under GDPR as well. In accordance with the clauses of this Directive, the video surveillance system shall not be used for the surveillance of the employees inside the workplace, with the exception of special, extraordinary situations where this is justified by the nature and the work conditions and is necessary for the protection of the health and safety of the employees or the protection of critical places in the enterprise (e.g., military production facilities, banks, high-risk facilities). For example, in a typical office in a workplace, video surveillance must be limited to the entrance or exit areas, without monitoring office or corridor spaces. Legitimate exceptions may be made for certain places such as cash registers, places with safes (strong-boxes), electromechanical equipment, under the condition that the cameras focus on the goods/assets that they are to protect, and not on the employees' working space.

522. Furthermore, in certain places, such as those with electromechanical facilities, the shift manager or the safety manager may observe the operators of high-risk machinery in real time, in order to intervene if a safety incident occurs. The operation of cameras and video-recording in locations within the enterprise that are not workplaces, such as restrooms, break-rooms, cafeterias or restaurants, cloakrooms, the immediate surroundings of the enterprise's premises, is prohibited.

523. Such places may come under surveillance only when there are exceptional circumstances, such as when there are well-founded suspicions that therein acts of violence or harassment are occurring or that there is trafficking or abuse of illegal substances. During the surveillance of the perimeter of such places, the recording of images from adjoining streets and sidewalks is prohibited, since there is the danger of the surveillance of passers-by.

524. The camera installation locations and the method of gathering the data must be defined in such a way that the data that are collected are no more than those necessary for the achievement of the purpose of the processing, and do not infringe fundamental rights of the employees or of other persons who are in the place under surveillance, and in particular do not to infringe that which may be considered 'a legal expectation of a certain degree of protection of private life' in the workplace.

525. This data must be kept for a specific time according to the purpose of processing in each case, and, in any case, from the making of visual recordings that are saved or made in real time, if there is no intervening event relevant to the pursued purpose, the data must be destroyed within fifteen working days.

526. Before any person enters an area under video surveillance, the data processing manager is under the obligation to ensure that this person is clearly and comprehensibly informed that he/she is entering a place under video surveillance.

527. The use of cameras able to turn and focus is allowed only in circumstances where the processing manager will watch the movements of natural persons in real time in order directly to intervene in order to avoid an incident (e.g., night shift in large areas such as factories, warehouses) and if all necessary technical measures for the limiting of the area of the video surveillance to that absolutely necessary have been taken (e.g., by the use of area concealment and/or the masking function). Except in certain exceptional situations, the processing of sound (audio) data is prohibited for the purpose of the protection of persons and goods.

528. Mutatis mutandis, all the above-mentioned points regarding the surveillance of the workplace also apply to the surveillance and monitoring of the employee's movements, including the monitoring of the movement of vehicles that have been allocated to the employee by the employer and have an installed GPS system.

C. Surveillance of PC and Telephone

529. More and more frequently, employers are resorting to the monitoring of the means of communication that are used by the employee, such as his/her telephone (fixed/landline and/or mobile), fax, radio, electronic and conventional correspondence and personal computer use (web pages visited, documents created or read, etc.).

530. The surveillance of the correspondence and the communication of the employee may concern external elements, meaning the information that defines the situations under which the communication is made and which personalizes it; that is, the names of the persons with whom the employee communicates, the phone or fax number, the e-mail address, the time of the communication and its duration, the geographical position in which the parties are located, etc. Surveillance may also concern internal elements: the content of the communication, which may be a phone message, sound or image, etc., meaning the content of the phone call, fax, SMS, MMS, etc. Correspondingly, the surveillance of visits to web pages may be limited to the detection of the web pages or to the listing of the content of the web pages that the employee visits or saves.

531. The purposes that justify the surveillance of the means of communication that are used by the employee are, for instance, the securing of classified information of the enterprise when there are suspicions that this is threatened by the employee, and the prevention or proof of criminal conduct by the employee, such as a sabotage of the enterprise's electronic systems, visiting child pornography web pages, hacking. However, these purposes may also be those that serve the daily operation of the enterprise, such as when the employee is absent or for the protection of an employee who is being harassed through e-mails from his/her colleagues.

532. In any case, it is forbidden that surveillance extend to phone calls, faxes, etc. that concern the private life of the employee, such as his/her personal correspondence.

533. In some cases, and in relation to the purpose pursued by the surveillance, this may be limited with the adoption of preventive measures, which are a less obtrusive measure compared to surveillance. If, for example, the purpose is to reduce illegal use of Internet with visits to sites of a specific content or with illegal downloading of material that is protected by legislation concerning intellectual property, software can be installed to block entry to such web pages. Indeed, there are programmes that allow visits only to those pages that are necessary for the execution of the employee's duties, or that warn the employee that the system has detected a forbidden use of the network and has taken measures for its prevention.

534. If the use of Internet is not necessary for the provision of work, the impossibility of connection to it constitutes a preventive measure. If the purpose is the control or limitation of the expenses of the enterprise in relation to the phone calls, a programme barring outgoing calls can be activated.

535. The fact that the equipment that is used (e.g., telephones, PC) belongs to the employer and has been conceded for use to the employee, or may have been conceded by the employer for ownership by the employee, does not justify uncontrolled surveillance of the employee.

536. Employees' protection as regards the surveillance detailed above does not mean that they are entitled to uncontrolled use of the company's technology for reasons that are not directly connected to the execution of their duties. The use of devices and technological equipment must be undertaken by the employee as needed for the provision of work, and only in exceptional situations for use for personal reasons, e.g., surveillance of minors or other dependent persons (e.g., elder members of the family or sick co-habitees), appointments with a doctor, etc. Contrariwise, the possibility of unconventional use by the employee does not justify uncontrolled surveillance.

D. Use of Biometric Methods

537. Biometric characteristics include fingerprints, the geometry of the fingers, the hand, the face, the ear, the iris, the retina, as well as body scent, the shape of the veins, the voice, body heat, the imaging of Deoxyribo Nucleic Acid, movement and body posture, the hand-written signature, the speech, the way of walking (gait), gestures, the manner of typing, as well as any other element, natural or behavioural, that appertains to the person and constitutes part of his/her 'personality'. Biometric data are data of personal character in that they contain data on natural characteristics and personal features that are unique to a person, as well as an element of the assignment of information to a particular person and subsequently form an element facilitating the recognition of the identity of the employee.

538. The use of biometric methods in companies takes place to a great extent for the ascertainment of the identity of the employees during their entry to and exit from most or all of the places of work. This use, in the view supported by the APDPX, is allowed only in those cases where this is imposed by specific security demands of the workplace and if there is no other means of achieving this purpose, e.g., for the controlling of access to extremely crucial areas and with the sole purpose of the protection of the persons and goods in these areas (e.g., military facilities, high-risk laboratories, places where enterprises' classified information is stored).

539. In contrast, it is not legal when it concerns, for instance, checking compliance with working time, watching the entrance and exit to the workplace and the movement of employees within the areas of enterprise, because in these cases the use of magnetic cards without biometric elements would be sufficient. Consequently, the employer is obliged constantly to balance on the one hand the existing risks and the extent of these risks with the existing alternate means of facing up to these risks, and on the other hand with the infringement of human personality and privacy that results from the use of such methods.

540. In accordance with the principle of proportionality,[259] the employer is obliged to choose the 'mildest' biometric system applicable to the case; e.g., the employer is obliged to choose the biometric system that is related to biological characteristics that do not leave traces over those systems that leave traces that are logged in a file.

E. Medical Examinations

541. The basic aim that justifies the submission of the employees to medical examinations is usually the protection of the employee's self, e.g., in order to assign duties that will not threaten his/her health or to find whether the workplace or duties assigned should be changed because of changes in the employee's health that render the preservation of the same duties and workplace hazardous. However, it is also possible that the aim is the better operation of the company, with the assignment of specific duties to employees who, because of their better physical and mental health, may better respond to these duties. In all such cases, medical examinations are the ultimate measure for accomplishing the proposed aim, and the conduct of the examinations as well as the results are confidential and are notified only to the employee concerned.

XI. Duty of Protection of Employees' Life, Health and Safety

542. A primary obligation of the employer is to secure employees' life, health and safety. This securing is set down as an obligation of the employer by Article

259. *See* para. 1030.

662 of the C.C., which stipulates that the employer is obliged to regulate the issues relevant to work and its location, as well as issues relevant to accommodation, facilities and machinery or tools, in such ways as to protect the life and health of the employee.

543. According to this provision, the employer is obliged to inform employees of any hazards that are involved in the provision of their work, to proceed to any necessary measures for their elimination and avoidance, to give instructions for the provision of the work that do not expose the employee to hazards, not to assign employees to duties that are not relevant to their skills and that expose them to dangers to their health and lives,[260] and to transfer the employee when, due to work conditions harmful to employee's health,[261] her/his health is damaged. In general, the employer is obliged to act in a way that protects the life and safety of the employee during the provision of work.

544. In the contrary case the employee, in accordance with Article 662 of the CC, has a direct claim against the employer for the adoption of the necessary measures and, depending on the case, for compensation, mainly in combination with the provisions for the protection of personality[262] and the fulfilment of contracts in bona fides.[263]

545. However, the protection of employees' life, health and safety is also attempted through a series of legal provisions of *jus cogens* in which specific employer obligations are set out. Of high importance in this field is Law 3850/2010 on the ratification of the Code of Laws on employee's health and safety. This Law codifies the regulations of Law 1568/1985, P.D. 16/1996, which incorporated Directive 89/654/EEC into national law, and P.D. 17/1996, which incorporated Directive 89/391/EEC into national law. Law 3850/2010 provides for a series of employer obligations for the protection of the health and safety of the employees in all aspects of their work. In accordance with Article 119 of Law 4488/2017 which supplements Law 3850/2010, an electronic report system under the auspices of SEPE is used for the reporting of occupational physicians and safety technicians.

546. The employer is obliged to:

(a) take all necessary measures for the protection of the health and safety of the employees, including all actions for the prevention of occupational hazards, for information and training, as well as for the creation of the necessary organization and the provision of the necessary measures;
(b) adapt the measures taken to changes that occur in the work;
(c) apply the advice of the technicians and labour health inspectors and in general to facilitate their work in the enterprise during inspections;

260. AP 2021/2007, AP 994/2001, AP 226/1987.
261. APol 937/1975.
262. Article 57 of the CC, Art. 5, para. 1 of the Constitution.
263. Article 288 of the CC.

(d) supervise the correct application of the measures for employees' health and safety;
(e) inform the employees of the occupational hazards of their work;
(f) establish a programme of preventive actions and amelioration of work conditions in the enterprise;
(g) ensure the maintenance and the monitoring of the safe operation of the means and facilities;
(h) encourage and facilitate employees' and their representatives' training and learning, as well as adopting collective measures for employee protection.

547. At the same time, employers are obliged to:

(a) evaluate the dangers to the health and safety of the employees, including, among others, those arising during the selection of work equipment, chemical and biological factors or products, during the physical arrangement of the workplace, as well as all dangers that are related to the manufacturing process;
(b) take all these factors into account when assigning duties to an employee;
(c) take care that the scheduling and the introduction of new technologies be an object of consultation with the employees and their representatives, concerning the consequences of the choice of equipment, of the work conditions and of the work environment for employees' health and safety;
(d) take care that only the employees who have received proper instruction shall enter zones of serious and particular danger. Measures for safety, health and hygiene during work may not entail, in any way, any economic liability for the employees.

548. Given the fact that in order to secure the life, health and safety of the employees, their own participation is necessary, employees are obliged to attend relevant seminars or other training programmes on issues concerning employees' health and safety. At the same time, the employees have further obligations, which emphasize that all employees are obliged to apply the health and safety regulations and to take care, to the extent of their capabilities, of their personal health and safety as well as the health and safety of other persons who are affected by their actions or omissions at work, in accordance with their training and the instructions given by their employers.

549. This general obligation is specialized in that employees must, more specifically, according to their training and the proper instructions from their employer to:

(a) correctly use machinery, appliances, tools, hazardous substances, transportation and other means;
(b) correctly use the personal safety equipment that is at their disposal and after its use must put it back in its place;
(c) refrain from disabling, deactivating, changing or arbitrarily relocating the safety mechanisms of the machinery, tools, appliances, facilities and buildings and to use all these safety mechanisms correctly;

(d) report immediately to the employer and/or to those that exercise the competencies of safety technician and occupational doctor any situations that can be fairly considered as presenting direct and serious hazards to safety and health, as well as reporting any omission or lack that is found in the safety systems;
(e) assist the employer and those that exercise the competencies of safety technician and occupational doctor, for such time as needed, in order to make possible the implementation of all the duties and requirements that are imposed by the competent Labour Inspectorate for the protection of health and safety of the employees during the work;
(f) assist the employer and those that exercise the competencies of safety technician and occupational doctor, for such time as needed, in order that the employer to be able to guarantee that the environment and the work conditions are safe and without any hazards to safety and health within their field of activity.

550. In the light of the great importance of ensuring the employees' health and their life, in every enterprise where at least fifty employees are employed there is an employees' Committee of Health and Safety, with advisory competencies.[264] In enterprises which employ more than twenty employees, the employees are entitled to choose their representatives, while in enterprises that employ up to twenty employees, the employees are entitled to consult and choose by majority their one representative for employees' health and safety.

551. Within the framework of its competencies, the employees' Committee of Health and Safety studies the work conditions and the work environment, proposing measures for their amelioration, monitors the adoption of measures concerning employees' health and safety and contributes to their implementation by the employees, suggests appropriate measures for the prevention of the repetition of severe accidents in the workplace or related events, points out occupational hazards in places or positions of work, contributes to the formation of the company strategy for the prevention of occupational hazards, is informed by the management of the number of accidents in the workplace and of severe illnesses that happen in the workplace, is informed by the management of new production processes, equipment, tools or materials or the operation of new facilities: all the above in relation to issues that affect the conditions for employees' health and safety. Furthermore, in case of an immediate, direct or severe danger, the Committee calls on the employer to adopt appropriate measures to prevent this, without excluding the stoppage of the operation of the facility or equipment that is causing the danger. Lastly, after an agreement with the employer, the Committee may seek the assistance of an expert on issues of employees' health and safety. Employees' representatives in smaller enterprises enjoy similar competencies.

552. In those companies that employ up to fifty employees, the employer is obliged to employ the services of a safety technician. In companies that employ fifty

264. Article 4 of L. 3850/2010. *See* below paras 1155 et seq.

employees or more, the employer is obliged to employ the services of a safety technician and of an occupational doctor. The safety technician provides the employer with suggestions and advice, in writing or orally, on issues concerning the health and safety of the employees, for the prevention of accidents in the workplace. The employer is obliged to receive and recognize these suggestions over his/her signature. The occupational doctor provides suggestions and advice to the employer, the employees and their representatives, in writing or orally, concerning measures that must be adopted for the protection of the physical and mental health of the employees. The employer, again, is to recognize these suggestions by signing for them. The skills and qualifications which are required by a safety technician or an occupational doctor are defined by law.

553. Employers who do not meet their obligations for the protection of the safety and health of the employees face administrative and penal sanctions. Furthermore, the employee may claim the adoption of necessary measures, may terminate the subordinate employment contract for reasons for which the employer is responsible, and may claim for compensation for moral and material damage.

XII. Duty to Protect Employees from Workplace Stress

554. In the NGCA of 2008–2009, the contractual parties included an agreement to increase awareness and knowledge on the part of employers, employees and their representatives concerning workplace stress, and to draw their attention to indicators that may reveal problems related to workplace stress. One aim of this agreement was to provide employers and employees with a framework for the identification, prevention and management of workplace stress. However, it was not intended to impose individual responsibilities on the employers.

555. The concept ‘stress’ refers to a condition that is accompanied by physical, psychological or social dissatisfaction or dysfunction which is created in employees who feel incapable of bridging the gap between reality and the requirements of the work or the expectations that the employer has of them.

556. Workplace stress may have a number of causes, such as the content of the work, the organization of work, the work environment, a lack of communication. Stress caused outside the work environment may lead to changes in behaviour and to the employee’s decreased efficiency. Stress is not a disease, but prolonged exposure to it may lead to decreased efficiency and may cause health problems.

557. Indications that may show the existence of workplace stress include a high level of absenteeism or personnel changes, or continuous conflicts among or grievances from the employees. The assessment of whether there is workplace stress may include the analysis of many elements, such as the organization of work and its procedures (management of working time, degree of autonomy, linking of the employees’ skills with the requirements of the work, workload, etc.), working conditions and environment (exposure to insulting behaviour/harassment, noise, heat, dangerous substances, etc.) communication problems (uncertainty about the requirements of the work, work perspectives or potential changes, etc.) and subjective elements (emotional and social pressure, feelings of inadequacy or lack of support, etc.).

558. Prevention, elimination or reduction of the causes of workplace stress may involve various measures, which may be collective, individual or both. They can be applied with the adoption of specific measures that have the aim of confronting identified causes of stress or may form part of a general strategy against stress, which includes preventive and suppressive measures.

559. In those workplaces where people have insufficient required specific knowledge, experts may be called in, in accordance with European and national legislation, with the collective agreement and with customary practices. From the time that they are applied, measures against workplace stress should be revised on a regular basis in order to evaluate their efficiency and the optimal cost-efficiency of their funding, as well as whether they are still necessary or appropriate. Such measures could include, for example:

(a) measures of management and communication, such as defining the company's targets and the individual roles of the employees in these, ensuring sufficient support to individual employees and groups of employees on the part of management, mapping of responsibilities and the supervision of work, and the amelioration of the organization of work and its procedures, conditions and working environment;
(b) training of managerial personnel and employees with the aim of increasing awareness and understanding of stress, its possible causes and ways to address and/or adapt to it;
(c) providing information to the employees and consulting with them or their representatives in accordance with European and national legislation, the collective agreement and customary practices.

560. When a problem of workplace stress is identified, immediate action must be taken for its prevention, elimination or reduction. The responsibility for taking appropriate measures lies with the employer. These measures are applied with the participation and cooperation of the employees and/or their representatives.

561. In accordance with Framework Directive 89/391/EC, all employers have a legal obligation to protect employees' occupational safety and health. This obligation concerns cases of workplace anxiety/stress insofar as this entails danger to the safety and health of the employees. All employees are under an obligation to comply with the protective measures set by the employer.

562. The addressing of problems related to workplace stress may also take place within the framework of a general process of risk evaluation, via a specific strategy related to stress and/or with specific measures targeted to address identified stressful factors.

XIII. Specifically for Accidents in the Workplace

563. Accidents in the workplace are, unfortunately, a common phenomenon. The phrase 'accidents in the workplace' refers to accidents suffered by an employee in a violent incident during his/her work or by cause of work which causes either incapacity for work for more than four days or the death of the employee. The last case applies when the accident is not the direct consequence of work but is connected to it by a causal link, in that because of the work, exceptional conditions were created which caused the incident to happen and which would not have existed without the work.[265] An incident that was deliberately caused by an employee is not considered as an accident in the workplace.

564. Physical damage to or disease of the employee that were brought about during the supply of his/her work or because of it and had as a consequence the partial or complete incapability of the employee to work or were caused by a sudden and unpredictable event and are unconnected to the individual organism of the employee, as well as the gradual decline and the damage that are related to the nature and type of work and the harmful conditions that are related to the work, are also considered to be accidents in the workplace.[266] The deterioration of an employee's previous illness which was caused by the continuance of his/her employment, even under normal conditions, is also considered to be a work accident, since in that case the employer bears some responsibility, being obliged to regulate issues related to work in such a way as to protect employees' life and security,[267] If he/she is aware of the illness, he/she is not to require the continuance of the sick employee's work and if the employer does not release the employee from duty, the working conditions become exceptional and harmful and assume the same character as a violent incident.[268] In that way, the causal link to the accident is not related exclusively to the organic or pathological predisposition of an affected employee whose accident would not have incurred without the work and its working circumstances.[269]

565. Issues concerning the responsibility of the employer in the case of an accident in the workplace are regulated by Law 551/1915. However, the importance of this Law is limited, since the affected employee is subject to the mandatory insurance of IKA and, as established by the provisions of EL 1846/1951 'on social security', he/she is fully covered by IKA. The employer is released from any obligation to compensation to the affected employee. If, however, the accident is due to wilful misconduct of the employer or his/her representatives in the workplace, the

265. AP 11/2012. *See also* AP 998/2012, which judged that the suicide attempt of an employee, while present in his workplace and during his working time, as a consequence of an intense conflict that he had with the employer over permanent matters concerning his work and that affected him psychologically, was considered an accident in the workplace, because of the psychological pressure that the employee experienced in combination with the fact that he had not suffered from a over depressive disorder.
266. AP 944/2001.
267. Articles 288 and 662 of the CC.
268. AP 1616/2003, AP 1432/2002.
269. APol 1287/1986.

employer is obliged to pay to the affected employee the difference between the amount of the compensation due under common law and the contribution from IKA. This exemption concerns not only cases where the accident was caused by an action or an omission by the employer, but also by his/her representatives in the workplace, who are also covered by this exemption.[270]

566. In the hypothetical case that the employee is not covered by IKA, the employer is obliged to pay compensation to the employee, the amount of which is legally defined in relation to severity of injury caused to the employee, or if the accident was fatal. This compensation may, under the judgment of the court, be reduced by half when the affected employee without reason breached provisions of law or regulations that set the standards of safety in the workplace and had been issued by the competent authority or the employer, if in the last case these provisions had been ratified from the outset. The responsibility of the employer is objective, meaning that he/she is liable to pay compensation regardless of the existence or otherwise of fault on his/her own part or that of her/his representatives in the workplace.

567. If the accident can be attributed to fraud of the employer or/and his/her representatives or when it occurs in a workplace or company where safety regulations were not followed, and the accident is causally linked with this breach, the affected employee (and in case of death his/her relatives as legally defined), may claim full compensation under the provisions of civil law. By regulations that govern safety terms are intended those that set out specific measures, means and ways to secure employees' safety, and it is not sufficient that the accident was a result of the breach only of those terms which are set by common opinion, the welfare obligation and the due diligence required in transactions, if these are not regulated by a specific provision of a law.[271]

568. In all other cases, the affected employee, and by analogy the members of his/her family, may maintain claims for financial compensation for moral injury or psychological grief against the employer or his representatives, if the accident is due to their error, meaning that it is enough for negligence to exist. Negligence towards the observing of safety conditions for the employees which are regulated by general or specific provisions also constitutes a fault.[272]

569. In the case of an accident in the workplace, the employer is obliged to notify the competent Labour Inspectorate, the nearest police authorities and the employee's insurance agency within twenty-four hours. Furthermore, the employer is obliged to report the accident in writing and under oath, within fifteen days, to the Magistrate's court (judge of the first instance court) of the region where the accident occurred.

270. APol 1267/1976.
271. APol 26/1995, AP 274/2000.
272. AP 412/2008.

XIV. Time Off for Finding New Employment

570. The employer who terminates the labour contract has a duty to allow his or her employee time off so he/she may search for and find a new job.[273] As the end of a labour contract of definite period approaches, the employer has the same duty. Legal theory and the courts accept that the employee does not lose the right to remuneration for this period,[274] while any agreement which infringes upon this right is considered null and void.[275]

273. Article 677 of the CC.
274. Article 557 of the CC.
275. Article 679 of the CC.

Chapter 4. Working Time, Annual Leave, Holidays

§1. Working Time

I. The Concept of Working Time

571. 'Working time' is the time during which the employee has the obligation and the right to be present at the workplace and at the disposal of the employer in order to provide his/her work. Seen from the other side, working time is the time during which the employer has the right to request the provision of work by the employee.

572. The quantity of work which the employer may obtain is irrelevant. This means that if the employer does not assign the employee tasks during the working time or if there is no work to be done, he cannot reduce the remuneration, provided that the employee has to be available.

573. The working time constitutes the time period during which the employee is allowed to provide his/her work, regardless of whether he/she will be employed by one employer, more than one employers or by the same employer under more than one employment relation.[276]

574. Under Law 4488/2017, employers are obliged to enter any change or modification of the working hours or the organization of the working time of employees into the Ministry of Labour' s information system (ERGANI) at the latest by the day of the change or modification, and in any case before the employees come on duty, as well as extra working hours and overtime before they start. A similar obligation is provided for by provisions specific to staff executing a construction work or a technical project.

II. Time Periods That Do Not Constitute Working Time

575. The following do not constitute working time unless it is otherwise specified by a term of a collective agreement or in the individual labour contract:[277]

(a) time spent commuting by the employee, regardless of whether this takes place with the employee's or the enterprise's means of transportation;
(b) time spent by the employee on preparation before work, e.g., putting on working clothes or uniforms, receiving the necessary materials or tools, and on preparation for leaving the workplace, e.g., handing in tools or changing into regular clothes;

276. Article 16 of PD 27.6-4.7.1932.
277. Article 14 of PD 27/1932.

(c) breaks, meaning short time pauses during the daily working time that are stipulated by legal provisions, such as the fifteen-minute break that is provided during six hours of continuous work.[278] Absence from the place of work for physical or urgent needs is not considered as a break but is included in working time;
(d) gaps or longer pauses in the work timetable, meaning longer breaks that intervene in the daily working time (continuous or fragmented) and are imposed by legislative provisions, such as the three-hour afternoon break in the daily working time in those shops that apply fragmented working time.[279]

III. Means for the Regulation of Working Time

576. All issues that concern working time are regulated by legislative provisions that include rules of unilateral *jus cogens* (legal time). Under clauses of collective agreements, there may be more favourable provisions (legal or collective or contractual time), and within the individual labour contract, there may be agreements more favourable than those of the collective agreements (contractual time).

577. Compliance with the legislation concerning working time is monitored by the competent public agencies (SEPE). Administrative and penal sanctions are imposed on offending employers.

IV. Calendar Periods for the Regulations for Working Time

578. Working time is regulated in accordance with the calendar periods of the calendar day (daily working time, daily rest), of the calendar week (weekly working time, weekly days of work, weekly rest) and the calendar year (annual leave, holidays, etc.).

§2. Duration and Limitations of Working Time

I. Daily Working Time

A. The Concept and the Maximum Duration of Daily Working Time

579. A working 'day' starts at 00:01 and ends at 24:00 of every calendar day. The daily working time may starts at any time of the day and may be continuous or interrupted. If it is not regulated by law or by a clause of a collective agreement or by a clause of the individual labour contract, the starting time of the working time and whether this will be continuous or interrupted are matters for the employer to decide.

278. Article 4 of PD 88/1999.
279. Article 42 para. 6 of L. 1892/1990.

580. The maximum duration of the legal working time is set at eight hours in most cases, such as for employees in industries, craft-industries, shops, which may be extended to nine hours when the work is provided on a five-day weekly basis. However, in many cases and according to the type of the enterprise, the legal form of the employer, the occupation of the employee or the hazardous work conditions, working time is shorter than eight hours. In a few cases, working time may be longer, such as for night watchmen, whose daily working time is ten hours.[280]

B. Night Work

581. Working time, as well as its extension, as is mentioned in a paragraph below, may partially or wholly cover the hours between 22:00 of one day until 06:00 the next day.[281] This time period is called 'night', and we refer to 'night work' and 'night worker'. For every hour of night work, the employee is paid in addition to the ordinary remuneration, an increment of 25% of the legal wage.[282]

582. Ministerial decisions have stipulated that night work shall be paid at a rate of time-and-a-quarter of the normal remuneration for the time after 22.00 hours until 6.00 hours in the morning. Additional recompense for night work is mandated by a common Decision of the Ministers of Labour and Finance, 18310/1946. More recently, Articles 2, 3, 4, 8, 9 and 11 of PD 88/1999 supplemented the provisions for night work.

C. Night Work and Children

583. Children's work (up to the age of 18) is forbidden in industrial enterprises during the night.[283] Exceptions exist for children above the age of 18 who are employed in retail shops during the night, for children above 14 employed in restaurants, hotels, etc., after 22.00 hours, and for children above 16 employed for reasons of apprenticeship or for other important reasons or in the public interest.

D. Flexible Daily Working Time

584. Working time may be flexible meaning that its start-time and its corresponding end-time may not be fixed absolutely, but be decided by the employee. Flexible working time may be regulated under a term of the collective agreement or by an agreement between the employer and the employee.

---

280. Article 7, para. 3 of EL 547/1937.
281. Article 2 of PD 88/1999.
282. Ministerial Decision 18310/1946.
283. Article 2 of L. 2272/1920 and Art. 3 of L. 4215/1961.

E. Daily Rest Period

585. During the twenty-four-hour day, the employee is entitled to a rest period of at least eleven consecutive hours.

F. Reduced Working Time for Parents of Children with Disabilities

586. In enterprises with at least fifty employees, the parents of children with disabilities, regardless of the children's age, are entitled to decreased working time of one hour per day in order to take care of their children. This decreased working time is accompanied, however, by a proportionally decreased remuneration.

II. Weekly Working Time and Weekly Working Days

A. The Concept and the Maximum Duration of Weekly Working Time

587. A week starts at 00:01 on Monday and ends at 24:00 on Sunday.

588. Weekly working time is defined, in accordance with legal provisions, to forty-eight hours.[284] However, from 1975 to 1984, this was gradually decreased to forty hours under terms of the NGCA. As things stand, under Article 4 of Law 2874/2000, as replaced by Article 1 of Law 3385/2005 and Article 74 paragraph 10 of Law 3846/2010, the legal weekly working time is set at forty hours. These provisions apply to the majority of employees.

589. Under sectoral collective agreements, there may be a shorter weekly working time for the employees of the sector, such as thirty-five hours for employees in foundries and thirty-seven hours for employees in banks.

590. Similarly, under enterprise-level collective agreements, a collective weekly working time of shorter duration may be defined.

591. Finally, under an agreement between the employer and the employee, a weekly working time shorter than the collective or the legal can be defined (conventional weekly working time).

B. Five or Six Working Days in a Week

592. For the majority of employees of the seven days of the week, working days are Monday until Friday included, while Sunday is a day of mandatory rest.

---

284. Article 2 of PD 24 Jun.–7 Apr. 1932.

593. In many cases, under special provisions, a system of a five-day working week applies, meaning that the employment of the employees is allowed only during five of the six working days, while on the sixth day, usually Saturday, the employment of the employees is prohibited, even though Saturday normally is a working day. Weekly working time, as examined in the following paragraphs, is calculated by case on five or six days, according to whether the employee is on a five- or six-day weekly work scheme.

594. Where work is normally provided during a five-day working week, any work provided on the sixth day shall be paid at the daily wage rate augmented by 30% irrespective of the sanctions which are applicable in such cases.

C. Distribution of the Weekly Working Time in Working Days

595. The weekly working time is distributed among the working days of the week that apply in a given circumstance. This distribution may be made equally or not to the working days of the week, but it is prohibited that the daily working time exceed the maximum duration of the daily working time that applies for the given period. Further, the aggregation of the working hours of more days is prohibited. Therefore, within the limits of eight hours per day for six-day weekly work and nine hours a day for a five-day week, the distribution of the forty hours may be made equally or otherwise among the five or six working days.

596. If in the enterprise there is a five-day weekly work scheme, the work of the employee on the sixth day, which is considered a non-working day, is prohibited. If the employee works on the sixth day, breaching the five-day scheme, for every hour of this day's work, he/she is entitled to the remuneration of the hour increased by 30%. However, those employed in hotels and catering enterprises are not subject to this provision.[285]

§3. Working Time in Excess of Daily and Weekly Limits

597. If special conditions cumulatively exist, as defined by law, work may be provided in excess of the maximum daily and weekly time limits that are stipulated for each case. In these cases we refer to 'overwork' and to 'overtime'.

285. Article 8 of L. 3846/2010.

I. Working Time in Excess of Daily Limits: Overwork and Overtime

A. The Concept of Daily Overwork

598. The exceeding of conventional standard daily working time until the completion of the collective or legal daily working time until the completion of the legal daily working time is called 'overwork'. Overwork is work provided in addition to normal daily work. The provision of this work may be requested by the employer on her/his judgment without the required existence of any precondition and without the need for compliance with any procedure.

B. Remuneration for Daily Overwork

599. For daily overwork additional remuneration is to be paid. The additional remuneration is agreed between the employer and the employee, and for every hour of additional work, it is, by rule, equal to the wage paid per regular working hour. This additional remuneration may, if there is a previous explicit agreement between the employer and the employee, be aggregated with the regular remuneration of the employee (paid remuneration) if the last is higher than the minimum legal remuneration and up to the amount by which it is higher than the minimum legal remuneration.

C. The Concept of Overtime Work

600. The exceeding of the maximum daily working time is called 'overtime'. Since the aggregation of the working hours of more than one day is prohibited, overtime exists even if with the provision of the additional work the maximum weekly time limits are not exceeded.

D. Remuneration for Overtime

601. For overtime additional remuneration is to be paid. The additional remuneration that is due is defined by law, and for every hour of overtime work, it is equal to the wage paid per regular working hour increased by 40.[286] If the overtime work exceeds, during the year, 120 hours, from the 121st hour the increment is 60.[287]

---

286. Article 1 of L. 3385/2005 as in effect after Art. 74, para. 10 of L. 3863/2010.
287. *Ibid.*

602. This additional remuneration is not to be aggregated with the regular remuneration of the employee (paid remuneration) even if the last is higher than the minimum legal remuneration.[288]

E. *Provisions for Overtime*

603. The provision of overtime may be requested by the employer only if special conditions, stipulated by law, cumulatively exist. The conditions are the following:

(1) an extraordinary need must exist as defined under limitation in the law:[289]
  (a) urgent work, the execution of which is necessary for the prevention of imminent accidents, the organization of rescue measures or the confrontation of sudden damage either in the material or the facilities or the building;
  (b) urgent work of temporary character or an exceptional urgent need to serve the public;
  (c) urgent repairs to ships or to land or air transportation means, or delays on routes of any type of transportation;
  (d) exception accumulation (backlog) of work;
  (e) the days before exempted holidays;
  (f) preparatory or complementary tasks, which due to their nature are executed outside regular daily working time;
  (g) for the completion of working hours that were lost because of a collective work interruption or pause which was notified to the competent public agency and was due to:
    – force majeure or urgent reasons, such as power cuts, natural disasters, lack of raw material;
    – national or local holidays (Sundays are not included);
    – changes in the weather, but only in industries or tasks that due to their nature are affected by changes in the weather.
(2) the Labour Inspectorate must be notified;[290]
(3) an overtime record book must be kept in the enterprise.

288. Article 8, para. 4 of L. 4020/1959.
289. Article 4, para. 1 of PD 27.6.1932, Art. 8, para. 4 of LD 515/1970, Art. 9, para. 3 of L. 4171/1961.
290. Article 9 of PD 27.6.1932.

F. Duration of Overtime

604. The duration of the overtime may be of up to three 3 hours per day,[291] while the total allowed hours for every calendar semester or year are set by ministerial decisions.[292]

G. Exceptional Overtime

605. Overtime that is provided in the absence of the aforementioned preconditions or for more hours than those referred above is called 'exceptional overtime', a term which replaces the previous term 'illegal overtime'.

H. Remuneration for Exceptional Overtime

606. The additional remuneration for exceptional overtime is defined by law and for every hour of exceptional overtime is equal to the wage paid per regular working hour increased by 80%.[293]

607. The total of this payment is classified by the law as compensation, and it is prohibited that it be aggregated to the regular remuneration of the employee (remuneration paid), even if the last is greater than the minimum legal remuneration.[294]

I. Common Remarks for Overwork and Overtime

608. For the provision of overwork or overtime, the employer must request it. The employer may request it even if it is not referred in the labour contract and the employee is obliged to provide it, if he/she is in a position to do so and if refusal would be contrary to bona fides.[295] In any case, the employee is entitled, for every hour of work additional to the hours of regular working time, to additional remuneration as mentioned in the previous paragraphs.

609. In contrast to the rules in effect covering regular daily and weekly working time for more than one employer, as already mentioned,[296] the exceeding of the daily or weekly time limit is considered an excess only for the employer for whom the employee worked during the regular working time.

291. Article 4, para. 2 of PD 27 Jun. 1932.
292. Article 4, para. 2 of PD 27 Jun. 1932, Art. 8, para. 4 of L. 515/1970 as replaced by Art. 74, para. 11 of L. 3863/2010.
293. Article 1 of L. 3385/2005 as in effect after Art. 74, para. 10 of L. 3863/2010.
294. Article 8, para. 4 of L.D. 4020/1959.
295. Article 659 of the CC.
296. Article 16 of PD 27 Jun.–4 Jul. 1932.

610. If the employer usually employs one employee with overwork or overtime, he/she is not obliged to continue to do so. The employer is entitled at any time to stop so employing the employee and to employ overwork or overtime a different employee. However, the employer is obliged to continue to employ the same employee, if this is overwork and either for the provision of the overwork there were, and still are, such conditions that lead to the conclusion that there is a tacit agreement for it or the overwork has been provided for a long period and the employer has not expressly reserved the right to terminate it.

J. Exceeding Daily Working Time That Is Not Overtime

611. A large number of special provisions have been defined to cover the possibility of exceeding daily working time without this being considered as overtime. The most important of these provisions are the following:

(a) If the employee does not work in the afternoon of the Saturday or of another day of the week, the daily working time of eight hours can be extended by one hour and this one hour is not considered as overtime, if he/she receives the remuneration for forty-eight hours working time and in total her/his working hours do not exceed forty-eight in the week in total.[297]
(b) The maximum limit of daily working time may be exceeded by up to one hour per day, which is not considered as overtime, under these conditions:
   - that these enterprises do not operate during the afternoon of a Saturday or of another working day of the week;
   - that the whole wage will be offered for these days; and
   - that the total of the hours worked shall not exceed forty-eight hours per week.[298]
(c) When the work is of continuous operation because of its nature and the continuity of the work is ensured with consecutive changes of personnel, subject to the precondition that the hours of the working time will not exceed on average fifty-six per week. In that case it is stipulated that (i) the sequence of work of the groups is changed weekly so that the night shift of one week will work during the day in the following week, and (ii) when a group works on Sunday, it is obligatorily provided with a twenty-four-hour rest period on another day of the week.[299]
(d) When the staff works in shifts, the duration of the work may be extended above eight hours per day and forty-eight hours per week, on the condition that the average number of working hours, calculated for a period of at least three weeks, does not exceed eight hours per day and forty-eight hours per week.[300]

297. Article 3 of PD 27 Jun. 1932.
298. Article 3 of PD 27 Jun. 1932.
299. Article 8 of PD 27 Jun. 1932.
300. Article 7 of PD 27 Jun. 1932.

K. *Shift/Work*

612. 'Shift work' is considered to be any method of organization of group work during which the employees succeed each other in the same work positions according to a given timetable, including a rotation timetable, and which may be continuous or may be segmented, which obliges the employees to execute work at different times over a given period of days or weeks.

II. Working Time in Excess of Weekly Limits: Overwork

A. *The Concept of Weekly Overwork*

613. The exceeding of conventional weekly working time of forty hours until the completion of forty-five hours, if the enterprise has a five-day weekly work scheme and until the completion of forty-eight hours, if the enterprise has a six-day weekly work scheme, is called 'overwork' or 'simple overwork', in order that they be distinguished from the 'legitimate overwork' that is mentioned in following paragraphs.

614. Since the aggregation of the working hours of more than one day is prohibited, weekly overwork may exist even if with the provision of the additional work there is no excess weekly work above the maximum weekly time limits.

615. Overwork is work provided in addition to normal weekly work. The provision of this work may be requested by the employer on her/his judgment without the required existence of any precondition and without the need for compliance with any procedure.

616. The exceeding of the forty-five or forty-eight hours is considered as overtime, and all the above mentioned on overtime (definitions, preconditions, consequences) are applicable.

B. *Distribution of Weekly Overwork to Weekly Working Days*

617. The distribution of the hours of legitimate overwork may be among any of the five or six days of weekly work, according to whether in the enterprise there is a system of a five-day or a six-day week, but must always comply with the daily legal working time.

C. Remuneration for Weekly Overwork

618. For weekly overtime additional remuneration is to be paid. The additional remuneration that is due is defined by law and for every hour of overtime work it is equal to the wage paid per regular working hour increased by 20%.[301]

§4. REST DAYS, HOLIDAYS

I. Day of Weekly Rest: Sunday

619. One weekly minimum continuous rest period of twenty-four hours (weekly rest) is ensured for the employees.[302] To these are added the eleven consecutive hours of daily rest, as previously mentioned.

620. The weekly twenty-four-hour rest period is primarily covered by Sunday, which is a day of mandatory rest for the majority of employees. Sunday is the last day of the week and starts at 00:01 and ends at 24:00.[303]

621. For employees in activities that operate during the whole of the twenty-four-hour period under a system of three consecutive working groups, Sunday may start at 06:00 or at 07:00 and end at the corresponding time on Monday.

622. During the day of weekly rest the work of the employees, regardless of their religion, is prohibited.

II. Legal Work on Sunday

623. Work on Sunday is allowed when defined so by law, as in the following cases:

(a) transportation of persons or objects of any type, as well as the tasks of sending, factoring, loading and unloading that are connected with this;
(b) repair and maintenance of means of transportation, and the related manufactured parts of means of transportation, by land, sea or air: tire repair workshops; motor vehicle fuel and lubricant service stations: parking facilities (car/vehicle parks);
(c) production, transformation and distribution of electric power, water, gas, steam or atomic energy;
(d) telecommunications, radio, television and filming motion pictures;

301. Article 1 of L. 3385/2005 as in effect after Art. 74, para. 10 of L. 3863/2010.
302. RD 748/1966, L. 435/1976, Art. 5 of PD 88/1999.
303. Article 5 of PD 88/1999.

(e) public and recreational shows and entertainment centres, public games and their connected work, lottery agencies, press agencies, any type of exhibition, museum, concert, sports event, horse-race, sporting organization, travel agency and club of any type;
(f) restaurants, pastry shops, bars, cafés/cafeterias, dairy shops, canteens and related shops;
(g) florists;
(h) baths or spas;
(i) hotels;
(j) medical offices, clinics and health institutions, as well as doctors and health practitioners in general;
(k) funeral homes, cemeteries and mortuaries;
(l) kiosks and similar shops, photo shops;
(m) the retail sale of nuts;
(n) non-daily newspapers and magazines.

III. Work on Sunday by the Free Choice of the Employer

624. If the employer maintains a sales facility the activity of which is not included among those which are allowed to employ employees on Sunday, as mentioned above, he/she may, by his/her own free choice, employ his/her employees and operate the shop on the following particular Sundays:[304]

(a) the first Sunday at the beginning of a sales period; should the first Sunday coincide with a holiday, this right is moved to the following Sunday;
(b) the last two Sundays before Christmas;
(c) Palm Sunday.

IV. No Application of the Provisions for Weekly Rest and Holidays

625. The provisions for weekly rest, Sunday and holidays are not applicable to specified classes of employees, such as (those in):

(a) agricultural, livestock farming, hunting and fishing businesses, undertakings and activities in general, except for the employees who have this as their basic employment in factories, workshops, offices or shops belonging to these categories of enterprise;
(b) enterprises in which only members of the employer's family are employed, provided that the work is not carried out in public and that no transitions are held;
(c) marine workers;
(d) domestic workers;

304. Article 16 of L. 4177/2013 as it is in effect after Art. 25 of L. 4208/2013.

(e) works carried out personally by householders and the owners of any kind of enterprise, if these are not carried out in public;
(f) for students of technical schools in general for their practical exercise, in places defined by the competent school.

V. Special Provisions

626. In enterprises of continuous three-shift operation, the provisions for mandatory rest on Sundays and holidays are not applicable in such cases as alcohol distillation enterprises, olive kernel oil extraction, hydrogenation of oil, if the hydrogenation is undertaken by pyrochemical methods, production of cement, production of glycerine and saturated fat, among others.

627. There is a large number of special provisions that refer to employees in pharmacies, theatres, taxis, restaurants, foreign press distribution, banks' currency exchange enterprises for the service of tourists and so forth.

VI. Consequences of the Provision of Work on Sundays

628. As mentioned above, the provision of work on Sundays is on principle prohibited but is allowed whenever the law states so. As such, the work may be regarded as being provided either in breach of the prohibition, in which case the agreement for the provision of the work is void or as being allowed by law.

629. In any case, regardless of the validity of the agreement concerning this employment and of other possible consequences, employees who work on Sundays are entitled to a compensatory weekly rest and additional remuneration, as in the following cases:

(a) An employee who has worked more than five Sunday hours is to be allocated a weekly rest period of twenty-four consecutive hours on a working day of the following week (compensatory weekly rest). The first fifteen minutes of an hour on Sunday is counted as a working hour. If the work is such as is permissibly provided on Sunday, the compensatory weekly rest must, for a period of seven weeks, coincide with a Sunday.
(b) If the employee has worked for up to five Sunday hours, he/she is entitled to claim a rest period of equal time on a working day in the following week.
(c) For every working hour on Sunday, the employee is remunerated with the paid hourly wage increased by 75% of the legal wage. If the employee is on a monthly salary, only this 75% increase is payable.

VII. Special Provision for the Employment of Employees Every Day of the Week

630. Enterprises that are not by nature of continuous operation may operate continuously, wholly or partially, under a system of four rotating working groups, if the employees that participate in these groups consent to do so.[305]

631. Furthermore, these enterprises may work continuously, wholly or partially, if for their operation on Saturdays and Sundays or on Sundays and Mondays, they hire additional staff to be employed in rotation in two groups for twelve hours per day. The total remuneration that is due for these twelve-four hours of work, included that which is stipulated for overtime, Sunday, holiday and night work, is equal to the remuneration for forty hours unless a shorter weekly working time is in application. The employee is to be insured for six days, although she/he is obliged to provide work for only twenty-four hours.

632. If the above enterprises or undertakings normally operate under a system of five-day weekly work, they may also operate wholly or partially for six days per week. However, they are obliged to provide a weekly rest period, contiguous to a Sunday, for each three-week period.

633. The employment of an employee in any of the above-detailed circumstances is not permissible without his/her consent.

VIII. Days of Holidays

634. As days of mandatory rest, the following holidays are stipulated:

(a) 25 March (Independence Day);
(b) the Monday after Easter (Easter Monday);
(c) the holiday of the Dormition of the Holy Virgin (15 August);
(d) Christmas Day (25 December) and the day after.[306]

635. During the above holidays the provision of work by adherents of every religion is prohibited.

636. Holidays start at 00.00 and terminate at 24.00 on the same day. For employees of enterprises that operate through the whole of the 24-hour period with a system of three working groups, this time may start at 06:00 of the day of the holiday and end at 06:00 of the following day.

637. The Minister of Labour may also define other days (five at most annually) as public holidays for certain districts.

305. Article 40 of L. 1892/1990.
306. Article 42 para. 1 of L. 4554/2018.

638. By decisions of lower-level administrative bodies, there may be holidays for specific towns, areas or regions.

639. If the employee provides his/her work on the above-mentioned holidays, he/she is entitled to a remuneration in accordance with that applicable for working on Sunday but is not entitled to the provision of free/rest time at a later date.

§5. Management of Working Time: Annualization of Working Time

640. With the aim of adapting working time to the needs that every enterprise faces, in 1990 provisions[307] were made which provided the possibility of exceeding the maximum daily and weekly legal and collective working time without this excess being considered as overtime or overwork and, because of that, without the employee being entitled to any additional remuneration for this excess. Such arrangements can only be made under an agreement between the employer and the representatives of the employees as explicitly defined by law.

641. In enterprises where a collectively or conventionally established working time of up to forty hours per week applies, it is permissible that during a certain time period (the period of increased employment) the employee should work on some days for two hours per day above the eight hours, subject to the condition that the additional time beyond the forty hours (or of a conventional working time that is shorter than this) must be deducted from the working hours of a different period (the period of decreased employment).

642. The length of periods of increased or decreased employment must not exceed six months in total within a period of twelve months (the reference period).

643. The average of weekly working time for the semester (the reference period here), in which hours of overwork and overtime during decreased employment periods are not included, remains at forty hours or, if a shorter contractual working time is in application, is equal to the number of hours of this shorter working time. The weekly number of hours must not exceed forty-eight, on average, in a period of six months, including the aforementioned hours of overwork and legal overtime.

644. It is permissible that, instead of the arrangement detailed in the previous paragraph, it may be agreed that up to two hundred 256 working hours of the total working time in a calendar year should be distributed as increased hours in specific time periods, which cannot, however, exceed in total thirty-two weeks per year, while this is accompanied by decreased working hours for the rest of the calendar year.

---

307. Article 41 of L. 1892/1990 as it was replaced by Art. 3 of L. 2639/1998, amended by Art. 5 of L. 2874/2000, replaced by Art. 2 of L. 3385/2005, by Art. 7 of L. 3846/2010 and finally by Art. 42 of L. 3986/2011.

645. The average of the hours of weekly working time over a calendar year (the period of reference here), in which the hours of overwork and legal overtime during periods of decreased employment are not included, remains at forty hours. or, if a shorter conventional working time is applied, remains at the number of hours set by this lesser working time, while with aggregation of the hours of overwork and legal overtime, the year-on average must not exceed forty-eight hours.

646. The employee has the right to turn down the provision of this additional work, if he/she is not in the position to provide it and if his/her refusal is not contrary to bona fides. Such refusal does not constitute sufficient reason to terminate his/her labour contract.

647. In place of the above reductions of working hours, all the following are permissible: the provision of fair resting time to the employee (repos), a combination of decreased working hours with resting days, a proportionate increase in annual leave with pay or a combination of decreased hours with rest days or days of leave.

648. During the period of increased employment, as detailed in paragraphs 1 and 2 above, daily working time may not exceed ten hours. Should daily working time exceed the legal daily working time at its higher limit of ten hours, or if weekly working time should exceed forty hours, the above-mentioned provisions for the extension of weekly working time do not apply.[308]

649. The remuneration paid due for the duration of an arrangement in accordance with paragraphs 1 and 2 is equal to the remuneration of forty hours weekly if the enterprise has a weekly working time of forty hours. If the enterprise has a weekly working time of less than forty hours, the remuneration paid for the duration of the arrangement is equal to the remuneration agreed or stipulated for that working time.

650. During the period of decreased employment (as in paragraphs (1) and (2)) the excess of the agreed decreased weekly working time, which is allowed as an exception, is remunerated as defined in Article 1 of Law 3385/2005, as replaced and in concurrent effect with paragraph 10 of Article 74 of Law 3863/2010.

651. The above working time management is defined either by enterprise-level collective agreements or by an agreement between the employer and the trade union in the enterprise or by an agreement between the employer and the works council or by an agreement between the employer and a legally constituted association of persons.

652. Enterprise-level and/or sectoral collective agreements may define a different system for the arrangement of working time, taking into account the specific characteristics of the enterprise or the sector.

308. Article 1 of L. 3385/2005 as replaced by Art. 74 para. 19 of L. 3863/2010.

653. If, for any reason, especially because of the resignation or dismissal of an employee, the arrangement of working time is not applied or completed in accordance with the current law, all those protective provisions that regulate the consequences of exceeding daily and weekly working time are applicable.

654. The above are also to be applied:

(a) in seasonal enterprises;
(b) for employees with a labour contract of less than one year.

655. Enterprise-level collective agreements and the above-mentioned agreements are to be submitted to the competent Labour Inspectorate.

§6. Paid Annual Leave (Annual Vacation)

I. General Remarks

656. The employer is obliged every year to allow employee free days for vacation, to pay the normal remuneration for these days, plus an additional amount. Contrary agreements between the employer and the employee or clauses in collective agreements are void.

657. The provisions for annual leave apply to all employees, including those having invalid labour contracts, regardless of the type of labour contract that they have concluded.

658. The time period of annual leave is considered to be a period of effective work for the calculation of the employees' benefits (seniority benefits, etc.), for the granting of the annual regular leave and the leave benefits, as well as for the calculation of the compensation in case of a dismissal and it is not aggregated with the annual leave or any other leave. 'Effective work' means effective workdays and assimilated days such as days of sickness, accidents at work, pregnancy.

II. Legislation

659. Since 1947 annual leave has been in force for several kinds of enterprises under EL 539/1945, as amended and supplemented later many times and by Laws 3227/2004 and 3302/2004, RD 376/1971, Article 38 paragraph 4 of Law 1892/1990 and clauses of NGCA. Numerous provisions in law and clauses in numerous sectoral and enterprise collective agreements introduce special arrangements for different categories of employees and increase the period of annual leave up to thirty days.

III. The General System in Force

A. *The Length of Annual Leave and the Conditions for Its Allowance*

660. Every employee is entitled to annual leave from the start of his/her work to an enterprise. The annual leave is twenty-four working days in the case of a six-day week and twenty working days in the case of a five-day week. The days are increased one day for every next year up to twenty-six and twenty-two days respectively. Sundays and public holidays that fall within the period of annual leave are not counted.

661. In the first calendar year of his/her employment, the employee has the right to receive two days of the annual leave for each month of effective work with proportional leave pay and leave allowance. If the employee does not ask for it, the employer is obliged, on his/her own initiative, by the end of the first calendar year to provide him/her with the proportionate annual leave, pay and allowance.

662. For each of the following calendar years, the employee is entitled to receive, as of 1 January of each year, full annual leave, full leave pay and leave allowance.

663. In the cases of intermittent work or work by rotation, the employee is entitled to two days leave, with the proportionate pay and allowance, for every twenty-five days of effective work.

B. *Leave Pay and Leave Allowance*

664. On the day that the annual leave starts employee receives his/her normal remuneration for the period of the leave (leave pay) plus an additional amount (leave allowance). The leave allowance is 50% of the paid leave pay limited to the 50% of the monthly remuneration for the employees remunerated by month and to thirteen daily wages for those remunerated by day.

665. Agreements, of any kind, for the conversion of free days to pay or vice versa are void.

666. Employees dismissed before getting the annual leave and the leave payments have the right to ask for them (leave pay and pay allowance).[309]

309. *See* L. 1346/1984, which provides for working students a complementary leave of fourteen days paid by OAED.

IV. Consequences of the Breach of the Law

667. The employer suffers penal sanctions if he/she does not allow the annual leave or does not pay the leave pay and the leave allowance to the employee.

668. If the employer does not allow the free days on purpose, the employee has the right to ask for civil penalty equal to 100% of the leave pay.

V. Arrangement and Spread of Annual Leave

669. Annual leave is arranged by the employer and the works council, according to bona fides and taking into account the needs of the enterprise. Parents of children of up to 16 years old or of children with a severe or chronic disease or disability have priority.

670. The law states that the annual leave for half of the staff should be given during the period from 1 May to 30 September so that each employee should have some opportunity to receive his or her annual leave during this period.[310]

§7. Other Leave

671. Besides annual leave, employees are also entitled, according to legal provisions or clauses of collective agreements, to leaves that are granted for various reasons.

I. General Remarks

672. Some of these leaves are with pay and some without. Provided that there are no contrary provisions, the time period of these leaves is considered to be a period of effective work for the calculation of the employees' benefits (seniority benefits, etc.), for the granting of the annual regular leave and the leave benefits, as well as for the calculation of the compensation in case of a dismissal and it is not aggregated with the annual leave or any other leave. The most important leaves are mentioned in the following paragraphs.

II. Leave for Exercising the Right to Vote

673. The special leave that is provided for exercising the right to vote is paid leave in the private sector. Its duration is proportionate to the distance (to the place where the employee is registered to vote) in kilometres. More specifically:

---

310. *See also* Art. 3 of L. 1346/1983.

(a) For employees working a five-day week:
- one working day for a distance of 200–400 km;
- two working days for a distance of 401 km and more;
- for the islands, up to three working days.

(b) For employees working on a six-day week:
- one working day for 100–200 km;
- two working days for distances of 201–400 km;
- three working days for a distance of more than 401 km;
- for the islands, up to three working days.

III. Marriage Leave

674. All employees are entitled to a marriage leave of five working days with pay for those under a five-day weekly working scheme and six working days with pay for those under a six-day weekly working scheme.[311]

675. Under more favourable collective agreements, a leave of marriage in excess of the five days may be granted, e.g., six days for accountants, personnel of Public Limited Companies and Limited Liability Companies, companies in general, staff of shops, supermarkets, staff of healthcare institutions and hospitals, seven days for oil and gas companies, nine days for shipping lines-shipping companies, architects, civil engineers, agronomists-topographers-engineers under an employment relation of private law, electrical engineers of the National Technical University of Athens.

IV. Maternity: Pregnancy Leave

676. Employed mothers are entitled to a maternity leave of a total duration of seventy weeks. Eight weeks are granted before the expected date of confinement and nine weeks after it. If the confinement takes place before the expected date, the rest of the eight weeks leave is granted after the confinement in order to complete the seventy weeks.[312]

677. Also, in the case of a birth of a child, the father is entitled to two days of leave with pay for every child.

V. Maternity Leave for Mothers of Surrogate Children

678. In accordance with Article 7 of the NGCA 2006–2007, in cases of having children under the procedure of surrogate motherhood, the parents are entitled to the leaves corresponding to the care and rear of the child similar to the case of natural

311. NGCA 2000–2001.
312. Article 7 of NGCA 2000–2001.

parents. For the duration of the breastfeeding, the decreased working time of Article 9 of the NGCA 1993, as in effect, is granted to both the surrogate and the mother that acquires the child.

VI. Breastfeeding Leave and Leave for the Care of Children

679. Employed mothers are entitled for a time period of thirty months, after the expiry of the maternity leave, to either come later to work or leave earlier one hour per day.

680. Alternatively, under an agreement with the employer, the daily working time of the employed mothers may be decreased by two hours for the first twelve months and by one hour for an additional period of six months.[313]

681. The leave of absence for reasons of childcare may be alternatively granted to the father, if the mother does not make use of it.

682. The decreased working time for the care of the children is considered, and remunerated, as working time.[314]

683. The right of absence from the work or for delayed arrival to the work or the early leaving of the mother, and alternatively of the father, for the childcare, in accordance with Article 9 of the NGCA 1993, is also granted to the parents of foster children of up to six years old.[315]

VII. Parental Leave for Child-Rearing

684. Parental leave is granted to the employees of all enterprises, regardless of the number of employed persons they employ. Moreover, in accordance with Law 2639/1998, the parental leave is granted to all parents in order of priority, without the limits that were set by Law 1483/1984 and the NGCA 1993 (8% of the employed persons in the enterprise). This leave is granted until the child completes the age of 3.5 years and its duration may reach 3.5 months for each parent.

685. The preconditions for the granting of the parental leave of child-rearing are the following:

(a) the completion of one year of working experience with the same employer;
(b) the other parent is employed outside of the house.

The duration of that leave starts at the date of the expiry of the maternity leave.

313. NGCA 2002–2003.
314. Article 9 of NGCA 1993.
315. Article 8 of NGCA 2000–2001.

686. In the case of more children, the leave is granted to the parent for every one of them, provided that since the date of the previous leave has passed one year of real employment of the parent.

687. If both parents are entitled for the granting of the parental leave of child-rearing, they decide under a common accord which one will be the first to make use of this right and for how long.

688. The right of the granting of this leave is also extended to those that have adopted a child. In the case of a divorce or a separation or widowhood or birth out of wedlock, the parent that has the custody of the child is entitled of the leave which is up to six (6) months.

689. After the expiry of the leave, the employee has the right to return to the same work in the same or similar position, which must not be, in any case, inferior to the one that he/she had before the leave.

690. The leave is without pay.

691. Under Article 5 of Law 2335/1995 for the calculation of the insurance period of the employee parent, the period of the leave is also included, provided that the parent will pay the whole of his/her and the employer's contributions.

692. For the first time, in Article 25 of Law 2639/1998, a provision entered stipulating that a termination of the labour contract that is made because of the exercise of the right for the granting of a parental leave is void.

693. To the widow employees as well as to the single parent employees, that have the custody of the child, a leave of six working days with pay is granted per year, additionally to the leave that they are entitled for under other provisions.

694. A parent of three or more children is entitled to a leave of eight working days. This leave is granted because of the increased needs of care of the children up to the age of 12 years old. It is granted once or segmented after an accord with the employer in accordance with the needs of the parent. This leave must not coincide with the start or the end of the annual leave.

VIII. Parental Leave for Child-Rearing in Accordance with Law 4075/2012

695. The employed parent is entitled to a child-rearing leave until the child completes the age of 6 years, in order to fulfil the minimum obligations of the child's rearing.

696. This leave is without pay, is granted for a time period of at least four months and is an individual right for each parent.

697. Unmarried mothers and uniparental parents employed in the private sector have the right to an eight months parental leave without pay for the rearing of the child until the child completes the age of 6 years.[316]

IX. Leave of Absence for Visiting the Children's School

698. If the employee has children of up to 16 years old that are students or pupils of elementary or intermediate education, he/she is entitled to be absent from work for some hours or for the whole working day in order to visit the school of his/her children. This leave is with pay and cannot exceed four working days per year.

X. Sick Leave to Take Care of a Family Member

699. In the case of a sickness of a child or other members of the family, a sick leave is granted to the employee under the following preconditions:

(a) the employee parent must be employed under an employment relationship of private law in an enterprise or an undertaking, regardless of whether he/she has a working experience of one year to the same employer; and
(b) the sickness of a dependent member of his/her family. 'Dependent' persons are children (natural or adopted) until the age of 16 years old and more than 16 years old if they suffer from a serious disease or a disability, a spouse that is unable to look after him/herself, parents or unmarried brothers or sisters who are unable to look after themselves.

700. This leave is without pay, can be granted once or segmented and its duration cannot exceed the six working days per year.

701. The duration of this leave may be extended to eight working days if the beneficiary protects two children and to twelve months if he/she protects more than two children.

XI. Leave for Thermal Baths and Aerotherapy Treatment of Invalid Employees

702. The invalid employees are entitled, in accordance with the provisions of L.Em. 1324/1949, to an additional leave of thirty days with full pay, in order to have treatment to thermal baths and aerotherapy centres. This type of leave is granted to war invalids that have a certificate of a special committee of the Ministry of National Defence.

---

316. Article 5 of L. 1483/1984 as completed and extended by Art. 25 of L. 2639/1998 and amended by Art. 7 of L. 4075/2012.

XII. Leave for Blood Transfusion

703. Employees having a working experience of until four years to the same employer and suffering from a disease that requires blood (or its derivatives) transfusion or blood dialysis, and the employer is notified of, are entitled to an additional annual leave of twenty-two working days per year with pay.[317]

XIII. Leave Due to the Death of Relatives

704. The employees are granted with a leave of two days in the case of death of a spouse, children, parents, brothers or sisters.[318]

XIV. Leave for Taking Examinations

705. Employees that are students or pupils of educational units of any type and level of the public sector or supervised by organizations of the public sector have the right of a leave without pay of a duration of thirty days per year, continuous or segmented, in order to take examinations.

706. This special leave is granted to all employees students without an age limit[319] but only for the provisioned duration of the studies incremented by two years, regardless of whether these studies were segmented or continuous and regardless of whether the employee has completed one year of working experience to the employer.

707. The status of the student or pupil and the participation in the exams is evidenced under a certification of the school, which the employee must give to the employer.

708. For the minor employees that are students, Law 1837/1989 stipulates that they are entitled a leave without pay of two days, continuous or segmented, for every day of exams in order to participate in them. This leave cannot be less than fourteen days and is paid by OAED and not by the employer.

XV. Leave for Trade Union Officials

709. In accordance with Article 17 of Law 1264/1982, the employer is obliged to facilitate the members of the Administrative Board, audit committees and the representatives of the first-level trade unions to the second-level trade unions for the

---

317. Article 8 of NGCA 2002–2003.
318. Article 9 of NGCA 2002–2003.
319. The threshold of 28 years was excluded under the NGCA 1998.

exercising of their duties. The same obligation exists for the administrative boards, audit committee and the representatives of the second-level trade unions to the third-level trade unions.

710. More specifically, employers are obliged to grant the following amounts of leave to the categories of individuals stated:

(a) leave for the whole term of their office to the members of the governing body of the most representative third-level trade union; the President and the General Secretary of the second-level trade unions, provided that the trade unions affiliated to them have more than 10,000 voting members; the President of the second-level trade unions, provided that the trade unions affiliated to them have between 1,501 and 10,000 voting members; and the members of the Executive Committee and the Secretariat of the ETUC.
(b) fifteen days per month to the President of the second-level trade unions, provided that the trade unions affiliated to them have no more than 1,500 voting members, and the Vice President, the General Secretary and the Treasurer of the most representative second-level trade union.
(c) leave for the duration of the conferences in which they participate to representatives of the second-level and third-level trade unions.
(d) three to nine days per month in other cases.
(e) thirty days per year to the above-mentioned persons under specific circumstances.

XVI. Leave for the Training of Trade Union Members

711. Union members that are employed in enterprises with more than 100 employees are entitled to a leave of fourteen days in order to participate in education and training programmes for union members under the preconditions that:

(a) they are selected by GSEE. The selected union members cannot be less than three and more than fifteen;
(b) a specific training programme has been concluded by GSEE.

Chapter 5. Remuneration

§1. The Concept of Remuneration

712. Remuneration constitutes an essential element of the individual labour contract. In principle, remuneration is everything that the employer supplies to the employee in exchange for the employee's work performance.[320]

713. Supply of subordinate labour cannot exist without remuneration and for that reason in every case of the conclusion of a labour contract, it is considered that a clause for the payment of remuneration must have been included, even tacitly.[321]

714. Only that which is offered in exchange for the work supplied by the employee is considered as remuneration.

715. Remuneration includes the amount offered by the employer for the provision of the work (wage), during the regular working hours, for overwork for legal overtime, for work on Sundays and holidays.

716. The employee is entitled to extra remuneration when the following cumulative conditions are met: (a) the work is carried out during the regular working hours; (b) the employee constantly provides extra work which is not included in their duties and is not related to the work originally agreed upon; (c) this extra work is, under ordinary circumstances, provided only in return for wages.[322]

717. In contrast, remuneration does not include benefits from the employer towards the employee that do not have as a main purpose the remuneration for the work provided by the employee, even if the employee takes advantage of such benefits. Therefore, remuneration does not include:

(a) benefits whose aim is not to pay the employee but to facilitate the operation of the enterprise or secure the life or the physical integrity of the employee, such as housing, work gear/equipment (protective clothing, tools, helmet, raw materials), training for the operation of machinery;
(b) funds to cover company expenses made by the employee, such as expenditures for buying equipment, the employee's travel expenses and the cost of the use of a car;
(c) benefits that have the legal character of compensation, such as severance pay, off-site work payment or the legal character of a civil penalty, such as compensation for the absence of annual holidays;

---

320. As it is evident from the provisions of Arts 648, 649, 653 and 361 of the CC, Art. 3, para. 2 of L. 2190/1920, Art. 5 para. 1 of L. 3198/1955 and Art. 1 of ILO Convention 95/1945 on the protection of wages, ratified by L. 3248/1955.
321. Articles 648, 649 of the CC.
322. AP 270/2017.

(d) tips from the customers of the enterprise (by custom or for any other reason) when it is agreed between the employer and the employee that they do not constitute remuneration.

§2. Voluntary Remuneration

718. A special type of remuneration is 'voluntary remuneration'. Voluntary remuneration is remuneration offered by the employer who is not so obliged by law or by a clause of the collective agreement or by the individual labour contract or by any other legal provision.

719. As such, voluntary remuneration is that offered by the employer beyond the requirements of the law or the clauses of the collective agreement, while remuneration offered by the employer who, even erroneously, believes that he/she is obliged to offer it, is non-voluntary. It is self-evident that this remuneration must be legal.

720. The continuation of the payment of a voluntary remuneration may be terminated (for the future) in the cases where the employer has explicitly maintained the right to revoke it. If a voluntary remuneration is paid continuously for a long period of time and the employer has not maintained the right to revoke it, a contractual obligation is created for the continuation of the remuneration and this remuneration is considered as part of the 'salary'.

721. Payment of voluntary remuneration by the employer is governed by the principle of equal treatment. The principle of equal treatment derives primarily from Article 288 of the CC in combination with Article 4 paragraphs 1 and 2 of the Constitution, and obliges the employer, who offers voluntary remuneration, not to exclude those employees for whom the cause that led to the offer of the voluntary remuneration is valid. In other words, the employer is forbidden to exclude from this remuneration those employees that are in the same position and works under the same conditions as those for whom the remuneration applies. Such employees are those who offer the same services, under the same work conditions, with the same skills, in the same economic situation, the same health conditions, etc. Exclusion is justified for reasons of bona fides, taking existing customs and practices into account.

§3. Types of Remuneration

722. The term 'remuneration of labour' is often used incorrectly as being synonymous with the terms 'benefits' and 'wage'. The term 'remuneration' describes the total of the funds allocated to the employee because of her/his labour and are distinguished as follows:

(a) 'primary remuneration', meaning the remuneration for work during the regular working hours and 'secondary or additional remuneration', meaning the remuneration paid for time in addition to the regular, such as overwork, work on Sundays and holidays, legal overtime;
(b) 'regular or ordinary remuneration', meaning the remuneration for work regularly offered in defined periods, such as monthly wage, Christmas or Easter bonuses, benefits paid every month, percentages of the gains or receipts or any other type of participation in the enterprise, if are paid to the employee in addition to his/her remuneration, are considered as ordinary remuneration only if there is a relevant agreement or customary practice.[323] It is the basis for calculating severance pay. Then there is 'extraordinary remuneration', meaning remuneration that is offered for work not made on a regular basis, such as for urgent (legal) work on some Sundays;
(c) 'usual remuneration', meaning the remuneration offered to the employee for a defined period of time, such as a monthly salary, work for one Sunday, additional remuneration for night work, which are the basis for calculating other payments, such as holiday pay;
(d) 'paid remuneration', meaning remuneration that is offered for regular work corresponding to a defined time period, that does not include the compensation for urgent additional work in the said time period or the remuneration for work of a longer time period (such as the Christmas bonus which corresponds to the work of the whole year).

§4. Systems for the Calculation of the Wage

723. The wage is calculated, as a rule, in relation to working time (time wage) and the amount of it is determined in accordance with legal provisions or with collective agreements, thus defining the 'time payment'. However, there are cases where wage is defined in relation to the quantity of the employee's output (as with piecework or as a percentage of/commission on sales) or as participation in the earnings of the company, of which the employer is obliged to inform the employee.[324] In some occupations, it is mandatory, on the basis of legal provisions or customs, optional payments of tips by the employer's customers to the employee. In such cases, after an explicit or tacit agreement between the employer and the employee, tips constitute wage. It is self-evident that total wage can consist of a combination of all the above types.

724. In any case, regardless of the manner of calculating wage, the final amount cannot be less than the amount of wage stipulated by law, as in the following paragraphs. Consequently, if the wage is defined in relation to the employee's performance and his/her share of company earnings or tips in the said time period is less than the minimum wage stipulated by law or by collective agreements, then the employer is obliged to cover the difference.

323. Article 3, para. 2 of L. 2112/1920, Art. 5, para. 1 of L. 3198/1955.
324. Article 654 of the CC.

§5. Time Wage

725. 'Time wage' is calculated in any of the following ways:

(a) per month (monthly wage) and refers to the calendar month, regardless of the number of days in the month. A monthly wage covers the working days per month, no matter how many they are, for a regular working timetable. It is the most usual way of calculating the salary;
(b) per fortnight. This is in essence a monthly salary paid in two equal fortnightly payments; it is not the time unit for the calculation of salary;
(c) per day (daily wage) and corresponds to a regular work timetable. This is the usual way of calculating remuneration for manual workers;
(d) per hour (hourly wage) and corresponds to each hour of work.

§6. Ways of Determining Remuneration

726. Remuneration can be determined in various ways:

(a) by legal provisions (legally provisioned wage, minimum wage). In this way, the minimum wage to which the employee is entitled is set out, as is the corresponding obligation of the employer to pay it. Remuneration calculated in any other way must not be less than the legally stipulated minimum;[325]
(b) under specific clauses of a collective agreement or an DA (collective agreement wage). This applies only to those employees whose individual work contracts are subject to the specific collective agreement/DA, in accordance with clauses referred to below;
(c) under an agreement between the employer and the employee[326] (contract wage). In those cases where wage is provided for by a specific clause of a collective agreement/DA, the amount of the contract wage must not be less than the collective agreement wage;[327]

325. Article 7, para. 3 of L. 1876/1990, Art. 1 para. IA sub-para. IA.11 s. 3 of Law 4093/2012.
326. Articles 631 and 648 of the CC.
327. According to settled case law: (a) the principle of favouring the employee (the 'favourability principle') is applied in the relationship between a collective agreement and a labour contract (i.e., an individual contract) and in the relationship between legal sources of varying rank regulating labour relationships (statutes, collective labour agreements, regulations, individual contracts). For this principle to apply, the rates of pay must be compared as single entities (e.g., the total remuneration set by the collective agreement must be compared with the total remuneration agreed between the employer and the employee), unless there is a special regulation to the contrary, and it is not possible to selectively choose one part of the remuneration from one source and another part from another source because it is not permissible to apply all these sources at the same time with regard to the concept of remuneration (e.g., APol 8/2015, APol 5/2011, AP 26/2007). (b) The favourability principle is not applied in cases involving sources of the same rank (e.g., in cases of remuneration established by successive laws or successive collective agreements of the same type). In these cases, more recent and special rules exclude the application of older or of general rules (e.g., AP 227/2018, AP 316/2017).

(d) in cases where wage is not defined in the above ways, an improbable case due to the general application of the legally provisioned minimum wage, then the employee is paid the wage of other employees who provide the same work, in the same region, under the same conditions and having the same typical and substantive skills and qualifications (customary wage).

§7. Current System for the Calculation of Minimum Wage: Safeguarding of Minimum Remuneration

727. In Hellas, there has long been a system of safeguarding minimum remuneration, meaning a system of defining the minimum wage that an employee is entitled to. The minimum wage has always been, and still is, defined as time wage.

728. Under Law 1876/1990, a minimum wage, monthly for white-collar employees and daily for blue-collar employees, at a national level was set by the NGCA for any employee under Hellenic law. In 2012, Law 4093 stipulated that from 1 April 2013, the minimum wage would no longer be determined by the NGCA, but by the law. In 2013, Law 4172 stipulated that the minimum wage would be determined by a Ministerial Decision, passed by the Minister of Labour, Social Security and Welfare, following the consent of the Cabinet Council, after a consultation between the social partners and the government during which scientific and researching bodies and institutions would offer their expertise on issues of economy, labour finance, social policy and labour relations. The new system was to be applied not earlier than 2017.

729. In 2012, for the first time, the minimum wage is defined by law, Law 4093/2012, and it covers only the employees in private sector. For that reason, it is made explicit in Law 4093/2013 that any reference in current legislation to a minimum wage under the NGCA should be to those minima provisioned by law. The amount of minimum wage is to be determined after consideration of the condition and prospects of the Hellenic economy and the job market (especially unemployment rates) and after government consultation with the representatives of the social partners, with experts and other agencies. This new system was enacted by Law 4172/2013 and will enter into effect after the Economic Adjustment Programme, meaning not earlier than 1 January 2017.

730. More specifically, this legal provision was enacted by Article First paragraph IA sub-paragraph IA.11 section 1 and 3 of Law 4093/2012, and its entry into effect took place on 1 April 2013. Under section 3 of the same sub-paragraph, and until the entry into effect of the new system, the minimum wage is as follows:

(a) for white-collar employees over 25 years of age, the minimum wage is set at EUR 586.08 a month, while for blue-collar employees over 25 years old, the minimum wage is set at EUR 26.18 a day;

(b) for white-collar employees of under 25 years of age, the minimum wage is set at EUR 510.95, while for blue-collar employees/workers under 25 years of age, the minimum wage is EUR 22.83 a day;
(c) the above minimum wage for white-collar employees of over 25 years of age is incremented by 10% for every three years of service and for up to three-year periods, thus in total by 30% for seniority of 9 years or more, while the minimum wage for blue-collar employees of more than 25 years of age is incremented by 5% for every three-year period for up to six such three-year periods, thus by 30% in total for seniority of more than 18 years. The above minimum wage for white-collar employees under 25 years of age is increased by 10% for every three-year period of work and for working for more than three years, while the minimum wage for blue-collar employees under 25 years old is increased by 5% for every three years of work and for up to two three-year periods, thus to total 10% increase after working six years or more;
(d) the above increases are paid to an employee with working experience for any employer and in any specialty as follow (aa) for the blue-collar employees after the completion of the 18th year of age, (bb) for the white-collar employees after the completion of the 19th year of age, and apply only to seniority acquired before 14 February 2012;
(e) apart from the regular increase because of the length of work experience (as above), no other increase is included in the legally defined minimum wage (monthly and daily);
(f) until unemployment rates fall below 10%, all increases of the legally defined minimum wage (monthly and daily) are suspended for work provided after the 14 February 2012.

731. The regime imposed by Law 4093/2012 was finally enacted by Article 103 of Law 4172/2013, which specifies that:

(a) after government consultation with the representatives of the social partners, with experts and other agencies, a legally stipulated minimum wage is defined, as well as the legally defined minimum wage, for full employment, for those workers and employees in the whole country whose remuneration is not determined by a collective agreement;
(b) the level of the legally provisioned minimum wage must be defined with regard to the state of the Hellenic economy and its prospects for development in terms of productivity, prices, competitiveness, employability, unemployment rate, incomes and wages;
(c) for the setting of the legal minimum wage consultation takes place between the social partners and the government, with the technical and scientific support of experts on economic issues and especially on the labour economy, social policy and labour relations, coordinated by a tripartite committee comprised of the President of OMED, acting as president, a high-profile representative of the Ministry of Finance and a high-profile representative of the Ministry of Labour and Social Insurance, with secretarial support from the services of OMED. The social partners that participate in the above consultations are:

– On behalf of the employees of the country: the GSEE and the other second-level trade unions, sectoral or of the same occupation, that represent the employees of the private sector on the national level. (ii) On behalf of the employers: representatives from their associations, among which we count the SEV, the Hellenic Confederation of Professionals, Craftsmen and Merchants (GSEVEE), the ESEE, the SETE and those other employers' associations that are proposed by them.

732. The above-mentioned consultations are concluded with the formulation of a Draft Consultation Finding which is completed no later than 31 May and is submitted to the Minister of Labour and Social Insurance, who in the second fortnight of the month of June of every year recommends to the Cabinet of Ministers the minimum wage for white-collar employees and the minimum wage for blue-collar workers. The recommendation takes into account the Finding of the Consultation, and then the Minister issues a decision for the determination of the minimum wage for white-collar employees and the minimum wage for blue-collar workers, following the assent of the Cabinet of Ministers.

733. By a Ministerial Decision issued (on 30 January 2019) by the Minister of Labour and adopted pursuant to Article 103 of L. 4172/2013, after taking into account, *inter alia*, the positions, memoranda and documentation of GSEE, SEV, GSEVEE and SETE, following oral consultations with SEV, GSEVEE, ESEE, SETE and FING, who responded to the call sent to GSEE, SEV, GSEVEE, ESEE, SETE and FING by the Coordinating Committee responsible for the consultations, and the consent of the Cabinet, the minimum monthly wage for employees (white-collar workers) is set at EUR 650.00 and the minimum daily wage for labourers and craftspersons (blue-collar workers) is set at EUR 29.04. The new rates came into effect on 1 February 2019 and apply to all workers, regardless of their age.

734. Neither individual labour contracts nor collective agreements may establish regular monthly wages or full-time employment wages that are less than the legally stipulated minimum salary or wage, or less than the pro rata minimum remuneration for part-time work contracts.

§8. Composition of the Wage

735. A wage is the result of a basic sum (basic wage) and may be supplemented by other sums (benefits) that are paid to the employee for specific reasons that concern the employee or the enterprise, such as family benefits (e.g., marriage benefits,[328] children benefits), seniority benefits, benefits for positions of responsibility or hazardous work. These benefits are defined either as a percentage of the basic wage or as a specified amount.

328. The court decision APol 8/2015 is of particular interest in this regard.

§9. Christmas and Easter Benefits

736. There is a special category that consists of holiday benefits that are paid to the employee every Christmas and Easter. These two benefits are equal to a monthly wage and to half of the monthly wage respectively. For employees who are paid per day, different provisions apply.

737. The benefits for Christmas, Easter and annual leave provided by any general or special law or clause or condition of a collective agreement or DA or individual employment contract, etc. for state employees, employees of legal persons governed by public or private law and municipalities and regional authorities were abolished with effect from 1 January 2013.[329]

§10. Money Remuneration

738. Remuneration is primarily, and usually, paid in money (money remuneration). The payment of the remuneration takes place in the currency that is in circulation and is primarily paid in cash. If it is so set out in regulatory provisions or is so legally agreed, then it is paid through a bank or by cheque. Remuneration may not be paid with securities (stocks, bonds, etc.), bills or other similar financial instruments. However, it is possible that part of the salary be paid in kind, meaning objects, services and rights produced or provided by the enterprise of the employer or by third parties.

§11. Time and Place for the Payment of the Wage

739. Remuneration is allocated in the workplace or in that place that is legally provisioned either by a clause of the collective agreement or by arbitration decision. However, pursuant to Ministerial Decision 22528/430/17.05.2017, effective 1 June 2017, employers are under the obligation to make salary payments to private sector employees exclusively via a deposit into the employees' bank accounts. Non-compliance with the above obligation is subject to fines from EUR 300 to EUR 50,000.

740. Concerning the time of payment, the following apply:[330]

(a) if there is no differing agreement or practice, remuneration is paid after the provision of the work;
(b) remuneration by time is paid at the end of the related time period;

329. *See* para. C sub-para. 1 of L. 4093/2012.
330. Article 655 of the CC.

(c) when remuneration is defined in accordance with the quantitative productivity of labour, then the employee has the right to be paid in advance in accordance with the circumstances, the type of work offered or those expenses that he/she may have undertaken;
(d) in every case of termination of a labour contract the remaining remuneration, up to the termination, becomes payable;
(e) overdue payment of wages places the employer in a legal position of defaulted payment,[331] and the employer is liable also to pay interest on the amount of the late payment.

741. In a valid labour contract claims for wage and remuneration in general are barred after five years.[332] In case of an invalid labour contract claims by suit for unjustifiable profit-making are barred after twenty years.[333]

§12. Deductions from the Wage

742. With responsibility of the employer and before payment, income tax, social insurance contributions and other amounts, as defined in law, must be withheld from the wage paid. All these amounts are transferred by the employer to the beneficiaries (the state, the insurance fund, etc.) in proper time as designated by the law; otherwise the employer is obliged to pay them from his/her income.

§13. Protection of Remuneration

743. Remuneration constitutes, among others, a means of livelihood for the employees. For that reason, the wage is protected against claims of the employer, the state and third parties. In order for the wage to be legally protected, it is forbidden that the whole or part of the wage be confiscated, held, cleared or allocated.

744. According to Article 56 of Law 4487/2017, any significant delay in the payment of accrued salary is considered to be a unilateral adverse change.

§14. Protection of the Wage

745. Remuneration serves, among other purposes, as the means of subsistence. For that reason, it is protected from claims by the employer, the state or any third parties. In order to protect the salary legislatively, the confiscation of any part of the remuneration, or of the net payment, the withholdings or of the transfer of the salary is prohibited.

331. Article 341, para. 1 of the CC.
332. Articles 250, 253 of the CC, Art. 2 of L. 5151/1970 which refers to remuneration in any type of overtime work.
333. Articles 904–913, 249 of the CC.

746. In accordance with Article 982, paragraph 2 section (d) of the Code of Civil Procedure claims for salary, pensions or insurance benefits are excluded from confiscation, except in the cases of a claim for alimony satisfactorily based on the law or of a provision in a will for a contribution to the needs of the family. In these cases up to half of the wage may be confiscated after taking into consideration the amount received by the beholden, the burden of the obligations that are created by his marriage for the care of the family needs and the number of the beneficiaries.

747. In accordance with Article 464 of the CC a wage is forbidden to be ceded elsewhere inasmuch as it is prohibited to be confiscated. In accordance with Article 664 of the CC, the employer cannot clear in his/her favour the payable remuneration by means of a claim against the employee since this remuneration is necessary for the support of the employee and his/her family. This prohibition does not apply to such clearance after a claim of the employer of a fraudulent damage caused by the employee during the execution of the labour contract. The salary, since it cannot be so cleared, neither can it be confiscated. If deductions have been agreed in the salary, then in the absence of any contrary agreement this is made for the cover of any potential damage to the employer.[334]

748. Finally, in accordance with Article 327 of the CC, the withholding of the wage is forbidden insofar as this is not subject to clearance.

749. Under a series of special clauses, different provisions are introduced, such as the claims of the employer against craftsmen and workers for rents of houses rented by the company or for the cost of food or other essentials that were provided by the company at wholesale prices.

750. When claims of the employees coexist with claims of other creditors of the employer and if there is an auction of the assets of the company, some claims by the employees are in a privileged position. Thus, in accordance with Article 675 of the Code of Civil Procedure, as replaced by Article 19 paragraph 10 of Law 4055/2012, those claims concerning the supply of dependent work are classified at the third level of priority; this includes compensation because of the termination of the work relation. Claims of teachers and lawyers are placed on the same level.

751. A similar classification exists for the claims of the employees in the case of the bankruptcy of the employer.[335]

334. Articles 664 and 665 of the CC.
335. Article 154 of L. 3588/2007, as amended by para. 5 of Art. 13 of L. 4013/2011.

§15. Remuneration Without Work

I. Non-provision of Work and Payment of Wage

752. The provision of work (supply of labour) is a timed provision, meaning that it must be made in a specific day and during the specific working time. If the work is not carried out, the employee has not the right and is not obliged to proceed to provide work at a different time. The non-provision of work in principle justifies the non-payment of wage for the time period of non-provision.

753. However, there are cases where the employee is entitled to remuneration, even though he/she does not supply work. These cases are made explicit in law and are as follows:

(a) when the employee does not supply work because he/she exercises a particular right, such as absence in order to vote in an election, absence on a holiday provided by law or a clause of the collective agreement or DA, in accordance with the above-mentioned paragraphs;
(b) when there is a major reason that is not related to the employee and the employee has worked for at least ten days from the beginning of the labour contract.[336] In such cases, the employer has the right to deduct from the salary that amount which because of the obstacle was paid to the employee by a compulsory insurance scheme. If the major reason appeared in the first twelve months of the labour contract, then the employee is entitled to claim his/her wage for half a month. If the major reason appeared at a later time, then the employee is entitled to claim one month's wages for every year of work. If within the above time limits more major reasons should appear, these time limits are not changed.

754. A 'major reason' is any incident that justifies, objectively and in accordance with bona fides, the non-provision of work on the part of the employee, regardless of the person under whose sphere of influence this incident occurs; e.g., a serious illness of the employee or his/her child, a blockade of the employee's residence by the police for the arrest of a serious criminal, an earthquake or a storm that affects the transportation of the employee to his/her place of work, a strike by third parties. Particularly in the case of a sick employee, there is relevant legislation included in the laws concerning social insurance, and the employer bears the payment of the remuneration only for the first three days of the employee's absence from work.

II. Non-acceptance of Work and Payment of Remuneration

755. Non-acceptance of work on the part of the employer in principle renders the employer 'in default' and in accordance with Article 656 of the CC, as replaced

336. Article 657 of the CC.

by Article 61 of Law 4139/2013, the employee has the right to claim to undertake her/his real employment at a subsequent time, as well as his/her remuneration for the time that he/she has not worked. However, the employer's default in acceptance of the offer to perform work is excluded if the employee is not in a position to perform it.

756. If the non-acceptance of the work is based on reasons that stem from the employer and are not caused by force majeure, the employee is not obliged to provide work at a subsequent time; however, he/she has the right to demand remuneration for the time that he/she had not worked.[337] The employer has the right to deduct from the remuneration any benefits that the employee derived from the suspension of work or from the provision of work at a different place.[338]

757. Force majeure refers to any unpredicted incident that is not the result of any fault of the employer and is, by its nature, exceptional in that it could not have been avoided by human capability even if the most extreme measures of diligence and prudence had been adopted.

758. However, the employer has the right to deduct from the salary anything that the employee gained as a benefit from the suspension of the work or from its provision elsewhere.[339] In accordance with the explanatory statement that accompanies the new provision, its purpose is to identify a general obligation of the employer to employ the employee since labour is considered as one of the most important factors for the development of human personality and the identification of the right of the employee to real employment is better harmonized with the obligation of care that the employer bears,[340] with the constitutional protection of the right to work,[341] with the free development of personality[342] and with respect towards the value of each person.[343]

337. AP 613/2018.
338. *Ibid.*
339. *Ibid.*
340. Article 288 of the CC.
341. Article 22 of the Constitution.
342. Article 5 of the Constitution.
343. Article 2 of the Constitution.

Chapter 6. Suspension of the Individual Labour Contract: Modification of the Individual Labour Contract

§1. Suspension of the Individual Labour Contract

I. General Remarks

759. In cases of suspension of the execution of the individual labour contract for reasons independent of the will of the parties, the contract between employer and employee remains in existence, while the duty of the employee to work is always suspended temporarily and the duty of the employer to pay remuneration in some cases is suspended or in other cases continues to exist. The secondary duties of both parties are not affected (e.g., liability, professional secrecy, providing for the employee). The suspension of the execution of the individual labour contract does not terminate the labour relation. The time of suspension is considered as time of service.

760. Suspension of the work relationship may come either by normative provisions or by an agreement between the employer and the employee.

II. Agreement Between the Employer and the Employee

761. When the parties agree that without the employee providing work the employer is or is not liable for payment of wages, the execution of their contract is considered to be suspended for the agreed period, e.g., in the case of uninstitutionalized leave.

III. Suspension Regulated by Law

762. In many cases when the employee executes his/her rights, the suspension of the employment relationship is the consequence of it, e.g., in the case of a leave, an annual leave, pregnancy leave, participation in exams, strike, conscription and illness.

IV. Military Service

763. The execution of the individual labour contract is suspended in the case of the military service of the man-employee who has already worked for at least six months for an employer under a valid contract.[344] The employee can request his return to his employer's business after the completion of his military service. The

344. In Hellas military service is a man's obligation.

request for his return has to be made within a month after the completion of the service and the application of readiness to start work within fifteen days after the request is made to the employer.[345]

764. Article 8 of Law 2054/1952, as interpreted by Article 34 paragraph 7 of LD 2961/1954, makes evident that the time of military service of the employees is calculated as a time of real work to the employer before the military service, for all the rights of the employee towards the employer.[346]

765. Firing of the employee is permitted only for a justified reason and after the approval of a certain committee of Article 7 of EL 244/1936. Without this approval, the employer has to pay the usual compensation for dismissal and further compensation equal to six months' pay.

766. During the suspension of the contract because of military service, the employee does not receive remuneration directly from his employer, but he receives insurance benefits issued by the OAED.[347]

V. Technical Disturbances or Economic Reasons

767. There is also suspension of the execution of the agreement in the case of disturbances caused by the employer or at the enterprise, e.g., the employer's inability to accept the work of the employee because of faulty organization or bad management, but not in the event of a temporary force majeure (Act of God). The employee is at the disposal of the employer or his or her duty to carry out alternative work at the enterprise is agreed, while the employer continues to be responsible for paying the employee's salary after deducting all other employee's profits or remuneration from another job during this period.

768. Article 10 of Law 3198/1955 provides for the suspension of the execution of the contract for economic reasons, i.e., those reasons which cause a fall in production. In this case only the employer, after his or her written announcement of the laying-off of employees for economic reasons and for a period which does not exceed three months in total, yearly, pays half of their normal remuneration. Mutual benefit associations having more than 5,000 employees need the previous approval of the Minister of Labour for a temporary lay-off; otherwise they are obliged to pay lay-off pay of the full remuneration.[348]

345. EL 547/1937, L. 519/1948 and L. 3514/1928.
346. AP 64/2002.
347. L. 2054/1952, L. 2961/1954.
348. Article 1 of LD 206/1974.

VI. Sickness

769. Article 3 of Law 4558/1930 defines the margins of a short sickness leave during which the labour relation is suspended. Relevant to the above are the provisions of Article 5 paragraph 3 of Law 2112/1920 and Article 8 of RD 16/18.7.1920.

770. When the absence of the employee because of sickness is more than the time limits set by the previous provisions, there cannot be an immediate termination of the contract nor it is considered that the employee is resigned.

771. In any case, a possible liability of the employee is examined, the potential return to the workplace and other factors that are shaped by jurisprudence in order to objectively judge the consequences of this absence on the work relationship.

772. It is only when it is absolutely impossible to continue the work, or for some other reason, the employee does not work, that the will of the employee has to be defined. In any case, the labour relation continues to exist for the period that the employer is willing to wait for the return of the employee without any further disturbance of the enterprise's operations, and after taking into account all relevant situations (e.g., deportation, preventive detention, violation of leave). The employee is not entitled on benefits during his/her absence because of sickness with the exclusion of some cases.

§2. Modification of the Individual Labour Contract

I. General Remarks

773. The terms of the individual labour contract are defined with provisions that are included in every source of labour law, such as legal provisions, terms of collective agreements, enterprise customary practices, agreements between the employee and the employer and any other lawful way. Similarly, those terms may be modified according to the future modifications of the law, etc. The new terms may be more or less favourable than the previous ones for the employees. The agreement between the parties may be explicit or tacit, however, in any case, it must be clear that a new agreement has been concluded as well as that the content of the new agreement and the term is specific.[349]

774. If the same terms are regulated by both legal provisions, clauses of collective agreements and new agreement between the employee and the employer, the

349. AP 1089/2006.

ones that are more favourable for the employee will apply, unless the legal provisions are of mandatory character. In the latest case, legal provisions take precedence over the clauses of the collective agreement and the terms of the agreement between the parties.[350]

II. Modification Based on Terms That Are Already Content of the Labour Contract

775. It is possible that the employer, under a term of the labour contract, has secured the right for himself to unilaterally change the terms of the contract. Such terms may not refer to a substantial clause of the contract, e.g., those that define the kind of the work and the relation between the work and the wage. The parties are not allowed to agree differently. In any case, the employer should exercise his/her said right in accordance with bona fides; otherwise it is examined for being abusive.

§3. Unilateral Modification by the Employer

776. A unilateral modification of the labour contract by the employer is prohibited, as in every unilateral change of the terms of any contract. The employer may unilaterally modify the labour contract, only if this is a right provisioned by the law or by any other normative provision. Where the employer proceeds to actions with the aim to unilaterally modify the labour contract, the employee may explicitly, orally or tacitly, accept it. If so, a new clause in the labour contract is deemed to have been concluded. If the employee does not accept it, he/she should express his/her objections in a fair time and insist on the existing clauses of the contract. Where the employer wishes to modify a clause of the contract, the latter's consent is required.

§4. Unilateral Modification to the Detriment of the Employee

777. A unilateral modification to the detriment of the employee is the modification of the labour contract that the employer tries to make and that causes material or moral damage to the employee.[351]

778. In such cases, the employee is entitled to exercise one of the following rights:

(a) The employee may reject the modification and insist on the previous work terms. On the employer's refusal, the employee may bring an action before the Labour Court to nullify the modification, even after it has entered into force. If

350. Article 7, paras 2 and 3 of L. 1876/1990.
351. AP 605/1996, AP 1227/1993.

the unilateral modification is nullified, both parties will revert to their respective situations before the modification entered into force.

(b) If the labour contract is of indefinite period, the employee may consider that the action of the employer is a tacit, and thereby wrongful, dismissal, and may bring an action before the Labour Court to nullify it or to claim severance pay.[352] If the labour contract is of definite period, the employee may consider that the action of the employer is an important reason for the employee to proceed to the termination of the labour contract in accordance with Article 672 of the CC[353] and claim for compensation due to the violation of the labour contract in accordance with Article 673 of the CC.

(c) The employee may accept explicitly, tacitly or orally, the modification, thus leading to the conclusion of a new clause in the labour contract that includes the modification.[354]

779. If the conditions under which the employer acts or modifies the labour contract offence the personality of the employee and cause moral damage to him/her, the employee is entitled to claim compensation on that ground.[355]

780. Jurisprudence has judged that unilateral harmful change of the working terms consists of, e.g., a delayed payment of remuneration in order to force the employee to resign,[356] the assignment of the employee to an inferior position,[357] the unjustified decrease of overtime[358] or the increase of working time.[359]

352. AP 211/2002, AP 559/2001, AP 94/1995.
353. Ef. Athens 2099/1994.
354. AP 48/2010, AP 1792/2001, AP 384/2001, AP 698/1989.
355. AP 596/1999, AP 542/1999, AP 674/1991.
356. AP 1203/1998.
357. AP 180/2010, AP 1306/2005.
358. AP 1342/1996.
359. AP 521/1984, AP 272/2017.

Chapter 7. Equal Treatment of Employees

§1. The Principle of Equal Treatment

781. The concept of the 'principle of equal treatment' defines elements such as:

(a) the obligation of the employer, when proceeding with voluntary provisions, not to exclude employees who are in the same position as those for whom the provisions are made;
(b) the obligation of the legislator, the employer and any other third parties not to discriminate among employees on the basis of sex, age, beliefs, origin, etc.

§2. The Principle of Equality: Article 4 Paragraphs 1, 2 of the Constitution

782. The concept of 'the principle of equal treatment' is sometimes wrongly confused with the concept of 'the principle of equality', which defines the obligation of the legislator to create similar provisions for similar conditions and dissimilar provisions for dissimilar conditions.

783. The principle of equality between all Hellenes, and more specifically between male and female Hellenes, is set out in Article 4, paragraphs 1 and 2 of the Hellenic Constitution. In accordance with the principle of sex equality, as an expression of the general principle of equality, the legislator and the employer (under the principle of third party applicability), are forbidden to treat in a different way, favourable or unfavourable, male and female employees, when these employees are found in similar situations.

§3. The Principle of Equal Pay for Equal Work

784. One specific expression of the principle of equality is the principle of equal pay for equal work.[360] In accordance with this principle, for work of equal value equal pay must be offered regardless of sex or any other distinction between employees.

§4. Measures Taken for the Promotion of the Principle of Equality Between Men and Women

785. Given the fact that women have been, and are, subjected to unfavourable treatment compared to men because of their sex, Article 116, paragraph 2 of the Hellenic Constitution stipulates that 'Positive measures taken for the promotion of the

360. Article 22, para. 1, sub-para. B of the Constitution.

principle of equality between men and women do not constitute discrimination. The state supports the removal of de facto inequalities, especially those unfavourable to women.' The aim of this provision is to dismantle that institutionalized inequality and inequality into practice which has been created against women and to promote not only institutional equality between men and women but also equal treatment of sexes into practice so that women may enjoy the same opportunities as men. Thus, any deviation or exclusion from the constitutionally regulated principle of equality is strictly forbidden. The only reasons that may justify the differentiated treatment of the two sexes are, in accordance with science, biological; for that reason, protection and support of maternity cannot be considered unconstitutional.

§5. Protection Against Discrimination: Equal Treatment Between Employees Irrespective of Sex, Age, Racial or Ethnic Origin, Religion or Belief, Disability or Sexual Orientation

I. The Legislation

786. In order to remove any discrimination against employees on the grounds of sex, age, racial or ethnic origin, religion or other beliefs, disability, sexual orientation, etc., Directive 2006/54/EC has been incorporated into law of the land by Law 3488/2006 and by Law 3896/2010 and Directives 2000/43/EC and 2000/78/EC by Law 3304/2005. Directive 2014/54 has been incorporated by Law 4443/2016, and Law 3304/2010 was repealed by Article 22 paragraph 1 of Law 4443/2016.

II. Equal Treatment for Men and Women

787. The present legal system fully supports the equal treatment of women and men in all fields of work, subordinate or not. However, in reality, discriminative conduct against women persists as to the amount of remuneration and as concerning promotion and the filling of administrative and high-responsibility positions.

788. Issues concerning the equal treatment of women and men were regulated by Law 3488/2006, which incorporated Directive 2006/54/EC into national law. This Law has been replaced by Law 3896/2010.

A. Direct and Indirect Discrimination

789. Law 4443/2016, such as the previous Law 3488/2006 and Law 3896/2010, forbids any type of direct or indirect discrimination on the basis of sex, especially in conjunction with marital status in all fields concerning employment.

790. Discrimination on the basis of gender is also constituted by:

(a) harassment, sexual harassment and any less favourable treatment that is related to the tolerance or acceptance of a harassment conduct;
(b) less favourable treatment for persons that have undergone a sex change operation;
(c) any order or regulation that includes discrimination against a person because of sex.

791. In the scope of application of the above Law, 'direct discrimination' refers to the case when an individual suffers, on the basis of sex, treatment less favourable than a different person in a similar situation. As 'indirect discrimination', we refer to those cases where an initially neutral act, criterion or practice may put persons of one sex into a disadvantageous position in comparison with persons of a different sex, unless this provision, criterion or practice is objectively justified by fair cause and the means of accomplishing the aim are effective and necessary.

792. The concept 'harassment' refers to undesirable behaviour that has to do with the sex of an individual, the aim or result being the abuse of the dignity of this person and the creation of a frightening, hostile, demeaning, humiliating or aggressive environment in the workplace. The concept 'sexual harassment' refers to the case where there is an expression of any kind verbal, non-verbal or physical behaviour with a sexual character, the aim or result being the abuse of the dignity of an individual, especially through the creation of a frightening, hostile, demeaning, humiliating or aggressive environment in the workplace.

793. Discrimination is also constituted by less favourable treatment of parents-employees because of childcare or care and adoption leaves.

794. Discrimination is not, however, constituted by the adoption or sustainment of special or positive measures that aim to eliminate existing discrimination against the less-represented sex and to achieve substantive equality in the fields included within the scope of Law 3896/2010.

B. Content of the Principle of Equal Treatment

795. The provisions of law set out to ensure the implementation of the principle of equal opportunities and of equal treatment for men and women in employment and work matters. This takes place in the fields of:

(a) access to employment, including career development and vocational training;
(b) working conditions and the terms of remuneration;
(c) social security systems (social insurance) as stipulated by Directive 2006/54/EC of the European Parliament and the European Council.

796. The prohibition of discrimination, corresponding to the enforcement of the principle of equal treatment, has the following content:

(a) It prohibits any reference to sex or marital status, or the use of criteria and evidence that lead to direct or indirect discrimination based on sex, in any notification, publication, advertisement, commercial, invitation, regulation or circular concerning the selection of persons for the filling of job positions, for the offer of vocational training, or for the granting of professional licences.
(b) It enforces equal pay for men and women for similar work or work of equal value.
(c) It extends to the planning and implementation of any systems for the assessment of personnel which are related to their progress on the pay scale.
(d) It involves the terms of entry to employment, including the criteria of choice and the terms of hiring, regardless of the sector of activity, and at all levels of the work hierarchy. Furthermore, it concerns the conditions of employment and work, promotions, and the planning and implementation of assessment systems for the employees, as well as to access to the content and the implementation of programmes. It applies in general to every field and sector that is directly or indirectly related to employment, such as the stipulation of the prerequisites for professional licences, and to participation in examinations for these; to diplomas or certifications, to the offer of scholarships and to any other educational or related benefits.

797. Termination in any way of the labour contract and any adverse treatment is forbidden:

(a) for reasons of sex or marital status;
(b) as an act of vengeance by the employer because the employee has not given in to sexual or other harassment;
(c) as a reaction of the employer or a person responsible for vocational training to a complaint, accusation, testimony or any other act of the employee, or his/her representative, in the workplace or the place of vocational training.

798. Moreover, direct or indirect discrimination based on sex or marital status is forbidden as concerns membership of or participation in trade unions, associations of persons or employers, or any union or professional body; this also includes the advantages that are offered by membership of such unions or associations.

799. Nevertheless, the establishment of an association that has members of only one sex is permitted when their main aim is to promote the equal treatment of men and women.

C. Persons Covered by Law 3896/2010

800. The provisions of Law 3896/2010 are applicable to persons who are employed or who are candidates for employment in the private and public sector under any type of labour contract. It also applies to persons on vocational training or are candidates for vocational training of any type. It also applies to the implementation of insurance systems.

D. Consequences of the Violation of Law 3896/2010

801. Any violation of the provisions of Law 3896/2010 brings administrative, civil and penal sanctions upon the person in question and to the aggrieved person a right to compensation.

E. Burden of Proof (Reversal of the Burden of Proof)

802. The person who claims that she or he has been discriminated against because of sex must report to the court or any other relevant authority facts that demonstrate probable cause of direct or indirect discrimination because of sex or sexual or other harassment and the opponent bears the burden of proof that there has not been a breach of the principle of equal treatment for men and women.

F. Institutions for the Implementation of the Principle of Equal Treatment

803. In order to fully implement in practice the principle of equal treatment of women and men, there are legally constituted institutions, public and non-public, that support the implementation of provisions promoting equality. There are also legal provisions regarding the obligations and jurisdiction of existing institutions so that these may contribute to the achievement of the principle of equal treatment regardless of sex.

804. The Hellenic Ombudsman is one of the agents for the supervision and promotion of the principle of equal opportunities and equal treatment of men and women in the application of the provisions of the current Law. Since 1984, there have been Departments of 'Gender Equality' in the Ministry of Labour, in the Supreme Council of Labour and in all Labour Inspectorates. Their aims include legislative initiative, with the processing of draft laws that are related to the application of the principle of equal treatment, the monitoring of international and communal law related to these issues, the monitoring of collective agreements and DAs, internal work regulations and all practices in the workplace, the provision of information to the employers, the employees, the trade unions and Non-Governmental Organizations that are engaged in the promotion of equality and any other related action.

III. Equal Treatment at Work Regardless of Age, Race, National or Ethnic Origin, Religious Belief or Other Criteria

805. Directives 2000/43/EC and 2000/78/EC were incorporated into national legislation by Law 3304/2005 and later by Law 4443/2016 in order to lay down a general framework for the fight against discrimination on the basis of racial or ethnic origin and for the fight against discrimination on the basis of religious or other beliefs, disability, age or sexual orientation, in the field of employment and work.

A. *The Concept of Discrimination and Its Scope of Application*

806. The concept of discrimination and its scope of application are similar to those previously mentioned as in Law 3896/2010.[361]

807. The adoption or continuation of measures for the prevention of or compensation for disadvantages that arise from religious or other beliefs, disability, age or sexual discrimination is not considered to be discrimination.

808. The adoption or continuation of measures concerning persons with disabilities, when these measures are related to ensuring health and safety in the workplace, or measures that create or maintain prerequisites or facilities for securing or promoting these persons' entry to employment, are not considered to be discrimination.

809. In particular, concerning discrimination on the basis of religion or other beliefs, age or sexual orientation, a provision, criterion or practice is not considered as discrimination when it is objectively justified by fair cause, the means being productive or necessary, or when it concerns persons with disabilities and measures are adopted in favour of these persons.

810. If the nature of the job offered requires a specific, substantive, fair and justified characteristic as an employment requirement, then differential treatment based on age, religion or other beliefs, sexual orientation or disability does not constitute discrimination.

B. *Different Treatment Due to Nationality*

811. The principle of equal treatment, as regulated by Law 4443/2016, for persons regardless of their religion or beliefs, disabilities, age or sexual orientation, is not applicable to cases where a different treatment is provided for because of nationality, so this principle does not infringe the provisions that regulate the entry to and residence in the Hellenic state of third-country nationals, or of persons of no nationality. Neither does the principle apply to the treatment of persons as far as this is related to their legal character as nationals of third countries or persons without nationality, concerning the benefits that are offered by public social insurance systems, nor to the military and security corps (police, coastguard), since in these institutions different terms apply concerning age and disability.

---

361. *See* above paras 786 et seq.

C. Persons with Disabilities

812. The employer, in order to comply with the principle of equal treatment for persons with disabilities, is obliged to adopt all necessary measures in order that these persons have access to jobs, are able to offer their work and to develop, as well as to participate in vocational training, on the condition that the cost of this is not considered disproportionate for the employer.

813. When evaluating the cost as disproportionate or otherwise, it is balanced against measures of protection taken in the field of policy-making concerning persons with disabilities.

D. Differential Treatment Due to Age That Does Not Constitute Discrimination

814. In particular, concerning age, differential treatment on the grounds of age does not constitute discrimination if such treatment is stipulated by legislation supporting employability, vocational training and the labour market in general. For the achievement of such aims, these measures are considered necessary and productive.

815. This differential treatment may include:

(a) the establishment of special conditions for the access to employment and vocational training and for employability and work, including terms of dismissal and remuneration, for young and older persons and for employees who financially support other persons, in order to facilitate their entry into employment and their protection;
(b) the setting of minimum age limits for access to employment or to certain advantages of employment, having regard to necessary previous work experience or seniority;
(c) the setting of a maximum age limit for hiring, on the basis of the required induction or training period for the job in question, or for the need for a sufficient period of work in order to complete a pension entitlement.

816. Finally, age as a criterion for entry or acceptance into professional systems of social insurance or disability funds does not constitute discrimination, as long as this does not lead to sex discrimination.

E. Consequences of the Violation of Law 4443/2016

817. The violation of the provisions of Law 4443/2016 brings administrative, civil and penal sanctions upon the offender and gives to the plaintiff the right to compensation.

F. Burden of Proof (Reversal of the Burden of Proof)

818. The person who claims to be the victim of discriminative conduct under the above-mentioned criteria must report to the court or any other relevant authority facts that demonstrate probable cause of direct or indirect discrimination and the opponent bears the burden of proof that there has been no breach of the principle of equal treatment as provided for in Law 4443/2016.

G. Institutions for the Implementation of the Principle of Equal Treatment

819. Under certain provisions of Law 4443/2016, public and non-public institutions have been created with the aim of supporting the implementation of the provisions that regulate the obligations and jurisdiction of existing institutions of this kind so that they may contribute to the achievement of the principle of equal treatment regardless of gender.

Chapter 8. Employees Nationals of EU Members and Third Countries

§1. Foreign Employees

820. Foreign employees who legally provide work under a labour contract are fully protected by the Hellenic labour law. There is a different legal status for the nationals of EU and the nationals of third countries.

§2. Nationals of EU: Freedom of Movement

821. Within the framework of the EU and according to the legal status of EU, nationals of Member States enjoy complete freedom of movement. So, they do not need any permission to enter in Hellas and to conclude an individual labour contract. They have equal standing with the national workers.

§3. Foreigners Not Nationals of EU: Permit for Work

822. Foreign workers that are not nationals of EU Member States can be employed with a labour contract only under the preconditions defined by Hellenic law.

823. Current legal provisions concerning the employment of foreigners are mainly included in Law 4071/2012 (Articles 22–41), in Law 4052/2012 (Articles 77–94) which incorporated Directive 2009/50/EC into national law, Law 4018/2011, Law 3386/2005, Law 945/1979 which ratified the entry of Hellas into the EEC and OA 448/1968.

824. In accordance with these provisions, foreigners may be employed with a labour contract if they possess a residence permit for subordinate employment. This permit is issued by the competent authorities if the foreigner:

(a) has a permit of entry for the provision of labour in Hellas;
(b) has concluded an employment contract by which it is evident that his/her remuneration is equal, at least, with the remuneration of an unskilled worker; and
(c) has presented all the supporting documents in accordance with the law.[362]

825. The presentation of a labour contract is not required for employment in the agricultural sector, construction sector, employment as private nurses and domestic workers for multiple employers, temporary workers in the tourism sector and in catering businesses as long as during the period of the renewal they receive unemployment benefits.

362. Article 15 of L. 3386/2005.

826. The renewal of the residence permit for subordinate employment is possible if it is requested by the foreigner two months before the expiry of his/her permit and if he/she presents all documents in accordance with the law, such as the ones showing that he/she has fulfilled his tax liabilities and that he/she has completed a minimum amount of wages with insurance cover.[363]

827. Employment of foreigners that are illegal residents of the country is prohibited.

828. Employers are obliged to request from foreign workers to have a valid residence permit which allows them to work. Employers are, also, obliged to keep a copy of this document and to present it to the competent authorities in case of an inspection.

829. Employers of foreign workers are obliged to notify the competent authorities (Foreigners and Immigration Service) for every hiring or change to the employment regime, such as in the case of an extension of the contract or a termination. If they do not comply with this obligation, they are subject to administrative and penal sanctions.

830. The employer of a foreigner that does not have a residence permit is punished by imprisonment. Similarly, penal sanctions are provisioned to the foreigners who are employed without a residence permit.

831. However, the employer who illegally employs foreigners is obliged:

(a) to pay all due remuneration. 'Due remuneration' is considered to be the minimum wage provisioned by the legislation or the collective agreements in accordance with prevailing practices to the specific occupation or enterprise, unless the employer or the employee prove that due remuneration was different in the framework of the current legislation;
(b) to pay to the competent authorities an amount equal to the contribution and tax that the employer would submit, if the foreigner had been legally employed, including administrative fines and their increments;
(c) to pay every cost associated with the mission of the payment to the country of origin of the foreigner, if the foreigner has returned or has been forced to return there.

832. Employment without a residence permit and with a subsequent issuing of an employment permit is allowed to foreign workers to industries or mines if (a) employment is urgent with a duration of up to three months for the repairing of damages of machinery, equipment or facilities; and (b) the employed foreign worker

363. *Ibid.*

possess technical or scientific skills that Hellenes unemployed persons do not possess or if there is a clause in the guarantee that provisions the repairing or maintenance only by foreign workers.[364]

§4. Special Provisions

833. There are special provisions for those employed in official foreign diplomatic missions or under bilateral international agreements or from European countries out of EU or from countries of Asia and Africa.

364. L. 448/1968.

Chapter 9. Minors, Women, Parents

§1. Minors

834. The employment of minors is regulated, mainly, by Law 1837/1989, as well as by PD 62/1998, which incorporated Directive 94/33/EC into Hellenic national law. Legal restrictions on the employment of minors are found in Law 4029/1912, in RD 590/1968, etc., which were modified by Article 11 of Law 1414/1984 and by Law 2918/2001, which ratified ILO Convention 182/1999 on the 'Worst Forms of Child Labour and the Actions Required for the Extinction of Child Labour'.

835. By the aforementioned Law 1837/1989, those who have not completed their 18th year are considered minors. Minors must not be employed in dangerous, heavy or unhealthy work, or in tasks that are a threat to their psychological health or that limit the development of their personality.

836. Before being employed in any capacity, minors must participate in vocational training programmes, which are organized and carried out by OAED, which grants certification to the minors participated in them.

837. Minors may not be employed without an employment card issued for the specific job or work area. For the issuance of this card, medical certification is required, showing that the specific job endangers neither the health of minors nor their mental and physical development. This certification is undertaken by medical services following medical examinations. These medical examinations are free of charges and include general examinations, as well as such specialized examinations as may be determined appropriate in the judgment of the doctor authorized to issue the medical certificate.

838. Minors under 16 years of age, as well as minors who study in high schools or vocational schools, public or private, that are certified by the state, are allowed to work for no more than six hours per day and thirty hours per week. Minors are entitled to a daily rest period of at least twelve hours, in which the time period of 10 pm to 6 am must be included. Overtime work for minors is forbidden.

839. Minors under 15 years of age may not be employed. However, under a licence from the Inspectorate of Labour, they may be employed in theatrical, musical or other cultural events, in television spots or advertisements, in fashion shows, in radio or television shows, in cinema, or as models, provided that neither their mental and physical health nor their morality will be harmed. For the employment of minors in cultural or similar events, vocational training and an employment card are not required. However, this type of work cannot exceed two hours per day forminors of no more than 6 years old, three hours for minors of 6 to 11 years, four hours for minors of between 11 and 13 years, and five hours for minors of 13 to 15 years of age.

840. Minors receive the remuneration set in accordance with the terms of the NGCA concerning unskilled workers, and in proportion to the hours that they are employed.

841. More favourable work conditions and higher remuneration can be set by collective agreements.

842. Minors have all the rights that arise from the valid individual labour contract, regardless of their contract is valid or void.

843. The employer, apart from the health and safety measures that are laid down for all employees, is also obliged to take additional protection measures for minors in the workplace, to inform them of any danger that threaten their lives, health and physical and mental development and to guide them towards the adoption of appropriate measures to avoid the above dangers.

844. The employer is obliged to protect minors from acts of violence, insult to their personality or harm to their morality.

845. Persons who have been convicted of sex crimes, sexual abuse, economic exploitation of sexuality or offences concerning the misuse of drugs, are barred from being employers of minors.

846. Penal sanctions are imposed on those employers, or their representatives, who intentionally or negligently breach the provisions of Law 1837/1989.

§2. WOMEN

847. There are no special provisions concerning women in the workplace. In accordance with the principles of equal treatment and of non-discrimination, any discrimination based on sex/gender is forbidden.

848. There are special provisions for the maintenance of equal treatment between women and men in actual practice.

849. The need to protect pregnancy, maternity and paternity have led to the adoption of specific provisions concerning mainly the granting of special leaves, the creation of flexible work time and protection from dismissal.

§3. Protection of Employees with Large Families, Persons with Disabilities, Veterans, Etc.

850. Some categories of employees are protected by special provisions that aim to facilitate their access to work positions.[365] These groups mainly consist of:

(a) employees from large families and their children;
(b) employees with disability of more than 50%, with limited capabilities for work because of a chronic physical or medical or psychological disease or damage (persons with special needs), as well as their parents, their siblings and the spouses of persons with disability of at least 67%;
(c) those who participated in the national resistance during the Second World War and their children;
(d) children, living spouses and living parents of persons who were executed or died from injuries or maltreatment because of their participation in the resistance to the military junta of 21 April 1967 to 24 July 1974;
(e) those handicapped and wounded by war or similar events, those who were rendered disabled by mistreatment while serving in any position in the armed forces or in the security corps and their children, victims of war including non-combatant civilian victims and their children, as well as those disabled in peacetime and their children.

851. Only one member of the above-mentioned families is protected.

852. The protection entails that the protected person is obligatorily hired by a company as described in the next paragraph, while special conditions of protection apply to their dismissal. The minimum age for their hiring or assignment to a post is 21 years, while the maximum age is 45.

853. Enterprises or undertakings, national or foreign, having their operation in Hellas in any form, as well as their subsidiaries, if they have more than 50 employees, are obliged to hire the above-mentioned groups of persons.[366] In enterprises so defined, protected persons are to be taken on to a percentage of up to 8% of the total of employees of the enterprise or the undertaking. Exceptions to the above are enterprises or undertakings that have shown a loss in their balance sheets in the two years previous to the job offer.

854. The selection and assignment to a post of a protected person, in accordance with the procedure and criteria defined by law, are made by a committee comprising a member of the Legal Council of the State or a higher administrative employee (with his/her deputies), as President of the Committee, two employees from the OAED, a representative of SEV, a representative from the Supreme Confederation

365. L. 3643/1998 with its supplements and complements.
366. This also applies to bodies of the public sector, banks and public owned companies. In these cases special provisions exist.

of Multi-Child Parents of Hellas (ASPE) or a representative from the National Confederation of Persons with Special Needs (ESAEA) or a representative of war veterans or of members of the national resistance. The choice of the Committee complements the choice of the employer and is notified to him or her. The labour contract between the selected employee and the employer is completed on the appearance of the person at the workplace. If the employer refuses the assignment of the employee, the employee is considered to be in a state of deferred employment and is remunerated accordingly.[367] The employee hired under the regime of protection is to receive equal treatment, in accordance with his/her skills, to the other employees, as concerns work terms, remuneration, promotion and work conditions in general.[368]

855. The labour relation of a protected person is ended:

(a) automatically when the person reaches the age limit set by the regulations of the enterprise, if he/she has the right to a pension because of old age or disability;
(b) with the termination of the labour contract with no severance pay if the protected person loses his or her civil rights;
(c) with the termination of the labour contract, following a decision of the Committee, for misconduct against enterprise regulations for which dismissal is provisioned as a sanction, for proven inefficiency or unsuitability for the work which cannot be attributed to her or his injuries or disabilities, or for antisocial or inappropriate conduct;
(d) with the termination of the labour contract after the completion of the prerequisites for a full pension.

856. Breaches of the provisions of Law 2643/1998 bring administrative sanctions upon the employer.

---

367. Article 656 of the CC.
368. AP 77/2009.

Chapter 10. Inventions and Copyright

§1. Inventions by Employees

857. Inventions are new technical creations, devices or innovations. In contemporary enterprises, they usually result from the activities of employees, where the employee has the chance to develop something new. These new inventions concern the discovery of new products, of new methods of production, or the improvement of existing methods. The problem which arises is that of how the protection of the rights to an invention may be assured for the person of the employee since the invention is mostly the product of his or her mind. Up to 1987, Article 668 of the CC was the basic law on inventions.

858. Then, in 1987, Law 1733/1987 abolished Article 668 of the CC, so issues related to employees' inventions have since been regulated by this Law. An invention that is created by an employee belongs to him or her (a free invention), *unless* this is a 'service invention', which belongs to the employer, or a 'dependent invention', where 40% belongs to the employer and 60% to the employee.[369] A 'service invention' is the product of a contractual relationship between an employee and an employer for the development of an inventive activity. In the case of the creation of a service invention, the employee is entitled to additional fair remuneration if the invention is beneficial to the employer.[370] 'Dependent inventions' are those inventions that are created by an employee with the use of means, material or information belonging to the company where he or she works. In that case, the employer can make use of the dependent invention, having priority for its use and pays the inventor in proportion to the value of the invention and the profits that the invention brings to the company.

859. The inventor of a dependent invention notifies his or her employer without delay, in writing, of the invention and provides the necessary means for the joint submission of an application for a patent. If the employer does not declare to the employee in writing and within four months of the initial notification, his or her interest in making a joint patent application, the application is submitted only by the employee, who now has full rights to the invention.[371] Any agreement that limits the aforementioned rights of either side is void.[372]

§2. Employees and Copyright

860. If the employee in the course of his or her work creates a piece of work that is an object of copyright, the primary beneficiary of the financial and moral rights is the creator of the work in accordance with Article 2 of Law 1733/1987. In

369. Article 6, para. 4 of L. 1733/1987.
370. Article 6, para. 5 of L. 1733/1987.
371. Article 6, para. 6 of L. 1733/1987.
372. Article 6, para. 7 of L. 1733/1987.

the absence of any agreement to the contrary only those benefits of the intellectual property right which are necessary for the fulfilment of the aim of the contract are automatically transferred to the employer.[373]

373. Article 8 of L. 2121/1993.

Chapter 11. The Ending of the Individual Labour Contract

§1. General Remarks

861. Employees' interest in maintaining their positions and the prevalence of job security is evident in the Hellenic labour law which is applied to the ending of the employment contract and especially to the unilateral termination by the employer or the employee. The right to work is also protected by the Constitution by Article 22 paragraph 1. As a consequence of this development of job security, the labour relation acquires freedom and certain remedies for the employee, when the good functioning of the enterprise is affected.

862. A general rule that everything that restricts the job security of the employee will be narrowly interpreted has an affirmative influence, e.g., on the ideas of the permanent position of employees or on justified dismissals or dismissals under certain conditions. Of course, the principle of freedom of labour must always prevail in labour relations, parallel to the above ideas.

863. The employer is obliged to enter (announcement) in the ERGANI information system (electronic platform) of the Ministry of Labour, any case of voluntary departure by an employee or dismissal of a labour contract of indefinite duration or natural ending of a fixed-term labour contract or of a contract of work no later than four working days from the date of the departure or the dismissal or the termination respectively. Otherwise, the labour contract is deemed not to have terminated.[374]

864. The hearing of an action or ordinary litigation means concerning a dispute over void dismissal, overdue salary payments or unpaid wages should be fixed on a date within sixty days of the filing of the action. Should the hearing be postponed, the date of the new hearing should be within thirty days of the last. The court's decision should be published within thirty days of the hearing.[375]

§2. The Protection of the Position of the Employee

865. The protection of the position of work is made with the following indicative ways:

(a) the enactment of rules of *jus cogens* that set the preconditions for the termination of the labour contract by the employer and that non-compliance with them brings the invalidity of the termination and therefore the continuance of the contract;
(b) that the termination is the last measure that can be taken by the employer since he has previously depleted the ability to proceed to a change of the contract in

374. Article 38 of L. 4488/2017.
375. Article 621 para. 3 KPolD as amended by Art. 47 of L. 4488/2017.

order to avoid the termination, as it is extensively described in the next paragraphs for the prohibition of the abusive exercise of the right of the termination from the employer;

(c) that the employer has been provided with the ability to put the personnel in temporary lay-off or to apply of work by rotation in order to avoid the termination of the contract in cases where the operation of the enterprise is decreased.

§3. Temporary Lay-off

866. Concerning the ability of the employer to put the employees in temporary lay-off the following apply.[376]

I. Provisions

867. If the economic activity of the enterprise has been decreased, the employer may, instead of proceeding to the termination of the contract, put a part or all of the employees of the enterprise in temporary lay-off. 'Temporary lay-off' is when the obligation of the employees for the provision of work is suspended, but they receive the half of the average of the usual remuneration of the last two months of regular employment.

II. Duration

868. The duration of the temporary lay-off cannot exceed three months per year. After the completion of the trimester, in order for the same employee to be put again on a reserve scheme, there must be an interval of three months.

III. Information and Consultation with the Employees

869. In order for the employer to put the employees in temporary lay-off previous information and consultation with the representatives of the employees must take place.

870. If there are no employees' representatives in the enterprise, information and consultation take place with the total of the employees.

871. Information must take place with a notice in an apparent and readily accessible place of the enterprise. Consultation takes place in a place and time defined by the employer.

376. Article 10 of L. 3198/1955 as completed by Art. 1 of LD 206/1974 and replaced by Art. 4 of L. 3846/2010.

872. The employer is obliged to notify the competent agencies of SEPE, IKA and OAED in any way, of the relevant notification for the temporary lay-off of a part or of the total of his employees.

IV. The Role of the Authorities

873. An authorization from the Minister of Labour and Social Insurance is required for a temporary lay-off if the enterprise is for public utility or employs more than 5,000 employees. This authorization is issued under a request of the employer and after the opinion of the Plenary of the ASE. If there is no response from the Minister in one month after the request of the employer, the employer may proceed without the authorization to the reserve scheme of the employees, in accordance with the procedure and the preconditions of the previous paragraph.

V. Consequences in Case of Illegal Temporary Lay-off

874. Enterprises of the previous paragraph that put their employees in temporary lay-off, in breach of the above preconditions, are obliged to pay full remuneration, even if the employees have accepted the temporary lay-off and have not provided their services.

§4. Work by Rotation

875. Concerning the ability of the employer to unilaterally impose work by rotation the following apply.[377] In the case where the operation of the enterprise is decreased, instead of the termination of the contract, the employer may unilaterally impose work by rotation. The duration of the rotation is prohibited to exceed nine months during the same calendar year and previous information and consultation with the representatives of the employees is required. The agreements or the decisions related with this paragraph are notified in a period of eight days from their conclusion or reception to the competent Labour Inspectorate.

§5. Different Ways for the Ending of the Individual Labour Contract

876. An individual labour contract may come to an end in different ways. Some of these also apply to the termination of contracts in general, such as:

(a) the death of the employee.[378] The heirs have the right to receive any outstanding earnings, compensation, holiday pay, bonuses, etc.;

377. Article 38 of L. 1892/1990 as replaced by Art. 2 of L. 2639/1998, Art. 2 of L. 3846/2010 and Art. 17 of L. 1899/2010.
378. Article 675, para. 1 of the CC.

(b) the death of the employer. In that case, the court may award, on its judgment, to the employee a fair compensation;
(c) the coincidence of the characteristics of employer and employee in the same person. There exists no such coincidence when the employee becomes a member of the legal person that is the employer, e.g., a company, because in such cases the legal person remains the employer;
(d) the expiration of the period for which the contract for a definite period was concluded;[379]
(e) by a party's unilateral decision, called 'resignation' by the employee and 'dismissal' by the employer (*stricto sensu* termination of the labour contract);[380]
(f) a condition in the labour contract for the termination of the contract;
(g) a new contract between the employer and the employee for the termination of the contract.

877. In the cases (f) and (g) it is highly possible that a termination of the contract is concealed by the employer as well as his/her effort to avoid the compliance with the preconditions set by the law for the termination of the labour contract. For that reason, when these ways of termination appear, this possibility must be thoroughly examined, and if it is found that a termination is concealed by the employer, the new contract for the termination of the labour contract or the condition in the labour contract is void and the contract is not terminated.

§6. Facts That Do Not Terminate the Labour Contract

878. The following do not terminate the individual labour contract:

(a) the fulfilment of the employee of all requirements for retirement;
(b) military service of the employee,[381] if he has already provided his work for six months and the labour contract is a valid contract of indefinite time;
(c) the bankruptcy,[382] the failure or the insolvency of the employer;
(d) the dissolution of the enterprise or part of it;
(e) the change of the person of the employer.

§7. Certification of the Work Performed

879. At the expiry of the contract, the employee may request from the employer a certificate for the type and the duration of the work performed. Certification of the quality of the work and/or of the employee's conduct is given, only by request of the employee.[383]

379. Article 669, para. 1 of the CC.
380. Article 669, para. 2 of the CC.
381. Article 1 of L. 3514/1928.
382. Article 34, para. 1 of L. 3588/2007.
383. Article 678 of the CC, Art. 2 of L. 2112/1920 and Art. 4 of RD 16/18.7.1920.

880. In any case, when the labour contract is terminated by the employer, the employer is obliged, in accordance with Article 9 of Law 3198/1955, to notify the termination to the public agency (OAED) in a time period of eight days. Similarly, the employer is obliged to inform of the resignation of the employee[384] and the expiry of the contract of definite time. The omission of these notifications brings administrative fines to the employer.

§8. Termination of the Individual Labour Contract

881. The termination (*stricto sensu*) is the usual way to end a labour contract of indefinite time. It is also the way to end a labour contract of definite time prior to the expiry of the term of the contract.

882. The termination is a unilateral action; it is called 'dismissal' when emanating from the employer and 'resignation' when emanating from the employee. In any case, the termination has to be announced to the other party in order to achieve its legal result.

883. Given the fact that the individual labour contract may be of definite or indefinite period, the termination of the contract is further examined in the following paragraphs. First, an analysis of the termination of the contract of definite period is quoted and an analysis of the termination of the contract of indefinite period follows.

§9. Termination of the Definite Period Labour Contract

I. Termination by the Employer or the Employee

884. To a labour contract of definite period, each party has the right to terminate the contract before its end (extraordinary termination) when an important reason exists.[385]

885. During the period of annual leave, the dismissal is not allowed for the employer.

A. The Concept of 'Important Reason'

886. 'Important reason' is a legal concept decided by the Supreme Court. An important reason exists not only with the liable breach of the obligations of the employee but also in cases or in the separate incident, because of which, after an examination and evaluation of the specific cases, such as the type of the work and

384. Article 6, para. 1(d) of L. 2972/2001 as replaced by Art. 65 of L. 3996/2011.
385. Article 672 of the CC.

the nature of the enterprise, is not possible to objectively, in accordance with bona fides and custom, be claimed by any of the parties, the continuation of the contract until the agreed or by law mandatory termination.[386]

887. This incident may be random or may be caused by force majeure, without being of interest which of the two parties created it.[387] Moreover, the important reason that allows the termination of the contract of definite time does not necessarily presuppose fault of that contractual party, against which, the termination is being made.[388] Bona fides does not require, in any price or sacrifice, the compliance with the agreed terms concerning the duration of the contract but sets certain limits of tolerance, which if surpassed, justify the exemption from the contractual obligation. The limit of the sacrifice, which may or not be claimed, is defined by the court in the specific case, after a general assessment of the specific circumstances and the balancing of all the conflicting interests of the parties. The above happens, after it is taken into account that the labour contract creates a relation of personal cooperation and mutual trust, the absence of which brings the unsuitability of the salaried for the work that he/she had been hired for.

888. Therefore, the substantial breach of the contractual obligations of the employee, such as the rejection of the provision of work, the breach of the faith obligation, the occupational inefficiency or incapability, the brutal or abusive conduct towards the employer or his/her fellow workers, are important reasons that objectively make the continuance of the employment relationship intolerable by the employer.[389] Even if the facts are outside of the sphere of action and responsibility of the employer and the employee, these may be important reasons, if they adversely affect the function of the contract and make intolerable its continuance.

889. Therefore, an important reason may be founded not only by a criminal conviction but also by the alleged commission of a criminal offence, especially when the employee is in a position of confidence, as well as the crisis of the confidence in the relationship of the employer towards the employee. Even the possible acquittal of the employee is not sufficient to reverse the existence of an important reason for the termination of the contract of the employee.[390]

890. The cause of damage to the employer or the danger of a cause of damage in the future from an unconventional behaviour of the employee, is not a precondition for the existence of an important reason, and the employee is kept in his/her position.[391] Economic problems that are not a threat to the substance of the enterprise and cash-flow difficulties of the enterprise are not considered as important reasons while an important reason is that the employee has fulfilled the preconditions for a full pension.

---

386. APol 10/1995, AP 451/2005, AP 824/2005, AP 20/2004, AP 112/2004.
387. AP 1533/2004.
388. AP 332/2000.
389. AP 1609/2003.
390. AP 112/2004.
391. Ef. Athens 4155/2008.

891. In cases of disagreement what constitutes an 'important reason' is up to the court to decide. For the definition of an incident as an important reason, bona fides and customary practices are taken into consideration, as well as the specific circumstances that accompany these incidents in the specific case. In the case of claiming, by the complainant of multiple incidents, the examination of one of them is sufficient if this incident truly justifies the premature termination of the contract. Otherwise, the total of these incidents is examined and if, cumulatively, burden the employment relationship in such degree, that the complainant cannot tolerate the contract's continuance.[392]

892. The knowledge of the complainant of the crucial facts for the establishment of the important reason is not a prerequisite for the validity of the termination and the complainant may claim in trial, for the validity of the termination, for first time new reasons, which pre-existed and they were known to him/her or came to his/her knowledge after the termination.[393]

B. No Severance Pay

893. According to the law, severance pay is not given due to the termination of the labour contract of definite period. Nevertheless, a severance pay may be due according to a condition of the contract or the applied collective agreement.

C. Cases in which Compensation Should Be Paid

894. There are specific cases in which, according to special provisions of law, a compensation should be paid due to the termination of the contract:

(1) obligation of any of the two parties for the payment of compensation: If the important reason, which justified the termination, is based on a breach of the contract, the person that breached the contract, either the complainant or the accuser, is obliged to pay compensation.[394] The amount of the compensation is defined by the court. The relevant claim must be made in a fair time from the termination of the contract;
(2) obligation of the employer for the payment of the compensation:
    (a) if the employer proceeded to the termination of the contract and the important reason was the change of his/her personal or economic situation, the court may, on his judgment, grand to the employee a fair compensation.[395] The relevant claim must be made in fair time after the termination of the contract;

392. AP 1515/2003, AP 1247/2002.
393. AP 112/2004.
394. Article 673 of the CC.
395. Article 674 of the CC.

(b) in accordance with Article 8 sub-paragraph a of Law 3189/1955, which, under some opinions, may be applied to the labour contract of definite time.[396] the employee may terminate the contract if the following exist cumulatively:
  - the employee has completed 15 years of service to the employer or his/her age for retirement in accordance with his/her insurer (obligatory insurance) and, in absence of such age limit, the 62 years old;
  - the employer concurs with the employee's removal from the work. In that case, the employer is obliged to pay half of the compensation to the employee that he/she would get if the termination was made by the employer without complying to a deadline. For this compensation, all the above mentioned concerning the compensation due by the employer when he/she proceeds to the termination of the indefinite time contract apply, without complying to the deadline and especially for the manner of the calculation and the time of the payment.

(c) in accordance with Article 8 sub-paragraph (b) of Law 3198/1955, as amended by Article 8 paragraph 4 of Law 3789/1957 and replaced by Article 5 paragraph 1 of Law 435/1976:
  - if the employee proceeded to the termination of the contract and the important reason of the termination was that the employee fulfilled the preconditions for full pension, the employer is obliged to pay compensation equal to the amount of the compensation that the employee would be entitled of, if the contract was of indefinite time and if the employer proceeded to the termination without complying with a deadline. This percentage is 40% if the employee is insured supplementary and 50% if he/she is not. For this compensation all the above mentioned concerning the compensation due by the employer when he/she proceeds to a termination of the contract of indefinite time without complying with a deadline will apply and especially for the manner of the calculation and the time of the payment;
  - if the employee is a white-collar employee and fulfils the criteria for full pension from his/her insurer (compulsory insurance), the employer is entitled to proceed to a termination of the contract by claiming that reason as an important one. In that case, the employer is obliged to pay the compensation mentioned in point (i).

D. No Contractual Exclusion of the Termination for an Important Reason

895. The termination of the contract of definite period for important reason may not be excluded under an agreement between the employer and the employee.[397] Specific reasons that, because of their specific circumstances and the nature of the

396. *See* contra AP 19/2013 that this is applied only in employment contracts of indefinite time.
397. AP 703/2006; Art. 672, sub-para. B of the CC.

work, can be characterized as important reasons may be included in the labour contract or in the work's regulation of the enterprise.[398] In that way, some incidents that objectively are not characterized as important reasons can be characterized as such. Similarly, some incidents that would be objectively characterized as important reasons can be defined as non-important reasons. Such agreements cannot refer to so many incidents that would, objectively, make possible the termination of the contract for any reason, nor can they exclude such incidents that would objectively prohibit the termination for an important reason.

E. No Need for Specific Type for the Termination

896. Law does not require the compliance with a specific type for the termination of the contract of definite period. However, in practice, the written type is usual in order for its evidence to be clear. The important reason, for which the termination is made, is not necessary to be part of the content of the document,[399] but if it is, the employer, in case that a trial takes place, may claim a different or more reasons in court.

F. No Need for Notice Period

897. There is no notice period for the above-mentioned termination. However, the termination must be made in a fair time from the appearance of the important reasons otherwise the right to terminate the contract is weakened and consequently the termination of the contract may be judged null and void.

G. Void Termination: Employee's Rights

898. If there is no important reason or if the proposed as important one is judged differently and therefore do not justify the premature termination of the contract, the termination is invalid, therefore null and void.[400] The invalidity is in favour of the employee, being the only one to claim it. Subsequently, the employee has the right to either (a) to consider that the termination is void or (b) to consider it valid. If he/she chooses (a), the employee may bring an action before the Labour Court to nullify the termination. The action must be introduced within three months of the dismissal.[401] If the termination is nullified, it is considered that it never took place and the employer has to pay the employee the wages from the day of the termination until the day of the final decision of the court. The employer is also obliged to

398. AP 220/2002.
399. AP 824/2005, AP 14/1999.
400. APol 10/1995, AP 824/2005, AP 1371/1999, AP 100/1996, AP 438/1993.
401. Article 6, para. 1 of L. 3198/1955.

continue the labour contract until the normal expiry with the completion of its definite period. If he/she chooses (b), it is considered that the employee resigned from the said right.[402]

H. Termination of Labour Contract and Equal Treatment

899. The claim by the employee that the employer treated in milder means other employees that erred in similar offences is not legal, because the principle of equal treatment does not concern issues of termination. Therefore, the termination of the contract of an employee is legal, regardless of the fact that other employees that had committed in the past similar offences simply had administrative penalties.[403]

§10. Termination of Labour Relation of Indefinite Time

I. Introduction

900. Each party, the employer and the employee, can terminate an indefinite time contract.

901. Laws lay down the manner to terminate labour contracts of indefinite time. For all the employees, with few exceptions, the dismissal is regulated by a great number of statutes. The most important of them are Laws 2112/1920, 3198/1955 and RD of 16/18 July 1920. Numerous amendments have been made in this legislation, with the important ones being in the period 2010–2018 especially by Laws 4093/2012, 4111/2013 and 4488/2017. The following paragraphs are a result of the combination of these provisions that were in effect on the date of this publication.

II. Termination by the Employer: Dismissal

A. Preconditions for Lawful Dismissal

902. The employer, in order to proceed to the termination of the labour contract of indefinite period, is obliged to comply with the following preconditions:[404]

(1) for a labour contract that lasted up to twelve months:

402. AP 1515/2003, Ef. Athens 264/2007.
403. AP 1407/2005, AP 474/1993, AP 1902/90.
404. Special provisions apply for the termination of the contract of the employees with a contract of subordinate employment in the public sector, legal persons of public law, associations of local authority and for the limitation of the amount of their compensation as well as for employees in public organizations and public utility organizations.

(a) employee covered by compulsory social insurance: the employee must be insured in the organization for the compulsory social insurance of the employees' (IKA);[405]

(b) the dismissal must be in writing: the dismissal must be in writing; otherwise it is null and void. The document of the dismissal must clearly indicate that the labour contract is terminated, must be signed by the employer or his/her legal representative and must be notified to the employee. The document is notified to the employee and the same time the contract is terminated (dismissal).[406]

(2) for a labour contract that lasted more than twelve months:

(a) employee covered by compulsory social insurance: the employee must be insured in the organization for the compulsory social insurance of the employees' (IKA);[407]

(b) the dismissal must be in writing: the dismissal must be in writing; otherwise it is null and void. The content of the document must clearly indicate that the labour contract is terminated and must be signed by the employer or his/her legal representative. The document must be notified to the employee and the labour contract is terminated as follows:

- if the employee is a white-collar one, immediately with the notification of the document in the case of dismissal without a notice period or after the expiry of a notice period in the case of dismissal with a period of time;[408]
- if the employee is a blue-collar one, immediately with the notification of the document.

(c) the payment of the severance pay to the dismissed employee:

- if the employee is a white-collar one, the amount of the severance pay depends on the monthly remuneration, the employee's seniority in the enterprise and the compliance or not by the employer with the notice period. The employer may comply a notice period, the duration of which depends on the duration of the labour contract until the date of its termination. In this case, he/she pays the minimum amount of severance pay. If the employer does not comply with the notice period, the amount of the severance pay is doubled. The employees that worked on 12 November 2012 and had a completed seniority of more than 17 years to the same employer are paid, whenever the contract is terminated, with an additional compensation which refers to the following table;[409]
- if the employee is a blue-collar one, the amount of the severance pay depends on the monthly remuneration and the employee's seniority in the enterprise.

---

405. Article 2, para. 4 of L. 2556/1997.
406. Article 5, para. 3 of L. 3198/1955.
407. Article 2, para. 4 of L. 2556/1997.
408. Article 74, para. 2 of L. 3863/2010.
409. Article 3, para. 3 of L. 2112/1920, Art. 12 paras 3, 4 of L. 4093/2012.

903. Tables for the above-mentioned severance pay and notice period are given in Annex 3.

B. Higher Severance Pay: Longer Period for Notice

904. Under customary practices higher severance pay may be paid, while under a term of a collection agreement or an DA or the individual labour contract higher compensation may be agreed or a longer term of notice.

905. The employer is due to the payment of the severance pay even when he/she terminated the labour contract for a liable non-fulfilment or inadequate fulfilment of the obligations of the employee. Non-payment of severance pay or a payment of a decreased severance pay is justified only in the cases explicitly provisioned in the law and which are mentioned in the following paragraphs.

C. Obligation for the Payment of Severance Pay in All Cases

906. The employer is obliged to pay a severance pay when he/she dismisses the employee, even if he/she makes the dismissal because the employee has breached the contract purposely.[410] No payment or payment of a part of the severance pay is legal only when the law regulates so explicitly, as it is analysed below.

D. No Obligation for the Payment of Severance Pay

907. In accordance with the legislation the employee is not entitled for severance pay if he/she provokes his/her dismissal by his/her malicious conduct in order to receive the severance pay (abuse of law).

E. Calculation of Severance Pay

908. The severance pay is calculated on the basis of ordinary remuneration of the last month of employment under the usual, ordinary conditions of the dismissed employee.[411] For the calculation of the compensation of an employee, the monthly remunerations that exceed the eight times of a daily wage of an unskilled worker, multiplied by thirty, are not taken into account.[412]

909. Especially for the calculation of the additional severance pay that the employees that were working on 12 November 2012 and had completed a seniority

410. AP 1691/2012.
411. Article 3, para. 1 of L. 2112/1920, as amended by Art. 1, para. IA sub-para. IA. Art. 12, para. 2 of L. 4093/2012, Art. 5, para. 1 of L. 3198/1955.
412. Article 5, para. 1 of L. 3198/1955.

of more than seventeen months to the same employee are entitled for, this is calculated on the ordinary remuneration of the last month up to the amount of EUR 2,000. This limitation does not apply for severance pay that is paid for the termination of the contract because of the retirement of the employee.[413]

910. When the employees are remunerated with percentages or in relation to the results of their work, the severance pay is calculated in relation to the average of their remuneration during the last two months before the termination of the contract. However, the amount of the remuneration may not be less than the wage of the employee's wage scale of his/her insurance.[414]

F. Cases in Which Reduced Severance Pay Is Paid

911. A reduced severance pay is paid in the cases explicitly defined by law:

(a) in accordance with Article 8 sub-paragraph (a) of Law 3198/1955, when the labour contract is terminated because the employee has completed 15 years' service to the employer or his/her age limit for retirement, as provisioned by his/her insurer (compulsory insurance), and in case of an absence of such limit, he/she is 62 years old, the employee receives half of the amount of the severance pay;
(b) in accordance with Article 8 sub-paragraph b of Law 3198/1955, as amended by Article 8 paragraph 4 of Law 3789/1957 and replaced by Article 5 paragraph 1 of Law 435/1976, when the termination is due to the retirement of the employee, the employee is paid 40% or 50% of the amount of the severance pay;
(c) in accordance with Article 4 of Law 3198/1955, if the employee leaves during the notification deadline with the consent of the employer, then the employer is obliged to pay half of the amount of the severance pay that the employee would be entitled of, if the employer proceeded to the termination of the contract without complying with the deadline;
(d) in accordance with Article 6 paragraph 2 of Law 2112/1920, if the employer proceeds to the termination of the contract because the operation of the enterprise has stopped due to a fire or other reason of force majeure and if the employer was insured for that risk, the employee is paid the two-thirds of the amount of the severance pay that is due for termination without notice.[415]

---

413. Article 3, para. 3 of L. 2112/1920, Article First para. IA under para. IA.12 para. 3, 4 of L. 4093/2012.
414. Article 5, para. 2 of L. 3198/1955.
415. Article 6 of 2112/1920, as completed by Art. 4 of L. 4558/1930, Art. 9 para. 2 of RD 16/18 July 1920.

G. Time for the Payment of Severance Pay

912. As already mentioned, the severance pay defined in Law 2112/1920 must be paid at the day of the termination of the contract.[416] However, when the severance pay exceeds the remuneration of two months, the employer is obliged to pay, on the day of the termination of the labour contract a part of the severance pay that corresponds to the remuneration of two months. The rest of the amount is paid on bimonthly instalments, and each of these instalments cannot be less than the remuneration of two months unless the amount that is due for the full payment of the severance pay is less. The first instalment is paid on the next day of the completion of the two months from the termination.[417]

H. Non-compliance with the Preconditions by the Employer

913. If the employer terminated the contract of indefinite period without complying with the written type, without paying the severance pay and without the employee being insured, the termination is void and is considered as it is not made[418] and the employer that rejects the work of the employee becomes default.[419] The invalidity of the termination is set in favour of the employee and is relevant; thus, the employee may (a) adhere to the invalidity of the termination and ask for due payments or (b) consider the termination valid and request the severance pay defined by law or the larger severance pay that has been agreed in the individual labour contract.[420]

I. Void Dismissal of a Void Labour Contract

914. However, if the contract that was terminated was void, the employee has only a claim on the payment of severance pay.[421]

J. Void Dismissal and Employees' Claims

915. If the employee wishes to doubt the validity of the dismissal and to make claims because of this invalidity, he/she may bring an action before the Labour Court within three months from the termination.[422]

---

416. Article 2 of L. 3198/1955.
417. Article 74, para. 3 of L. 3863/2010.
418. Article 180 of the CC, Art. 5, para. 3 of L. 3198/1955 as replaced by Art. 2, para. 4 of L. 2556/1997.
419. Articles 349, 350 of the CC.
420. AP 590/1994, AP 701/1991, AP 947/1982, AP 816/2002, Ef. Athens 8731/2000.
421. AP 983/2000, AP 1022/1993.
422. Article 6, para. 1 of L. 3198/1955.

916. When the severance pay established by Law 2112/1920, has not been paid, all or a part of it, and the employee wishes not to challenge the validity of the termination for that reason, but only to request the payment of the severance pay, he/she may bring an action before the Labour Court. The action must be introduced within six months of the termination.[423] That time period does not apply, when the employee claims a severance pay established otherwise, e.g., a clause of a collective agreement or an DA or of the individual labour contract.

917. If the termination is nullified, it is considered that it never took place and the employer has to pay the employee the wages from the day of the termination until the day of the final decision of the court. The employer is also obliged to continue the labour contract.

K. Removal of Employer's Default

918. Furthermore, from the combination of the provisions of Articles 648, 656, 669 paragraph 2 of the CC, Articles 2 and 5 of Law 3198/1955 and Articles 1 and 3 of Law 2112/1920, it is evident that the employer that proceeded to a dismissal and became default, may repeal the default with the rehiring of the employee or with a statement that he/she accepts the services of the employee under the same employment conditions or with a subsequent valid dismissal of the same contract. This second new dismissal, which may be made by the employer subsidiary, meaning without prejudice to the previous termination and with the purpose to repeal the overdue concerning the acceptance of the services of the employee, is legally accepted and brings the termination of the contract. The validity of this dismissal is not affected by the fact that during the time of the termination the employer defaulted or by the fact that the first dismissal was not finally judged as void since the employer directly aims at the termination of the contract and the repeal of his/her default.[424]

L. Termination of the Contract with No Obligation for the Payment of Severance Pay and for Compliance with a Notice Period

919. Remuneration is always paid independently of the cause of the termination of the contract. However, it is possible for the employer to terminate the contract without the payment of a severance pay in the following cases, explicitly provisioned by the law:

(a) in the case of a bankruptcy of the enterprise severance pay is normally due; however, if it is not paid, this is not a reason for invalidity of the termination;[425]

423. *Ibid.*
424. AP 497/2011.
425. Article 34, para. 2 of L. 3588/2007.

(b) if the employer has brought an action against the employee for a criminal offence that was made during the provision of his/her work;[426]
(c) if a criminal proceeding has been made against the employee for any offence, at least of a misdemeanour, which adversely affects the continuance of the employment relationship.[427]

920. In cases (b) and (c) if the employee is acquitted with an acquittal order or a court decision, he/she is entitled to notify the employer and the employer is obliged in fair time to pay to the employee severance pay, otherwise the termination of the contract is void and the employer is due to default wages from the notification of the acquittal order or a court decision.[428] However, since the ratification of the (revised) European Social Charter by Law 4359/2016, dismissals are no longer permissible without valid grounds relating to the capacity or conduct of the employee or based on the operational requirements of the undertaking, establishment or service.[429]

M. The Dismissal Is Without Justification

921. The dismissal is without justification, meaning that its validity is not dependent on the existence of a reason that justifies it or from the legitimacy of that reason.[430] That is why, unless a different explicit legal provision exists, there is no need to include the reason of the termination in the document, and if it is included, the employer may invoke any other reasons as well.

N. Abusive Dismissal and Abuse of Law: Consequences of the Nullity of the Dismissal

922. From Article 669 paragraph 2 of the CC, 1 of Law 2112/1920 and 1 and 5 of L. 3198/1955, it is evident that the termination of the labour contract of indefinite period is unilateral unwarranted legal act, and therefore its validity is not dependent on the existence or the inadequacy of the cause because of which it was made but is a right of the employer. The exercise of this right, as in the exercise of any right, is subject to the limitation of Article 281 of the CC, meaning the non-exceedance of the limits set by bona fides, customary practices and the social or economic purpose of the right. The exceedance of these limits makes the dismissal

---

426. Article 5, para. 1 of L. 2112/1920, Art. 7 of L. 3198/1955, Art. 6, para. 2 of R.D. 16/18 July 1920.
427. *Ibid.*
428. Article 5, para. 2 of L. 2112/1920, Art. 7, para. 2 of L. 3198/1955, Art. 6, para. 3 of RD 16/18 July 1920.
429. MPLasithiu 17/2019.
430. AP 244/2017 held (like other decisions earlier) that a dismissal is not regarded as unfair in cases where there is no real or obvious reason.

void, in accordance with Articles 174 and 180 of the CC.[431] The court examines the possible abusive character of the dismissal only after a relevant claim is made by the employee.

923. The dismissal is void, as being abusive, if it is dictated by employer's humble causes that do not serve the purpose of the right of dismissal, as it happens in cases where the dismissal is made because of hate or aggression against the employee, reasons of revenge, as a result of a previous disliked conduct of the employee to the employer.[432] Similarly, when the dismissal is made for economic reasons, meaning for the reorganization of the enterprise that make necessary the decrease of the staff, if these reasons are ostensible and conceal hate or malicious conduct or when these financial reasons are real but the choice of the dismissed employees is not made with objective criteria (service or social).[433]

924. The abusive character must be based on specific reasons that must be claimed and proven by the employee, because of which reasons, the exercise of the relevant right of the employer obviously exceeds the limits set by the Article 281.[434]

O. Cases of Non-abusive Dismissal

925. A case of an abusive dismissal does not exist when no reason exists, since, in the light of all those exposed for the unwarranted character of the dismissal and its exercise in exceedance of the limits of Article 281 of the CC, in order for the termination to be considered as void or abusive, the claim that the reasons posed from the employer are false or that there was no apparent reason at all is not sufficient.

926. Finally, a dismissal is not abusive, when it has as a real motive the inadequate execution of the duties of the dismissed or, from the side of the employee, the breach of the contractual obligations; also when this is caused by real and wanted and inappropriate behaviour towards the employer or the legal representatives of the employer or his/her co-workers that disturb the orderly function or the disciplinary legal order of the enterprise.[435]

P. Dismissal by Modification of the Labour Contract

927. Where there is a reason for the termination of the labour contract by the employer, because, e.g., the employee is unable to respond efficiently to his/her

431. AP 247/2012.
432. *Ibid.*
433. AP 1649/2012.
434. *Ibid.*
435. AP 247/2012, AP 1649/2012, AP 1698/2012.

duties or behaves offensively to the clients of the enterprise or is surplus to requirements, the employer is obliged, if at all possible, to propose to the employee a proper modification of labour contract as an alternative to the dismissal. It is up to the employee to accept or reject the proposed modification and, respectively, to avoid or not the dismissal.

928. Usually the employer sets a deadline for the employee to respond, whether he/she accepts or rejects the dismissal by amendment. If the possibility of such modification exists, the employer is not allowed to proceed to a dismissal. The primary purpose is the modification of the labour contract and not the termination of it.

929. The employer may not exercise the said right in an abusive way and the judicial review to determine, whether such an abuse occurred, extends to:

(a) the reasons for the modification, which must be reasons that can support the dismissal. If the employer cannot proceed to dismissal, he/she cannot proceed to dismissal after refusal of modification of labour contract;
(b) the proposed modification, which must be justified, e.g., by the behaviour of the employee or the needs of the company;
(c) the content of the proposed modification, which (i) must, on the basis of bona fides, be potentially acceptable by the specific employee, in the specific light of her/his skills and qualifications, (ii) must be in fair relation to the cause of the amendment to the contract.

Q. Specific Cases of Dismissal

930. According to law, different procedures should be followed and certain reasons should exist for the dismissal of employees who belong in special categories, such as:

(a) Dismissal and annual leave: the dismissal of the employee is not allowed during the period of the annual leave.[436]
(b) Dismissal and military service: the dismissal of the employee is not allowed during the period of his military service. An employee who returns to his job after his military service may not be dismissed during a period of one year after his return unless the special committee of Article 7 of Law 244/1936 decides that a justified cause exists for his dismissal. If his dismissal takes place without the special committee's decision, the dismissed employee may demand (within a period of a year from the day of his dismissal), besides the common severance pay, an additional compensation equal to six months' remuneration.
(c) Dismissal and large families with special needs: parents of large families and one of their children, persons with special needs (with disability of more than

436. AP 1683/2012; Art. 5, para. 6 of E.L. 539/1945.

50%), those that participated in the National Resistance and their children), disabled and injured of war or warlike events and all those persons defined in the law, such as Article 1 of Law 2643/1998, are dismissed only for the reasons and with the procedure that is defined in Article 11 of the same Law.

(d) Dismissal and family obligations: family obligations of the employees are not a reason for dismissal.[437]

(e) Dismissal, pregnancy and childbirth: the dismissal of a pregnant employee by the employer is prohibited and absolutely void for the periods during the pregnancy, for 18 months after the childbirth and during her absence for a greater period because of an illness that is caused by the pregnancy or the childbirth, unless an important reason exists for the dismissal. A possible decrease in the efficiency of her work cannot be considered as an important reason.[438] The employer is obliged to justify in writing the dismissal and to proceed to a relevant notification to the competent Labour Inspectorate.[439]

(f) Dismissal and legal union action:
   - dismissal for legal union action is prohibited, and if it is made, it is void;[440] e.g., the employer cannot dismiss an employee who took part in a legal strike or protest or is a member of an employees' committee;
   - dismissal of the officers, members of the regular or founding or temporary Administrative Board of the trade union is prohibited for the duration of their term of office as well as for a year after the expiry of the term of office, unless if there is a reason defined by law. Law lays down a limited number of reasons, the occurrence of which justifies the termination of the employment contract of trade unionists. The reasons provided by law that make it exceptionally permissible to dismiss trade unionists include the deception of the employer, the unjustified refusal to perform work. Article 18 of L. 4472/2017 prescribes that: (a) an unjustified absence from work for more than three days constitutes a legitimate reason for the dismissal of a trade unionist. According to the previous legislative regime, the dismissal of a trade unionist was justified after seven days of absence without leave; (b) the termination of a trade unionist's employment contract is permissible when the trade unionist has committed theft or embezzlement against the employer or a representative of the employer; (c) the deception of the employer, the unjustified refusal to perform work, the disclosure of industrial secrets; (d) the falsification of credentials by the employee during the hiring process or in order to receive additional. The number of the protected members is defined by the law in relation with the number of the members of the trade union.[441] Law establishes a specific administrative procedure to ascertain whether such reasons occur in each particular case. In any case, the statutory provision under which the termination of a trade unionist's employment contract for any reason is null and void if the Special Committee for

437. Article 14 of L. 1483/1984.
438. Article 15, para. 1 of L. 1483/1984, as replaced by Art. 36, para. 1 of L. 3996/2011.
439. Article 10, para. 3 of PD 176/1997.
440. Article 14 of L. 1264/1982 as amended by Art. 7 of L. 1446/1984, Art. 34 para. 11 of L. 2956/2001, Art. 18 of L. 4472/2017.
441. Articles 14, 15 of L. 1264/1982.

the Protection of Trade Unions has not previously convened and ruled remains in force. The Committee is a collective administrative body, and its decisions constitute administrative acts subject to cassation by the StE.

(g) Dismissal and illness of the employee: an abstention of the employee from his work that is due to a relatively small duration illness is not considered as a termination of the contract from his/her part. As 'small duration illness' is considered the one that has a duration of one month for employees that have worked for four years, three months for employees that work for more than four years and up to fifteen years and six months for employees that work for more than fifteen years.[442] If the abstention is of greater duration, the conditions, possible liability of the employee, the behaviour of the employee and the employer during the abstention are examined and are evaluated objectively in order to define whether this abstention constitutes a resignation or justifies the termination of the contract by the employer.

(h) Dismissal and transfer of the enterprise: the transfer of the enterprise by itself is not a reason for the dismissal of the employees.

§11. Collective Redundancies

I. The Concept of 'Collective Redundancies'

931. Collective dismissals are regulated by Law 1387/1983, as amended by numerous laws, mainly by Article 15 of L. 2736/1999, Article 14 of L. 3863/2010, Article 21 of L. 3488/2006, Article 17 of L. 4472/2017.

932. Hellenic law considers as collective redundancies those which take place in enterprises employing more than twenty employees for reasons not connected with the face of the dismissed and exceed for every calendar month the limits set by the law. The limits, above which the redundancies are considered as collective are defined by the number of employees that are employed at the beginning of the month and are the following:

(a) up to six employees for enterprises or undertakings that employ from 20 to 150 employees;

(b) a percentage of 5% of the personnel and up to 30 employees for enterprises or undertakings that employ more than 150 employees. This percentage is defined for every calendar semester and in relation to the conditions of the labour market under a Decision of Minister of Labour, which is issued after an opinion of the ASE and is published in the Hellenic State Gazette (HSG).

933. For the calculation of the number of the redundancies, all ways of the termination of the labour contract that are made under an initiative of the employer for

---

442. Article 5, para. 3 of L. 2112/1920, as completed by Art. 3 of L. 4558/1930.

one or more reasons, which are not related to the face of the employees, are taken into account and are equalized with the redundancies, under the condition that these redundancies are at least five.

934. An employment relation is the one that is created by the effective employment of the employee regardless of the validity of the labour contract.

II. No Application of the Provisions for Collective Redundancies

935. The provisions for collective redundancies do not apply to:

(a) employees with a definite period labour contract, a contract of work, a contract for the execution of specific works unless the redundancies are made before the expiry of the contract or the completion of the work;
(b) the personnel of the public sector, associations of local authorities, legal persons of public law that is employed with an employment relationship of private law;
(c) employees that are dismissed from contracting firms because of a stop or suspension of the works that are caused by the owner of the work when this is the public sector or a legal person of public law;
(d) ship crews;
(e) dismissals that are made for reasons related to the person of the dismissed such as unconventional behaviour, lawsuits, retirement, illness, inadequacy.

III. Consultations with the Representatives of the Employees

936. The employer, before he/she proceeds to collective redundancies, should proceed to consultations with the representatives of the employees, in order to examine the possibility of avoiding the dismissals or decrease the number of the dismissals. More specifically, the employer is obliged:

(1) to provide to the representatives of the employee all useful information; and
(2) to notify them in writing of:
  (a) the reasons of the plan for the dismissals;
  (b) the number and the categories of the under dismissal employees;
  (c) the number and the categories of the usually employed employees;
  (d) the time space of the proposed dismissals;
  (e) the criteria for the choice of the employees who will be dismissed.

937. These obligations are applied regardless of whether the decision for the collective redundancies is made by the employer or by an enterprise that controls the employer.

938. For breaches of the obligations of the information, consultation and notification, the argument of the employer that the enterprise that decided the collective redundancies has not provided him with information cannot be taken into account. The lack of information of the employer from the enterprise that made the above-mentioned decision does not remove this obligation from the employer.

939. As representatives of the employees we refer to the legal representatives of the union of the employees in the company or undertaking that has as members at least 70% of the employees of the company, as well as the majority of those dismissed.

940. As part of the consultations with employees' representatives, the employer may bring to the attention of the employees a social plan concerning the employees to be dismissed, i.e., measures designed to alleviate the effects of redundancies.[443]

IV. The Time Period for the Consultations

941. There is a time period of thirty days for the consultations, which starts with the invitation of the employer to the representatives of the employees.

V. The Results of the Consultations: Proceedings Before ASE

942. The result of the consultation between the employer and the employee representatives shall be recorded in minutes signed by both parties (or, by one side, as the case may be) and submitted, together with other documentation, to the Collective Redundancies Control Division of the ASE.[444]

943. If an agreement is reached during the consultations, the redundancies should proceed accordingly following a lapse of ten days from the submission of the consultation minutes.

944. If no agreement is reached, the ASE should issue a decision, within ten days from the submission of the consultation minutes, regarding the employer's compliance with the information and consultation obligations.

945. If the ASE decides that the employer has complied with its information and consultation obligations, the redundancies should be implemented after a lapse of twenty days from the issue of the decision. If not, the ASE decides either to extend the consultations period or to set a deadline for the employer to comply.

946. If the ASE decides that the employer has met its obligations, the redundancies should be effected after the lapse of twenty days from the issue of the decision.

443. Article 3 and 5 of L. 1873/1983 and Art. 17 of L. 4472/2017.
444. Article 5 of L. 1387/1983 as amended by Art. 17 para. 3 of L. 4472/2017. Article 17 of L. 4472/2017 replaces the decisive intervention by the administration (the state intervention in collective redundancies through the Prefect or the Minister of Labour) with the proceedings before the ASE.

947. In any case, the redundancies become effective sixty days after the submission of the consultation minutes to the ASE.

948. Collective redundancies effected in breach of the provisions of the law are invalid.[445]

949. Current legislation concerning a valid dismissal and paid of the severance pay apply on collective redundancies.

VI. The Termination of the Enterprise's Activities and the Collective Redundancies

950. Should the employer willingly decides the termination of the enterprise's or establishment's activities, it is necessary that he/she notifies the representatives of the employees and makes consultations with them, as mentioned above; otherwise the dismissals are null and void.[446]

951. The same applies where the termination of the enterprise's or establishment's activities is due to a judicial decision. However, proceedings before the ASE do not apply to collective redundancies arising from termination of the enterprise's or establishment's activities where this is the result of a judicial decision.

§12. The Termination of the Labour Contract of Indefinite Period by the Employee (Resignation)

952. The employee who wishes to resign from the labour contract of indefinite period is obliged to follow a notification deadline, which duration is the half of the employer's notification for the dismissal, but its maximum duration is three months.[447] If the employee does not follow the deadline, he is obliged to pay to employer compensation equal to his/her remuneration of the notification deadline, which cannot be more than the remuneration of three months.[448] The payment of such a compensation is rare in practice

953. The non-compliance with the above obligations does not harm the validity of the resignation.

954. The resignation is tacitly or informally without a written statement, but without leaving any misinterpretation about the will of the employee to terminate the labour contract.[449]

---

445. AP 786/2017.
446. APol 37-40/2007, AP 1541/2011.
447. Article 4 of L. 2112/1920.
448. Article 4 of L. 2112/1920.
449. AP 221/1993, AP 315/1969.

955. Arbitrary absence from the work is usually considered by the legislation as resignation.[450]

956. If the employee has been forced by the employer to leave his/her job, the termination is considered as dismissal and the employee may ask for compensation.

957. If the white-collar employee resigns after a service of fifteen years or when he/she fulfils the precondition for receiving his/her pension at a certain age (or the 65th year of age if a different eventuality is not foreseen in a special law), the employee may ask for severance pay amounting to half of the sum for the severance pay due to dismissal without notice period. If the employee has fulfilled or fulfils the preconditions for a full pension he/she also receives 50% of the severance pay due to dismissal without notice or 40% of it if he/she is eligible to receive assisting insurance from his/her fund.

450. APol 32/1988.

Chapter 12. Transfer of the Enterprise

§1. Law 2112/1920 and PD 16/1920

958. Hellenic legislation has for many years ensured the preservation of employees' rights in cases where, during a dependent employment relation, the employing enterprise is transferred to a third party and the identity of the employer changes. Article 6 paragraph 1 of Law 2112/1920[451] as well as Article 9 paragraph 1 of RD 16/1920[452] stipulate that a change in the identity of the employer, in whatsoever manner that this may take place, does not affect the application of those provisions favourable to employees in the case of the termination of the employment contract.

I. The Protection of Employees

959. In accordance with these provisions, and a large number of others of similar content, jurisprudence has formed the legal rule that the person whom for any reason and by any legal form (e.g., by law, by contract or de facto) succeeds the employer (is the 'successor') in the enterprise, automatically takes on the position of the initial employer (referred to henceforth as the 'transferor') and automatically assumes the rights and obligations that arise concerning the employment relationship; here, the consent of the employee, the wishes of the transferor or the wishes of the successor are neither required nor relevant.[453]

960. The specific legal manner of the transfer and the validity of this act are not a concern of labour law. Rather, what matters is the real fact that a third party assumes the status of the employer, even temporarily, and that the identity of the enterprise and its economic activity remains the same.[454]

II. The Concept of the 'Undertaking'

961. The term 'enterprise' covers an enterprise, an undertaking, part of these. Hellenic labour law does not define the concept of the enterprise or the undertaking; it is however mentioned that an enterprise is an organization of capital and labour with the aim of profit, while an undertaking is any organized economic unit for the attainment of a technical, scientific or productive aim.

962. When the enterprise is organized in a centralized way in one production unit, the concepts of enterprise and undertaking coincide. When the enterprise is

---

451. 'The change of employer, however this may take place, does not affect the application of the favourable provisions for the employees of the current Law.'
452. 'The change of the identity of the employer, in any way that it may occur, does not in any way affect the application of the those provisions of this Law favourable to the employee.'
453. AP 1900/1987, AP 1113/1987, AP 187/1979.
454. APol 5/1994, AP 1673/2002, AP 1850/2006.

organized in a decentralized way, into various distributed production units, these concepts may be distinguished, and the enterprise may comprise multiple separate undertakings, each having functional (administrative), economic and legal autonomy.[455]

III. The Transfer of an Enterprise or an Undertaking

963. The transfer of an enterprise or an undertaking refers to any type of acquisition or continuation of the economic activity by a third party, if the identity of the enterprise and undertaking is not changed, meaning that the same enterprise, as an economic unit, continues and preserves its identity, under the control of the new party, with the same or a different title or form.[456]

§2. PD 178/2002

964. In parallel with these provisions, PD 178/2002 by which was incorporated into national law Directive 98/50/EC for the protection of the employees in the case of the transfer of an enterprise, an undertaking or part of them.[457]

I. The Regulations of PD 178/2002

965. The application of PD 178/2002 is extended to those cases where the transfer of the enterprise takes place with transfers made by contracts or by law. In accordance with prevailing opinion in jurisprudence and theory, and under the regime of PD 178/2002, a transfer of an enterprise is the acquisition and continuation of the economic activity by a third party, if the identity of the enterprise or of the undertaking remains the same, meaning that it continues, as an economic unit, to function as an enterprise, facility or department.

966. For the transfer of an enterprise, or undertaking, or its departments, to take legal effect, this transfer has to be made in such a way that the transferred assets will preserve their functional unity and will be capable, under the new employer, of potentially attaining the targeted profit, economic or technical aims. This means that the transferred enterprise preserves its identity under its new owner. The change concerns only the identity of the owner/employer, not the enterprise (etc.) itself.

967. Any judgment as to the preservation or not of the identity of the economic unit, and so whether the transferred enterprise, undertaking or department is to be

---

455. APol 36/2005, AP 170/2009, AP 175/2000, AP 443/1999, AP 174/1999.
456. AP 1723/1995, AP 1364/1992, AP 942/1992, AP 889/1992, AP 610/1991, AP 18/1991, AP 227/1990, AP 602/1980. AP 259/2006, AP 564/2005.
457. Previously, PD 572/1998 was in effect, incorporating Directive 77/187/EC into national law.

assumed still to be 'an ongoing concern', will depend on the general evaluation of the conditions in the particular case. In the framework of this overall evaluation, the following factors are crucial:

(a) the transfer or otherwise of tangible assets (buildings, machinery, etc.);
(b) the transfer of intangible assets and their value;
(c) the employment or otherwise of a significant number of the employees of the transferred (enterprise by the new employer/successor;
(d) the transfer or otherwise of the former clientele of the enterprise;
(e) the degree of similarity of the activities that take place before and after the transfer; and
(f) the duration of any possible break or suspension of these activities.[458]

968. It is crucial that a judgment be made based on the overall evaluation, as to whether the successor indeed assumes responsibility for an organization that had been created by a different person for the attainment of a continuous and stable economic aim, which organization the successor maintains for the attainment of the same basic aim.

969. The identity of the enterprise is not changed by the fact that the successor has added new assets to those transferred (new machinery, facilities, hiring of new personnel, extension of its activities, production of new products, etc.) A lengthy break or suspension of the functioning of the enterprise may be considered as a change to its identity, because in that case, the organization, its clientele, and its reputation may have disappeared. However, apart from any such suspension, other elements must also be evaluated in order to judge whether the transfer of an enterprise has taken place. A temporary suspension of operations does not as a matter of course change the identity of the enterprise.

II. The Consequences for Employees

970. On the transfer of an enterprise, these are the consequences for its employees:

(a) Successor assumes the position of the transferor as an employer.
(b) This assumption is automatic by law, regardless of the will and/or consent of the employee, the successor, the transferor; even if it is contrary to the will of any of these.
(c) The successor assumes and continues to have all the obligations of the previous employer towards the employees concerning their subordinate individual

458. AP 1850/2006.

employment contracts, whether under the terms of collective agreements or of DAs, or as deriving from work regulations, or from enterprise practices or by law, etc.[459]

An exception is made for rights that have arisen from pre-existent systems of occupational or bi-occupational insurance, whether in the form of a group programme with an insurance company, or in the form of a fund that operates within the enterprise, or as a group programme that exists as a private pension fund (private pension fund).

(d) The successor, together with and on equal terms with the transferor, is liable without limit of time for those obligations and liabilities of the transferor towards the employee(s) that had arisen up to the time of the transfer of the enterprise.[460]

(e) The transfer of the enterprise by itself is not a reason for the dismissal of the employees; neither can it justify any detrimental change to the terms of employment. Further, if the contract of subordinate employment is terminated on the basis that the transfer entails a substantive change to the terms of employment that is detrimental to the employee (e.g., because the successor is insolvent), it is considered that the termination has been caused by the employer. If the transferor or the successor proceeds to a reorganization (restructuring) of the enterprise, termination of the contract as a part of this reorganization is not considered termination on account of the transfer.

971. These consequences do not arise when the transferor is undergoing a bankruptcy process or is in any other similar condition of insolvency, where this is being undertaken so as to liquidate the assets of the transferor, and is being carried out in accordance with applicable procedures under the supervision of the relevant authority.

III. The Consequences for Representatives of Employees

972. While the enterprise preserves its autonomy, the composition of the representatives of the employees remains the same. When the enterprise loses its autonomy, the representatives remain in office until the election of new ones.

IV. The Obligation to Inform the Representatives of Employees

973. The transferor and the successor are obliged to inform the representatives of the employees that are affected by the transfer of the following:

(a) the date or the proposed date of the transfer;
(b) the reasons for the transfer;
(c) the legal, economic and social consequences for the employees of the transfer;

459. AP 1688/2012, AP 796/2001, AP 339/2011, AP 200/2009, AP 1801/2008.
460. AP 1688/2012, AP 796/2001, AP 339/2011, AP 1468/2008, AP 647/2003.

(d) proposed measures concerning the employees.

974. The transferor is obliged to provide this information to the employees' representatives within a reasonable time before the transfer takes place.

975. The successor is obliged to provide this information to the employees' representatives promptly, and in any case before the employees are affected directly by the transfer, as concerns their work and working conditions.

976. When the transferor or the successor has the intention of adopting measures changing working conditions, and labour relations in general, in the enterprise, they are obliged to proceed to consultation concerning these measures with the employees' representatives in order to reach an agreement.

977. The results of the consultation process and the final positions of the interested parties should be in writing.

978. The above obligations befall regardless of whether the decision for the transfer has been made by the employer or by an enterprise that controls the employer. Moreover, the non-provision of information by the enterprise that controls the employer is not considered as a justification for any breach of the employer's liability.

Chapter 13. Settlement of Individual Labour Disputes

979. Disputes that arise in the workplace are settled in courts. No other way of settlement is provisioned such as by other organs.[461] Terms of collective agreements or by any other type of agreements between the trade unions and the employers' associations may not exclude the settlement of the dispute from courts.

980. Arbitration, as an institution of procedural law, meaning a means of settlement of labour disputes, is not provisioned in the Hellenic legislation. On the contrary, arbitration is explicitly forbidden in these cases.[462]

981. Labour disputes are judged under special provisions[463] which lay down a very simple and quick special procedure for their settlement and have the purpose to reduce the time required for the completion of the settlement of the dispute and to facilitate the proof of the facts that the parties in the dispute invoke. All means, documents and others, proving the facts of the case must be submitted pre-evidently to the court for its judgment.

982. Labour disputes, as they are mentioned in Article 614 paragraph 3 of the KPolD, are especially the following:

(a) differences which have arisen from the supply of subordinate work or from any other reason or because of it, between employees or their successors or of any employee and their employers or their successors;
(b) differences which arise from the supply of subordinate work, or from any other cause because of the implementation of the work, between those commonly employed by the same employer;
(c) differences which arise from the implementation of a collective agreement between those covered by the contracting parties or from regulations of equal value to collective agreements between the covered parties or between them and third parties;
(d) differences between employers of small businesses and handicrafts or between them and their customers, arising from the supply of work or products manufactured by them;
(e) differences between social security funds and their insured persons or their successors, or those indirectly protected by the social insurance fund beneficiaries.

983. Concerning labour disputes from points (a) and (b) of the above, a trial date is set in no more than fifteen days from the submission of the application in court, while the decision must be published in a month from the discussion of the dispute

461. KPolD was radically amended by L. 4335/2015 and by subsequent laws such as L. 4509.2017, 4512/2018.
462. Articles 591, 614 para. 3, 621, 622 of the KPolD.
463. Articles 663–576 of the KPolD.

in court. The service of the claim to the defendant is made in five days. Respectively, the above mentioned apply for the case of an appeal or a reversal.[464]

984. Courts are also competent to decide on disputes that arise concerning the legitimacy of a strike and of a collective agreement.

985. The competent court for the settlement of all the disputes is the Magistrate's court (Court of First Instance), while for disputes with economic claims of up to EUR 20,000, the competent court is the One-Member Court of First Instance (*Monomeles Protodikeio* – higher to Magistrate's Court), often called 'Labour Court'.

986. The above differences may be settled in the district court of the place of work even if the contract is terminated.

987. Mediation and arbitration are provisioned only in the cases for the conclusion of a collective agreement or for the settlement of a collective dispute with an DA.

988. More than one employee may be litigants in the same trial if their rights and duties have arisen from the same legal cause.

989. If the employee is a member of a trade union, the union cannot substitute him in court nor is obliged to cover the expenses for the trial. Yet, legally recognized trade unions and employers' associations, or their unions or chambers of commerce are eligible for:

(a) exercising rights by regulations of a collective agreement or by other regulations considered of equal value to those of a collective agreement, in the name of their members, unless the employee has explicitly expressed his/her opposition;
(b) intervening in favour of one of the litigants if he/she is one of their members or a member of one of their unions or associations;
(c) intervening in any trial which concerns the interpretation or implementation of a collective agreement or the equivalent to collective agreements' regulations which they are following, for better protection of collective interest by the court decision.

990. Specifically for the disputes that arise from the infringement of the principle of equal treatment and non-discrimination for racial or ethnic origin, religion or other beliefs, disability, age or sexual orientation,[465] legal persons that have the purpose to secure the principle of equal treatment may represent the employee in

464. Article 32 of L. 1545/1985.
465. *See* L. 3304/2005.

court as well as in any administrative authority or administrative organ, since the concerned employee has expressed in writing his/her consent.[466]

991. Similarly, for the disputes that arise from the infringement of the principle of equal treatment of men and women,[467] legal persons and associations of persons that justify the said legal interest may exercise, in the name of the employee, an appeal to the competent administrative or legal authorities after the consent of the concerned employee. They can also intervene in favour of the employee before administrative and other authorities.[468]

992. For the disputes that arise from the infringement of the principle of equal treatment of men and women, the employee may ask for a mediation proceeding from the Hellenic Ombudsman, which is the competent authority for monitoring and promoting the implementation of that principle.[469]

993. Concerning the disputes that arise from the infringement of the principle of equal treatment, when the employee presents facts from which a direct or indirect discrimination is evident, the adverse party bears the liability to prove that there have been no occasions where this principle has been breached (reversal of the burden of proof). This does not apply to the penal trial.[470] The same reversal of the burden of proof arises in the cases where the concerned employee claims facts or evidence that speculate direct or indirect discrimination based on gender or in the cases of sexual or moral harassment.[471]

466. Article 13 para. 3 of L. 3304/2005.
467. *See* L. 3896/2010.
468. Article 22, para. 1 and Art. 25 of L. 3896/2010.
469. *Ibid.*
470. Article 14, paras 1 and 2 of L. 3304/2005.
471. Article 19, paras 1 and 2 of L. 3896/2010.

Part II. Collective Labour Law

Chapter 1. Collective Labour Law, Collective Labour Relations and Collective Labour Conflicts

Viktoria Sp. Douka

§1. Collective Labour Law

994. Collective labour law or the law of collective labour relations is constituted by the laws that regulate collective employment relations and collective employment conflicts. It is the branch of the law which regulates the organization, functioning and activities of trade unions.

995. Collective labour law is defined as the law created in order to support employees' collective organization and collective action for the safeguarding of and promoting fair working terms, remuneration and labour relations via collective action.

996. Correspondingly, the same applies to employers.

997. Collective labour law regulates:

(a) the basic right of SD and labour of association (freedom to organize);
(b) the parties to collective labour relations and to collective disputes, which are the trade unions and the employers' associations (so, by implication or extension, the rights of trade unions);
(c) the means that trade unions enjoy in order to exert pressure on employers or the state with the aim that these parties will accept the unions' demands, these means being labour conflict and especially the strike (the right to labour conflict and the right to strike);
(d) the manner of (peaceful) settlement of collective disputes by the parties, this being the conclusion of a collective agreement after free negotiations (the rights to collective negotiations and collective agreements).

§2. Collective Labour Relations

I. Definition

998. Collective labour relations are those relations that are created in the field of subordinate work in which the employees' side, at least, must be a collective entity. It mainly concerns the founding of trade unions and the membership of these unions, as well as the collective actions of these unions, of which the conclusion of collective agreements and the resort to strike action are the most important.

II. Subjects

999. The subjects of collective labour relations are, on the one side, the trade unions, and, on the other side, the employers' associations, or individual employers. These subjects are called 'social partners' or 'social adversaries' or, simply, 'the parties to collective labour relations'.

III. Conflict of Interests

1000. A characteristic of collective labour relations is that there is a conflict of the parties' interests and rivalry between them, as social groups in the economic system, this conflict or rivalry being broader than and having a different quality from the conflicts between individuals as parties to the subordinate employment contract.

§3. Collective Labour Disputes

I. Definition

1001. The concept of the collective labour dispute refers to those disagreements that are created by the conflict between the collective interests of employers and those of employees. In collective labour disputes, the existence of the existing rules is not disputed and neither is their content, but it is denied that these are appropriate, capable and convenient in regulating working terms and remuneration or labour relations in general, in a fair manner. In a collective labour dispute, the aim is to create new rules for the regulation of working terms and labour relations in general; for that reason, these disputes are settled by the creation of new rules of law and not by the application of existing rules of law.

II. Ways of Settlement

1002. The settlement of collective labour disputes takes place with the creation of new rules either (a) by the state with new legislation or (b) by the conclusion of a collective agreement.

III. Characteristics of Collective Labour Disputes and Differences Between Them and Legal Disputes

1003. To further define the differences between collective labour disputes and legal disputes, the following table shows these characteristics.

Characteristics of collective labour disputes	*Differences between collective labour disputes and legal disputes*
(a) They arise from the conflict of interests.	(a) Legal disputes arise from the conflict of rights.
(b) They are between trade unions and employers' organization(s) employees or one/more employers.	(b) Legal disputes are between specific persons.
(c) They put in question the efficiency of current rules in regulating labour relations fairly.	(c) Legal disputes put in question the interpretation of law provisions
(d) They aim at the creation of new rules for the working terms and remuneration.	(d) They aim at proper interpretation and application of the law in the said dispute.
(e) They are settled by collective bargaining and the conclusion of a collective agreement (or an DA)[472] or by passing a new law.	(e) Legal disputes are settled by courts or by arbitration as regulated by Articles 867–888 of the Code of Civil Procedure.

IV. Relation Between Collective Labour Disputes and Legal Disputes

1004. Collective labour disputes may arise by legal disputes and vice versa. Such a transformation may occur when, for example, the behaviour of the employer has already created a legal dispute, e.g., because the employer refuses to pay wage, but at the same time disputes the collective interests of the employees, e.g., because he/she also refuses the right of the employees to regulate the rate of the wage by collective agreements. In such cases, the collective labour dispute does not necessarily have the aim of creating new rules, as mentioned above, but it has the aim of safeguarding the collective interests of the employees in a different manner, e.g., to force the employer to recognize the right of the employees to regulate wage via collective agreements.

1005. The possibility of such transformations are of great importance for strikes when the question arises of whether a legal dispute may create a legitimate strike. Both jurisprudence and theory accept this possibility.

472. *See* below paras 1385 et seq.

Chapter 2. SD (Freedom of Association)

Viktoria Sp. Douka

§1. General Remarks

1006. In Hellas the first association that could be called 'trade union' was created in 1879, short after the establishment of the newer Hellenic State in 1833, by the wood workers in the Syros (the island of Hellas, in Aegean Sea) shipyards. In October 1918, the GSEE, the most important third level trade union in Hellas, was established.

1007. The trade union movement is organized on the basis of the occupation of the employees either by sector or inter sectors.

1008. Employees in both private and public sector are organized in the GSEE, while public servants – working under a public law relation – are organized in the ADEDY.

§2. Concept and Content

1009. 'SD' refers to the right of every employee to associate with others independently, and, being so organized, to act independently in order to defend, safeguard and promote their common collective interests of any kind, such as financial, professional, concerning social insurance.

1010. SD includes a number of rights and has both a positive and a negative aspect. Employers enjoy the same freedom.

1011. 'SD' is not only of great importance for collective labour law, it is a fundamental right because collective labour law is the law that regulates SD given that it comprises provisions for the trade unions, their organization and acts, the mechanisms for the resolution of collective disputes regulates.

§3. Positive Aspect: Organization and Action

1012. The positive aspect of SD includes the following rights:

(a) Every employee is entitled to exercise the right to organize, meaning:
  - to found, together with other employees, a trade union or to become a member of an already existing trade union, to participate in the bodies of the trade union and in its internal procedures (right of organization);

  - to participate in the actions, acts of industrial action included, decided on by the trade union which covers his/her interests or of which the employee is a member (right of action).

(b) Every trade union, as a legal entity of independent existence, is entitled:
  - to formulate its statute, which content includes the union's name and head office address; its coverage in terms of personnel, branch of activity and geographical area; its objectives and duration (in cases where the union is not being formed for an indefinite period); rules on granting and withdrawing membership, and members' rights and obligations; disciplinary code; composition, election and functioning of the General Assembly and governing bodies; financial administration, budget and accounts system; creation and functioning of branches and other forms of decentralized organization; procedure for amending the rule book; and winding-up, disbandment and consequent liquidation and distribution of assets (right of internal autonomy);
  - to work together with other trade unions for the founding of further trade unions or to become a member of an existing trade union, to participate in its bodies and its internal operation procedures (right of organization);
  - to independently choose, manage and implement activities of any kind (e.g., conclude collective agreements, call for a strike) that promote its purposes with the sole criterion its own choices and the sole limits those imposed by law (right of external action, tight of collective action);
  - the specific right to free collective bargaining and to conclude collective agreements consists of the 'collective autonomy' and the specific collective action of strike consists the right to strike.

Employers and employers' association enjoy the above rights as well.

1013. Under the Hellenic legal system the establishment of a trade union is the first act for the exercise of SD; it is a *sine qua non* precondition for the development and exercise of any other right related to the SD, e.g., the internal organization, the strike, the collective agreements. Thus it functions as a right-uterus from which all related rights become; that is why it is considered as 'basic right' called 'freedom/right to organize/unionize' and this term is usually used to define only the right to establish or join a trade union.

§4. Negative Aspect

1014. The negative aspect of the freedom includes the right of not exercising the above. The holders of SD enjoy the negative aspect of SD, meaning the freedom not to join any or a particular trade union and the freedom to leave a trade union. They are entitled to choose not to exercise the SD,[473] e.g., join or remain a member

473. StEol 52/2008.

of a trade union. Expressions of the negative aspect of the freedom are the prohibition of union membership clauses (closed-shop clauses), the right not to pay membership dues to a trade union to which an employee is not a member.

1015. However, the SD is stipulated and protected by the law as a right of a collective dimension, the purposes of which can be achieved effectively only in relation to participation rate. Therefore, the protection that the positive aspect of SD enjoys is a sine qua non-condition for the very existence of the freedom, while the protection of the negative aspect is necessary only to such an extent as to secure that the employee is not under pressure in order to exercise the freedom in question.[474] For that reason, is void due to opposition to the Constitution any provision or agreement that sets the employee's membership in a trade union as a precondition for his/her insurance cover[475] or for his/her employment or for his/her dismissal or discrimination in promotion, lay-off, training opportunities, transfer.

§5. Free Exercise

1016. The trade union right, in any of its expressions, is exercised independently, meaning that it is a matter of the choice for the holders, without any intervention or pressure by third persons; such third persons may be employers, employment agencies, state officers, employers' associations, trade unions or any other person is prohibited to intervene trying to make the employee change his/her mind, e.g., by offering him benefits or by threatening to penalize him.

1017. The holders of the right independently and primarily decide on whether they will exercise their right and choose the manner, the time and the place to act respectively. Third persons are forbidden to intervene in any way to influence or coerce the employees or the trade union to exercise or to abstain from the exercise of the right. Trade unions are voluntary associations and become a member of one is an act of free choice.

1018. Bar Association, Medical Association, Technical Chamber of Hellas, Hellas Chamber of Commerce and other similar legal entities of public law function, among others, as professional associations, but they are not trade union as membership is obligatory.

§6. Holders of SD

1019. Holders of SD are both the employees and the trade unions:

(a) every employee regardless of the validity or the duration of the labour contract (e.g., part-time employees, employees for a definite period), the type of work

474. Article 5, para. 1 and Art. 22, para. 1 of the Constitution, Arts 57–59 of the CC, etc.
475. AP 65/2003.

he/she provides and the tasks the employee is given, the duties he/she exercises, the wage rate, the amount and type of remuneration or any other characteristic;

(b) every trade union, regardless of its legal form, its membership or any characteristic;

(c) every employer, legal or natural person, regardless of the type of legal entity (e.g., company, foundation, consortium), of the kind of its activity, of the sector of its activity;

(d) every employers' association, regardless of its legal form, its membership or any characteristic in general.

§7. Prohibition of Gender Discrimination

1020. SD is stipulated by the law, included the Articles 22 paragraph 2 and 23 of the Constitution, to every employee. Further to this, in accordance with Laws 3304/2005, 3488/2006 and 3896/2012, any discrimination concerning the right to organize on the basis of gender, racial or ethnic origin, religion or other beliefs, disability, age or sexual orientation is prohibited.

§8. Extension to Other Individual Persons Who Supply Work

1021. The right to organize is also assigned to persons that work, but they are not employed under a labour contract, meaning they are not working under subordination.

1022. Such persons are:

(a) public servants, in general, meaning private individuals providing their work under a public law relationship in the public sector, in legal entities of public law, in local authorities organizations. Nevertheless, the SD of judicial functionaries and those serving in the security corps, e.g., police and military corps, is limited in accordance with special provisions, such as Article 23, sub-paragraph b of the Hellenic Constitution. These persons' right to organize is regulated by a series of special provisions, such as Article 23 paragraphs 1, 2 sub-paragraphs (b)-(d) and Article 22 paragraph 3 of the Constitution, Article 9 paragraph 1 of the ILO Convention 87/1948, Article 5 paragraph 1 and Article 6 of the ILO Convention 98/1949, Article 1 paragraph 2 and Article 3 of the ILO Convention 154/1981, ILO Convention 151/1978 ratified by Law 2405/1996, Articles 30, 30A and 30B of Law 1264/1982 and Law 2738/1999;

(b) seafarers, who are subject to special provisions such as O.L. 3276/1944 and Law 1376/1983 for foreign seafarers;

(c) journalists' associations, in which members may become journalists whether they are employees or not.[476]

§9. Institutional Identification of SD: Legislation

I. Institutional Identification

1023. The SD is recognized and protected by Hellenic law, EU law and international conventions.

1024. This institutional identification means, among others, that international community and legal order recognize the contradiction between employees and employers, accept that this produces conflict of their interests. Furthermore, they accept that exercising SD and especially exercising the right to industrial action may disrupt the normal function of the enterprise, affect the economy and social life. The institutional identification of SD embeds industrial conflicts and the means to solve them, primary collective agreements and strike, in the structure of the economic and in social system. This thesis leads to the conclusion that causing damage to employer, economy or society due to the exercise of either of the above rights, e.g., strike, is acceptable by law, provided that the right is legally exercised.

1025. The legislation for collective labour relations in the private sector of Hellas consists of the following.

II. Legislation

A. International and ILO Conventions

1026. In relation to collective labour relations in the private sector of Hellas, the following ILO Conventions apply:

(a) ILO Convention 87/1948 concerning Freedom of Association and Protection of the Right to Organize (Entry into force: 4 July 1950), ratified by LD 4204/1961;
(b) ILO Convention 98/1949 concerning the Application of the Principles of the Right to Organize and to Bargain Collectively (entry into force: 18 July 1951), ratified by LD 4205/1961;
(c) ILO Convention 135/1971 concerning Protection and Facilities to be Afforded to Workers' Representatives in the Undertaking (entry into force 30 June 1973), ratified by Law 1767/1988;
(d) ILO Convention 154/1981 concerning the Promotion of Collective Negotiations (entry into force: 11 August 1983), ratified by Law 2403/1996;

476. Under Art. 1, para. 2 of L. 1264/1982 the journalists' associations enjoy some of the rights that Law 1264/1982 provides for trade unions.

(e) IC of Rome (4 November 1950) for the Protection of Human Rights and Fundamental Freedoms, as well as the Additional Protocol of Paris of 20 March 1952;
(f) European Social Charter, ratified by Law 1426/1984;
(g) the International Covenant on Economic, Social and Cultural Rights, ratified by Law 1532/1985.

B. EU Legislation

1027. The whole of EU legislation regulating collective labour relations in the private sector.

C. National Legislation

1028. The most important national laws that regulate collective labour relations are the following:

(a) Article 22 paragraph 2 and Article 23 of the Constitution, likewise Article 12 paragraphs 2, 3 set the constitutional framework for the legal system of collective labour relations. Constitution enshrines SD in fairly broad terms, as in other European countries and as in the Universal Declaration of Human Rights and ILO Convention No. 87/1948, as a fundamental right, identifies all of its expressions and support within the limits of the law. Article 23 paragraph 1 recognizes SD and the 'related' rights, as expressly stated, which are the establishment and internal organization of a trade union, the participation in it, collective autonomy in general, the conclusion of collective agreements, the right to strike, etc. In addition, Article 22 paragraph 2 recognizes collective autonomy/collective agreements, collective bargaining, arbitration and Article 23 paragraph 2 recognizes strike. Article 23 of the Constitution is included among those constitutional regulations that may be suspended in extreme or emergency situations, in accordance with Article 48 paragraph 1 of the Constitution;
(b) Law 1264/1982 on the Democratization of the Union Movement and the Safeguarding of Union Rights, regulating trade unions and strike as amended by a several Laws, such as Laws 4331/2015, 4446/2016, 4472/2017, 4517/2018, 4578/2018;
(c) Law 1876/1990 on Free Collective Negotiations and Collective Agreements as amended by a large number of Laws, such as Laws 3846/2010, 3899/2010, 4019/2011, 4024/2011, 4046/2012, 4093/2012, 4303/2014, 4310/2014, 4320/2015, 4331/2015, 4336/2015, 4472/2017, 4475/2017, 4485/2017, 4549/2018 regulating collective negotiations, collective agreements, mediation and arbitration as institutions supportive to collective negotiations;

(d) Cabinet Law 6/28 February 2012, regulating, *inter alia*, collective agreements and arbitration;[477]
(e) provisions throughout the legislation that regulate specific issues.

D. *Obligations of the State*

1029. The state shall adopt due measures safeguarding the freedom to unionize and the unhindered exercise of related rights against any infringement thereon within the limits of the law. The state, its authorities and bodies, are required to proceed to any kind of state action. The public authorities shall refrain from any intervention which would restrict this right or impede the lawful exercise thereof. In relation to legislation, this means that the law shall not be such as to impair this freedom and in relation to justice this means that law shall be so applied as not to impair the said freedom as well. Legislation and jurisprudence shall support it.

E. *Protection Within the Limits of the Law*

1030. The safeguarding, unhampered exercise and protection of SD and related rights are provided by the Constitution under reservation of law. The executive laws, dictated in order to ensure the fullest application of the said freedom and rights may, secondarily, entail the enactment of restrictions, which must be justified by serious reasons of overall interest must meet the purpose for which they are enacted, must be necessary and appropriate (principle of proportionality), and must not disprove the core of the said. So, the law cannot abolish them, nor can it attribute to them a narrower content than that attributed by the Constitution.

F. *Prohibition of Waiver*

1031. Waiver or the above-mentioned rights is prohibited and does not result in legal consequences. That means, for instance, that a clause in a labour contract by which the employee agrees not to join a union is de jure void.

477. Article 3 of Cabinet Act 6/2012 was annulled (its paras 1, 2, 3) by Decision 2307/2014 of StE and repealed (para. 4) by Art. 1 para. 6 of L. 4046/2012 as amended by Art. 14 of L. 3899/2010, Art. 4 of L. 4303/2014, Art. 55 para. 8 of L. 4310/2014, Art. 15 of L. 4549/2018.

Chapter 3. The Trade Unions

§1. Definition and General Remarks

1032. A trade union is a free association of employees, that is created in order actively to safeguard and promote their collective interests. Mixed associations of employees and employers are explicitly prohibited by law.[478]

1033. Trade unions are always legal entities, meaning that they have legal personality. Associations of employees that are not legal entities, e.g., random groups of employees, are not trade unions; thus they do not have the rights of a trade union; e.g., they cannot call for a strike or conclude a collective agreement.

1034. Trade unions have the legal form of a *somatio*[479] regardless of their type. If there is no trade union in the enterprise, then an association of the employees in it may be for a time period of no more than six months, called 'union of persons'.[480]

1035. Law 1264/1958 is the basic law for trade unions and regulates, among others, the purposes, financial resources, types and structure, bodies of them, the preconditions and process for membership, the election system and process for the all the bodies, the protection of the officers.

1036. The state is obliged to adopt due measures safeguarding the freedom to unionize and the unhindered exercise of related rights (e.g., the establishment and autonomous function of trade unions) against any infringement thereon within the limits of the law.[481]

§2. Trade Union Purposes

1037. The right to establish and organize a trade union is recognized exclusively for the achieving of specific purposes, meaning to defend, safeguard and promote their common collective interests, as mentioned above in accordance to the

478. Article 14, para. 3 of L. 1264/1982.
479. The term *somatio* (*somatia* in plural) as a legal term in Hellenic legislation, defines a legal entity that has a legal personality and is regulated by a special legislation regime provided by Arts 61–106 of Civil Code. Trade unions have the legal form of *somatio*, so the term *somatio* is used in the present text at times henceforth, as no other term quite captures the meaning of it. The same stands for the term 'unions of persons'.
480. It is a legal entity, non-profit association of persons, established in compliance with the law and regulated by Art. 107 of the CC. EfofEasternKreta 78/2017 held that a 'union of persons' is a trade union.
481. Article 14 of L. 1264/1982.

purposes of SD as a holistic and basic freedom regulated by the Constitution (principle of specific purposes).[482] These may be labour, trade union, insurance or economic interests, as well as any other interest the achievement of which ameliorates the economic and social position of the employees. Interests may be material, such as an increase in remuneration, or intangible, such as protection from harassment. In any case, these interests must be collective and not individual, even though sometimes this distinction may not be clear. Unions with other purposes are not trade union even if their members are only employees.

1038. Profit-seeking, meaning the systematic conduct of activities with the aim of gaining profits to distribute to the members or for capitalization, is prohibited as a purpose of or as a continuous activity by trade unions.[483] On the other hand, occasional profit-seeking is not prohibited, e.g., sale of objects, lotteries, sale of tickets for events, union training courses with payment, in order to cover the costs that are necessary for the operation of the trade union, e.g., lodging costs, benefits and insurance costs for the employees of the trade union, or the financing of trade union purposes. It is explicitly permitted that, without profit-seeking, trade unions may found consumer or credit cooperatives, maintain meeting rooms and libraries, provide training courses to their members, and create special funds to serve urgent needs for solidarity and mutual assistance for their members.

1039. Political purposes and political activity are forbidden, but political acts as means to achieve trade union purposes are accepted.

1040. In order to achieve its purposes a trade union may use means, e.g., to refer to the administrative and other authorities on any matter concerning the interests of their members, the violation of the provisions of labour law, to cooperate with other trade unions, to resort to industrial action.

§3. Economic Independence, Funding of the Trade Union

1041. In order to secure that a trade union will not be under the influence of anyone, e.g., employers, employment agencies, state officers, employers' associations, trade unions or any other person, Article 5 of Law 1264/1982 promotes trade union's financial independence and defines that trade union funding may come exclusively from the following sources:

(a) registration fees and membership dues. The method of defining them and the rate of each of them are regulated in the statute (by-law) of the trade union;[484]

482. Article 4 of L. 1264/1982.
483. Article 4, para. 2 of L. 1264/1982, Art. 1, para. 3(b) of L. 1712/1987.
484. Under the interpretative clause of Art. 22 of the Constitution, the general working conditions (determined by law and supplemented by collective, as stipulated by Art. 22 para. 2 of the Constitution) include the definition of the manner of collection and the agent obliged to collect and return to trade unions membership fees specified in their respective by-laws.

(b) voluntary contributions from the members;
(c) income from the exploitation of the property of the trade union. The property of a trade union that is necessary for its operation cannot be sequestered;
(d) revenues from donations, inheritances, bequests and from various events and festivities. Such donations and grants must always be made eponymously.

1042. The trade unions are forbidden to accept contributions and grants from employers or the employers' associations unless they are trade unions of first level, their members are employees in employer's enterprise, money is given for trade union's benefit purposes.

1043. The trade unions are forbidden to receive funding and support from political parties or any other political organizations.

§4. Protection Against Interventions by A Third Party

1044. Employers or persons who act on their behalf or any other are forbidden to proceed to any action or omission that hampers employees or trade unions from independently exercising their rights on membership and on functioning respectively. More specifically, it is prohibited:[485]

(a) to exercise influence on employees for the founding or non-founding of the trade union;
(b) to impose or hamper in any way or by any means the affiliation of employees to a specific trade union;
(c) to demand from employees any declaration of membership or non-membership of or exit from a trade union;
(d) to support a particular trade union by economic or other means;
(e) to intervene in the governance, function and activity of a trade union;
(f) to treat employees favourably or unfavourably due to their membership of a specific trade union.

1045. Employees and their unions are protected as regards the exercise of their trade union rights in the workplace.[486]

1046. Violation of the above prohibitions carries penal sanctions for the employer.[487]

485. Article 14, paras 2, 3 of L. 1264/1982.
486. Article 16, para. 1 of L. 1264/1982.
487. Article 23, para. 1 of L. 1264/1982.

§5. Bodies of a Trade Union

1047. The internal organization of the trade union provides for the bodies, as key issues of internal democracy in trade unions, which may be distinguished to mandatory bodies, meaning those that are provided by *jus cogens*, and optional, meaning those that the trade union wishes to exist.

I. Mandatory Bodies

A. *General Assembly*

1048. The General Assembly is comprised of all the members of the trade union and is its highest body.[488] It is a body of internal operation, meaning that it formulates the will of the trade union but does not express this will to third parties, does not proceed to actions for the execution of this will and does not proceed to transactions with third parties. The General Assembly always decides by vote, never by acclamation. A secret ballot is required for any vote on the election of an administration board, audit or electoral committees, or of the representatives to be sent to second-level and third-level trade unions. A secret ballot is also required for the selection of a second-level degree trade union for representation at the third-level, for confidence issues regarding the administration, as well as for accountancy authorization, personnel issues, and the calling of a strike. The Electoral Commission is a mandatory body functioning as part of the General Assembly in cases of an election process.[489]

B. *Board of Directors*

1049. The number of members of the board of directors is defined in the union's statute; however, there must be at least three.[490] Their term of office cannot exceed three years. Its members are elected by the General Assembly and are accountable to it.

C. *Audit Committee*

1050. The audit committee is competent to monitor and supervise the board of directors as concerns the financial management of the trade union.[491] The number of its members and the method of its operation are defined in the statute of the trade union. The term of office of the audit committee always follows the term of office

488. Article 8 of L. 1264/1982.
489. Articles 11, 12 of L. 1264/1982.
490. Article 9, para. 1 and Arts 10–13 of L. 1264/1982.
491. Article 9, para. 3 of L. 1264/1982.

of the members of the board of directors. The elections for the board of directors and for the audit committee are conducted simultaneously.

D. The Representatives

1051. In cases that a first-level trade union is a member of a Federation or a Workers' Centre and a second-level trade union of a Confederation, a number of individual persons, consisting the body that is called 'representatives', is necessary for the participation of the trade union in the General Assembly of the one of higher level.[492]

E. Electing the Members of the Bodies

1052. The members of mandatory bodies are elected by the General Assembly, the election process is held under the auspices of the Electoral Commission, elections are conducted in secret using paper ballots (lists of candidates), voting is compulsory as an obligation due to membership and the electoral system is the simple proportional representation one, namely a plurality system where the winner is the candidate with the most number of votes, though not necessarily an absolute majority of votes. The statute of the trade union cannot provide differently.

II. Non-mandatory Bodies

1053. The statute of the trade union may provide for other bodies, such as a disciplinary committee, a committee for union action, a public relations committee, the number, type, composition, competencies and any other issues of which are regulated by the statute of the trade union.

§6. Registration and Acquisition of Legal Personality

1054. Since the trade unions have the legal form of a *somatio*, in accordance with the relevant provisions of the Law 1264/1982 and CC, the following are required for a trade union to be founded:

(a) A decision of:
  - at least twenty employees for a first-level trade union;
  - at least two first-level trade unions for a second-level trade union;
  - at least two second-level trade unions for a third-level trade union.

(b) the election, by a secret ballot, of a temporary board of directors by the above persons;

---

492. *Ibid.*

(c) the drawing-up, by the above persons, of a document which includes their decision to found the trade union, is dated and signed by them;
(d) the drawing-up, by the above persons, of the statute of the trade union, which is dated and signed by the founder members;
(e) the documents (c), (d) a list of the full names of the members of the temporary board of directors and an application are submitted to the Magistrate's court (of the district of the headquarters of the trade union).

1055. If the legal conditions are met, then the Magistrate decides and:

(a) ratifies the statute of the trade union;
(b) orders an abstract of the statute, including the essential elements, to be published in the press;
(c) that the trade union will be registered in the record of trade unions that is kept by the court.

1056. The trade union acquires legal personality from the date of this registration.

1057. The statute is notified to the public prosecutor and is deposited in the archives of the first instance court.

1058. The decision that accepts the application may be appealed by either the public prosecutor of the first instance court or by anyone who has a legal interest.

1059. A decision rejecting the application may be appealed only by the applicants.

§7. Statute of the Trade Union

1060. Trade unions have the right to elaborate its own statute within the limits of the law. The minimum contents of a statute[493] are the purpose of the trade union in accordance with Article 4 of Law 1264/1982, the registration terms of its members (status, qualifications, hindrances, that the members must or must not possess, e.g., to be in the same occupation or in the same sector of economy or in the same enterprise – as well as the registration process and the competent body), the terms of removal from and cancellation of membership and the administrative bodies or organs of the trade union. Other issues, e.g., discipline process within the trade union, may be regulated by the statute if the members decide so.

493. Article 80 of the CC.

§8. Dissolution of a Trade Union

1061. The manners in which a trade union may be dissolved are the following:

(a) by the decision of the General Assembly for whatever reason by a decision of its General Assembly. In order for this decision to be made, a quorum of at least half of the members of the General Assembly is required. The decision must be taken by a majority of three-quarters of those present. A special quorum and majority are required if the dissolution is decided on in order for the trade union to consolidate with a different trade union;[494]
(b) *ex lege*: a first-level union may be *ex lege* dissolved if the number of its members drops below ten;
(c) by court judgment for violation of the law or of a substantial provision of its statute.

1062. Financial liquidation procedure follows the dissolution.

§9. Types of Trade Union

1063. There are several types of trade unions defined by *jus cogens* law[495] and social partners may not create new ones.

I. Enterprise, Sector and Occupation Trade Unions

1064. Trade unions of first level and federations are classified as follows:[496]

(a) trade unions of enterprise level, the members of which are, correspondingly, either employees or the *somatio* of the enterprise;
(b) sector trade unions, the members of which are the employees or the *somatio* of a specific sector of the economy, e.g., chemical industries, food trade, banks;
(c) same-occupation trade unions, the members of which are employees that exercise the same occupation or a similar occupation or a *somatio* of employees that exercise the same or a similar occupation, e.g., engineers, accountants, cleaners.

II. Local or National Trade Unions

1065. Trade unions of first level and federations are either local, when their members work in a given town or area, or national, when their members work throughout the country.

494. Article 8, para. 3 of L. 1264/1982.
495. Article 1, para. 3 of L. 1264/1982, Art. 7 of L. 1264/1982.
496. Article 1, para. 3, Art. 1 para. 3(b) and Art. 7, paras 1, 2 of L. 1264/1982.

III. Trade Unions of Primary/First, Second and Third Level

A. *Somatio, Union of Persons, Local Branches*

1066. The members of first-level trade unions are employees individually acting. These trade unions of first level are:

(a) legal entities having the legal form of *somatio*;
(b) union of persons;
(c) local branch, that is a part of a first-level trade union of a broader region or of a national level, provided that it is laid down in the statute of the union. Local branches are not legal entities and they exist only by being affiliated to the local workers' centre.

1067. Members of first-level trade unions may be, as mentioned above, only employees, regardless of their position or duties. Moreover, it is of no importance whether the labour contract of the employee is valid or void, of definite or indefinite time, full- or part-time. However, if the employee is minor or foreigner then she/he must be legally employed.[497] Unemployed persons may be members of a trade union if they have worked for at least two months in the time period of 12 months that precedes the date of the application for registration with the trade union. This means that the long-term unemployed do not have this capability. Finally, retired persons cannot be members of a trade union.

B. *Federations and Workers' Centre*

1068. Their members are trade unions of first level; the second-level trade unions are:

(a) federations: the association of two or more trade unions of first level, *somatio*, of the same sector or of the same occupation;
(b) workers' centres or centres of labour unions: the association of two or more trade unions of first level, *somatio* or local branch. They were created to play an active role as trade unions that safeguard and promote the interests of the employees at a local level, narrow or broad, regardless of the enterprise or the sector or the occupation of the employees.

1069. A *somatio* may join only one federation, the one of the same sector or occupation, and one workers' centre.[498]

497. Article 7, para. 1(b) of L. 1264/1982.
498. Article 7, para. 2 of L. 1264/1982.

C. Confederations

1070. Their members are trade unions of second level; the trade unions of third level are the confederations, namely the association of two or more trade unions of second level and of any type. They were founded to secure, safeguard and promote the interests of the whole of the employees in the country and they are of national level. A federation or a workers' centre may join only one confederation.[499]

D. Specifically for Trade Unions Within an Enterprise

1071. At enterprise level the following types of trade union may be:

(a) first-level trade unions, such as *somatio*;
(b) federation, the members of which are *somatia* of enterprise level;
(c) if there are no trade unions in the enterprise, the establishment of a union of persons is allowed provided that requirements of the law are met. Unions of persons are trade unions of first level of temporary character and enjoy limited rights. The law provides for the establishment of a union of persons as follows:
  - in order to call a strike,[500] if there are up to forty employees in the enterprise and there is no trade union of the first level having at least half of the employees as its members;
  - for the conclusion of an agreement with the employer for the management of working time;[501]
  - for the conclusion of an enterprise-level collective agreement,[502] if a trade union capable for the conclusion of such an agreement does not exist and at least third-fifths of the employees in the enterprise join the union.

E. The Most Representative Trade Unions

1072. Trade unions, regardless of their type and specific characteristics enjoy the same rights and protection. However, in some cases, law assigns some rights only to the most representative trade union. The most representative trade union is the one that may proceed to the conclusion of a collective agreement[503] and to the appointment of security staff.[504] When there are more than one similar trade unions in an enterprise, a sector or an occupation, only one is the most representative. The criterion of representativeness is based, in accordance with Article 6 paragraph 2 of Law 1876/1990, on the number of employees that participated in the most recent

499. Article 7, para. 2 of L. 1264/1982.
500. Article 1, para. 3, s. a, subs. gg of L. 1264/1982.
501. Article 41, para. 6 of L. 1892/1990 as replaced by Art. 42 of L. 3986/2011.
502. Article 3, para. 5 of L. 1876/1990 as replaced by Art. 37, para. 1 of L. 4024/2011 in combination with Art. 1, para. 3(gg) of L. 1264/1982.
503. Article 6, para. 1 of L. 1876/1990.
504. Article 21 of L. 1264/1982. *See* below paras 1346 et seq.

elections for the Administrative Board. When in an enterprise, a sector or an occupation, there is only one trade union, then this union is the one that proceeds to the conclusion of a collective agreement and the appointment of security staff. The representativeness may be challenged by another trade union of the same type. The complaint will be examined by the Committee set up under Article 15 of Law 1264/1988 and the decision of the Committee is not subject to appeal. This matter does not fall within the courts' jurisdiction.

IV. Registration

A. *Preconditions for Registration*

1073. The following preconditions for registration in a trade union exist:

(a) Employees have the right to decide whether they want to join a union and, if so, which union. According to Article 7 paragraph 1(a) of Law 1264/1982, which includes a provision of *jus cogens*, the employee who submits for registration must:
   - have worked for at least two months in the enterprise, sector or occupation (depending on the type of the trade union to which he/she applies) in the twelve-month period before the date of the application;
   - fulfil the requirements set by the statute of the higher trade union; the trade union is obliged not to set conditions that would entail the denial of registration of new members unjustifiably and contrary to bona fides, otherwise internal autonomy is deemed to have exercised by the trade union in an abusive way, e.g., when the interest of the trade union is not served by the specific term or the exclusion of the applicant is not justified;[505]
   - not be a member of another similar trade union; and
   - not be a member of two other trade unions of any type.

   When the employee fulfils the above, he/she acquires a right to join the trade union and the trade union is obliged to accept the application.

(b) Trade unions of first level may join a trade union of second level, when the requirements set by the statute of the trade union of second level are fulfilled.

(c) Trade unions of second level may join a trade union of third level, when the requirements set by the statute of the trade union of third level are fulfilled.

B. *Registration Process: Registration by Court Judgment*

1074. The registration process is defined in Article 7 paragraphs 5, 6 of Law 1264/1982. The body of the trade union competent, on the basis of its statute, for the examination of the application, must come to a decision on the day of its first meeting following the submission of the application. If the competent body rejects

505. *See* AP 1402/1991, AP 633/1989.

the application or if within a period of one month has not announced his/her decision to the applicant, the last is entitled to bring an action to the court and claim his/her registration in the trade union. If the court accepts the claim, court decision is served on the trade union; from and by the service of the court decision the employee or the trade union, respectively, becomes a member of the trade union.

V. The Principles of Multiplicity and of Multiple Memberships

1075. Employees are free to establish more than one trade unions of the same type, meaning that their members are drawn from the same group of employees, e.g., the same enterprise, the same sector, the same occupation, same region (the principle of multiplicity), provided that each employee is member-only of one of them.

1076. However, the last trade union may not have a name similar to that of the previous one, when this would be likely to cause confusion as to the identity of the trade union.[506]

1077. Every employee has the right to become a member of no more than two trade unions, which shall be of different type (the principle of multiple memberships).[507] However, the statute of a trade union may provide that its members are prohibited to join any other trade union.[508]

§10. Protection of the Members of the Board of Directors

1078. In order to guarantee that members of the board of directors of trade union shall be free to perform their duties, special provisions provide for their protection and special leaves of absence are granted to facilitate the performance of their duties:

(a) termination of the labour relation on the grounds of legal union activity is void;
(b) termination of the labour contract of the members of the board of directors of the trade union, during their term of office and for a year after the expiry of the term of office, is allowed only for specific reasons defined by law and the existence of which must be confirmed by the decision of a special committee, the Committee for the protection of union members.[509] The same protection applies, with certain conditions, to the first twenty-one members of the earliest-founded trade union in an enterprise, sector or occupation;

506. AP 1374/2005, AP 764/2005, AP 1842/1984, AP 821/1981.
507. AP 1374/2005, AP 1469/1992, Art. 7, para. 1 of L. 1264/1982.
508. Article 7, para. 4 of L. 1264/1982.
509. Articles 14 and 15 of L. 1264/1982.

(c) the reassignment of these persons is only allowed with the consent of the relevant trade union, even if such reassignment is explicitly mentioned in the labour contract that has been concluded or in a work regulation of the enterprise.

§11. Facilitation of the Trade Union Activity in the Enterprise

1079. For the facilitation of union activity within the enterprise, the following apply:[510]

(a) First-level trade unions are entitled to have a notice board in the workplace and in places agreed between the employer and the trade union.
(b) Ordinary or extraordinary meetings of the most representative trade union of the enterprise will convene apart of working time, in a suitable place in the workplace outside the production area. If in the company there are at least eighty employees, the employer is obliged to provide the place provided that this is possible. Alternatively, the employer may cede or rent a suitable place within a radius of up to 1,000 m from the workplace.
(c) The employer or her/his authorized representative is obliged to meet with the representatives of the trade unions on their request, at least once per month, and to attend to the settlement of the issues that are of concern to the employees or their trade union.
(d) The employer is obliged to make available to the trade union of the enterprise with the most members an office provided that the employees of the enterprise are more than 100 and that this is possible.
(e) Trade unions of every level are entitled to distribute their notices in the workplace apart of working time.
(f) Representatives of the board of directors of the trade union of enterprise or the local area's workers' centre if there is no trade union, will be entitled to attend inspections carried out by the competent officers of the Ministry of Labour and to submit comments.

1080. If there are disputes between the employer and the trade union concerning the above-mentioned issues, these are settled by the competent Labour Inspector. If the employer does not comply with the decision of the inspector, the inspector imposes a fine on the employer.

§12. The Greek General Confederation of Labour

1081. The GSEE was founded in 1918, is the third-level organization of the union movement of Hellas which represents all employees in Hellas. At the end of 1918, following an initiative by the workers' centres of Thessaloniki, Piraeus and

510. Article 16 of L. 1264/1982.

Volos, the first Panhellenic Labour Conference was held in Athens on the 21–28 October 1918, and then in Piraeus, which concluded with the founding of the GSEE. federations and workers' centres are registered as members of GSEE and are more than 200. The main objective of a trade union is to defend, promote and safeguard the interest of the whole of employees of the country and, as it has been said, it is 'the country's umbrella union for private sector worker'. It is the negotiating and contracting part on the employees' side for the conclusion of NGCA and it calls all employees on strike in case the need arises. The GSEE has established a number of supporting institutes to help it achieve its goals.

§13. Employers' Organizations

I. General Remarks

1082. Employers' organizations are legal entities, the legal form is *somatio* or union of persons, and their members are professionals and business persons; their purposes are the defence, safeguarding and promotion of professional and business interests which concern them as employers. Employers' organizations are vocational organizations.

1083. In contrast to what applies to the trade unions, there is no particular legal provision concerning employers' associations. Employers' organizations are regulated, apart from the ILO Conventions and the EU legislation that refer to the right to organize in general, by the provisions of the Hellenic Constitution mentioned above and by the provisions of the CC concerning *somatia.* As for merchants, craftsmen and other entrepreneurs, Law 1712/1987 on 'the modernization of professional organizations of merchants, craftsmen and other entrepreneurs' apply, which, however, does not cover the country's hotel enterprises.[511] Employers' organizations under that law are of primary, second or third level.

1084. Employers may independently decide upon the type of their affiliation; they usually are affiliated on the basis of the sector that employers operate in, e.g., the ESEE, the SETE. However, they may be affiliated on the basis of the legal form of their enterprises or the basis of any other criterion proposed by the interested parties, e.g., the SEV.

1085. Employers' organizations' purpose is to secure and promote the common economic, social and occupational interests of their members. Organizations of Law 1712/1987 do not exercise profit-making activities. However, they may encourage their members to be found productive, consumer, purchasing or credit cooperatives, to found libraries and to organize training programmes for their members.

1086. In order to achieve these purposes, professional organizations may engage in consultation, on any matter which has to do with their professional interests, with

511. Article 7, para. 7 of L. 2160/1993.

public authorities, local authorities, cooperative organizations, agricultural associations, trade unions both within the country and abroad, as well as with representatives of various social groups.

II. The Most Important Employers' Organizations

1087. The most important employers' organizations, signing the NGCA on the employers' side are the following.

A. *Hellenic Federation of Enterprises*

1088. Its regular members are legal entities that have the form of a limited liability company, carrying out industrial or other business activities in accordance with the principles of private enterprise, and having their statutory headquarters or a legal facility in Hellas. Furthermore, Hellenic sectoral, regional or local associations of such companies may be members of the SEV.

1089. Enterprises and employers' organizations from other sectors of the economy may also become members of SEV since they contribute to industrial development. In addition, those enterprises of the wider public sector that function under private enterprise criteria are also members. The main body of SEV membership is comprised of secondary industrial companies, with their corresponding sectoral or regional associations. The majority of enterprises represented by SEV are classified as 'small-to-medium' in size, according to the criteria set by the European Commission; this accords with the general size of enterprises both nationally and across Europe.

B. *The Hellenic Confederation of Professionals, Craftsmen and Merchants (GSEVEE)*

1090. This was founded in 1919, in response to a perceived need for Hellene professionals and craftsmen to join forces, initially under the name Hellenic Craftsmen's Association.

1091. It is a third-level organization and constitutes the major and largest association of professionals, craftsmen and merchants in the country. The GSEVEE incorporates (a) 88 federations, of which 59 are local, 28 sectoral and 1 of pensioners, (b) 1,100 main unions with 160,000 natural persons (entrepreneurs) registered. It represents small and medium-sized enterprises (micro (up to 10 employees and ≤ EUR 2 million turnover); small (up to 49 employees and ≤ EUR 10 million turnover); medium-sized (up to 250 employees and ≤ EUR 50 million turnover)) and the self-employed (330,000 enterprises).

C. The Hellenic Confederation of Commerce and Entrepreneurship

1092. The Commercial Associations Coordinating Council was formed in 1961 and was incorporated in 1987, taking the form of a federation.

1093. This confederate organization represents Hellenic Commerce on both domestic and international levels. The founding of the National Confederation of Hellenic Commerce was the result of an arduous and lengthy effort on the part of representatives of Hellenic Commerce for the establishment of their own high-level organization. Its establishment was made possible by the cooperation of local commercial associations active in Hellenic society since the end of the nineteenth century and the early twentieth century.

1094. The founding members were ten commercial association federations, organized on a regional basis, covering the entirety of commercial activity in Hellas. Nowadays, the National Confederation of Hellenic Commerce has a membership of 14 commercial federations and 283 commercial associations, representing the entire territory of Hellas, even small towns.

D. The SETE

1095. It was established in 1991, as the result of a meeting between nine entrepreneurs from the broader tourism sector.

1096. SETE members fall into two general categories (a) national tourism associations and (b) independent tourism enterprises.

1097. Unions of tourism enterprises at the national level represent accommodation providers, travel agencies, transport (air, land and sea) and all other tourism sectors in general.

1098. Individual tourist enterprises, regardless of size, come from the entire range of direct and indirect tourist activities.

1099. SETE members are (a) ordinary members: 14 unions of tourism enterprises and 457 tourism enterprises, representing more than 50,000 enterprises belonging to a wide range of economic activities. These include small and large hotels, rented accommodation, travel and tourism agencies, car and boat renting businesses, tourist buses, marina holdings, coastal shipping enterprises, catering chains and conference organizers; (b) extraordinary members: 50,367 tourism enterprises and 5 unions of individual persons.

1100. The sector employs more than 400,000 workers and contributes about 16% of the country's employees

E. The Federation of Industries of Northern Greece

1101. The FING was established in 1915. Since its foundation, it has been active in its efforts to promote not only industrial development but also economic and social progress in Northern Greece. It proposes and contributes to actions aimed at establishing and promoting the competitive advantages of Northern Greece, as well as to the promotion of the overall economic development of the region.

1102. The main aims of FING's development strategy have, for many years, been based on overall regional growth and development, as well as on the industrial development and international competitiveness of Greek industries, and on Balkan and Black Sea economic cooperative ventures. Over the years, FING has worked ceaselessly to achieve these goals and will continue its efforts to maximize and channel the benefits of these activities not only towards industrial development but, on a more general level, also towards the economic and social progress of the regions of Makedonia, Thrace and Epirus.

1103. Members of the federation are manufacturing companies and industrial organizations.

Chapter 4. Institutionalized Relations Between Employers' and Employees' Representatives

Vasileios Th. Koniaris

§1. Representation at Management Level

1104. Legally based participation of workers at the level of management is now provided for in Hellenic legislation. Of course, during the previous years and on many occasions, temporary committees representing employees or employees and employers jointly at the enterprise were formed. Such de facto participation of employees in assisting the correct application of labour legislation was formed mainly in industry and was formal in tobacco factories, in Hellenic railways and in certain banks, during periods of trade union unrest (e.g., in the 1920s and later even before the Second World War).

I. Works Councils

A. National Works Councils

1. Scope and Area of Implementation

1105. IC 135 of ILO and works councils were introduced into Hellenic legislation by Law 1767/1988. The notation of works councils, familiar to European labour movements, had been unknown to Hellenic legislation. Opinion giving by the employees, exchange of views and transmission of information by the employer to employees' representatives were never fully applied in Hellas.

1106. All the employees having normal employment (full or part time) in an undertaking or a workplace under the same employer may participate in the elections for a works council. In every enterprise, its branch or establishment in a different area[512] which employs at least fifty persons or twenty persons if a trade union does not exist, the employees have the right to elect and organize a works council for their representation in the undertaking.

1107. The provisions of Law 1767/1988 are not applied to employees of merchant shipping enterprises. They were also not applied to employees of those 'socialized' enterprises of Article 2 of Law 1365/1983. Later, Law 1767/1988 was extended to 'socialized' enterprises of public (state) character or of common utility by Article 8 of Law 2224/1994. Any dispute is subject to mediation and arbitration in accordance with Articles 15 and 16 of Law 1876/1990 as revised.

512. Article 1, para. 6 of L. 1256/1982.

1108. In works regulations in special collective agreements of public utility enterprises and banks, disciplinary and service councils were already provided for. But these councils had member representatives of the employer and employees with managerial responsibilities in the enterprise.[513]

2. Organs of Representativeness of Employees: Composition

1109. The representatives of the works councils are elected by and represent all the employees of the enterprise (workplace, workshop, undertaking, branch, etc.). They have three members in enterprises with 50–300 employees, five members for enterprises having 301–1,000 employees and seven members for enterprises with more than 1,000 employees. If there is no trade union in an enterprise with at least twenty employees, then they may also vote for a works council. Works councils are considered representatives of employees by the notion of Article 3 of IC 135/1971 of ILO, which IC is implemented by Article 18 (Chapter B) of Law 1767/1988.

3. General Assembly of Employees: Elections

1110. The rights of the meeting of the members and its representatives are described in Law 1767/1988.[514] There are ordinary (every six months) and extraordinary meetings of the General Assembly. In the meetings, the works council elects at least three members as organs for the chair of the meeting. The meeting of the members or General Assembly needs a quorum, half of the number of the employees of the undertaking. For calling an extraordinary meeting, at least one fourth of the employees of the undertaking are required. The leadership of the trade union of the employees of the undertaking, or at least one tenth of the employees has the right to call the first meeting. The composition of the meeting must be validly constituted according to the law.

1111. Elections for the works council's officials take place every two years and all the employees, who have normal employment for at least two months in the undertaking, have the right to participate and or be also elected. A three-member committee supervises the electoral proceedings.

4. Composition, Functions, Protection and Enabling of Employees' Representatives

1112. Works council members elect among them the president, the vice president and the secretary. Their valid decisions need a special quorum of more than half of the members and a special majority of the present members. An ordinary

513. Nevertheless, in certain EU countries there are mixed works councils having as members the employer and the employees of the enterprise.
514. *See* Arts 3–11 of L. 1767/1988.

meeting takes place every month and an extraordinary when at least one third of the members call for it. All members and the employer have the right to propose issues for discussion to the president, who prepares the agenda. For a valid decision, half of the members should be present and a simple majority of the present members is needed.

1113. The employer is obliged to provide economic assistance to the members of the works council exercising their functions on information and consultation. The members enjoy the protection provided also in Article 14 paragraph 10 and Article 15 of Law 1264/1982. Employers should not intervene, obstruct or influence members.

1114. Paid leave not exceeding two hours a week is granted to the president of the works council or his substitute. Also, all members of the works councils have the right to receive payment for their leave from the undertaking, for the period of their participation in conferences with experts or meetings having to do with education programmes organized by the most representative third-degree trade union or a special educational organization providing experts. This leave should not exceed twelve days during their office, and the employees must present to their employer proof of their participation in each meeting conference in order to receive paid leave.

1115. The employer and the members of works council meet, in the first ten days of every second month or extraordinary when one of the parties asks to discuss issues in common.

5. Competence and Relation with Trade Unions

1116. The representatives of the works council do not constitute bodies for the confrontation of workers' interests with those of the employers, as trade unionists would have it: rather, they have been given by the legislator some competencies in common with the trade unions with the aim of protecting workers' rights within the company. Their function is mainly cooperative and opinion-giving aiming to improve the work conditions of employees in relation to the development of the enterprise.

1117. The relationship between the works council and the professional organizations of an enterprise's personnel is laid down in Law 1767/1988. What is more interesting, Article 8 of Law 2224/1994 recognizes the supremacy and precedence of the trade unions. There is no danger that the works council will weaken the influence of the trade unions among the workers. The representatives of the Council may conclude agreements that do not differ essentially from the collective agreement and these have regulatory validity.[515]

515. *See* Metzitakos, in EED 55 (1996), No. 22, pp. 997–1002, Art. 12 of L. 1767/1988.

1118. Agreements between the employer and the works council do not bind trade unions, which are free to ameliorate them in a collective agreement. The works council decides with the employer only on matters which are not regulated in a collective agreement or when a trade union does not exist in the enterprise. In particular, by paragraph 4 of Article 12 of Law 1767/1988, they decide on:

(a) the preparation of the working regulations for the undertaking;
(b) the works regulations concerning health and safety in the undertaking;
(c) the planning of information programmes on new organization methods and the use of new technologies;
(d) the programming of training, continuous vocational training and retraining of personnel, mainly following upon technological changes;
(e) the means of checking the presence and the behaviour of personnel, in relation to the protection of the employee's privacy, including the possible use of audio and visual surveillance;
(f) the programming of yearly paid leave;
(g) the reintroduction of employees of the undertaking, having suffered a work accident, into suitable positions;
(h) the planning and organization of cultural and social events and of equipment for the same.

For all the above-mentioned topics (a)–(h) a written agreement is concluded.

1119. In a conflict between the employer and the works council, a Hellenic competent regional mediation body, should decide.

6. Information and Consultation

1120. Law 1767/1988 on National Works Councils in Article 13 stipulates all topics on which the works council is empowered to be effectively informed. The employer is required to provide data on the following topics:

(a) changes of the legal status of the undertaking;
(b) total or partial moving, extension or reduction of the installations;
(c) introduction of new technologies;
(d) changes in the structure of the personnel: reduction or increasing the number of employees, and the taking on or laying-off of employees or the introduction of rotating employment;
(e) the yearly planning of investment for the improvement of work hygiene and safety in the undertaking;
(f) the employer provides all information requested by the works council on matters included in Article 12 of this Law;
(g) the programming of overtime work.

1121. Work councils are also empowered to be informed on the following topics:

(a) the general trends of the undertaking in the economic area and production programming;
(b) the budget and the balance sheet of the undertaking;
(c) the accounts of the undertaking.

1122. The employer is bound by the law to supply timely and clearly information at least once a year on a prearranged day. Extraordinary meetings may take place if the works council asks for them and the employer is obliged to respond in twenty working days. But certain information or data from the employer could cause serious damage to the undertaking if revealed. The employer is not obliged to disclose data, such as the information covered by the concepts of banking or legal confidentiality, matters of national security and patents, which are matters characterized as confidential by the Hellenic legislation.

1123. Paragraph 5 of Article 13, provides that the members of works council are obliged of not revealing to third parties the information which has expressly been provided to them in confidence. The obligation of not revealing confidential information shall continue to apply wherever the members of the works council and their experts who assist them are, even for five years after the expiry of their term of office.[516]

1124. A specific procedure before a competent tribunal for the determination of the status of information, whether it can or may not be disseminated, is provided by paragraphs 4 and 5 of Article 13 of Law 1767/1988.

1125. Article 14 of Law 1767/1988 stipulates that the works council exchanges views and establishes dialogue between them and the employer. Article 14 becomes more specific, because it stipulates that the works council has a right to consult with the employer, if a trade union does not exist in the undertaking, about the following:

(a) in cases of group redundancies, according to the law on the control of group redundancies;
(b) in cases when consultation is foreseen in general or special laws.

1126. Under Article 15, works councils have the right to apply to a labour inspection office and ask for its assistance to resolve a conflict and in inexistence of a trade union in the enterprise the works council may express an opinion on any topic concerning the implementation of work legislation, of collective agreements and of other pro-employees conditions in the workplace.

---

516. Article 17, para. 3 of L. 1767/1988.

1127. Whoever fails to comply with obligations deriving from this Law shall be subject to imprisonment and fine in accordance to law.[517]

B. European Works Council

1. Implementation into National Law

1128. By PD 40 of 20 May 1997 on Workers' rights to information and consultation in Community-scale enterprises (undertakings) and groups of enterprises, Hellas implemented the Directive of 94/45/EC into Hellenic law. This PD provided for the establishment of a European works council (EWC) or a procedure in a Community-scale undertaking located in Hellas, or a Community-scale group of undertakings having its controlling undertaking (central management) located in Hellas, for the purposes of improving the employees' right to information and consultation.[518]

1129. Law 4052/2012 of 1 March 2012, in Articles 43 to 76 (Chapter 12), repealed the above PD 40/1997 and now incorporates the provisions of Directive 2009/38/EC of the European Parliament and of the Council of 6 May 2009, which is the new law. The arrangements for informing and consulting employees are defined and implemented in such a way as to ensure their effectiveness and to enable the undertaking or group of undertakings to take correct decisions. Information and consultation of employees are to occur at the relevant levels of the management and the procedures governed by this Law are limited to transnational issues as defined in the Law.[519]

1130. For the purposes of the Law, Community-scale undertaking is any undertaking with at least 1000 employees within the Member States and at least 150 employees in each of at least two Member States. Also, Community-scale group of undertakings is any group of undertakings that employs at least 1000 employees within the Member States:

(a) has at least two group undertakings in different Member States;
(b) includes at least one group undertaking that employs at least 150 employees in one Member State and at least one further group undertaking that employs at least 150 employees in another Member State.

1131. The prescribed thresholds for the size of the workforce shall be based on the average number of employees, including part-time employees, employed during

517. *See* Art. 458 of the PC, Art. 16, paras 8, 9 of L. 1264/1982 and Art. 16 of L. 146/1914.
518. T.B. Koniaris, 'Hellas', in R. Blanpain (ed.), *Labour Law and Industrial Relations in the European Union* (Kluwer Law International) pp. 89–95.
519. *See* V.T, Koniaris & T.V. Koniaris, 'European Works Council Greece' in R. Blanpain (ed.), *International Encyclopaedia of Laws: Labour Law, and Industrial Relations* (Kluwer Law International, 2013).

the previous two years. When calculating the number of employees, work contracts of defined duration that have expired or contracts for part-time employment are extended to the full yearly term of employment which is applied by the undertaking or the employees branch of employment.

2. Scope of Application

1132. The powers and competencies of the EWC and the scope of information and consultation procedures established to achieve the purpose specified above shall cover all the establishments of a Community-scale undertaking located within the Member States, and, in the case of a Community-scale group of undertakings, all group undertakings located within the Member States. Within a group of undertakings, the undertaking which is able to exercise a dominant influence over another undertaking is called the controlling undertaking, as in the case of ownership, financial participation or other rights deriving from its rules or statutes.[520] The provisions of this Law do not apply to merchant navy crews.

3. Establishment of an EWC or a Procedure

1133. The central management is responsible for creating the conditions and providing the means that are necessary for the setting of a EWC or of a procedure for information and consultation in accordance with the Law and the Directive. The management of a member undertaking, as well as the central management or the presumed central management as defined in the Law,[521] are responsible for obtaining and transmitting to the parties concerned with the application of this Law, the information required for the opening of the negotiations in particularly concerning the structure of the undertaking or group of undertakings and the number of employees.

4. Special Negotiating Body

1134. To further the objective of establishing an EWC or a procedure of informing and consulting employees, a special negotiating body (SNB) is established as follows:

(a) The members of SNB shall be elected or appointed in proportionate number to the number of employees who are employed in each Member State by the Community-scale undertaking or Community-scale group of undertakings, allocating for each Member State one seat per portion of employees employed in

520. Article 52 of L. 4052/2012.
521. Article 53, para. 2 of L. 4052/2012.

the Member State, a portion being equal to 10% of the number of employees employed in that Member State, or a fraction thereof.
(b) The central management and local managements as well as competent European employees' and employers' organizations shall be informed of the establishment of the SNB and of the commencement of negotiations.

1135. The SNB has the task, together with central management, of determining by written agreement, the scope, composition, duties and term of office of the EWC(s) or the arrangements for implementing a procedure for the information and consultation of employees. The SNB may be assisted by experts of its choice in its task. The SNB may decide by a majority of at least two-thirds of votes not to open negotiations or not to continue those already in progress, thus bringing to an end the procedure for concluding the agreement in writing concerning the details of the implementation of employee information and consultation in particular to transnational matters. For concluding agreements in accordance with provisions of the Law, the SNB shall decide by a majority of its members.

5. Subsidiary Requirements for the Establishment of an EWC

1136. In the case that the SNB and the central management so decide or the central management refuses to begin negotiations or the parties are unable to conclude an agreement, the law provides the manner that a EWC is formed. Its members shall be elected or appointed in proportion to the number of employees employed in each Member State by the undertaking or the group allocated as follows for each Member State: one seat for each portion of employees employed in the Member State, a portion being equal to 10% of the number of employees employed in the total of the Member States, or a fraction of this portion. The EWC for coordination reasons shall elect a select committee of a maximum of five members, with conditions enabling it to carry out its activities on a regular basis. The central management shall be informed of the composition of EWC.

1137. Employee's representatives who participate in the SNB or the EWC are elected together with their substitutes, in the fallowing order of priority:

(a) by existing trade union organizations;
(b) by workers councils that have assumed their duties in accordance with Law 1767/1988;
(c) by direct election by the employees in accordance with Articles 12 of Law 1264/1982 and 4 of Law 1767/1988.

6. Competence of the EWC

1138. The EWC shall adopt its own rules of procedure as stipulated by Article 49 paragraph 2 of the Law. It shall receive information particularly on the structure, financial situation, and possible development of activities, production and sales of the undertaking. The information of and consultation with the EWC relate in particular to the state and trends in employment, investments, organizational changes, introduction of new working methods or production processes, transfers, mergers, closures and collective redundancies.

1139. The EWC has the right to meet with the central management once a year so as to be informed on the basis of a report from central management. The select committee or the EWC must be kept informed of any exceptional situation having significant impact on employees' interests. The select committee has the right to meet, at its request, with central management or any other competent managerial body, so as to be informed and to express its opinion. In that meeting Members of EWC directly affected by the exceptional circumstances or decisions have the right to participate. Four years after its establishment the EWC shall examine whether it is necessary to open negotiations for the conclusion of the agreement with the central management on the details of the implementation of employee information and consultation,[522] or whether to continue to apply the above provisions. In certain cases referred by law,[523] the SNB is replaced by the EWC.

7. Functioning of the EWC

1140. If no agreement is reached between the central management and the employees' representatives, then an employees' representative shall preside over the information and consultation meeting. Before each meeting with the central management, the EWC or the select committee has the right to meet without management being present with the assistance of experts. The central management shall provide the operating expenses (of the select committee and of one expert), financial resources, material means, and it shall take on the expenses of organizing meetings, interpretation expenses, transport and accommodation expenses of members or the EWC and the select committee.

8. Confidential Information

1141. The members of the SNB and of the EWC and the experts who may assist them, are not permitted to reveal to third parties any information made known to them explicitly as confidential, in accordance with Article 13 paragraphs 4 and 5 of Law 1767/1988. The same applies to employees' representatives within the framework of a procedure for information and consultation. This obligation remains valid also after the expiry of their terms of office. Central management and the EWC work together in a spirit of cooperation.

522. Article 56 of L. 4052/2012.
523. Articles 56, 57 of L. 4052/2012.

1142. The members of the EWC and the central management may make common decisions on the data that will be made available to third parties. The central management is not obliged to inform the EWC on matters which are classified as confidential.[524] In case of disagreement on the matter of the transmission of information, the provisions of Article 16 paragraphs 8 and 9 of Law 1264/1982 shall apply.

9. Role, Protection, Relationships

1143. The members of the EWC, without prejudice to the competence of other bodies or organizations of employees, shall inform representatives of employees or the workforce as a whole, of the content and outcome of the information and consultation procedure. For the exercise of their representative duties on an international level, members of the SNB and of the EWC shall be provided with training without loss of wages.

1144. The members of the SNB and of the EWC and the employees' representatives engaged in functions within the framework of an information and consultation procedure enjoy the protection provided by Article 9 paragraph 1 of Law 1767/1988. They shall get paid leave of absence for the time of their participation in actions that have to do with the Law after presenting to the employer documentation of their attendance in order to obtain the relevant paid leave of absence. The members of the EWC are granted paid leave of absence of up to two hours per week, which leave may not exceed fifteen days per year.

1145. The management of establishments, which function within Hellas, as well as employees' representatives involved in the process of information and consultation, whether or not the central management is located in Hellas, must abide by the obligations laid down by Law 4052/2012, in order to have the protection of the law. Arrangements for linking information and consultation between the EWC and the national employee representative bodies shall be established in an agreement referred to in this Law.[525] This agreement is valid without prejudice to the provisions of national legislation or national practice regarding the information and consultation of employees.

1146. The current law does not affect employees' rights to information and consultation found in Hellenic law and obligations arising from this law to an agreement in force shall not apply in accordance with Article 68 of the law. The law provides for the application, extension, expiry and renegotiation of the agreement. Undertakings functioning in Hellas and subject to the provisions of Law 4052/2012 are obliged to inform in writing the competent body of Labour Inspectorate of the Ministry of Labour and Social Insurance as to the number of employees and of their representatives.

---

524. Article 14, paras 4, 5 of L. 1767/1988.
525. Article 56 of L. 4052/2012.

1147. As already mentioned, all employees are not eligible voters. The election or appointment of the members of the EWC shall be carried out in accordance with the Hellenic legislation,[526] which considers employees-voters only those who perform services in relationship of subordination and in exchange for remuneration (normal employment). Persons working in furtherance of an apprenticeship contract, as having normal employment, are equivalent to employees, among which are also those carrying labour contracts of definite duration or contracts for part-time employment and all are eligible voters, as law provides. Interim workers and another number of atypical employees are not included. Also, homeworkers who may have a contract of employment, but different from the ordinary contract of employment, are also excluded.

II. Health and Safety of Employees

A. *The Committee for Health and Safety of Employees*

1148. A code of laws has been enacted on 2 June 2010, in accordance with Article 76 paragraph 7 of the Constitution, with provisions concerning the health and safety of the employees.[527] For that purpose, this law includes general principles concerning the prevention of occupational hazards and the protection of health, the abolition of the risk factors and workplace accidents as well as occupational diseases, information, consultation, equal participation, training of the employees and their representatives as well as rules for the application of all the above principles.

1149. The provisions of Law 3850/2010 are applied in all works, undertakings, etc. of the private and public sector, as well as to the staff of the armed forces, but not to the domestic workers.[528] Special provisions exist for the sea transportations[529] as well as for the sector of mines and quarries.

---

526. Article 12 of L. 1264/1982 and Art. 4 of L. 1767/1988.
527. The most important provisions before issuing the code on health and safety at work are found in L. 1568/1985, in Art. 13 of L. 2874/2000, in Arts 3 and 9 of the NGCA for the years 1991–1992, in PD 16/1996, 17/1996 and 88/1999 which brought the Hellenic legislation into line with European Union Directives 89/391 and 91/383.
528. Article 2, para. 3 of L. 3850/2010. In the case of domestic workers, health and safety of the personnel must be ensured as regards to the purposes of the Law.
529. In accordance with para. 4 Art. 2, especially for sea transportation, the provisions of LD 187/1973 apply for the code of the maritime legal system, L. 486/1976 which ratified ILO Convention 134 concerning the Prevention of Accidents for Seafarers, L. 948/1979 which ratified ILO Convention 147 concerning merchant shipping (minimum standards), L. 1314/1983 which ratified International Convention concerning the Standards of Training, Certification and Watchkeeping of Seafarers and all the PDs related to these laws.

1. Role of the CHSE

1150. A committee for the health and safety of the employees (CHSE) is provisioned for the amelioration of the working conditions in the enterprise. For enterprises with less than twenty employees, the employees are entitled to choose with a majority voting their representative in the committed with a term of office of two years, while for enterprises with more than twenty employees, the employees are entitled to choose their representatives with a special competency on issues of protection of the health and safety in accordance with the law. The employees in enterprises with more than fifty employees are entitled to elect their representatives to the Committee of Health and Safety of the Employees. All employees of the undertaking participate in electing the representatives to the Committee and conflicts arising are presented to the Labour Inspector and take recourse to the Justice of Peace of the area.[530]

1151. The committee for health and safety of employees or the elected representative acts as an advice-giving organ and their competencies are defined in accordance with Article 5 of the law. Among others, their competencies include the monitoring of the work conditions, the compliance of the measures and to proposition of new additional measures for the prevention of serious workplace accidents, points occupational risks and is informed by the enterprise for every change that affect the conditions of health and safety in the workplace. The Committee calls the employer to take measures and asks for the assistance of experts on matters of health and safety at work. A meeting is organized on an agenda presented by the Committee, the employer or the representative of the employees and records of the meeting are kept in duplicate. The CHSE, or the representative of the employees, meet with the employer or his/her legal representative in the first ten days of every quarter. The occupational doctor and the safety technician also participate in these meetings, in accordance with Article 8 of the Law.

2. Composition of the CHSE

1152. The number of the elected representatives for the CHSE is two members in an undertaking of 20 to 100 employees, three members in undertakings of 101 to 300 employees, four members for undertakings of 301 to 600 employees, six members in undertakings of 1,001 to 2,000 employees and seven members in undertakings of more than 2000 employees.[531] The employer is obliged to facilitate the Committed or the representative of the employees in any relevant case.[532]

530. Article 4 of L. 3850/2010.

531. L. 1568/1985 on health and safety of the employees provided for an elected representative of the employees in an enterprise of 20–50 employees, or an elected workers' committee at an enterprise with more than 50 employees for consulting the employer regularly every three months, in common meetings with the safety technician and the work doctor. Companies whose workforce exceeded a yearly average of 50 were obliged to employ a workplace doctor and a safety technician. The workers in these companies had the right to consult a health and safety committee.

532. Article 6 of L. 3850/2010.

1153. Works councils propose the members for the CHSE from (among) their members. If in the enterprise, there are no representatives or works councils, the employees elect in a General Assembly which is called especially for this purpose, every two years, the members of the External Service for Protection and Prevention (EXSPP) or their representative, for the health and safety of the employees with a direct and secret vote.[533]

1154. In the enterprises with less than fifty employees, the employer is obliged to use the services of a safety technician.[534] In enterprises with more than fifty employees, the employer is obliged to use the services of a safety technician and an occupational doctor.[535] The employer makes available to the safety technician and the occupational doctor, the necessary personnel, place, facilities and any other necessary means by bearing all the costs of the above. The employer is also obliged to facilitate the participation in training courses in accordance with Article 22 of Law 3850/2010.

B. *Safety Technician and Occupational Doctors*

1155. It is possible for the employer to assign the position of the safety technician and/or the occupational doctor to employees in the enterprise or to persons outside the enterprise with a contract with EXSPP in accordance with Article 23 of the before mentioned Law[536] or a combination of the above. The employer is obliged to notify the related Labour Inspectorate on the skills, employment to other enterprises, working time of the assigned employees as well as to submit to the Labour Inspectorate a list with all logistics and personnel for the cover of its obligations and a list of the logistics and services provided by the EXSPP. These notifications in accordance with Article 119 of Law 4488/2017 can be made at the Unified Information System of SEPE electronically.

1156. The services of the safety technician and the occupational doctor which are provided in an enterprise by wholly owned enterprises or legal persons outside of the enterprise, called EXSPP, exert their authorities and have the duties and obligations of the safety technician and the occupational doctor, after a relevant permission that they are obliged to possess in accordance with the provisions of Article 14 of the Law. There is an opinion-giving committee in the Ministry of Labour and

533. Article 7 of L. 3850/2010.
534. Article 12, para. 4 of L. 3850/2010.
535. In accordance with Ch. B of Law 3850/2010.
536. The creation of the EXSPP facilitated the application in practice of the existing framework for the improvement of health and safety at work. Workplace doctors and safety technicians had been unable to function correctly: this lead to the establishment of the EXSPP. Full application of the provisions for health and safety at the workplace was not possible. Hellenic government tried to ease the malfunctioning procedures by putting a limit on doctors' and safety technicians' working hours and by putting the notification of the monthly disposition of their working hours and their working timetable in a visible location in the workplace.

Social Insurance which provides the permissions for the operation of EXSPP.[537] Under PDs, after an opinion of the Supreme Council of Labour and a proposal of the Minister, the application of the provisions of Chapter B (Articles 4–25) of the Law, is extended to special categories of enterprises with an increased occupational risk.[538]

1157. The labour contract of the safety technician and the occupational doctor to existing employees of the enterprise is made in writing and a copy of the document is notified from the employer to the local Labour Inspectorate. If these competencies are assigned to an EXSPP, before the assignment, the employer is obliged to notify the competent Labour Inspectorate of a written contract, which includes all the necessary elements defined by the law. An Internal Service for Protection and Prevention (ISPP) must be created in enterprises that are obliged to full time employ two safety technicians. The ISPP are allowed to also operate as EXSPP and to be used by other enterprises in accordance with the conditions set by the Law.

1158. In order to define the working hours of the safety technician and the occupational doctor, as well as their required level of expertise,[539] the enterprises and the work are classified in categories, whose sector of economic activity are marked with a code number that is included in the code. The safety technician must possess the skills required by the law and is subject directly to the management of the enterprise.

1159. At the Supreme Council of Labour (ASE) of the Ministry of Labour and Social Insurance and Solidarity, there is a body, competent and opinion giving exclusively for issues concerning the health and safety of the employees. This body is called CHSE in accordance with the specific provisions of Article 25 of PD 368/1989 (Organization of the Ministry of Labour) as is in effect until today. Under PDs, that are issued with a proposal of the Minister of Labour and Social Insurance, and the by case competent Minister, after an opinion of the Council of Health and Safety of the Employees, the specific level of knowledge and the specialty of the safety technician are defined, in relation to the number of the employees in the enterprise and the type of activity of the enterprise.[540]

537. For the first time in Hellas, by Art. 13 of L. 2874/2000 in the Ministry of Labour, Social Insurance and Solidarity, there was established an advisory committee on matters concerning the issue of operating permits to EXSPP. It was the task of this committee to inspect EXSPPs that are applying for permits and to give relevant advice to the competent General Directorate of the Ministry. The opinions of minority members of the Committee were included in the advisory report.

538. Article 25 of L. 3850/2010.

539. The required level of knowledge and skills of the safety technician are described in Art. 10 of L. 3850/2010 and the specifications of the safety technicians in accordance with the sector of activity of the enterprise are described in Art. 13.

540. The Council of Health and Safety of Employees should register the enterprises and the sectors of economic activity, for which documents on their special dangers should have been drawn up. In these documents all means and materials for confronting special dangers in the enterprise, the responsibility for reporting a work accident within twenty-four hours, the duty to keep a register of accidents in the enterprise, etc., must be mentioned. Employers should ask the opinion of employees or their representatives and allow employees' participation in matters of work and health safety.

1160. The safety technician provides to the employer suggestions and advices, in writing or orally, on issues concerning the health and safety of the employees and the prevention of accidents in the workplace. These written suggestions are registered by the safety technician in a special booklet of the enterprise, which is paged and signed by the Labour Inspectorate. The safety technician gives advice to the employer on issues of managing the production process and controls the safety of the facility and the technical means, while being morally independent from the employer and the employees and keeping the confidentiality of the enterprise.

1161. The occupational physician must possess and exercises the specialty of his medical work, as certified by the related medical association. Under extraordinary conditions, the services of the occupational doctor, as these are defined in the Law, may be provided by doctors without the above-mentioned specialty, who had previous contracts of provision of services of occupational doctor. This is made in accordance with the conditions of the law as provisioned in Article 16 paragraph 2 of L. 3850/2010 and amended by Article 46 of Law 4578/2018. The occupational doctor is directly subject to the management of the enterprise and has the auxiliary personnel of Article 16 paragraph 5.

1162. The occupational physician provides suggestions and advices to the employer, the employees and their representatives, in writing or orally, in relation with the measures that must be adopted for the physical and psychological health of the employees. The written proposals are registered in a special booklet as defined by Article 14. The occupational doctor proceeds to medical examinations of the employees, according to their position, after their hiring or the change of their work, as well as to periodical medical examinations, after a judgment of the Labour Inspector and after a request made by the EXSPP, when this is not provisioned by the Law. Also, the occupational doctor supervises the application of the protection measures of the health of the employees and of prevention of workplace accidents and for that reason, he/she supervises the workplaces, propose measures of protection and the proper use of personal safety measures, executes programmes of vaccination and reports through the enterprise to the Labour Inspectorate of any possible sickness of the employees that is related to the work. If the enterprise does not have the proper infrastructure, the occupational doctor is obliged to send the employees, without any financial cost for them, to EXSPP or the related units of the insurance organizations. For every employee, the occupational doctor keeps a relevant medical file, which includes the medical booklet of occupational hazard. In case of a termination of the labour contract, this booklet is given to the employee.[541]

1163. A Ministerial Decision, after an opinion of the Supreme Council of Labour, further regulated the specific issues that concern the keeping and the content of the personal booklet of occupational hazard the collection and processing of

---

But the whole system of protection did not function as it was expected. As a response, Art. 13 of Law 2874/2000 set in motion the handing over of health and safety services to EXSPP.

541. Article 18, para. 9 of L. 3850/2010.

additional information with the consent and diligence of the employee and the imposing of administrative and legal penalties that are defined by the Law.[542]

1164. The safety technician and the occupational doctor are obliged, during the provision of their services, to cooperate with the EXSPP or the representative of the employees and to provide advices on issues of health and safety of the employees. In the case of a conflict between them and the employer, this conflict is settled only by the Labour Inspector.

1165. The minimum real annual working time of the safety technician and the occupational doctor for each of the categories of enterprises, per employee, cannot be less than the defined by the Law.[543] Under decisions of the competent Ministers, after an opinion of the Supreme Council of Labour, the execution of training programmes for the safety technicians, the occupational doctor, the members of the EXSPP and the representatives of the employees are approved and conducted in the related ministries, or education or public organizations and certified training centres.[544]

1166. In any prefectural authority, there is a collective opinion-giving body which is called Regional Committee of Health and Safety of Employees.[545] Also, in any region or city, there are mixed committees for the supervision of work conditions and safety of the work for the building industry and construction sites. Also, there are mixed supervision committees in the ship-building and ship-repair zones of Piraeus-Drapetsona-Keratsini-Perama-Salamina.[546]

1167. Chapter D of the Law (Articles 29–33) refers to the building demands of the workplace, size of the places, work positions in accordance with ergonomic conditions (Article 29), plans of escape and the designing of emergency exits (Article 30), the maintenance and supervision of workplaces (Article 31), the unhampered circulation in the workplace (Article 32) and the criteria for the formation of the workplace as well as the airing, ventilation, temperature and lighting (Article 33).

---

542. Article 18, para. 11 of L. 6850/2010.
543. Article 21 Law 3850/2010.
544. Article 22 of L. 3850/2010. In Art. 13 of L. 1568/1985, following the opinion of the Council for Health and Safety at Work, training programmes for safety technicians, works doctors, members of the committees and other persons of the ministries, etc., involved in health and safety work, were approved after a common decision by the Minister of Labour and the competent minister in the case. Other ministerial decisions regulated the organization and function of these programmes, as well as the period of training and the remuneration of the persons involved. We should also mention that by National General Collective Agreement for 1991–1992 of 3 Apr. 1991, in Art. 6, the founding of the Institute of Hygiene and Safety at Work was decided. Its running was the responsibility of the social partners Also, by Art. 9 of the same National General Collective Agreement (NGCA) the contractual parties had decided to set up mutual committees to study problems concerning the economy, society and employees, such as development, training, employment social insurance, productivity problems.
545. Article 27 of L. 3850/2010.
546. Article 28 of L. 3850/2010.

1168. The prevention of occupational dangers and accidents from the use of old and new machinery or their repetition is included in Article 34 of the Law 3850/2010, where the obligations of the manufacturers, importers and suppliers of machinery, tools and appliances are described. Article 36 refers to the manufacturing conditions and of proper placements of the machinery and the adoption of protective measure during their use.

1169. Chapter ST refers to the protection of the employees form natural, chemical and biological 'factors'[547] and the obligations of the employers, manufacturers, importers and suppliers of factors that they produce, import, put into circulation or given in any for professional use. The employer is obliged to adopt all the measures that are described in Article 38 paragraph 2 of the Law 3850/2010, in order to prevent or minimize the exposure of the employees in such factors. In any case the degree of this exposure must be less than the one defined as 'marginal level of exposure'.[548]

1170. The medical examination of the employees that are exposed to the abovementioned factors is an obligation of the employer. The employer is obliged to subject the employee to medical examinations, after his/her hiring in regular time spaces and before any possible change of position. The employer takes care in order for a booklet of medical examinations to be kept and updated as well as a personal file of the employees that are exposed in such factors. This file is kept by the occupational doctor and is considered as medical secrecy. The representatives of the employees in the Committee of Health and Safety or, in case of absence of such representatives, all the employees of the enterprise are entitled to be informed by their employer on the risks that exist in the enterprise, e.g., by the exceeding of maximum levels of exposure, and have the right to be informed for the results of their personal clinical and biological examinations that are indications of their exposure to the factors.

1171. Under PDs that are issued after a proposal of the competent Minister of Labour and the by case any other competent Minister, after an opinion of the Supreme Council of Labour, the minimum levels of the factors are defined, as well as the accepted levels of exposure, the manner of the clinical examinations of the employees, the levels of the biological indexes, the keeping of lists of the employees that are exposed in the factors and the manner by which these factors are notified to the Labour Inspectorate in accordance with the Law.[549]

---

547. This is every physical, chemical and biological factor that exists during the work and may be harmful to the employee, regardless of his natural condition.
548. The maximum level of exposure of the employees to a factor, which is defined by the provisions of this chapter as the maximum level of concentration or intensity in the workplace, above which level the employees are not allowed to be exposed. As marginal level, it is considered the maximum accepted concentration of a factor, which is calculated directly to the body tissues, body fluids or exhaled air or indirectly through the condition of the organism.
549. Article 41 of L. 3850/2010.

1172. Chapter Z of the Law describes the obligations of the employer and the employees. The employer is obliged to secure the health and safety of the employees by adopting all appropriate measures. The obligations and the liability of the employer continue to exist after the hiring of an EXSPP for the appointment of a safety technician and/or an occupational doctor. Under the framework of his/her general obligations, the employer applies all the measures that are provisioned in Article 42 paragraph 4 of the Law 3850/2010, in accordance with the general principles of prevention that are also included in the same article. Article 43 includes special provisions of the employers and Article 44 refers to the special provisions concerning the employees in public services, legal persons of public law and local authorities, as those concerning the benefit of hazardous work and the provision of personal safety material.

1173. The employer is obliged to take all necessary measures, adapted to the type and the size of the enterprise, concerning first aid, fire safety and the evacuation of the workplace by the employees. The employer is also obliged to appoint those that are responsible for the application of the measures and to provide to the employees any assistance for the addressing of any risk.

1174. The employers consult with the employees and their representatives and facilitate their participation in the framework of all the issues that are related to the health and safety in the workplace. Article 46 stipulated consultations and participation of the employees, above the provisions that are referred in the competencies of their representatives and the EXSPP of Article 4 of the Law and of the Law 1767/1988 concerning works councils. The employees and their representatives participate in the meetings and consult with the employer in order that the employer adopts specific measures and the employees may be present during the inspection that is conducted by the related Labour Inspectorate. They may also present their proposals during the inspection without being subject to less favourable treatment because this activity.

1175. The employer facilitates the employees in order to be informed for the legislation concerning the health and safety in the enterprise and secures the proper and adequate training of the employees and their representatives with information that is written in a special book and in a catalogue that are provisioned in cases b and c of paragraph 2 of Article 43 of the Law, as well as instructions. The employees are obliged to apply these rules of health and safety, to properly use the machinery, to assist the employer and the safety technician and occupational doctor, to participate in the relevant seminars and to express their solidarity towards each other, especially for the issues of health and safety.[550]

550. Articles 48, 49 of L. 3850/2010.

1176. Every employer that employs minors keeps a registry with their information, as defined by the law.[551] The same applies in any Labour Inspectorate concerning the minors that have been provided with a labour booklet from the related Inspectorate. Every employer is obliged to adopt additional measures for the protection of minors in the workplace.[552]

1177. The employer or his/her representatives that breach the provisions of the law are subject to legal and administrative penalties.[553] The control of the application of the provisions of the law is entrusted to the competent bodies of the Ministry of Labour, Social Security and Welfare.

III. Work Regulations

1178. Generally, the disciplinary right at the level of the factory was imposed by the employer. Now, the works council, together with the employer, decides upon the works regulations of the enterprise, the regulations on health and safety for the employees of the enterprise, the programming of the yearly leave of the employees, etc. Thus, the directing right of the employer could be limited.

1179. Works regulations were provided obligatorily by LD 3789/1957 for all enterprises with more than seventy employees. But according to Law 1767/1988 and Law 1876/1990 works regulation is no longer one-sided.

IV. The Spirit of Representation

1180. On the enterprise level, the workers' representatives (trade unionists, members of works councils, of health committees, etc.) and the employer have already come to a crossroad. In an effort to refurbish their image, social partners[554] are experimenting with new orientations, new social thinking for a 'shared ideology', new organizing tactics and strategies for overcoming conflicts of interest between them by free negotiations. This is no longer a question of 'exploitative choices', but a question of choosing an organizing and administrative system in each enterprise which makes machines, technology and factory production subordinate to men. It also means that the practical utility of unlawful Activities is now being questioned.

1181. It remains to be seen whether management and trade unions in Hellas have considered that the time has come for a return to certain more positive and permanent principles of traditional virtue according to which greed is bad, double-crossing is wrong and mere love of money is odious. If both social partners are to

551. Article 58 of L. 3850/2010.
552. Article 65 of L. 3850/2010.
553. Articles 67 et seq. of L. 3850/2010.
554. *See* Art. 3 of L. 2232/1998 on social partners.

become prime movers in factory-level negotiations and the conclusion of collective agreements, one main challenge the social partners face is the CVT of the employees, if they wish to combine a new model of production with the use of new technologies and to incorporate new social relationships in the form of collective agreements, with goodwill. As a first step, concession negotiations would be brought into play in a period when mature collective negotiations were not yet adequately developed.

§2. Relations at the Branch of Activity

1182. In accordance with Development Law 1892/1990, OAED, through its regional services, plans programmes for occupational re-orientation of employees facing dismissal, the unemployed, etc. Law 2009/1992 founded regional educational centres and institutes for occupational training for organizing and administering certain levels of training leading to a certificate or recognized occupational diploma. Article 6 of Law 2640/1998 organizes technical professional institutes (TEE) for higher levels of training, and now Article 17 of Law 2874/2000 amends the above-mentioned Article 6 and permits the functioning of a higher second cycle of studies in the TEE of OAED.

1183. Committees and institutes are undertaking in Hellas initial, continuing and adult education training at the level of the prefectures and regions. For these institutions, the law lays down new forms of cooperation between employers, trade unions, government agencies and local authorities (municipalities, etc.).

1184. The workers' centre is the representative trade union in the prefecture or a region. Workers' centres coordinate labour activities between national or local unions of a certain region. The correct application of legislation and of collective agreements is their primary concern. They are the caretakers of correct enforcement of the suggestions and circulars of the confederation. They are showing willingness to participate in tripartite bodies of their district for implementing their new roles, agreed or imposed by laws.

1185. In Hellas there are no joint committees at sectoral level to play important roles in labour relations, as happens in other European countries. The strength of labour has been entrusted to workers' centres and not to federations. However, a system of federations has long existed in Hellas. The federation is the link between specific trade unions of the same sector to problems of enterprises as a whole of the same or identical occupations. Nowadays, this link has been seriously damaged with the transfer of the collective negotiations to the enterprise level.

§3. Participation in National Administrative and Other Opinion-Giving Tripartite Bodies

1186. Industrial democracy was something vague in Hellas. Social partnership is a new concept, which is examined with great caution. Employees are considered not to be equal to employers, and the state is still preoccupied with the idea that economic progress should be free from all obstacles. This perception is in total contrast with the progressive protective legislation on labour topics. The state and political parties interfere with and control the Activities of workers and employees. This intervention resulted in the controlled development of trade unions and labour relations and the development of institutions which did not facilitate the relation of the interested parties of employers and employees.

1187. Workers' participation in administrative organs or opinion-giving councils which, besides the representative(s) of the state, also have an employers' representative(s) and workers' representative(s) have not offered the expected results, which were to lead to a real industrial democracy. This was due to the fact that most of the time the employees' representatives did not follow up the wishes of the workers, but tried to abide by the will of the government.

1188. After the revolution of 1909, a trade union resolution to the Revisionist Parliament stated that the trade unions asked for the passing of labour legislation, aimed at the betterment of the hygienic, ethical and economic conditions of the working classes and thus for the elevation of the masses. The possibilities for the labour class to participate in some spheres of administration arose as a consequence of the state being forced to assuage internal stresses and profound strains deriving from social, political and economic changes.

1189. The state took a very real interest in the phenomenon of the trade unions. Legislation with regard to labour of this period, after 1909, has been cited as proof of this. Representatives of trade unions could participate in the boards of labour insurance institutes and government organizations: in the Supreme Council of Labour of 1911, in the Supreme Economic Council of 1930 and elsewhere. In the Supreme Council of Labour eleven workers' representatives and eleven employers' representatives participated, besides those members representing government, Parliament, etc. Its aim was to assist social provision.

1190. The Hellenic Constitution of the 3 June 1927 (following the revolution of N. Plastiras in 1922 and the Pangalos dictatorship in 1925), established the system of two Houses, founding a Congress as an opposing force to the existing Parliament. One-sixth of the 120 seats of congressmen were elected by the trade unions of the country, according to Law 3786/1929 about the formation of Congress. The institution of trade union representation in the administration of the nation through Congress was partially introduced. Four seats of the Congress were for the trade unions and thus GSEE had to appoint congressmen out of its elected representatives.

1191. The disagreement about the distribution of these four seats contributed much to a new split of GSEE officials. Even if it is written that the labour class did not have the chance of sending consistent representatives to these high positions, this early state recognition of trade unions' respective legitimate interests was a fact that new economic circumstances, at least, justified these associations. In fact, trade unions made great headway, though during periods of political unrest legitimate recognition was suspended.

1192. The need for an advisory body in the economic field was felt by the Venizelos government. It is true that even if the decision belonged to one man, the advice of many in the creation of the preconditions was a necessity. Thus, the Supreme Economic Council was founded. The labour class was also represented by trade union officials. Unfortunately, the representatives of the classes in the Council were not prepared for the task. They had not realized what a collective contribution to the economic development was. Thus, their mission was a futile effort in labour tactics due to their lack of social and economic education.

1193. In accordance with the PD of 9 November 1931 the Council of Labour was founded. Four workers' representatives and four employers' representatives participated in its administration. Other members were representatives of the government and two professors. The study, research and opinion-giving on drafts of laws concerning labour topics or hygiene, job security, work relations and labour law enforcement were the task of the Council, which operated until 1957.

1194. By Law 2053/1952, a new Collective Tripartite Council for the arbitration of disagreements on wages was founded. Among its sixteen members there were five trade union representatives. This Board for Regulation of Collective Relations and Disagreements did not succeed until Law 3239/1955 abolished it and introduced collective agreements again.

1195. Only compulsory arbitration for collective disputes was recognized by Hellenic law when negotiations were not concluded. According to Article 10 of Law 3239/1955, a four-member first-degree administrative arbitration court could be founded in a city where an inspectorate of the Labour Office existed. One member of the court, as well as his or her replacement, was a representative of labour, appointed by GSEE or by the trade union which GSEE had appointed. The president of the court was a permanent judge. Two members of the appeal courts were appointed by GSEE or by the trade union which GSEE had entrusted. Second-degree six-member administrative courts were located in the most populated cities of Hellas, presided over by the presidents of the courts of appeal, or a judge of this court.

1196. Article 28 paragraph 1 of Law 3239/1955 (as amended by Articles 9 and 10 of LD 3755/1957) stated that a National Advisory Board on Social Policy should be set up under the Ministry of Labour as a body for consultation. Paragraph 2 provided that the board should consist of the following members:

(a) one member of the liberal professions, having special knowledge of social policy matters, as chairman;
(b) five senior civil servants and an equal number of substitutes;
(c) five employers' representatives and five substitutes designated by the SEV, the Athens Merchants' Association, etc.; and
(d) five employees' representatives and five substitutes designated by GSEE.

1197. LD 184/1969 founded the Supreme Board of Labour, where four representatives of civil servants, one specialist in labour policy, one representative of workers and one of the employers were proposed by their organizations and appointed by the Minister of Labour as administrators of the board. The board is divided into three departments: the department of remuneration and hours of work of the private sector, the department of settlement of disputes on paid leave and unhealthy work conditions and the department of work regulations as an opinion-giving organ on all matters concerning work regulations.

1198. After a joint decision of the then Ministers of Coordination and Programming the Opinion Giving Board of Labour and Social Policy was founded in 1976. Four civil servants, four representatives of workers and four of employers, nominated by their trade unions, constitute this board. Its task is to put forward solutions to problems of labour relations or to find solutions for ministers who face problems of social policy.

1199. After two years, in 1978, by Decision 1096/1978 of the Prime Minister, the Board of Social and Economic Policy was founded, as an advisory organ to the government. Five members of its board are specialists in the area and forty-five are representatives of workers, farmers and employers.

1200. Employers' organizations and trade unions are also represented on the boards of the OAED, on employment office advisory committees on the Board of Social Insurance (with two representatives relatively in its nine-member council), on the Central Supervisory Council (one representative of employers and one of workers) and on Boards of Organization of Public Utility. Law 1365/1983, on the 'socialization of the public nature or public utility organizations', introduced the participation of the employees in the ASKE, the Administrative Council, and the central and the regional labour councils of each of these organizations.[555]

1201. Law 1365/1983 was amended in August 1987 in regard to the opinion-giving committees of Article 2 (their opinion, though not obligatory, was no longer required), and by Law 1766/1988 which abolished the 'notorious' Article 4, which was introducing provisions creating obstacles to the free exercise of the right to strike in the socialized organizations.

1202. There are also representatives of employers' organizations and trade unions on national or district committees, e.g., of Article 15 of Law 1264/1982 as

555. In the beginning, Law 1767/1988 on works councils was not applied to the socialized enterprises.

replaced by Article 25 of Law 1545/1985 for the examination of the validity of the argument on the existence or otherwise of a sufficient (important) reason for the dismissal of a trade union protected representative from his or her work.

Chapter 5. Collective Negotiations: Collective Agreements

Viktoria Sp. Douka

§1. Introduction

1203. Even before the Second World War, collective labour law was introduced and applied in Hellas, and the institution of collective negotiations and collective agreements between trade unions and employers' organizations was established. At intervals or during politically uncertain periods, statutes and ministerial orders on issues of labour relations took the place of collective agreements.

1204. After World War II the system of collective negotiations and collective agreements was regulated by Law 3239/1955. Law 3239/1955 focused primarily on the resolution of collective labour disputes and on wage control, while the support of the collective negotiation and of the freedom of the social parties to conclude a collective agreement were not its goals. The law did not provide sectoral and enterprise-level collective agreements. Collective negotiations were given a substitute role and no importance was attributed to their success or failure. For that reason, Law 3239/1955 introduced and insitutionalized compulsory arbitration conducted by specific administrative committees of first and second instance, called 'Administrative Arbitration Court',[556] composed of one regular judge as president having double vote, one employee of the Minister of Labour, one representative of the employers and one of the employees. The first two members were appointed by the Minister of Labour. Where the negotiating parties should not conclude a collective agreement, they were obliged to resource to compulsory arbitration and the dispute was solved by its decision, called DA, being fully equivalent to a collective agreement. In order for the collective agreement and the DA to take on the normative force, the Minister of Labour had to issue a decision published in the Government Gazette. The Minister of Labour could amend the content of the collective agreement and of the DA or refuse to issue its decision if they were opposed to government policy. These settlements caused intense social conflicts, successive and dynamic strikes, judicial interventions, denunciations and appeals to international organizations (ILO), etc.

1205. In 1990 under a coalition government and as a result of broad political and social consensus, Law 1876/1990 on 'free collective negotiations and other provisions' was passed aiming to promote the freedom of collective negotiations without the state's intervention. It was an innovative law that replaced almost all the provisions of Law 3239/1955 and other relevant regulations, especially it replaced the obsolete and rigid system of collective negotiations and arbitration provided by Law 3239/1955. Contrary to Law 3239/1955, the new law's main goals were to secure

556. Using the term 'Arbitration Court', one must have in mind that an 'Arbitration Court' is not a 'court' *stricto sensu* and does not solve legal disputes; it solves collective disputes (disputes of interests).

free collective negotiations, to turn it into a mechanism for the social partners to regulate their interests by themselves and to exclude the state's intervention at the stage of collective negotiations and at the stage of the settlement of collective disputes (especially at arbitration) as well. Law 1876/1990 ensured a multilevel decentralized collective negotiations system, national general, sectoral, same occupation, enterprise levels. The social partners could choose independently the level to negotiate. The NGCA, known under its Hellenic initials as the *Ethniki Geniki Syllogiki Symvasi Ergasias* – covered all employees of the country, regardless of whether they were members of a trade union, and ensured for them a minimum safety net for wage and working conditions in general. The other types of collective agreements could not include provisions less favourable for the employees. For settling labour disputes Law 1876/1990 provides for three types of extra-judicial, of absolutely voluntary character mechanisms, being conciliation, mediation and arbitration. That system is auxiliary to and supportive of the collective bargaining but does not substitute them. In order for the collective agreement and the DA to take on normative force, an original copy of it shall be filed with the competent authority. Aiming to support free collective negotiations, Law 1876/1990 established the OMED. Mediators and arbitrators constitute two separate bodies; they are hired and remunerated by OMED, and they are fully independent in the execution of their duties.

1206. Under the regime of Law 1876/1990 wage and the whole of labour relations, individual and collective, had been shaped by clauses of collective agreements. The NGCA's main purpose was to determine minimum levels of pay, wage and benefits and some important working conditions, e.g., working time, training, teleworking and other issues of an institutional nature. Its normative clauses covered the whole of the employees in private and public sectors. Sectoral and same-occupation collective agreements shaped wage, benefits and other working terms according to the specific working conditions of the said sector and occupation respectively. The same applies to enterprise-level collective agreements.

1207. The last years, from 2010 to 2018, Law 1876/1990 was frequently amended and modified by Laws 3846/2010, 3899/2010, 4019/2011, 4024/2011, 4093/2012, PIS 6/2012, 4303/2014, 4310/2014, 4320/2015, 4331/2015, 4336/2015, 4472/2017, 4475/2017, 4485/2017, 4549/2018.

1208. The system of collective negotiations and collective agreements stipulated by Law 18765/1990 has been notably reformed and overthrown by the new legislation leaving space to the freedom of contact to regulate the individual labour contract and the labour relations in general.

1209. The purpose of those amendments is to create a new system of collective negotiations, collective agreements and arbitration in order to transfer the collective setting of the wage and the working conditions closer to enterprise level.

1210. The first results of the implementation of those provisions are reflected in Annex 4 of this monograph. The numbers of sectoral and same-occupation collective agreements have been sharply decreased; they even are on zero level, and they were led to marginalization. On the contrary, enterprise-level collective agreements have been sharply increased.

1211. Additional to the above-mentioned structural modifications, transitional provisions aiming to immediately decrease the cost of work as it has been formed by collective agreements' clauses under the regime of the Law 1876/1990, such as the following:

(a) the abnormal, *ipso jure* from 14 February 2013 until 14 February 2015, termination of the collective agreements in force on 14 February 2012;[557]
(b) the *ipso jure* suspension of clauses that grant wage increases. From 14 February 2012 onwards clauses of collective agreements and provisions of laws that provide for any increase in wage in connection of 'service maturity', meaning the completion of a predefined time period of work, e.g., seniority benefits, are suspended until the unemployment rate in Hellas reaches a percentage lower than 10%;[558]
(c) the annulment of DAs. Article 51 of law 3871/2010 provides that DAs are not allowed to grant, in any way, wage increases for the years 2010, 2011, 2012. DAs issued by this publication, pursuant to procedures of the OMED resolving collective disputes are deemed invalid and do not engender any legal consequence, should they award, in any way, wage increases for 2010 and the first half of 2012. In addition these awards are deemed invalid and have no legal consequence if any wage increases for the period from 1 July 2011 to 31 December 2012 are awarded in any way apart, from the following: (i) as of 1 July 2011, any increase in the minimum wages and daily remuneration as established on the 31 December 2009 in the NGCA for the years 2008–2009, by a percentage equal to the annual change in the European inflation rate for the year 2010. (ii) As of 1 July 2011, an increase in minimum wage and daily remuneration levels as established on 1 July 2011 as cited above in (a), by a percentage equal to the average change in the European inflation rate for the year 2011. Mediation agreements cannot exceed the limits set out in paragraph 1 for the three-year period 2010–2011–2012.[559]

1212. Arbitration could only take place on wages and until 2012, the awards could not exceed the limits set by Article 51 of Law 3871/2010, i.e., the average EU inflation rate. In case non-wage issues had been regulated by an older collective agreement, they would have to be settled through negotiations.

1213. The implications of current collective agreements' regime must be assessed jointly with the current trade unions' regime, especially the modifications

557. Article 2, para. 2 Cabinet Act 6/2012.
558. Article 2, para. 4 Cabinet Act 6/2012.
559. Article 51 of L. 3871/2010.

on the types of trade unions, described above. In general, the provisions of all above-mentioned law from 2010 afterwards aim at restricting the role of social partners, especially the trade unions, in the regulation of employment issues and limiting their influence on labour market regulation.

1214. Under all the new provisions is more than obvious that a transition from collective bargaining to individual negotiations seems to be promoted.

1215. Despite this hostile legal framework, which, among others, diminished the political, social and economic role of the NGCA, and despite the high rate of unemployment, the main social partners the GSEE, on the employees' side, and the Hellenic Confederation of Professionals, Craftsmen and Merchants (GSEVEE), the ESEE, the SETE, on the employers' side, came to the negotiation table and, after three consecutive meetings, on 14 May 2013 they concluded the NGCA for 2013. This was the first time that SETE participated as a social partner in collective negotiations for the conclusion of the NGCA and that the SEV did not, though it always was one of the NGCA's contraction parties. The NGCA was given a retrospective effect from 1 January 2013 and will be valid until 31 December 2013.

1216. It was of great importance that the contracting social partners declared, in writing and as a part of the NGCA's content, that they recognize the need to maintain the National General Collective Employment Agreement as an active institution and to restore its political, social and economic role.

1217. The content of that NGCA is, in its main part, as following: (a) the 'contracting parties' should commit to take joint initiatives to the government to tackle unemployment and combat uninsured and undeclared employment. They should also work towards amending the new legal framework that imposes restrictions on collective autonomy, restoring the full and universal validity of the NGCA and expanding collective agreements. (b) They will consult on how competitiveness and the economy can be strengthened, not through reducing wages but by looking at structural factors. These might include transport, energy and other costs and the tax system. (c) The marriage benefit should remain in force and shall be granted to all employees regardless of sex, as stipulated by the NGCA of 1988. (d) All the institutional working conditions agreed in previous NGCA and the corresponding DAs should remain in force. These would include maternity leave, confinement leave and sabbatical leave. (e) Any favourable working conditions which may be provided for by laws, decrees, ministerial decrees, collective agreements, DAs, by-laws, customs, business practice or individual employment contracts, should also remain in force.

1218. The current system of collective agreements is presented below.

§2. Concept and Legal Nature of Collective Agreements

1219. A collective agreement is an agreement between a trade union and, one or more, employer's associations or, one or more, employers, which regulates wage, remuneration, working terms and conditions of employees.

1220. Collective agreements are the outcome of free collective bargaining and regulate the remuneration, the work conditions and the labour relations in general of those employees who fall into the scope of their application. They are agreements under private law since they are concluded between private persons and regulate private interests.

1221. Collective agreements are a means for the creation of rules of law for the regulation of labour relations they are 'normative contracts'. Their prescriptive function is to regulate the content of individual labour contracts.

1222. Therefore, they constitute a source for labour law, both private and collective, and more specifically, a source of law of occupational origin that follows sources of state origin in the hierarchy of sources.

1223. They are rules of protective law setting rights in favour of employees, and respectively obligations of employers, within the scope of the collective agreement. They apply to all labour contracts within their scope of the collective agreement, regardless of whether the labour contracts are valid or void, full- or part-time, of definite or of indefinite time, etc.

§3. The Characteristics of Collective Agreements

1224. These agreements are of 'exceptional' character having the following characteristics:

(a) The clauses of collective agreements have 'normative power' meaning that they function as law provisions. They are an expression of the right to collective autonomy and action of the trade unions and the employers' organizations.
(b) Their primary and main purpose is the enactment of new rules of law for the settlement of collective disputes in the workplace and not the regulation of the relations of the parties involved in the process.
(c) The issues that can be regulated by a collective agreement are defined by the law, and the contracting parties may independently formulate the content of the agreement, within the framework set by the law.
(d) The contracting parties are defined by the law, and they are trade unions, employers' associations or separate employers.

§4. Purpose and Function (Conventional and Normative) of Collective Agreements

1225. Therefore, collective agreements are conventional in their origin and conclusion, and normative in their function; that is, they have a double legal nature, both normative and conventional.

1226. Collective agreements are given a law-making function. Their normative-regulatory effect shows the principle of protection of the collective agreement that the employer is not able to reduce the working conditions stipulated in the collective agreement to the employees' disadvantage. The object of the collective agreement lies in the lessening of the negotiations disadvantage that the employee is presumed to have when he/she negotiates work conditions and remuneration individually, meaning the case of the labour contract with the employer.

1227. Though, the conclusion of the collective agreement does not aim to abolish contractual freedom in the area of labour relations. For that reason, clauses of a collective agreement that define ceilings for the protection of the employees are void, and the parties to the labour contract may agree upon the working terms and remuneration provided that their agreement is more favourable to the employee.[560]

1228. The rule is that the collective agreement can contain provisions more favourable than the law and the individual labour contract can contain provisions more favourable than the collective agreement.

§5. Collective Autonomy: Relation Between Collective Agreement and Law

1229. The Constitution of 1975, in Article 23 paragraph 1, stipulates the safeguarding of SD and the unhindered exercise of related rights. Further, Article 22 paragraph 2 declares that 'General work conditions shall be determined by law, supplemented by collective agreements concluded through free negotiation and, in case of the failure of such, by rules stipulated by arbitration.' Both law and collective agreements may determine general working conditions. The harmonized interpretation of the above-mentioned two provisions, in combination with the provisions of the Constitution that regulate the country's economic environment, leads to the correct interpretation of Article 22 paragraph 2 of the Constitution as being that the law introduces the minimum levels of protection for employees and leaves to the collective agreement (i) the regulation of such conditions in a way more favourable to the employees, (ii) the extension of the provisions of the law to employees that are not covered by them (iii) the regulation of working terms that are not regulated by the law.

---

560. Article 7, para. 2 of L. 1876/1990.

1230. The conclusion of the collective agreement represents the most important expression of collective autonomy, which is the right of the social partners independently to agree on provisions on every issue concerning labour relations, private or collective.

1231. In practice the regulation of remuneration, its size and composition (basic wage, benefits, etc.), and working terms in general was left to the collective agreements. It is notable that the first general application provision for the setting of a basic wage and basic salary by law was made by Law 4093/2012. Until then, remuneration was regulated only by collective agreements and only exceptionally, in case of the absence of a trade union, it was set by Cabinet Acts.[561]

1232. Given the fact that collective agreements are source of law, therefore they are subject to compulsory rules and minimum rights set by the referred sources. In a case of concurrence of law and collective agreements, the clauses most favourable to the employee are applied[562] (principle of favourability).

§6. CONTENT OF A COLLECTIVE AGREEMENT

I. General Remarks

1233. The content of the collective agreements is defined in relation to their conventional origin and to their normative purpose. Therefore they contain the typical clauses of a private law contract; they may contain clauses to stipulate rights and obligations of the contracting parties and contain normative clauses which have the purpose of normatively establishing the remuneration and working terms and conditions in general. The last is the rules that the labour contracts, entered into between the parties embraced by the collective agreement, have to comply with. Given the normative nature of collective agreements, the normative clauses are the ones that mainly characterize the content of the collective agreements.

II. Typical Content

1234. The collective agreement shall state the names of the contracting parties, the trade union and the employers' organizations or employees, the names of their representatives, the personal, temporal, geographic and functional scope, the place and the date on which it was drawn up.

561. *See* EL 435/1968.
562. Article 3, para. 2 in combination with Art. 7, paras 2, 3 of L. 1876/1990.

III. Contractual Content: Contractual Clauses

1235. The 'contractual clauses' are the contractual content of a collective agreement, regulate the relations between the contracting parties and they have a binding effect only on the contracting parties, while they are not binding on the members of the contracting parties.

1236. A collective agreement may contain the following clauses of contractual nature:

(a) the duty to implement the agreement. This is the essence of the agreement and coincides with its minimum legal content;
(b) the duty to influence the members of the organization participating in the agreement in order to apply its normative part It is a natural part of the agreement and requires the parties, using every legal means, to induce members to live up to the agreement. This implies that the members do not conclude labour contract that go against the collective agreement. The parties have to exert influence on their members, without at the same time being able to deliver a guarantee on their members' behaviour. This is generally admitted that those two obligatory stipulations are of the essence of the collective agreement, even without being explicitly agreed and mentioned in the text of the collective agreement;
(c) the peace obligation: the peace obligation means that the contracting trade union will refrain from industrial action (e.g., strike) with regard to the effects of the collective agreement for as long as the collective agreement is in force. If a peace clause is not explicitly agreed and mentioned in the text of the collective agreement, then the contracting trade union is free to resort to strike during the period the agreement is in force in order to resume demands regarding new normative provisions even immediately after signature. The peace obligation ceases with the expiry of the collective agreement. In any case, it always remains possible for the contracting trade union to resort to industrial action for different demands bearing on issues not regulated in the agreement;
(d) matters relating to rights and obligations of the contracting parties on labour relations;
(e) issues related to the process and the terms for the conclusion of a future collective negotiation and/or clauses for the mediation and arbitration.[563]

1237. By clauses of a collective agreement, the terms of recourse to mediation and arbitration may also be regulated, as well as the whole of the process that may take place leading up to the subsequent similar collective agreement.[564] If such clauses are not included in a collective agreement, there may be an agreement on these issues during the stage of collective bargaining. In the absence of such agreement, the provisions of Articles 15 and 16 of Law 1876/1990 will apply.

563. Article 14, para. 2 of L. 1876/1990.
564. *See* Art. 2, para. 8 of L. 1876/1990.

IV. Normative Content: Normative Clauses

1238. The 'normative clauses' are the normative content of a collective agreement, create rights to the employees in the context of the employment, regulate the entire working life of the employees with a great variety of provisions both at a collective and at an individual level, and become mandatory in the labour contracts and labour relations in general of all employees and employers that fall within the scope of the collective agreement.

1239. The normative clauses have a binding effect only on third persons, meaning not the contracting parties but individual employees and employers.

1240. The contracting parties enjoy complete autonomy in determining working terms and conditions to be incorporated into individual labour contracts.

1241. The issues that may be regulated in a collective agreement are referred to, mainly, in Article 2 paragraphs 1–6 and 10 of Law 1876/1990 and are the following:

(a) matters concerning the establishment, terms of application and duration of labour contract, e.g., the conclusion, operation and termination of labour contracts, wages, benefits in money and kind, the place, time and manner of payment.(remuneration terms), work time, reduction and arrangement of work time, increments for overtime and overwork, breaks and leave of different types, promotions within the hierarchy, discipline in the company, hiring and dismissals, such as competitions, probationary periods, drawing up of the contract in writing, skills required for hiring, justified dismissals;
(b) matters concerning the exercise of trade union rights in the undertaking, the provision of facilities to trade union officials, procedures for the deduction at source of trade union dues and the transfer of the latter to the appropriate organizations;
(c) matters related to the exercise of the right to organize in the enterprise, the provision of facilities to the trade union and the manner of withholding trade union dues and their payment to the entitled unions;
(d) matters arising in respect of social security, in so far as the provisions of the agreement on such matters do not contravene constitutional provisions or the policy laid down by the state social insurance institutions. Matters relating to pensions, to the employers' and employees' contribution in compulsory social security and other relevant matters are excluded;
(e) matters concerning the management of the enterprise insofar as it directly affects labour relations;
(f) matters concerning the interpretation of the normative clauses of the said collective agreement or similar previous ones;
(g) matters concerning the provisions of Article 12 of Law 1767/1988 (workers' councils) without prejudice, however, to the powers vested in the workers' councils;

(h) matters relating to the modification or supplementation of the provisions of law on part-time and on the additional shifts.

V. Mixed Content: Mixed Clauses

1242. Some clauses are in between the normative and the contractual clauses because they neither create rights to the employees nor create obligations to the contracting parties. Whether a clause of a collective agreement is contractual, normative or mixed is a matter of interpretation and legal characterization of its content. Since the normative effect of a collective agreement is the predominant, when in doubt about the content of a clause, the normative should be accepted.

§7. The Conclusion of a Collective Agreement

I. Collective Bargaining by Free Choice and in Bona Fides: Information Given to the Parties

1243. The conclusion of a collective agreement is the end of successful collective bargaining.

1244. Collective bargaining is not only a right but also an obligation for the parties[565] involved. Trade union, employers' organizations and individual employers shall have the right and the obligation to negotiate with a view to conclude a collective agreement. The parties do not represent individual interests, theirs or that of third parties; they represent the collective interests of the employees and the employers with the aim of creating new rules of law.

1245. Collective bargaining shall be free,[566] meaning shall be the free choice of the parties and intervention by any third person, e.g., the state, public agencies or authorities, other trade unions, is prohibited.

1246. The negotiation shall be conducted in bona fides, meaning that they are to be undertaken with the purpose of the settlement of the collective dispute. To ensure this, the parties are obliged to submit clear proposals and counterproposals, to justify their positions and their oppositions, not to stall or to undermine the negotiation.[567]

1247. Negotiation generally advances through a series of meetings. The process can be quick or it can take years to reach an agreement. Proposals are the basis for

565. Article 4, para. 1 of L. 1876/1990.
566. Article 2, para. 2 of the Constitution.
567. Article 4, para. 3 of L. 1876/1990.

the negotiations. Each party has an opportunity to present and make arguments for their proposals, and in some cases proposals may lead to counterproposals by the other party.

1248. The employers' side and the public agencies are obliged to provide the employees' side with comprehensive and precise information and any other information likely to facilitate negotiation on the issues under consideration. This shall apply to information on the financial situation, economic policy and personnel policy of the enterprise.[568] The representatives of the parties are bound by confidentiality.

1249. The state authorities, for their part, shall supply all necessary information on national economic developments, on the employment situation in the various sectors of the economy and on prices and wages.

II. The Collective Bargaining Process

1250. The process for a collective agreement to be concluded is regulated by Articles 4 and 5 of Law 1876/1990.[569]

1251. The party intending to exercise its right to collective bargaining shall notify the other party in writing (invitation to negotiate) of the place where the negotiations are to be held, of the issues to be addressed and of the persons empowered to conduct the negotiation in question.

1252. The invitation to negotiate is filed with the competent public agency, as an act of public announcement of the beginning of the negotiations' process having the aim of concluding a collective agreement, entailing the creation of new rules of law. This notification is subject neither to control of its legitimacy (of the invitation and its content, that is) nor to any requirement for any licence or approval on the part of the public agency.

1253. The other party shall agree to the negotiations and appoint its representatives within 10 working days of the date on which it is notified of the issues to be addressed in the negotiations.

1254. The said time limit of ten days may often be reduced to twenty-four hours, where the matters at issue are of such a nature as to require immediate settlement.

1255. The representatives of the trade union organization empowered to negotiate shall be appointed by the executive committee of the organizations concerned unless otherwise stipulated by their rules or statutes.

568. Article 4, para. 4 of L. 1876/1990.
569. *See also* Art. 2, para. 8 of L. 1876/1990.

1256. The notification of the invitation effectively expresses the existence of a collective dispute, and for that reason in Article 4 paragraph 3 of Law 1876/1990 there is explicit mention of the 'settlement of a collective dispute' through negotiation and the conclusion of a collective agreement. That is to say, there is an expression of a conflict and of the intention to settle this conflict through a collective agreement. The listing of the issues to be negotiated defines both the content of the collective conflict and the framework of the negotiation. During the negotiation, the issues may be specified, extended, enhanced or limited, among other possibilities.

III. Conclusion, Type and Entry into Force

1257. The collective agreement must be written. It is signed in three copies.

1258. In order for the collective agreement to take on normative force and entries into force, one of the copies shall be filed, by an authorized person, with the competent authority,[570] the Labour Inspectorate or the Ministry of Labour. The official in charge shall make out and sign a certificate of registration of the original copy of the agreement; this certificate shall also be signed by the person filing the agreement.

1259. If negotiations fail, the parties may either terminate the process without the settlement of the collective dispute or conclude a common contract or recourse to the services of a third party, e.g., conciliator, mediator, arbitrator, as will be analysed below.

§8. Institutionalized Types

1260. Under Article 3 paragraph 1 of Law 1876/1990, there are four types of collective agreement by the criterion of the group of employees that fall under their scope. As these types are defined by *jus cogens* law, social partners may not create new ones.

1261. The institutionalized types of collective agreements are the following:

(a) NGCA for employees all over the country regardless of their occupation or the sector or the enterprise they work to;
(b) sectoral collective agreements for the employees of a sector of the economy (of a number of similar undertakings) in a city or a region (regional) or the country (national);
(c) enterprise-level collective agreements for the employees of an undertaking or an enterprise;
(d) same-occupation collective agreements for employees of the same profession/occupation in a city or a region (regional) or the country (national).

570. Article 5 of L. 1876/1990.

1262. The conclusion of a collective agreement does not prevent collective negotiation for the conclusion of a collective agreement of another type.

§9. RELATIONSHIP BETWEEN COLLECTIVE AGREEMENTS OF DIFFERENT TYPES

1263. In the previous legislation,[571] NGCAs determined the minimum working terms and conditions and the minimum remuneration for all the employees in private and public sector, regardless of whether they were or not members of the contracting trade union. Similarly all employers were bounded. Consequently, no other collective agreement could regulate the same issues in a way less favourable to the employees (principle of favour).

1264. In the current legislation, according to Article 3 paragraph 2 and Article 8 paragraph 1 of Law 1876/1990, as amended and modified by Law 4093/2012, the principle of favourability does not apply. The following apply:

(a) The normative clauses of the NGCA, which regulate non-remuneration issues, determine the minimum levels of working terms and conditions for all employees in the private sector. Therefore, the normative clauses of other collective agreements may not regulate the same issue in a less favourable way for the employees.
(b) The normative clauses of the NGCAs that regulate remuneration issues do not determinate the minimum remuneration levels for all the employees in the private sector. Therefore, the normative clauses of other collective agreements may regulate remuneration issues in a way more or less favourable for the employees not covered by NGCA. But, in case of an enterprise-level collective agreement, if the contracting employer is a member of the employers' association that signed the NGCA, then the enterprise-level collective agreement may not include for the same issues clauses less favourable for the employees of the said enterprise.

§10. COLLECTIVE AGREEMENTS IN CONFLICT: CONCURRENCE OF COLLECTIVE AGREEMENTS

1265. Concurrence of collective agreements occurs if a labour contract simultaneously falls within the scope of more collective agreements of different types, which regulate the same issues differently. In such a case the following apply:

571. Article 3, para. 2 of L. 1876/1990 stated that 'Sectoral, company level and national or regional collective occupational collective agreements may not allow or include work terms less favourable to the employees than the terms of the NGCA', while Art. 8, para. 1 stated that: 'National General Collective agreements define the minimum levels of work for the employees of the country. These employees include those with an employment under private law in the public sector, legal persons of public law and local authorities organizations.'

(1) in case of the concurrence of an NGCA and an enterprise-level collective agreement:
  (a) for the non-remuneration clauses, the more favourable shall apply (there can be a combination of the clauses of both the collective agreements);
  (b) for the remuneration clauses:
    – if the employer being one of the contracting parties to the enterprise-level collective agreement is a member of (at least one of) the employers' associations being contracting parties to the NGCA, the clauses that regulate the remuneration in a way more favourable for the employee shall apply (there cannot be a combination of the clauses of both the collective agreements);
    – if the said employer is not a member of (at least one of) the employers' associations being contracting parties to the NGCA, the clauses of the enterprise-level collective agreement shall apply, regardless whether they are more or less favourable for the employee.

(2) in case of the concurrence of an NGCA and a sectoral or same-occupation collective agreement, the agreement more favourable for the employees shall take precedence;[572]

(3) in case of the concurrence of a sectoral and same-occupation collective agreements, the sectoral agreement shall apply, regardless of whether it is more or less favourable for the employee;[573]

(4) until the end of the Economic Adjustment Programme, that means until 20 August 2018, in case of the concurrence of a sectoral and an enterprise-level collective agreement, the latter shall apply, regardless of whether it is more or less favourable for the employee.[574] As from 21 August 2018 in the same case the agreement more favourable for the employee shall apply;

(5) in case of the concurrence of a same-occupation and an enterprise-level, the latter shall apply, regardless whether it is more or less favourable for the employee.[575]

1266. If different work conditions are simultaneously regulated by collective agreements of different types, all of them shall apply.

§11. Succession of Collective Agreements

1267. We refer to 'succession of collective agreements' when a collective agreement is followed by a similar one. The succession of collective agreements is regulated by the principle of order under which 'the most recent law shall take precedence over the older one'. Consequently, the most recent collective agreement shall apply, regardless of whether it is or not less favourable for the employees.[576]

---

572. Article 3, para. 2 (as amended after L. 4093/2012) and Art. 10, para. 1 of L. 1876/1990.
573. Article 10, para. 2 of L. 1876/1990; AP 43/2017.
574. Article 10, para. 2 of L. 1876/1990 as amended by Art. 5 para. 1 L. 4475/2017.
575. Article 10, para. 2 of L. 1876/1990 with the supplement of Art. 37, para. 6 of L. 4024/2011.
576. AP 227/2018, AP 316/2017.

1268. Since collective agreements are, among others, the means for the adaptation, in a short and fair time period, of work conditions and remuneration to the changing socio-economic environment, on the expiration of one collective agreement one other similar follows for working terms, conditions and remuneration to be continuously regulated by collection agreement.[577] This was of great importance given the lack of regulations by law on those issues.

§12. Parties to the Collective Bargaining and Collective Agreements (Contracting Parties)

1269. The ability to conclude a collective agreement and to conduct the relevant negotiation is an act of the right of collective autonomy and is recognized, only by the provisions of the law, as special ability conferred on specific persons.[578] These persons are trade unions, employers' associations and specific separate employers.[579] Withdrawal from that ability is void.

1270. On the employees' side this ability is assigned only to trade unions. More specifically, for the employees' side, this ability is recognized for the following trade unions according to the type of the collective agreement that is to be concluded:

(a) For the conclusion of an NGCA, to the third-level trade unions.[580]
(b) For the conclusion of a sectoral collective agreement to the first- and second-level sectoral trade unions with constituting members drawn from all the employees of the said sector.[581]
(c) For the conclusion of same-occupation collective agreements to the first- and second-level trade unions of the same profession/occupation with constituting members drawn from all the employees in the country with the said occupation.[582]
(d) For the conclusion of an enterprise-level collective agreement to the enterprise-level trade union with members drawn from all the employees in the said enterprise's. In the absence of such a trade union to the association of persons with members drawn from all the employees in the said enterprise.[583] In the absence of such an association to the respective first-level sectoral trade union.

577. Or at least, this was the standard until the entry into effect of Act of Cabinet (PIS) 6/2012.
578. Article 3, paras 3–7 and Art. 6 of L. 1876/1990.
579. Professional Associations having the legal form of Legal Persons of Public Law are not free associations and they are neither trade unions (*see* Art. 1 para. 2 last verse of L. 1264/1982) nor employers' associations. Some Legal Persons of Public Law were excluded in accordance with Art. 6 para. 1 s. g of L. 1876/1990 in order to make possible the collective regulation of work terms and remuneration of employees in law offices, notaries' offices and certain other offices; *see* ILO Convention 154/1983, ratified by LD 2403/1996.
580. Article 3, para. 3 of L. 1876/1990.
581. Article 3, para. 4 of L. 1876/1990.
582. Article 3, paras 6, 7(b) of L. 1876/1990.
583. Article 3, para. 5 of L. 1876/1990 as amended by Art. 37, para. 1 of L. 4024/2011.

1271. On the employers' side the same ability is assigned to the follows:

(a) for the conclusion of a national same-occupation collective agreement to an employers' association of wider representativeness or nationwide range;[584]
(b) for the conclusion of sectoral collective agreements to an employers' associations that represent the employers' side in the said sector;[585]
(c) for the conclusion of a sectoral collective agreements in banking sector, the collective agreements may be concluded by employers represented by a common representative or representatives, provided that either they employ at least the 70% of the employees in the banking sector or they are at least the five of the biggest employers in the banking sector, on the criterion of the number of the employees they employ. Other employers may participate in the collective bargaining and sign the collective agreement;[586]
(d) for the conclusion of a national same-occupation collective agreement to an employers' association of wider representativeness or nationwide range and of a local same-occupation collective agreement to a local employers' association;[587]
(e) for the conclusion of an enterprise-level collective agreement to the employer of the said enterprise regardless of the number of the employees;[588]
(f) for the conclusion of collective agreements for employees in lawyers', notaries' and other similar offices to the relevant associations, which are legal entities of public law and representative bodies of the employers of these employees, who (employers) as practitioners are forced by the law to be members to these associations.

1272. The power to conclude a collective agreement is called 'the ability to conclude collective agreement'[589] and we may refer, correspondingly, to an 'able' trade union or employers' organization. Every 'able' trade union or employers' organization is not competent to conclude a specific type of collective agreement. Law defines, as mentioned above, which trade union or employers' organization is competent to conclude a specific type of collective agreement.

1273. A collective agreement concluded by a not 'able' trade union or employers' organization does not non-exist, while the one concluded by a non-competent trade union or employers' organization is null and void.

---

584. Article 3, para. 3 of L. 1876/1990.
585. Article 3, para. 4 of L. 1876/1990. In some cases this ability is assumed by separate employers, such as in the case of the banking sector in accordance with Art. 3, para. 4 of L. 1876/1990.
586. Article 3, para. 5 of L. 1876/1990 as amended by Art. 37, para. 1 of L. 4024/2011.
587. Article 3, paras 6, 7 of L. 1876/1990.
588. Article 3, para. 5 and Art. 6 para. 1 s. b of L. 1876/1990; in the previous provision of Art. 6 para. 1 s. b, in order for an enterprise-level collective agreement to be concluded, there was a threshold of fifty employees in the enterprise.
589. Article 6, para. 1, s. a, sub-para. a of L. 1876/1990.

§13. The Most Representative Trade Union

1274. On the employers' side, more than one competent employers' associations may act jointly.

1275. On the other hand, on the employees' side, only one trade union may act, in accordance with Article 6, paragraph 1 section a parts b, c of Law 1876/1990. These provisions refer to the cases where it is possible that more than one able and competent trade union exist. In such a case, not all of the existing trade unions have the power to conclude the collective agreement. Only the most representative of them has the power. The criterion of representativeness is based, in accordance with Article 6 paragraph 2, on the number of employees that participated in the most recent elections for the Administrative Board. The number of trade union's members is irrelevant. The power of the most representative trade union to conclude a collective agreement is called 'representativeness to conclude collective agreement' and, correspondingly, we refer to 'the most representative trade union'.

1276. In the case of doubts raised against the representativeness of the trade union, the law provides for a recourse to a tripartite committee, which is composed of one lawyer of the state, one representative of the employers and one representative of the employees, and which makes the relevant decision based on the abovementioned criterion. More specifically, when the conclusion of a collective agreement is pursued by a trade union which is able and competent, it addresses to the related employers' side (employers' association or single employer) the invitation to negotiate. When the initiative is received by the employers' side, this side addresses the invitation to negotiate to the trade union which is able and competent. The invitation is notified to the competent Labour Inspectorate.[590] In a case where there is more than one able and competent trade union and one of them doubts the representativeness of the trade union called on, it may claim, in accordance with Article 6 paragraph 2 verses b-st, the right to negotiate and conclude the collective agreement. In that case, the trade union appeals, within the deadlines set by the law, to a committee formed under Article 15 of Law 1264/1982, for the issue of representativeness to be decided. The Committee is the only competent organ to decide on the issue; the courts have no competence. If this appeal is not made within the deadline set by the law, then it is presumed irrefutably that the trade union called on is legitimized for the negotiation and the conclusion of the collective agreement. The collective agreement that is concluded in this case is not void for that reason.

§14. Intervention in Collective Bargaining

1277. In some cases, during the negotiations' process for the conclusion of an enterprise-level, sectoral or same-occupation collective agreement, although only one trade union can conclude the collective agreement, more than one trade union can participate by exercising the right to intervene in accordance with Article 4,

590. Article 4, para. 2(b) of L. 1876/1990.

paragraph 5 of Law 1876/1990. This intervention is performed with a unilateral declaration, in writing or orally, which is notified to the parties in negotiation. The parties are obliged to accept the intervention. The interveners are not part of the collective dispute and if the collective agreement is concluded they are not referred as contractual parties. They can only participate in the negotiations. They may also sign the concluded collective agreement. If they do so, they are covered by the agreement.[591]

§15. The Binding Effect

I. The Personal Scope

1278. As mentioned above the contractual terms of a collective agreement bind the contracting parties and the normative ones bind the employees and employers within the scope of the collective agreement.

1279. Article 8 of Law 1876/1990, as modified by Law 4093/2012, determines the scope of collective agreements and their binding effect as follows:

(1) For the employees:
   (a) for an enterprise-level collective agreement, only the employees of the said enterprise regardless of union affiliation are bound;[592]
   (b) for a sectoral or a same-occupation collective agreement, only the employees who are direct or indirect members of the contracting trade union[593] are bound with the trade union membership being a requirement;[594]
   (c) for an NGCA, there is a distinction to be made in accordance with the content of the normative clauses included:[595]
      – by the normative clauses that regulate non-remuneration issues, all the employees in the private sector are bound; trade union membership is not required;
      – by the normative clauses that regulate remuneration issues, only the employees who are employed by employers that are members of the employers' contracting parties are bound; trade union membership is not required for the employees.

   Conclusively, trade union membership is required only for employees to be covered by a sectoral or a same-occupation collective agreement.

(2) For the employers:

591. In view of Art. 8, paras 2, 3, this brings legal consequences only in relation with sectoral and same-occupation collective agreements.
592. Article 8, paras 2, 3 of L. 1876/1990.
593. *Ibid.*
594. AP 874/2018.
595. Article 8, para. 1 of L. 1876/1990 as modified by L. 4093/2012.

(a) for an enterprise-level collective agreement, only the employer of the said enterprise;[596]
(b) for a sectoral or a same-occupation collective agreement, only the members of the employers' contracting parties are bound;[597]
(c) for a sectoral collective agreement concluded by employers acting individually, only the said employers;
(d) For an NGCA, there is a distinction to be made in accordance with the content of the normative clauses included:[598]
   - by the normative clauses that regulate non-remuneration issues, all the employers in the private sector are bound;
   - by the normative clauses that regulate remuneration issues, only the employers that are members of the employers' contracting parties are bound.

Conclusively, the membership of an employers' organization is required but for the employers to be covered by the normative clauses of an NGCA regulating non-remuneration issues.

II. The Consequences of the Binding Effect

1280. Given the fact that collective agreements regulate work conditions and remuneration, in order for a collective agreement to be applied, both the parties to a labour contract should be within the scope of the collective agreement.

1281. Where the status of membership is required, once a labour contract (meaning, both parties) falls within the scope of a collective agreement, the binding effect of the collective agreement remains even if either or both of them cease to be members.

1282. The binding effect takes place automatically with the conclusion of the collective agreement.

1283. The normative clauses of the collective agreement are automatically and compulsorily applied to the individual labour contracts already concluded or to those that will be concluded in the future until the termination of the collective agreement. The provisions of the collective agreement are not definitively incorporated into the individual contracts instead of the same provisions they contain. They are only provisionally accepted in the individual contract until either a new similar collective agreement is concluded (succession of collective agreements) or until, after the termination of the collective agreement, the parties to the labour contract make a new individual agreement *in malus* or *in pejus* to the employee.

596. Article 8, paras 2, 3 of L. 1876/1990.
597. Article 8, para. 2 of L. 1876/1990.
598. Article 8, para. 1 of L. 1876/1990.

§16. The Extension of a Collective Agreement and the Suspension of the Extension

1284. As mentioned above, the sectoral and same-occupation collective agreements have a binding effect only for the members of the contracting parties. A collective agreement of that type may be declared as generally compulsory for all of the sector's or the occupation's employers, and employees provided that it already binds employers who employ 51% of the sector's or the occupation's employees (extension of a collective agreement).[599]

1285. The Ministerial Decision is issued by the Minister of Labour, following an opinion delivered by the Supreme Council for Labour. The Minister acts ex officio or upon the submission of a competent trade union, even if the latter is not the most representative one and did not participate in the conclusion of the collective agreement or intervened during the collective negotiations.

1286. The ministerial decision, extending the scope of a collective agreement, will start producing its effect from the date of its publication in the Government Gazette, no retroactively from its date of issue, or from the date of submission of the relevant trade union's demand. The Council of State in its case law before the crisis had pointed out that the extension mechanism serves the public interest and the cohesion of the collective negotiations system.

1287. The extension was a frequent practice in almost every sector and profession.

1288. In accordance with paragraph 6 of Article 37 of Law 4024/2011, this prerogative of the Minister of Employment had been suspended until the end of the Economic Adjustment Programme, that means until 20 August 2018.[600]

1289. Given the fact, as mentioned above, that the sectoral and same-occupation collective agreements have a binding effect only for the members of the contracting parties, the suspension of extension mechanism urges employers to leave the organization in which they are members and opt out from the binding effect of the sectoral and same occupationally collective agreement.

§17. Accession to a Collective Agreement

1290. Trade union organizations and individual employers not bound by a collective agreement may jointly accede to any collective agreement concerning them.[601] Workers' trade union organizations may accede to any collective agreement already binding upon their employers.

599. Article 11, para. 2, 3 of L. 1876/1990.
600. Article 10, para. 2 of L. 1876/1990 as amended by Art. 5 para. 1 L. 4475/2017.
601. Article 10 of L. 1876/1990.

1291. Accession to a collective agreement shall be effected by private contract; such contact shall be notified to the parties of the agreement and filed with the local branch of the Labour Inspectorate, which shall enter it in the special register of collective agreements. An enterprise agreement shall not be open to accession by an employer or a trade union from another establishment.

§18. Bound by Agreement Between a Trade Union and an Employer: Bound by Agreement Between the Parties to a Labour Contract

1292. A trade union and an employer that are not bound by a collective agreement, may accede to it by mutual agreement, irrespective of whether the said collective agreement concerns the sector of the employers' enterprise or the employee's occupation.[602]

1293. On the basis of Article 361 of the CC, an agreement between an employer and an employee in which the latter will receive as payment for the work he/she provides to the former the amount provided for in a currently valid or in the future to be valid collective agreement that does not concern them or that lays down conditions that are not met by the employee in question may be considered valid. For such an agreement to be valid, no formal written agreement is necessary and it may be either explicit or tacit in form.[603] In such cases, the terms of the collective agreements referred to in the agreement between the employer and the employee are contractually valid for both parties.[604]

§19. Duration and Termination of a Collective Agreement

I. Duration

1294. Collective agreements are by nature continuous contracts. In accordance with current legislation,[605] their duration is set from a minimum of one year up to a maximum of three years. The parties may expressly agree upon the duration within the limits set by the law.

1295. Under previous legislation, the duration of the collective agreement could be of definite or indefinite period. However, it could not be less than one year and where the collective agreement lasted more than one year it was deemed to have been concluded for an indefinite period.

602. Article 11 para. 1 of L. 1876/1990.
603. AP 874/2018, AP 1109/2017 AP 773/2017, AP 567/2004.
604. AP 874/2008, AP 692/2014.
605. Article 9 of L. 1876/1990 as amended by Art. 2 of Act of Cabinet (PIS) 6/2012 and Art. 12 of L. 1876/1990.

1296. The collective agreement comes into force the day of its submission to the competent public service.[606]

1297. Though, the contracting parties may agree, that a collective agreement shall have retroactive effect as from the date on which the previous collective agreement ceased to apply, either because its duration had expired or because it had been terminated by a notice of termination. In such a case the duration of the new agreement shall begin that date. Where there was no previous collective agreement, the new one shall have retroactive effect as from the date on which negotiations began.

1298. The contracting parties may also agree that the collective agreement, all or part of it, will come into force at a subsequent time.

II. The Termination

A. The Normal Termination

1299. A collective agreement expires either on the completion of the third year or the agreed shorter duration or the conclusion of another similar collective agreement or when either of the parties gives a notice of termination to the other.

1300. A collective agreement may be terminated by a notice of termination one year as from the date on which it came into force. A notice of termination may be given during the first year, only in case of an appreciable alteration of the socio-economic conditions prevailing at the time of its conclusion.

1301. Notice of denunciation has to be in writing and served by a bailiff both on the other party and on the local branch of the Labour Inspectorate with which the agreement was filed. The official in charge of the branch of the Labour Inspectorate shall make a notification in the margin of the special register in which the collective agreement was registered.

1302. Notice of denunciation shall be accompanied by a brief statement of the grounds for it and of the issues to be the subject of the future collective bargaining. Those grounds may be the occurrence of events that make onerous for the complainant's side the continuance of the collective agreement and that, if the contracting party had had knowledge of or could have foreseen these events, it would have not concluded the agreement in its original form. In accordance with a different interpretation approach, this occurrence of events significantly distorts the balance that had been achieved through the collective agreement so as to justify the provision of new terms before the passage of the minimum duration of one year or of the agreed duration of the collective agreement. Such events may be related to the

606. Article 5, para. 3 of L. 1876/1990.

increase in the cost of living, an issue that can be used for the termination of every type of collective agreement, or an increase of the operational cost in the sector or the enterprise.

B. The Results of the Termination

1. Contractual Clauses

1303. The termination of a collective agreement entails the expiry of the contractual clauses, except for those that, due to their content, still apply after the termination.

2. Normative Clauses

a. Clauses Remaining in Force for a Three or Six-Month Period (Constructive Continuation of the Collective Agreement)

1304. The normative clauses remain in force for an additional period of three months, starting from the termination of the collective agreement.[607,608] Especially for the NGCA this period is for six months, and the NGCA shall apply to the employees engaged (i.e., new recruits are included), provided that in the meanwhile a new similar collective agreement has not been concluded.[609]

b. Clauses Remaining in Force Afterwards ('After-Effect', *Metenergia* of a Collective Agreement)

1305. After the completion of the three-month period, the normative clauses that regulate issues other than remuneration still remain in force.[610] New employees however would not acquire them.

1306. The normative clauses still remain in force those that regulate the basic wage, per month or per day, and benefits for seniority at the level that this benefit will have reached for each employee until 14 February 2012, children, studies and dangerous work.

1307. These remaining clauses acquire a contractual character, meaning that they may be changed either by an agreement between the employer and the employee as a content of the individual labour contract or by the normative clauses of a new similar collective. In both cases, the new individual agreement and the new clauses may be *in malus* or *in pejus* to the employee.

---

607. Article 40 of L. 4320/2015.
608. Article 2, para. 4 of Cabinet Act 6/2012.
609. Article 40 of L. 4320/2015.
610. Article 2, para. 4a of Cabinet Act 6/2012.

1308. The employer is not obliged to continue paying other benefits stipulated by the terminated collective agreement and he/she may stop paying them without the employee's consent.

1309. In previous legislation, during the period of *metenergia* all normative clauses would remain in force, irrespective of their content.[611] They all acquired a contractual character, meaning that they could be changed either by an agreement between the employer and the employee as a content of the individual labour contract or by the normative clauses of a new similar collective. In both cases, the new individual agreement and the new clauses could be *in malus* or *in pejus* to the employee.

1310. Under both sets of legislation, the previous and the current one, new employees would not acquire the wage and the benefits of the terminated collective agreement.

C. The Abnormal Ipso Jure Termination of Collective Agreements by PIS 6/2012

1311. On 14 February 2012, the date that Cabinet Act 6/2012 entered into force, numerous collective agreements of different types were still in force.

1312. The termination of those was regulated by Article 2, paragraphs 2, 3, and 4 sub-paragraph b of Cabinet Act 6/2012.

1313. Collective agreements being in force for at least 24 months on 14 February 2012, were terminated on 14 February 2013.

1314. Collective agreements being in force for less than 24 months on 14 February 2012, will terminate after three years as from the date on which they came into force, meaning until 14 February 2015.

1315. In both cases, the collective agreements may be terminated earlier by a written notice of termination, as referred to above.

1316. In all cases, the three-month period and the period afterwards referred above shall follow the termination.

611. Article 9, para. 5 of L. 1876/1990.

Chapter 6. Strike

Viktoria Sp. Douka

§1. The Concept of Strike

1317. The social partners may engage in industrial conflict. There no legal rules laying down a particular course of action for solving such conflict. Legal rules are laying down only if the action is strike. These rules are found in Articles 19–22 of Law 1264/1982 On the Democratization of the Union Movement and the Safeguarding of the Union Rights of Employees, and are legally enforceable in court.

1318. A strike is the collective temporary abstention of employees from work, decided by a trade union, with the aim (the immediate goal–means) of exerting pressure on the employers' side, mainly, or on the state, in order (a further goal) that employees may safeguard or promote their common collective interests of any kind, e.g., financial, labour, trade union and insurance interests.

I. Abstention from Work

1319. Abstention from work may take the form:

(a) of the cessation of all work: employees can either be present at the workplace (a sit-down strike) or absent (a walk-out);
(b) of the continuation of work but at a pace slower than usual, where the volume of work is considerably decreased in relation to that offered under ordinary conditions ('white-strike' or 'go-slow'); when the decrease in work volume is attributed to the fact that the employees are strictly following those rules or instructions that should be applied in the workplace ('work-to-rule');
(c) of covering the whole of the working time or the day (twenty-four hours); if it covers part of them, it is called 'work-stoppage'.

1320. Abstention from work is temporary, meaning that it takes place along with the intention of the strikers to continue their work normally after the strike is terminated.

1321. During the strike, there is a temporary cessation (whole or partial) of the operation of the enterprise or a temporary state of non-ordinary operation, whole or partial, thus creating a loss for the employer, the economy as a whole, society and the state. This loss is the means by which pressure is applied for the adoption of the demands of the strike, and is included in the concept of strike. Consequently, this loss is not a criterion by itself or an argument for the issuing of legal decisions that characterize the strike as illegal or abusive.

II. Collective Character

1322. The collective character of the strike arises from the collective character of the demands and the promotion of collective interests by that means and is not related to the number of employees who participate in that action or to those employees as persons.

§2. Constitutional Guarantees

I. Article 23 of the Constitution

1323. To strike is identified as a constitutionally regulated right in accordance with Article 23, paragraphs 1 and 2 of the Constitution and specifically as an act of the SD; a strike may be declared only by a legally established trade union and only for the safeguarding and promoting the financial and the general labour interests of the employees.

1324. According to paragraph 2 of Article 23 of the Constitution, strikes of any nature and form whatsoever are prohibited to judicial functionaries and those serving in the security corps. Despite this prohibition, strikes have been undertaken by the above groups mainly in the last two decades. According to the same provision, the right to strike is subject to specific limitations under law regulating this right in the case of public servants, employees of local government agencies and of public legal persons, as well as in the case of the employees of all types of enterprises of a public nature or of public benefit, the operation of which is of vital importance in serving the basic needs of the social entity. These limitations may not be carried to the point of abolishing the right to strike or hindering the legal exercise of this right.

II. Article 48 of the Constitution

1325. Article 48 of the Constitution lays down that the Parliament or the President of the Republic, at the suggestion of the government, may suspend, throughout the state or in part of it, the force of the provisions of Article 22 (right to strike, etc.), in case of war or mobilization owing to external dangers, in the case of serious disturbances or of evident threat to public order and the security of the state. Moreover, Article 22 of the Constitution lays down that 'special laws shall determine the requisition (conscription) of personal services in case of war or mobilisation or to face urgent social emergencies'.

§3. A Right under the Private Law

1326. To strike is a right of private law since its holders are private persons (employees), it is decided upon by private legal persons (trade unions) and it is exercised within a relationship between private persons (labour relations) and the settlement of legal disputes about a strike are under the jurisdiction of civil courts.

§4. Holders of the Right

I. Every Employee

1327. Holder of the right to strike is 'every employee', in accordance with Article 19 paragraph 1 of Law 1264/1982, regardless of any characteristic of his/her labour contract, e.g., regardless of whether it is void or not of definite or indefinite period, regardless of the type of work that the employee provides, the position of the employee in the enterprise.

II. Every Trade Union

1328. However, the decision to strike is not taken by the employees, in person or in groups, but exclusively by legally established trade unions, as referred to in Article 23 paragraph 2 of the Constitution and Article 19 paragraph 1 of Law 1264/1982, which are responsible to act according to law in order for the strike to be legal. A strike that has been called by a not legally established trade union is absolutely illegal.

1329. A strike that takes place without the previous decision of a trade union is illegal, but it can be legalized if, during the strike, the trade union which could legally have called the strike takes a decision to 'adopt' the strike. There is some debate as to whether this 'adoption' of the strike confers legitimacy from the beginning of the strike, or from the time of the adoption.

III. Participation in the Strike

1330. When a legally established trade union decides on a strike, the employees that are members of the trade union participate in the strike. When the trade union is a federation, a workers' centre or a confederation, the employees that have the right to participate in the strike are the members of the primary trade unions that are members of the federation, the workers' centre or the confederation. However, since the right to strike is a right of every employee and not only of those that are members of a trade union, in the strike can participate employees that are not members provided that they could be members. These employees are considered as 'potential members' of the union. This is the final interpretation of the provision of Article 20 paragraph 1 of Law 1264/1982, which declares that 'Employees of the sector or the enterprise who are not members of the trade union that called the strike may also participate in it.'

§5. The Decision for the Strike: Trade Union's Competent Organs

1331. In accordance with Article 20 paragraph 1 of Law 1264/1982, a strike can be called as follows, depending on the type of union. Any decision by the General Assembly to take strike action requires the presence of at least half (1/2) of the fully paid-up members for the debate and decision to declare the strike.[612]

I. First-Level Trade Union

1332. In a first-level trade union a strike can be called by:

(a) the General Assembly of the union;
(b) the board, except where otherwise provided by statute, when:
  - the strike will take the form of work-stoppages that will not take place on the same day or in the same workweek;
  - the trade union is of broader regional or national scope.

1333. In accordance with Article 8 paragraphs 1, 2, 3 of Law 1264/1982, the decision for the strike is to be made by secret ballot, with a quorum determined by the applicable provisions.

1334. In first-level trade unions that have the legal character of a union of persons, the decision is made by a secret ballot of the whole body of employees, with a majority ruling.[613]

II. Federations, Workers' Centres, Confederations

1335. In federations, workers' centres, confederations, unless provided for otherwise by the statute, a strike can be called by the board.

§6. Aims of a Strike

1336. In accordance with Article 23 paragraph 2 clause a of the Constitution and Article 19 paragraph 1 of Law 1264/1982 the right to strike is identified as a right

612. Article 8, para. 2 of L. 1264/1982 as amended by Art. 211 of L. 4517/2018.
613. Article 1, para. 3 verse A case GG of L. 1264/1982.

carried out exclusively for the attainment of specific purposes, being the safeguarding and promoting the collective interests of the employees. The achievement of these aims justifies and legalizes every act of industrial action.

1337. In accordance with Article 19 paragraph 1 of Law 1264/1982, a strike is identified as:

(a) a means of safeguarding and promoting the economic, labour, association and insurance rights of employees;
(b) an expression of solidarity for the attainment of the above aims (sympathy or solidarity strike);
(c) an expression of solidarity with employees of multinational companies or multinational groups of undertakings abroad, under the specific provisions of Article 19 paragraph 1 sub-paragraph b of Law 1264/1982.

§7. Strike's Demands

I. Collective Interests

1338. In accordance with the purposes of a strike, a strike's demands must promote and support the collective interests of those employees who strike or of those in support of whom a sympathy/solidarity strike takes place. As to content, a strike's demands must have to do with to the economic, labour, union or insurance interests of the employees, as stated above.

1339. The safeguarding and promotion of the collective interests of the employees, which is the aim of the freedom of trade union in general and of the right to strike in particular, is undertaken by means of the submission of specific demands by trade unions to those parties that may accept and satisfy them, that is, to employers or to the state, as recipients of these demands. If the demands are rejected, the trade union may call a strike as a means of exerting pressure for the acceptance of these demands. Therefore, every strike necessarily entails specific demands which define the aim of the strike in the particular case, and these demands legitimize the strike as an attempt to achieve the aims of the union. Once a strike is called, the recipients of the demands become objects of the strike. The demands of the strike must promote and support the collective interests of the employees who strike, or of the employees on whose behalf a sympathy strike takes place. As to content, demands must relate to the financial, labour, union and insurance and other collective interests of the employees.

II. Solidarity Strike

A. *General Remarks*

1340. As an expression of solidarity, a strike can take multiple forms. A strike can take place in order to support employees of a different enterprise, who are on strike, when the interests of the employees of both enterprises are similar. A strike may also take place in order to support one or more employees of the enterprise or the sector of economy, when, at the expense of the said individuals, abusive measures and decisions have been taken. These abusive measures and decisions must be considered to harm not only the interests of the said employees but the collective interests of the strikers as well. In that case, the individual legal dispute that has been created following the adoption of the abusive measures has created the disruption of a collective interest. The strike is called to address this disruption in order that it may not happen again in the future.

B. *Solidarity Strike and Multinational Companies*

1341. A special case of a strike as a means of solidarity is provided for in Article 19 paragraph 1 verse B of Law 1264/1982 concerning employees in a multinational enterprise or in a multinational group of enterprises. Here, a precondition for the strike to be called is that the employees of the enterprise or group of enterprises abroad are already on strike and that the outcome of that strike will have an effect on the employees of the enterprise in Hellas. The legitimacy of this strike is based on the fact that the employer of the whole of the employees, nationally and abroad, is the same entity. The group of companies or enterprises are included in this case due to the fact that there is a common centre of decision-making that regulates labour relations of the whole of the employees of the group. The above case leads to the creation of a community of employees' interests regardless of the country in which they work. The direct consequence of the above is that, by objective evaluation, it is expected that the acceptance or decline of the demands of the strike abroad may have analogous effects on the employees within the country, although it does not necessarily imply that the acceptance of the demands of the employees abroad will necessarily have a similar effect on the labour relations of the employees at the in-country national level.

III. Lack of Collective Interests

1342. Demands not associated with collective interests of the employees or having a different character from those mentioned above cannot be legitimate strike demands and thus cannot render the strike legal. Demands that do not have a collective character or are not associated with collective interests in their content, as by Article 19 paragraph 1 of Law 1264/1982, cannot create collective disputes and thus cannot justify the strike.

IV. Collective Disputes and Legal Disputes

1343. However, collective disputes can give rise to legal disputes, as mentioned above. It is possible for a legal dispute to create a collective dispute, if and when the behaviour of the employer (that caused the legal dispute) infringes not only the rights of one or more specific employees, but also constitutes a threat to the collective interests of the employees by denying these interests or is an abusive act of the managerial prerogative that concerns the whole or the majority of the employees of the enterprise or reveals the need for a more efficient safeguarding of the collective interests of the employees through the creation of a new regulation. It is not given, therefore, that from a legal dispute a collective one will arise. In order to clarify whether a legal dispute can become a collective one or an infringement of rights become an infringement of collective interests must be carefully examined. In case of a collective dispute, a strike can be called in order to safeguard the collective interests, e.g., if the rehiring of an employee was a breach of a clause of collective agreement. The strike is called regardless of whether there will be a trial or not. The settlement of a legal dispute, in general or in a specified manner in accordance with the interests of the trade union that calls the strike or of the interest of the specific employees that are parties to the legal dispute, cannot be a demand of the strike.

§8. Trade Union's Obligations

I. In Private Sector

1344. The trade union that calls for a strike has certain obligations stipulated by law and being preconditions for the legitimacy of the strike. These obligations are as follows.

A. *Employer's Notification (Announcement of the Strike)*

1345. The trade union that calls for a strike is obliged to notify the employer or the respective employers' association at least twenty-four hours before the start of the strike.[614] The purpose of this notification is that the strike may not be characterized as abusive because of the unawareness of the employer and his/her consequent inability to make preparations to minimize the damage that will be caused by the disruption of enterprise's operation due to the strike. The twenty-four-hour period is counted to the minute by the clock. It is not compulsory for the notification to be made in writing; however, given the fact that the trade union is responsible for proof of notification, it should be in writing so that it may constitute clear and direct proof.

614. Article 19, para. 1 of L. 1264/1982.

B. Security Staff

1346. The trade union that calls the strike is obliged to safeguard that, during the strike and due to the strike, no damage shall be caused to the facilities of the enterprise and to prevent damage and accidents.[615] For that purpose, trade union must make available security staff for the period of the strike, who, during the strike, will provide their work in order that the facilities of the enterprise shall remain safe and to prevent accidents.

1347. Members of the security staff are not strikers, they are paid as normal, they provide their work under the managerial prerogative of the employer, but their duties are restricted to acts for preventing damage and accidents and they have the right to refuse any other work, including work that they would normally carry out under regular conditions.[616]

1348. Any issues relevant to the security staff and its tasks are regulated by the clauses of a collective agreement.[617] Otherwise, by a specific agreement between the most representative trade union and the employer, which is concluded each year by 25 November and takes effect for any strikes that may be called in the enterprise during the year to come. If this is not the case either, the security staff is appointed by, and as a responsibility of, the trade union that calls the strike.[618]

C. Voluntary Public Debate

1349. The trade union, before or during the strike, may call on the employer, in writing and the document served by a bailiff, to participate in a public debate about the demands of the strike.[619] The debate, conducted by a mediator, aims at settling the dispute that has given rise to the strike or at averting the strike. The same may an employer do after he/she has been informed of the demands of the strike or the call for the strike or he/she is of the opinion that the strike will disrupt peace in the workplace.

II. In Public Sector, in Companies of a Public Nature or of Public Benefit, Etc.

1350. In public sector, in regional and local government agencies, in public organizations, in companies of a public nature or of public benefit whose function is vital to serving society, the trade union that calls for strike has further responsibilities, as the following.

615. Article 21 of L. 1264/1982.
616. Article 21, para. 3 of L. 1264/1982.
617. Article 21, para. 9 of L. 1264/1982.
618. Article 21, para. 1 of L. 1264/1982.
619. Article 3 of L. 2224/1994.

A. Mandatory Public Debate

1351. The trade union, under Article 19 paragraph 2 of Law 1264/1982, is obliged to call on the employer to participate in a public debate on the demands of the strike.[620] As mentioned above, the debate, conducted by a mediator, aims at settling the dispute that has given rise to the strike or at averting the strike. The same may an employer do after he/she has been informed of the demands of the strike or the call for the strike or he/she is of the opinion that the strike will disrupt peace in the workplace.

B. Announcement of the Strike

1352. The trade union that calls for a strike is obliged to notify the employer(s), the competent Ministry(ies) and the Ministry of Labour of the demands of the strike and the reasons on which these demands are founded.[621] This notification is made in writing and is served by a bailiff no less than four days before the date of the strike. After the strike is called, demands different than those already set out in the notifying document is forbidden to be made.

C. Basic Needs of Society

1353. The trade union that calls the strike is obliged, besides the previously mentioned security staff, to make available an additional security staff in order to serve the basic needs of the society.[622] Those mentioned above for the security staff apply for these employees as well. The basic needs of the society are defined by clauses of collective agreement or by the other means mentioned above for the security staff in private sector.

§9. Termination of the Strike by Court Judgment

1354. According to the prevailing opinion on current legislation and theory, when the strike is illegal, whosoever calls on and justifies a legal interest (e.g., the employer) can take legal action against the trade union that called for the strike and claim the strike to be declared as abusive and illegal. If the action is accepted, the court judgment is not directed against the strikers (such claim would be contrary to Article 22 paragraph 4 of the Constitution) and does not oblige them to stop the strike. It is up to the strikers to stop the strike and return to the work or not. However, if the strikers decide not to return, this may cause their dismissal, as set out below.

620. *Ibid.*
621. Article 20, para. 2 of L. 1264/1982.
622. Article 21, para. 2 of L. 1264/1982.

1355. A claim for cessation of the same strike in the future is not legal since no future strike can be the 'same' as the one that was examined in court, given the fact that the different time by itself, entails different conditions which differentiate the strikes. Every strike is unique for it is called under the specific conditions that apply at the time of the strike, regardless of the content of the demands, which may be the same.

§10. Methods for the Effectiveness of the Strike

1356. In accordance with Article 22 of Law 1264/1982, in order to ensure the effectiveness of the strike:

(a) During the strike, no strike-breakers can be hired. The term 'strike-breaker' may refer to existing employees that have the right to participate in the strike that takes place. It may also refer to employees that are hired from outside by an employer in order that the operation of the enterprise may continue during the strike, by replacing the strikers. The latter definition is the one used in the above prohibition.
(b) Lockout is forbidden. The term lockout refers to the refusal of the employer to accept the work of the employees, as a means of pressure for the settlement of the collective dispute in the interest of the employer.
(c) The termination of the strike by legal interim measure is forbidden by law.

1357. Since in the case of legal temporary measures the court judgment is based on probable cause, meaning that a full proof is not necessary,[623] it is self-evident that it is not legally acceptable that an issue of such high importance, such as the legitimacy of the strike and its continuance, can be judged on probabilities. It must be based on full proof.

§11. Legal Strike

1358. To summarize all the above, a strike is legal when the following preconditions are met:

(a) the decision to strike is made by a legally established trade union;
(b) the decision is made by the appropriate body of the trade union;
(c) the content of the demands of the strike is legal;
(d) there is an announcement of the strike;
(e) security staff is available;
(f) there is a public debate, where this is mandatory.

623. Article 690, para. 1 of the KPolD.

§12. Illegal and Abusive Strike

I. Cases

1359. The strike is illegal and abusive in the following cases:

(a) Any one of the above-mentioned preconditions is not met.
(b) Its demands are not legal; for example, they are not collective or they do not have appropriate content as mentioned above. However, in the case of multiple strike demands, the legitimacy of at least one demand applies to the whole, unless it is proven that the one valid demand has been falsely promoted in order to avoid the illegal character of the strike.

II. Consequences for the Strikers

1360. If the strike is judged to be illegal by a court judgment, the strikers face the following consequences.

1361. The strikers are obliged not to participate in the strike or to return to their work with the terms of employment and remuneration that were in effect before the strike. However, they cannot be forced to do so, as stated explicitly in Article 22 of the Constitution.

1362. The absence of the strikers from their work is arbitrary and they are not entitled for a pay for this reason, in accordance with Articles 374, 380 and 648 of the CC.

1363. When the decision for the strike has been made by a legally established trade union, it is accepted that the employee is in excusable error concerning its legitimacy, and, for that reason there can be no consequences. The employer, however, can call on and prove facts shown that a specific employee, by acting as a prudent employee, could have been aware of the illegal or abusive character of the strike.

1364. In the above case, the labour contract is not automatically terminated but the period of participation in the illegal strike is characterized as an arbitrary absence from work, meaning that it can be used as a reason for the termination of the labour contract, regardless of whether it is of definite or indefinite period. Moreover, it can justify the deduction from the striker's salary of an amount equal to the salary for the period that he/she participated in the illegal strike.

1365. After the court judgment, that characterizes the strike as illegal, is published and after the employer notifies the employees respectively and calls on them to return to their work, if the employees decide to continue the 'strike', the concept of excusable error as to the illegal character of the strike ceases to exist. However, even in that case, participation in the illegal strike does not automatically entail the termination of the individual labour contract.

1366. In accordance with Articles 30, 30(a) and 30(b) of Law 1264/1982, there are specific provisions on the union freedoms and the rights of those working in the public sector, in the police and in the National Security Agency under contracts of public law.

Chapter 7. Conciliation, Mediation and Arbitration

Viktoria Sp. Douka

§1. General Remarks

1367. Collective bargaining for the conclusion of a collective agreement may fail.

1368. As mentioned above,[624] under Law 3239/1955 in such cases, the parties were obliged to resource to compulsory arbitration, conducted by the so-called Administrative Arbitration Courts, and the dispute was resolved by its decision (DA), and compulsory arbitration was in essence the only way of settling collective labour disputes, given that no provision was made for mediation, and the conciliation process was limited to a formal procedure whose purpose was to bring the collective dispute to compulsory arbitration. The Minister of Labour had the power to amend or to refuse to approve the DA if its content was opposed to government policy.

1369. On the contrary, Law 1264/1982 is based on the view that the conflict of collective interests between employers and employees forms an inherent part of collective labour relations and that social dialogue is considered to be the most appropriate means of resolving collective labour disputes. Thereof, it provides three types of mechanisms for resolving collective disputes with the assistance of a private third party: conciliation, mediation and arbitration. Aiming to support free collective bargaining, Law 1876/1990 established the OMED.[625]

1370. According to Law 1876/1990, should collective bargaining fail, the parties may decide on the assistance of a third party, who may provide his/her assistance in three ways, as conciliation, as mediation, as arbitration and will assist in continuing the negotiations or in concluding the collective agreement or (as an arbitrator) will resolve the collective dispute by his/her decision (DA).

1371. Conciliation means that a third person assists the contracting parties to continue their negotiation in order to achieve the conclusion of the collective agreement.[626] The third person, called 'conciliator', facilitates the contact between the parties. The conciliator has no power to resolve the collective dispute conflict or to formally submit a proposal to the parties.

1372. Mediation means that a third person participates in the negotiation in order to facilitate the conclusion of the collective agreement by the parties.[627]

---

624. *See* above para. 1396.
625. *See* above para. 233.
626. Article 13 of L. 1876/1990.
627. Article 15 of L. 1876/1990.

1373. Arbitration means that a third person or committee, called 'Arbitrator' and 'Arbitration Committee' respectively, resolve the collective dispute by his/her own decision, where the parties have failed to conclude a collective agreement.[628] Article 22 paragraph 2 last section of the Constitution introduces arbitration as the institution for solving collective disputes if collective bargaining fails. Arbitration issues norms, with the power of an act of compulsory law, under that constitutional provision.

1374. The assistance of the third party is supportive to the parties, meaning, among others, that the third party is bound by the agreements of the parties and that his/her primary task and mission is to convince the parties to conclude the collective agreement.

1375. Furthermore, on the basis of the above, recourse to the assistance of a third person is subject to the following:

(a) the recourse is optional and is exclusively on free choice of the parties. Any intervention by the state or the employers' side or any other is forbidden;
(b) the parties are not obliged to exhaust each mechanism before proceeding to the next;
(c) the right to recourse is explicitly assigned to the parties that participate directly in the negotiations;
(d) the parties may agree on the conditions and the procedure for the recourse to mediation and arbitration, as well as on the procedure for the mediation and arbitration (in practice no contractual regulations have yet been recorded).[629] If such agreement has not been reached, the provisions of Article 15 and 16 of Law 1876/1990, as amended, shall apply and only persons listed in the respective lists held by OMED, in accordance with Article 17 of Law 1876/1990, may act as mediators and arbitrators.

§2. MEDIATION

1376. The parties may apply for mediation at any stage of the negotiation process.[630] They may jointly apply or any of them unilaterally. The parties may, at any time, suspend or abolish the mediation process and either conclude a collective agreement or stop the negotiations or apply for arbitration.

1377. The mediation could deal with any issue that might be regulated in a collective agreement, provided they have already been the subject of the relevant negotiations unless the recourse to mediation is specified for some of them.

628. Article 16 of L. 1876/1990.
629. Article 2 s. 8 and Art. 14, para. 2 of L. 1876/1990.
630. Article 15 of L. 1876/1990, as amended by Art. 14 of L. 38899/2010, Art. 4 of L. 4303/2014, Art. 15 of L. 4549/2018.

1378. The parties have the right to select a mediator independently from the list held by OMED (Mediators' list) by joint agreement, in writing. Otherwise, a selection by lot will take place.

1379. The mediator, in no more than five working days, calls on the parties to joint or separate meetings. The mediator shall conduct separate hearings with each party, examines the economic conditions, the overall competitiveness of the productive activity referred to in the collective dispute and the development of purchasing power of wages, conducts enquiries, fact-finding examinations and any other research or enquiry on the labour conditions, assisted by one or more experts of his/her choice.

1380. If the collective agreement is not concluded within twenty working days, the mediator submits a reasoned proposal, namely a draft of the intended collective agreement, to the parties.[631] The time period of twenty working days is indicative, meaning that the mediator has no right to submit the proposal earlier. The mediator may not submit a proposal only by a reasoned decision of him and set the parties a deadline of three to six working days (extended by agreement of the parties) to continue the negotiations. Should not the parties conclude the collective agreement within those days, the mediator submits his/her reasoned proposal. The mediator may publicize the proposal via the mass communication media

1381. Should the parties, within five working days, do not accept, in writing, the proposal, it is assumed that the proposal has been rejected. The acceptance or the rejection of the proposal is notified to the other party. If the proposal is accepted by both parties, the mediator calls them to sign the collective agreement, its content being as that of one of the proposal.

1382. Given that on the employers' side there may act more than one employers' association or more than one individual employers, if only some of them accept the mediator's proposal, the collective agreement is signed between those and the trade union. Between the rest of them and the trade union the mediation may continue.

1383. During the mediation process, the employer and every competent service are obliged to provide data to the mediator and to assist his/her task.

1384. The mediator is bound to observe confidentiality with regard to all information obtained in carrying out his/her tasks.

631. *See* Art. 15 para. 6 of L. 1876/1990 as amended by Art. 4 para. 2 of L. 4303/2014 for the exact content of the mediator's proposal.

§3. Arbitration

1385. The parties may apply for arbitration at any stage of the negotiations' process or mediation.[632] The (exercise of the) right to strike is suspended for ten days from the day of the submission of the arbitration appeal.

1386. The parties may apply jointly by agreement between them or either party may apply unilaterally (i) if the other party refuses the mediation, (ii) if the applied accepts the mediator's proposal which the other party rejects.[633]

1387. Under the previous regime, the parties could apply for arbitration (a) under Article 3 paragraph a 1 of Cabinet Act 6/2012, only by joint agreement of the parties; (b) under Article 16 paragraph 1 of L. 1876/1982 by joint agreement or unilateral by either side (i) if the other side refused mediation, (ii) regarding national, sectoral or occupational collective agreements, by trade unions if they had adhered to the mediator's proposal and the employers' side had rejected it, (iii) regarding company-level collective agreement, by either party that accepted the mediator's proposal which was rejected by the other side.

1388. The arbitration may deal with any issue (e.g., wages, working conditions) that might be regulated by a collective agreement. The DA is equivalent to a collective agreement (meaning that it may have the same content, it has normative power, the types of the DAs are the same as those of the collective agreements, binds the employees and the employers that are bound by the respective types of collective agreements, expires in the same way as a collective agreement, etc.) and is in force from the day following the submission of the mediation application, unless otherwise agreed by the parties.[634]

1389. Under the previous regime (a) under Article 3 paragraph 2 of Cabinet Act 6/2012, the content of the DA was restricted only to the basic wage, monthly or daily; (b) under Article 16 of L. 1876/1982 in the version which applied prior to Cabinet Act 6/2012, the content of the DA was the same as today.

1390. The arbitration shall be conducted by an arbitrator or, at one party's request and in the case of unilateral recourse to arbitration, by a Three-Member Arbitration Committee (first instance of arbitration).

---

632. Article 16, 16A, 16A of L. 1876/1990 at present, as amended and replaced by L. 3899/2010 (Art. 14), L. 4303/2014 (Art. 4 para. 3), L. 4310/2014 (Art. 55 para. 8), L. 4549/2018 (Art. 15), Cabinet Act 6/2012 (Art. 3).
633. Article 16 para. 1 of L. 1876/1982 as replaced by Art. 4 para. 3 of L. 4303/2014 and as amended by Art. 15 para. 3 of L. 4549/2018.
634. The Areios Pagos (AP 223/2001) held that the arbitrator may give retroactive effect to the arbitration award to be delivered, which dates back to a period prior to the day following the submission of the mediation request.

1391. The parties have the right to select the arbitrator or the members of the Committee from the list of arbitrators held by OMED by joint agreement, in writing. Otherwise, a selection by lot will take place.

1392. The arbitrator and the members of the committees undertake their task within five working days of their appointment, and in order to carry out their task they enjoy the same rights and they are subject to the same obligations as mediators.[635] They are not bound by the proposal of the mediator.

1393. The arbitrator and the Committee study all the evidence and findings which were compiled during the mediation and arbitration proceedings, such as the economic and financial data, the development of competitiveness and the economic situation of the economically weaker undertakings of the productive activity referred to in the collective dispute.[636]

1394. If mediation has taken place, the DA is issued within fifteen days from the day the Arbitrator or the Arbitration Committee assume duties, otherwise within thirty-five working days.

1395. An DA issued either by an arbitrator or the Three-Member Arbitration Committee (DA of first level) may be appealed by either party (second instance of arbitration). Appeals must be lodged with the Secretariat of the Mediation and Arbitration Organization (OMED) within ten days of the notification of the award.

1396. Appeals are examined by a Five-Member Arbitration Committee of Second Instance, which is composed of two arbitrators (selected by lot) from the list of arbitrators held by OMED, two judges from the Supreme Courts (one from the StE and one from the Areios Pagos) and one member (lawyer) of the Legal Council of the State.

1397. The enforcement of an DA of first level is suspended until a decision is issued in the second instance proceedings.

1398. The Five-Member Committee of Second Instance functions under the same rules as the Three-Member Arbitration Committee, and its members enjoy the same rights and are subject to the same obligations as the members of the latter. The decision should be based on the evidence submitted to the Three-Member Arbitration Committee and should be issued within twenty days of the date on which the Committee of Second Instance assumed its duties.

1399. The decision of the committees is made unanimously or by majority.

---

635. Article 16, para. 5 of Law 1876/1990 and Art. 3, para. 3 of Cabinet Act 6/2012.
636. *See* Art. 16 of L. 1876/1990 as replaced by Art. Fourth of L. 4303/2014.

1400. The arbitrator and the committees are bound to come to a decision (DA), meaning that they are not entitled to deny to resolve the collective dispute brought before them.[637]

1401. The DA (either of first or second instance) shall be reasoned and shall provide a well-founded justification. The completeness of the reasoning is subject to judicial review.

1402. Where no appeal has been brought to the Five-Member Committee of Second Instance, either party is entitled to bring an action over the validity of the DA (issued by the Committee of First Instance) before the Civil Court of First Instance (Monomeles Protodikeio). The action shall be brought within ten days after the expiry of the deadline for the above appeal.

1403. Where an appeal has been brought to the Five-Member Committee of Second Instance, either party may bring an action (against the other and not against OMED)[638] over the validity of the decision of this Committee before the Court of Appeal (Efeteio). The appeal shall be brought within ten days of the notification of the decision by the Five-Member Arbitration Committee of Second Instance. In such a case, the Court of Appeal may also decide on the validity of the DA (issued by either an arbitrator or the Three-Member Arbitration Committee).

1404. In both cases, the decision of the court shall apply to the parties bound by the DA.

1405. The court has no jurisdiction to amend the DAs[639] or to examine their expediency. The court is empowered to deal only with the legality of the DAs.[640] The same applies to the collective agreements and labour contracts.

1406. The arbitrator and the members of the committees must observe confidentiality with regard to all information they are given during the performance of their duties.

1407. The arbitrator and the members of the committees shall be completely independent in performing their tasks.

§4. Mediators and Arbitrators

1408. Mediators and arbitrators are specialists in labour relations; they constitute two special bodies, autonomous of each other, and are appointed by OMED after a public call of interest announcing the availability of mediator and arbitrator

637. EfAthens 110/2016.
638. EfAthens 110/2016, MPAthens 4291/2017.
639. EfAthens 110/2016.
640. StEol 2307/2014, APol 25/2004, AP 223/2001, EfAthens 110/2016.

positions.[641] The board of directors, after examining the candidates' files, and possibly after a face-to-face interview, selects the most capable candidates, issues a unanimous decision of the seven members of the board of directors. Mediators and arbitrators perform a civil (public) function without being civil servants and enjoy complete independence. They are hired for a three-year tenure which is renewable, with the possibility of converting appointment as a mediator into appointment as an arbitrator, and vice versa.

§5. Distinction Between Arbitration Regulated by Law 1876/1990 and Arbitration of the KPolD

1409. Arbitration as an institution for the settlement of collective disputes, regulated by Law 1876/1990 as modified by PIS 6/2012, is similar only by name to that arbitration as an institution for the settlement of legal disputes that is regulated by Articles 867–903 of the KPolD. These are two completely different institutions, of which the former falls within the broader scope of the right to organize, while the latter is part of the system for the settlement of legal disputes. For that reason, Articles 867–903 of the KPolD do not apply, neither directly nor by analogy, to arbitration as an institution for the settlement of collective labour disputes.

641. Article 17 paras 8–11 L. 1876/1990 as replaced by Art. 14 of L. 3899/2010.

Selected Bibliography

Legislation

Kazakos A., Zerdelis D., Douka Sp. V, *Labour Legislation*, ed. Sakkoulas, Thessaloniki, 2012.
Koukiadis I., *Basic Labour Legislation*, ed. Sakkoulas, Thessaloniki, 2006.
Leventis G., *Labour Legislation A*, ed. Sakkoulas, 1986.
Papadimitropoulos V., *Pandectes of Law of Collective Agreements (Codification) Nos. 1 and 2,* Athens, 1939.

Collective Agreements, Conventions, Tables of Wages (Collections).

Institute of Social Insurance, Collective Agreements, 196. Supplement IKA Bulletin, Athens, 1968.
Karali A., Potiri I., *The Evolution of Lowest Limits on Wages and Salaries*, Athens, No. 1, 1957, No. 2, 1960.
Keranis D., *Labour Law and Labour Legislation*, Sakkoulas, Athens, 1986.
Tsimpouki Ch., *Code of International Conventions of Labour*, Athens, 1947.

Periodicals

Bulletin of Labour Legislation (Deltion Ergatikis Nomothessias), Fortnightly since 1945 (direction: Dimitrakopoulou).
Economy and Labour Law (Oikonomia kai dikaion ergasias), K. Kalantzopoulou (ed.), circulated during 1947–1948 and in 1958.
Labour Law (Ergatikon Dikaion), Gr. Kassimatis (ed.), circulated during the years 1942 and 1943.
Labour Law Survey, EErgD *(Epitheorissis Ergatikou Dikaiou)*, T. and Ch. Tsimpouki (eds), Fortnightly since 1941.

Books

Agallopoulou P., *Introduction to Labour Law,* Athens, 1958.
Agallopoulou P., *Labour Law, The Labour Relations*, Athens, 1958.
Deliyanni I. & Koukiadi I., *Labour Law, A+B* (volume), ed. Sakkoulas, 1976, 1978.
Dimitrakopoulos E., *Labour Legislation,* ed. D, Athens, 1972.
Douka Sp. V., *The Protection of Personal Data in Labour Relations*, ed. Sakkoulas, 2010.
Douka Sp. V., *Part-Time Employment Contract*, ed. Sakkoulas, 2005.

Selected Bibliography

Douka Sp. V., *The Transfer of the Enterprise and Its Impact on Labour Relations*, ed. Sakkoulas, 1998.

Douka Sp. V., *Individual Labour Contract in Public Sector*, ed. Paratiritis, 1991.

Kalomoiris K. D., *Labour Law, Part I, 'General principles'*, 1969.

Kalomoiris K. D., *Contemporary Tendencies of Labour Law*, 1972.

Karakatsanis A., *Individual Labour Law*, ed. Sakkoulas, 1987.

Karakatsanis A., *Collective Labour Law*, 1988.

Kardaras A., *Regulations of the Terms of Employment Contract at Enterprise Level*, ed. Sakkoulas, 1996.

Kazakos A., *Collective Labour Law*, ed. Sakkoulas, Thessaloniki, 2013.

Koukiadis I., *Labour Law: Individual Labour Relations*, ed. Sakkoulas, 2017.

Koukiadis I., *Labour Law: Collective Labour Relations, Collective agreements*, 2017.

Leventis G., *Collective Labour Law*, ed. Sakkoulas, Athens, 2011.

Lixouriotis G, *Labour Law, Individual Labour Relations*, ed. Nomiki Vivliothiki, 2013.

Lixouriotis G, *Collective Labour Relations*, 2013.

Mantzoufas P., *General Principles of Labour Law*, ed. Sakkoulas, 1961.

Ntasios L., *Labour Law*, 5 Volumes, ed. Sakkoulas, 1987–1995.

Zerdelis D., *Individual Labour Law*, ed. Sakkoulas, 2013.

Zerdelis D., *Collective Labour Law*, ed. Sakkoulas, 2017.

Annexes

Annex 1. Evolution of Employment Agreements

New employment agreements (with a work schedule different from the legal one) submitted to Labour Inspectorates, 2007–2012. The data on working time flexibility are not plentiful. Data on how many paid employees are officially in part-time employment or job-rotation schemes (i.e., working full time less than five or six days/week) show that working time flexibility is increasing sharply.

Year	*Part-time employment*	*Job rotation*	*Total*
2012	332,167	94,021	375,843
2011	300,230	84,519	384,749
2010	340,619	90,158	430,777
2009	272,561	57,825	330,386
2008	332,695	46,212	378,907
2007	282,255	47,275	329,530

Amendment of full-time employment agreements to agreements with a work schedule different from the legal one, submitted to Labour Inspectorates, 2009–2012. Data on amendment of full-time employment to part-time employment or job rotation schemes show that the number of paid employees who had to change their working time due to the economic crisis has risen sharply.

Annex 1

Year	*From full to part-time employment*	*From full-time employment job rotation*	*Total*
2012	49,640	21,478	71,118
2011	32,420	26,542	58,962
2010	18,713	7,540	26,253
2009	11,622	4,839	16,461

Source: Labour Inspectorate.

Annex 2. Conventions Ratified by Hellas up to 1 April 2019

L. 4096/2012 (HSG A' 232/23.11.2012): ratification of the Amendment to Article 20 paragraph 1 of the Convention concerning the Elimination of All Forms of Discrimination against Women (CEDAW), as adopted in the meeting of the member states on 22.5.1995 and approved by the General Assembly of the U.N. on 22.12.1995.

L. 4078/2012 (HSG A' 179/20.9.2012): Ratification of the Maritime Labour Convention, signed in Geneva on 23/2/2006.

Decision Φ.054/5/ΑΣ 435/Μ.5356/2002: Announcement for the Seafarers' Hours of Work and the Manning of Ships Convention, signed in Geneva on 22.10.1996 and of the Protocol of 1996 concerning the Merchant Shipping (Minimum Standards) Convention, signed in Geneva on 22.10.1996.

L. 2974/2001 (HSG A' 293/31.12.2001): Ratification of the ILO Convention 180 concerning the Seafarers' Hours of Work and the Manning of Ships, signed in Geneva on 22.10.1996 and of the Protocol of 1996 concerning the Merchant Shipping (Minimum Standards) Convention, signed in Geneva on 22.10.1996.

L. 2918/2001 (HSG A' 119/15.6.2001): Ratification of the ILO Convention 182 concerning the Worst Forms of Child Labour, signed in Geneva on 17.6.1999.

L. 2405/1996 (HSG A' 101/4.6.1996): Ratification of the Convention concerning the Protection of the Right to Organise and Procedures for Determining Conditions of Employment in the Public Service, signed in Geneva on 22.5.1951.

L. 2403/1996 (HSG A' 99/4.6.1996): Ratification of the ILO Convention 154 concerning the Promotion of Collective Negotiations, signed in Geneva on 3.6.1981.

L. 1879/1990 (HSG A' 38/21.3.1990): Ratification of the ILO Convention 126 concerning the Accommodation on Board Fishing Vessels, signed in Geneva on 21.6.1966.

L. 1855/1989 (HSG A' 14/1.6.1989): Ratification of the ILO Convention 141 concerning the Organisations of Rural Workers and their Role in Economic and Social Development, signed in Geneva on 23.6.1975.

L. 1856/1989 (HSG A' 141/1.6.1989): Ratification of the ILO Convention 142 concerning Vocational Guidance and Vocational Training in the Development of Human Resources, signed in Geneva on 23.6.1975.

L. 1817/1988 (HSG A' 252/15.11.1988): Ratification of the ILO Convention 160 concerning Labour Statistics, signed in Geneva on 25.6.1985.

L. 1767/1988 (HSG A' 63/6.4.1988): Ratification of the ILO Convention 135 concerning the Protection and Facilities to be afforded to Workers' Representatives in the Undertaking, adopted in Geneva on 23.6.1971.

L. 1672/1986 (HSG A' 203/24.12.1986): Ratification of the ILO Convention 122 concerning the Employment and Conditions of Work and Life of Nursing Personnel, signed in Geneva on 21.6.1977.

L. 1639/1986 (HSG A' 109/18.7.1986): Ratification of the ILO Convention 71 concerning Seafarers' Pension, signed in Geneva on 28.6.1946.

L. 1637/1986 (HSG A' 107/18.7.1986) Ratification of the ILO Convention 92 concerning Crew Accommodation on Board Ship (Revised 1949), adopted in Geneva on 18.6.1949.

L. 1549/1986 (HSG A' 65/19.5.1986): Ratification of the ILO Convention 133 concerning Crew Accommodation on Board Ship (Supplementary Provisions), adopted in Geneva on 30.10.1970.

L. 1576/1985 (HSG A' 218/23.12.1985): Ratification of the ILO Convention 156 concerning Equal Opportunities and Equal Treatment for Men and Women Workers: Workers with Family Responsibilities, signed in Geneva on 23.6.1981.

L. 1556/1985 (HSG A' 100/28.5.1985): Ratification of the ILO Convention 159 concerning Vocational Rehabilitation and Employment (Disabled Persons), adopted in Geneva on 20.6.1983.

L. 1546/1985 (HSG A' 94/22.5.1985): Ratification of the ILO Convention 150 concerning Labour Administration: Role, Functions and Organisation, signed in Geneva on 26.6.1978.

L. 1430/1984 (HSG A' 49/18.4.1984): Ratification of the ILO Convention 62 concerning Safety Provisions in the Building Industry, signed in Geneva on 23.6.1937.

L. 1424/1984 (HSG A' 29/14.3.1984): Ratification of the ILO Convention 111 concerning Discrimination in Respect of Employment and Occupation, signed in Geneva on 25.6.1958.

L. 1423/1984 (HSG A' 29/14.3.1984): Ratification of the ILO Convention 122 concerning Employment Policy, signed in Geneva on 9.7.1964.

L. 1342/1983 (HSG A' 39/1.4.1983): Codification of the International Convention of 1979 of the United Nations concerning Equal Payment for Equal Work between Men and Women.

L. 1302/1982 (HSG A' 133/29.10.1982): Ratification of the ILO Convention 103 concerning Maternity Protection (Revised 1952), signed in Geneva on 7.9.1955.

L. 1181/1981 (HSG A' 195/24.7.1981): Ratification of the ILO Convention 115 concerning the Protection of Workers against Ionizing Radiations, signed in Geneva on 22.6.1960.

L. 1182/1981 (HSG A' 19324.7.1981): Ratification of the ILO Convention 138 concerning the Minimum Age for Admission to Employment, adopted in Geneva on 26.6.1973.

L. 1176/1981 (HSG A' 184/13.7.1981): Ratification of the ILO Convention 144 concerning Tripartite Consultations to Promote the Implementation of International Labour Standards, signed in Geneva on 21.6.1976.

L. 1175/1981 (HSG A' 183/13.7.1981): Ratification of the ILO Convention 124 concerning Medical Examinations of Young Persons for Fitness for Employment Underground in Mines, signed in Geneva on 23.6.1965.

L. 1174/1981 (HSG A' 182/13.7.1981): Ratification of the ILO Convention 106 concerning Weekly Rest in Commerce and Offices, adopted in Geneva on 26.6.1957.

L. 1173/1981 (HSG A' 181/13.7.1981): Ratification of the ILO Convention 78 concerning Medical Examination of Children and Young Persons for Fitness for Employment in Non-Industrial Occupations, adopted in Montreal on 9.10.1946.

L. 1171/1981 (HSG A' 180/13.7.1981): Ratification of the ILO Convention 77 concerning Medical Examination for Fitness for Employment in Industry of Children and Young Persons, adopted in Montreal on 9.10.1946.

L. 1163/1981 (HSG A' 154/18.6.1981): Ratification of the ILO Convention 68 concerning Food and Catering for Crews on Board Ship, adopted in Geneva on 27.6.1946.

L. 1131.1981 (HSG A' 39/13.2.1981): Ratification of the ILO Convention 73 concerning the Medical Examination of Seafarers, adopted in Geneva on 29.6.1946.

L. 1130/1981 (HSG A' 38/13.2.1981): Ratification of the ILO Convention 23 concerning the Repatriation of Seamen, adopted in Geneva on 23.6.1926.

L. 948/1979 (HSG A' 167/25.7.1979): Ratification of the ILO Convention 147 concerning Minimum Standards in Merchant Ships, adopted in Geneva on 29.10.1976.

L. 492/1976 (HSG A' 332/11.12.1976): Ratification of the ILO Convention 136 concerning Protection against Hazards of Poisoning Arising from Benzene, adopted in Geneva on 23.6.1971.

L. 486/1976 (HSG A' 321/3.12.1976): Ratification of the ILO Convention 134 concerning the Prevention of Occupational Accidents to Seafarers, adopted in Geneva on 30.10.1970.

L. 46/1975 (HSG A' 105/3.6.1975): Ratification of the ILO Convention 100 concerning Equal Remuneration for Men and Women Workers for Work of Equal Value, adopted in Geneva on 29.6.1951.

LD 53/1974 (HSG A' 256/20.9.1974): Ratification of the Convention for the Protection of Human Rights and Fundamental Freedoms as amended by the Protocol 2 of Paris on 20.3.1952.

ML 366/1968 (HSG A' 88/27.4.1968): Ratification of the ILO Convention 55 concerning the Liability of the Ship-owner in Case of Sickness, Injury or Death of Seamen, adopted in Geneva on 24.10.1936.

L. 4318/1963 (HSG A' 88/11.6.1963): Ratification of the ILO Convention 5 concerning Fixing the Minimum Age for the Admission of Children to Employment at Sea, adopted in Geneva on 24.10.1936.

L. 4317/1963 (HSG A' 87/11.6.1963): Ratification of the ILO Convention 69 concerning the Certification of Ships' Cooks, adopted in Geneva on 27.6.1946.

L. 4316/1963 (HSG A' 87/11.6.1963): Ratification of the ILO Convention 108 concerning Seafarers' National Identity Documents, adopted in Geneva on 13.5.1958.

LD 4204/1961 (HSG A' 174/19.9.1961): Ratification of the ILO Convention 87 concerning Freedom of Association and Protection of the Right to Organize, adopted in San Francisco on 9.7.1948.

LD 4205/1961 (HSG A' 174/19.9.1961): Ratification of the ILO Convention 98 concerning the Application of the Principles of the Right to Organize and to Bargain Collectively, adopted in Geneva on 1.7.1949.

LD 4221/1961 (HSG A' 173/19.9.1961): Ratification of the ILO Convention 105 concerning the Abolition of Forced Labour, adopted in Geneva on 25.6.1957.

LD 4215/1961 (HSG A' 170/19.9.1961): Ratification of the ILO Convention 6 concerning the Night Work of Young Persons Employed in Industry, adopted in San Francisco on 10.7.1948.

L. 3924/1959 (HSG A'1/2.1.1959): Ratification of the ILO Convention 89 concerning the Night Work of Women in Industry (Revised 1948), adopted in San Francisco on 9.7.1948.

L. 3251/955 (HSG A' 140/2.6.1955): Ratification of the ILO Convention 102 concerning Minimum Standards of Social Security, adopted in Geneva on 28.6.1952.
L. 3250/1955 (HSG A' 139/2.6.1955): Ratification of the ILO Convention 88 concerning the Organisation of the Employment Service, adopted in San Francisco on 9.7.1948.
L. 3249/1955 (HSG A' 139/2.6.1955): Ratification of the ILO Convention 81 concerning Labour Inspection in Industry and Commerce, adopted in Geneva on 11.7.1947.
L. 3248/1955 (HSG A' 138/2.6.1955): Ratification of the ILO Convention 95 concerning the Protection of Wages, adopted in Geneva on 1.7.1949.
L. 2082/1952 (HSG A' 117/28.4.1952): Ratification of the ILO Convention 116 concerning the Partial Revisions of the Conventions Adopted by the General Conference of the International Labour Organisation at its First Twenty-Eight Sessions for the Purpose of Making Provisions for the Future Discharge of Certain Chancery Functions Entrusted by the Said Conventions to the Secretary-General of the League of Nations and Introducing therein Certain Further Amendments Consequential upon the Dissolution of the League of Nations and the Amendment of the Constitution of the International Labour Organisations, adopted in Montreal on 9.10.1946.
L. 2078/1952 (HSG A' 116/28.4.1952): Ratification of the ILO Convention 17 concerning Workmen's Compensation for Accidents, adopted in Geneva on 10.6.1925.
L. 2081/1955 (HSG A' 109/25.4.1952): Ratification of the ILO Convention 52 concerning Annual Holidays with Pay, adopted in Geneva on 24.6.1936.
L. 2077/1952 (HSG A' 109/25.4.1952): Ratification of the ILO Convention 11 concerning the Rights of Association and Combination of Agricultural Workers, adopted in Geneva on 25.10.1921.
L. 2079/1952 (HSG A' 108/25.4.1952): Ratification of the ILO Convention 29 concerning Compulsory Labour, adopted in Geneva on 28.6.1930.
L. 2080/1952 (HSG A' 108/25.4.1952): Ratification of the ILO Convention 18 concerning Workmen's Compensation for Occupational Diseases, adopted in Geneva on 21.6.1934.
RD 10-9/1937 (HSG A' 405/14.10.1937): Concerning the Safety of those Employed in the Woodworking Industry.
LD of 30-10/1935 (HSG A' 508/31.10.1936): Ratification of the ILO Convention 19 concerning the Equality of Treatment for National and Foreign Workers as regards Workmen's compensation for Accidents, adopted in Geneva on 5.6.1925.
ML of 30-10/1935 (HSG A' 509/31.10.1935): Ratification of the ILO Convention 45 concerning the Employment of Women on Underground Work in Mines of all Kinds, adopted in Geneva on 21.6.1935.
ML 30-10/1935 (HSG A' 509/31.10.1935): Ratification of the ILO Convention 27 concerning the Marking of the Weight on Heavy Packages Transported by Vessels, adopted in Geneva on 21.6.1929.

Annex 3. Severance Pay for White-Collar and Blue-Collar Employees

Table 1 Concerning the White-Collar Employees

Duration of the contract until the termination	*Notice period in months*	*Year of the contract, during which, the termination is made*	*Severance pay (equal to the remuneration of the following months + 1/6 of it)*	
			With a notice for the termination	*Without a notice for the termination*
Up to 12 months	-0-	1st	-0-	0
13–24 months	1	2nd	1	2
3–4 years	2	3rd		
4th	1.5	3		
5–9 years	3	5th		
6th–7th	2	4		
8th–9th	2.5	5		
10th year and over	4	10th	3	6
11th	3.5	7		
12th	4	8		
13th	4.5	9		
14th	5	10		
15th	5.5	11		
16th and over	6	12		

Annex 3

Table 2 For White-Collar Employees Who Worked on 12 November 2012, the Day of the Entry into Effect of Law 4093/2012, and Have Completed in the Same Employer a Seniority of More Than 17 years Are Paid, in Addition to the above Severance Pay, the Following Amounts

17th	6.5	13
18th	7	14
19th	7.5	15
20th	8	16
21st	8.5	17
22nd	9	18
23rd	9.4	19
24th	10	20
25th	10.5	21
26th	11	22
27th	11.5	23
28th and over	12	24

Table 3 Concerning Blue-Collar Employees

Duration of the contract until its termination	*Severance pay (daily wages) (equal to the remuneration of the following days + 1/6 of it)*
Up to 12 months	0
13–24 months	7
3–4 years	15
5–9 years	30
10–14 years	60
15–19 years	100
20–24 years	120
25–29 years	145
30 years and over	165

Annex 4. Evolution of Collective Agreements, per Type, for the Period 1961–2013 (Source: Ministry of Labour, Social Insurance and Welfare at www.ypakp.gr)

	Period of effect of L. 3239/1955												
	NGCA		*Same occupation*				*Special*		*Total*			*%*	
			National		*Sectoral*								
	CA	*AA*	*CA*	*AA*	*CA*	*AA*	*CA*	*AA*	*CA*	*AA*	*CA+AA*	*CA*	*AA*
1961	1		12	21	36		14	19	63	40	103	61.2	38.8
1962	2		14	12	19		35	18	70	30	100	70	30
1963			10	24	31		20	24	61	48	109	56	44
1964		1	27	27	21		29	32	77	60	137	56.2	43.8
1965	1		21	30	59		40	29	121	69	190	63.7	36.3
1966			28	29	40		37	39	105	68	173	60.7	39.3
1967	1		10	24	26		26	15	63	39	102	61.8	38.2
1968	2	1	14	38	24		23	32	63	71	134	47	53
1969			13	33	16		21	17	50	50	100	50	50
1970		1	20	22	3		30	20	53	43	96	55.2	44.8
1971			17	33	7		22	19	46	52	98	46.9	53.1
1972			44	19	11		33	18	88	37	125	70.4	29.6
1973			47	25	18		93	28	158	53	211	74.9	25.1
1974			21	44	15		34	29	70	73	143	49	51.1
1975	3		30	59	13		85	48	131	107	238	55	45
1976		1	30	52	24		90	40	144	93	237	60.8	39.2

Annex 4

	Period of effect of L. 3239/1955												
	NGCA		*Same occupation*				*Special*		*Total*			*%*	
			National		*Sectoral*								
	CA	*AA*	*CA*	*AA*	*CA*	*AA*	*CA*	*AA*	*CA*	*AA*	*CA+AA*	*CA*	*AA*
1977	1	1	29	80	15		101	70	146	151	297	49.2	50.8
1978			37	65	14		115	131	166	196	362	45.9	54.1
1979		2	42	94	15		116	126	173	222	395	43.8	56.2
1980		1	56	112	25		140	159	221	272	493	44.8	55.2
1981			54	130	26		153	170	233	300	533	43.7	56.3
1982		1	70	141	42		188	52	300	194	494	60.7	39.3
1983			9	46	8		40	25	57	71	128	44.5	55.5
1984	1		47	170	22		182	79	252	249	501	50.3	49.7
1985	1		51	103	29		194	45	275	148	423	65	35
1986	1		18	43	7		18	16	44	59	103	42.7	57.3
1987		1	21	41	11		44	19	76	61	137	55.5	44.5
1988	1		83	43	28		98	18	210	61	271	77.5	22.5
1989	1		90	63	24		161	33	276	96	372	74.2	25.8

Period of effect of L. 1876/1990															
	NGCA		*Same occupation*					*Sectoral national Local*	*Enterprise level*			*TOTAL*		*%*	
			National		*Local*										
	CA	*AA*	*CA*	*AA*	*CA*	*AA*	*CA*	*AA*	*CA*	*AA*	*CA*	*AA*	*CA+AA*	*CA*	*AA*
1990	1		65	41	20	18	46	34	53	9	185	102	287	64.5	35.5
1991	1		37	30	35	20	89	25	125	12	287	87	374	76.7	23.3
1992			28	12	14	5	66	8	63	7	171	32	203	84.2	15.8
1993	1		50	11	26	2	98	15	105	2	280	30	310	90.3	9.7
1994	1		44	14	26	2	99	17	117	4	287	37	324	88.6	11.4
1995	1		41	14	25	4	64	13	108	2	239	33	272	87.9	12.1
1996	1		46	16	20	6	76	18	242	3	385	43	428	90	10.1
1997			44	14	25	8	69	96	143	4	281	52	333	84.4	15.6
1998	1		51	13	16	10	87	28	137	7	292	58	350	83.4	16.6
1999			23	20	18	9	70	19	115	3	228	51	279	81.7	18.3
2000	1		54	15	22	4	98	17	122	6	297	42	339	87.6	12.4
2001			34	12	24	1	60	22	146	5	263	40	303	86.8	13.2
2002	2		43	19	32	6	96	20	175	11	348	56	404	86.1	13.8
2003			28	25	26	8	52	26	168	5	274	64	338	81.1	18.9
2004	1		37	16	43	4	101	22	216	10	398	52	450	88.4	11.6
2005			37	18	24	8	84	15	234	20	379	61	440	86.2	13.8
2006	1		42	17	34	6	100	24	224	7	401	54	455	88.1	11.9
2007			23	14	20	3	73	19	202	7	318	43	361	88.1	11.9
2008	1		43	17	27	2	117	25	215	15	403	59	462	87.2	12.8
2009			15	11	12	5	47	30	215	12	289	58	347	83.3	16.7
2010	1		33	8	14	6	31	21	227	11	306	46	352	86.9	13.1

Annex 4

Period of effect of L. 1876/1990															
	NGCA		Same occupation					Sectoral national Local	Enterprise level			TOTAL		%	
			National		Local										
	CA	AA	CA	AA	CA	AA	CA	AA	CA	AA	CA	AA	CA+AA	CA	AA
2011			15	5	7	1	23	12	170	9	215	27	242	88.84	11,15
2012			4	1	6	7	19	7	975		1004	8	1012	99.2	0.8
2013	1		4		10		9		409		433		433	100.0	0.0
2014	1		3		5	2	10	2	286		305	2	307	99.3	0.7
2015	1		5		7	11	6	11	263	1	282	12	294	95.9	4.1
2016	1		2	3	6	7	7	7	318	4	334	4	338	96.0	4.0
2017	1		4	1	6	2	10	2	244	2	265	5	270	98.1	1.9

Index

The numbers here refer to paragraph numbers.

Index

Made in the USA
Monee, IL
18 October 2026

66041414R10214